A Passion for Polka

A Passion
for Polka

Old-Time Ethnic Music in America

Victor Greene

UNIVERSITY OF CALIFORNIA PRESS

Berkeley / Los Angeles / Oxford

Acknowledgment is made to the following for permission to reprint excerpts from song lyrics:

Nicola Paone, Scarsdale, N.Y.: "Yakity, Yak" and "The Big Professor" by Nicola Paone.

Songs Music, Inc., Scarborough, N.Y.: "Uei Paesano!" by Nicola Paone (English translation).

Ethnic Music Co., Hasbrouck Heights, N.J.: "Roumania, Roumania" by Aaron Lebedeff (Banner Record BAS 1007); "Die Greene Koseene" by Hyman Prizant, © 1937 J&J Kammen Co.; "Bei Mir Bistu Shein," lyrics by J. Jacobs, © 1933 S. Secunda, © 1937 J&J Kammen (English translation).

Mills Music, Inc.: "BLUE SKIRT WALTZ." Frank Yankovic & Mitchell Parish. Copyright © 1948 by R. A. Dvorsky. Copyright renewed. Exclusively published in the United States and Canada by Mills Music, Inc. A Division of Filmtrax Copyright Holdings Inc. Published in the rest of the world by International Music Publications, England.

Warner/Chappell Music, Inc.: "BEI MIR BIST DU SCHON" (Sholom Secunda, Jacob Jacobs). © 1937 WARNER BROS. INC. (Renewed). All rights reserved. Used by permission.

University of California Press
Berkeley and Los Angeles, California

University of California Press, Ltd.
Oxford, England

Library of Congress Cataloging-in-Publication Data
Greene, Victor, 1933–
    A passion for polka : old-time ethnic music in America / Victor Greene.
        p.   cm.
    Includes bibliographical references and index.
    ISBN 0-520-07584-6 (alk. paper)
    1. Folk music—United States—History and criticism.   2. Music—United States—History and criticism.   3. Music and race. I. Title.
ML3551.G696   1992
781.62′00973—dc20   92-954
                                                                          CIP
                                                                           MN

Printed in the United States of America
9 8 7 6 5 4 3 2 1

The paper used in this publication meets the minimum requirements of American National Standard for Information Sciences—Permanence of Paper for Printed Library Materials, ANSI Z39.48-1984.
∞

Contents

Photographs following page 112

Preface

This work deals with a subject paradoxically both popular and little known. Three factors prompted me to write it: the character and ambience of the city in which I live, Milwaukee, Wisconsin, one of the nation's centers of ethnic pluralism; my personal experience, particularly my memory of the extraordinary wide appeal of certain ethnic tunes in my youth; and the recent trend in American social historiography to deal with popular music.

Teaching immigration history for three decades and establishing an academic program in ethnic studies at my university, an urban institution in an ethnically diverse city, made me intimately aware of the area's many ethnic communities and their cultural life, especially their music and dance. Ethnic dancers, musicians, and bands performed often, not only at the city's major metropolitan folk festival each fall but on many other occasions throughout the year. Milwaukee's ethnic-music activities have earned the city the identity of which it boasts, the "City of Festivals." The familiar phenomenon of ethno-cultural music and dance performed outdoors and in taverns, supper clubs, and cafes struck me as somewhat anachronistic in the late twentieth century, long after the end of large-scale European immigration. At any rate, such an apparent anomaly certainly merited a historian's attention.

Of course I soon learned that Milwaukee and Wisconsin were not unique in the persistence of active ethnic musical groups; other cities also had an ongoing group musical life. Yet while the public was well acquainted with such entertainment as a common part of urban cultural life, academicians had either totally neglected it or simply had not accounted for its persistence. Neither classical nor "popular" in the general sense, ethnic music seemed to be absent from the standard surveys of American music, a surprising circumstance in view of the fact that many people enjoyed listening and dancing to this music. One rare student, Charles Keil, has referred to it as "Polka Happiness." The situation of a common and familiar activity chiefly among American working classes, one which scholars had ignored, attracted my attention.

Besides the genre's enigmatic popularity in urban ethnic centers, another paradox attracted my interest. I had been aware of the extraordinary popularity of this ethnic music in my youth in the 1930s. A student of the piano accordion, I recalled two ethnic song hits in particular that had swept the country at the end of the 1930s, the Jewish-Yiddish "Bei Mir Bist Du Shön" and the Czech-German "Beer Barrel Polka." The great enthusiasm for these works a half-century ago appeared to contradict general scholarly opinion about social life of that time. Conventional assessments of our popular culture referred to the powerful homogenizing impact of the media and our popular music. However these two pieces, best known from the versions by the Andrews Sisters, seemed to prove not that popular culture assimilated ethnic cultures but possibly the reverse, that ethnic music had become popular. This second apparent flaw in conventional opinion also encouraged me to reassess the impact of ethnic music.

The final spur for me to examine ethnic music was a recent trend in scholarship itself. Over the 1980s a few social historians and allied scholars have become interested in the recreational and leisure-time activities of the masses. One of the central questions raised by this line of inquiry has concerned how popular culture, or mainstream American norms, affected the way of life of the ethnic masses. Although scholars initially concluded that mass culture assimilated the multicultural working class, more recent analyses disagree. A few studies have suggested that lower-class non-white and minority ethnic groups maintained their racial and ethnic identities through their leisure-time activities.

All these factors motivated me to look into how immigrant ethnic groups established and maintained their musical life on these shores and to assess the influence, if any, of their vernacular music on the mainstream. To my surprise, I learned that the forms of musical entertainment fashioned by immigrants in the United States were not only viable in terms of ethnic group life but were also in certain instances influential to the development of mainstream American music. This work is therefore both a study of the organization of that recreational life in music and an examination of its musical elements that became popular nationally.

Of course the subject of ethnic music and its impact is wide-ranging, and I had to be selective, particularly as to which groups I could study in detail. Among the obvious omissions in this project are the Cajuns of Louisiana and the many groups of immigrants from Asia. I designed my work to focus especially on the musical lives of relatively neglected European immigrant groups about whom I could obtain information, resulting, then, in a study that admittedly is more of an introduction than a comprehensive conclusion to the subject of ethnic music.

As the reader will discern from the citations, the sources for such a study still remain largely in private hands, and I was fortunate to be able to view many materials made available to me by ethnic entertainers, members of their families, and their friends and fans. Because the field has lacked serious attention and because I was a neophyte in music history, I had to learn a new vocabulary, and I was heavily dependent on many individuals, mostly nonscholars, to assist me with sources.

While my effort could not be completely comprehensive I met a large number of enthusiasts, a few of them academics but most of them ordinary people—aficionados, families of musicians, music businesspeople, and amateur collectors, all of whom were most gracious in showing me their archives. In some cases these individuals had tens of thousands of phonograph records, as well as illuminating documents, including newspaper clippings, photographs, sheet music, and similar materials. As is obvious from my notes and bibliography, the extent of my indebtedness to the families and friends of my subjects is sizable. The research experience was a revelation to me in historical methodology, as I discovered from field experience a huge community of amateur "collectors" that the scholarly community would do would well to reach, recognize, and consult. Scholars must acknowledge that important sources for research have been preserved not only by public institutions and archives but also by millions of individual Americans.

Since I started this study in 1985, I have been fortunate to receive support from a number of agencies, including the Association for Recorded Sound Collections, the National Endowment for the Humanities, the University of Wisconsin–Milwaukee, and the New Jersey Historical Commission, all of whom provided financial assistance. The Association of the University of Wisconsin Professionals, AFL-CIO, provided important material support.

Unlike all my previous research, this project, as discussed above, drew mostly on private collections and materials. Although my detailed acknowledgements appear in the source notes to this book, here I wish to list several people who were both generous and hospitable with their advice and criticism. Richard Spottswood, the most knowledgeable authority on ethnic music, provided enormous help. My colleague James Leary of Madison, Wisconsin, whose research I valued, also offered helpful criticisms. I also benefited from the substantial generosity and general support of Pekka Gronow of Helsinki, Finland; Bob Andresen of Duluth, Minnesota; Ray Tump, John Steiner, and the members of Milwaukee Area Radio Enthusiasts; Bob Norgard of Clinton, Ohio; Brian Juntikka of Fort Myers, Florida; Janet Kleeman of Providence, Rhode Island; LeRoy Larsen of Coon Rapids, Minnesota; Greg Leider of Fredonia, Wisconsin; Henry Sapoznik of Brooklyn, N.Y.; Anne-Charlotte Harvey of Lemon Grove, California; Emelise Aleandri of New York; and Joseph Bentivegna of Loreto, Pennsylvania.

Among the amateur collectors who graciously shared with me their huge files and the benefit of their expertise were four in particular: Philip Balistreri of Milwaukee on the Italians; Frederick P. Williams of Philadelphia on band music; Bob Freedman of Philadelphia on Jewish music; and Don Sosnoski of Parma, Ohio, who has an immense library on polka music.

A number of musicians and their families offered hospitality that made field work a pleasure. Among the most generous were Victoria and Peter Karnish of Rosedale, New York; Frank Wojnarowski of Bridgeport, Connecticut; E. Theodore Krolikowski III of Devon, Connecticut; Mr. and Mrs. Lucian Kryger of Wilkes-Barre, Pennsylvania.; Mr. and Mrs. Dennis Wilfahrt of St. Paul; Mr. and Mrs. Staś Jaworski of Toms River, New Jersey; the late Bernard Witkowski and Mrs. Mariane Witkowski of Hillside, New Jersey; the late Alvin Sajewski of Chicago; Leon Kozicki of the International Polka Association, Chicago; Walter Ossowski of Philadelphia; "Connecticut"

Staś Przasnyski of Bristol, Connecticut; and, of course, the "Polka King" himself, Frankie Yankovic of Euclid, Ohio. Mr. and Mrs. Nicola Paone of Scarsdale and New York City were particularly gracious, opening their home and business to me in a manner that was simply overwhelming. And I must add my appreciation to Seymour Rexsite and Miriam Kressyn of New York for revealing the delights of old-time Yiddish vaudeville.

In the fall of 1990, the staff and students at the Centre for the Study of Social History, University of Warwick, Coventry, England, provided me with a perspective on my subject I could never have obtained in my own country. I am especially grateful to Tony Mason, the Centre's Director of Studies.

As always, I must offer my most profound gratitude to my wife, Laura, whose literary skill I continue to admire. As in the past, she has helped my drafts make sense.

Introduction

In 1986 an important event took place in American cultural history that eluded the attention of most students of our society. The National Academy of Recording Arts and Sciences, the major arbiter of American popular music through its Grammy awards, established a new award category, polka music. Inclusion of the new category was notable not just for recognizing the quality of particular record albums; it also represented a much-belated formal acceptance of a new kind of music in American popular culture—not a new musical genre, for polka music had been around for some time, but a new level of serious attention to the significance of polka music on the American musical scene.

The recording artist honored with the first Grammy in the polka-music category was the appropriate recipient; a seventy-one-year-old Slovenian American bandleader from Cleveland named Frankie Yankovic, known for several decades as "America's Polka King." Although there have been other claimants to such a title, unquestionably Yankovic's claim was paramount. He had attained the widest popularity in that field and in fact had been "crowned" in a ceremony in the late 1940s, at the peak of polka's golden age. In any event, by adding this musical genre to country-western, pop, rock, and the other popular music forms recognized with Grammy awards, several decades after the polka's glory days, the National Academy gave the genre new professional status, an honor that certainly thrilled all polka aficionados. Presentation of the phonograph statuette to Yan-

1

kovic did more than make his fans happy, however; it also signified an important cultural change, the formal acceptance of polka music into this nation's popular culture.

The long neglect of this musical genre has been unfortunate, because its presence and performance have represented a little-known but vital aspect of American social life. The reason for the oversight reflects a general misunderstanding of the term "polka music" itself, which is an ambiguous and therefore misleading designation. Even the standard references about polka music are confusing: the dictionary definition, for example, defines the term too narrowly, identifying it as a lively dance of Bohemian origin done in a hop-step-close-step pattern in 2/4 time.[1] While that designation is true as far as it goes, the polka is far more than just a type of musical recreation; it is also one of a group of many traditional dance elements in what should be known as the "old-time ethnic" music tradition. Old-time ethnic music is what Yankovic and his colleagues play and what in truth the National Academy cited. Instead of "the polka," the terms "polka-style" or "polka music" are preferable, suggesting a far broader genre.

"Polka music," such as that played by Yankovic and his colleagues, is in current discourse the popularized version of many varied tunes and dances of the European immigrant folk past. The normal repertoire of "polka" bands is not simply one type of dance music but rather a variety of pieces, including waltzes and marches, which are in fact dances once common among European peasants. In addition, polka music includes or stems from dance forms associated with specific ethnic groups, such as the German *laendler,* the Czech *sousedska,* the Polish *oberek,* the Hungarian-Gypsy *czardas,* the Ukrainian *kolomyika,* the Swedish schottische, the Italian tarantella, and even the dances of Yiddish klezmer ensembles. The National Academy's "polka music," then, is really the commercialized version of music derived from America's European immigrants.[2]

Because the term "polka" is so ambiguous, a more accurate term is obviously essential; fortunately, history provides one. At the height of the popularity of this kind of ethnic music, from around World War I through Yankovic's heyday, record companies and popular-music publications referred to this musical genre as "old-time" and occasionally "international" music.[3] The term "old-time" presents a problem, however, because it has also been used by popular-music critics to describe another traditional genre, the folk-type music that came out of the Southern Appalachian region, also known as "hill-billy" and later as "country-western" music. To distinguish the term more precisely for our purposes here, it is necessary to add "ethnic" to the designation "old-time."[4] Unfortunately, the matter cannot rest there because this project cannot deal comprehensively with the music of *all* ethnic groups; music of this nation's Oriental, African, and Middle Eastern peoples is not examined here.[5] Still, while concentrating almost exclusively on Euro-American cultures, this work suggests conclusions that may illuminate the lives of America's non-Western groups as well.

Perhaps because of the complexity of "ethnic old-time" music, ethnomusicologists and music historians have generally ignored or even deliberately avoided a genre that has also been referred to as "people's" music.[6] They have preferred to give their serious attention to the better-known musical forms, such as the more traditional folk, jazz, rock, and country-western genres, the popular tunes of the nineteenth century and Tin Pan Alley, and, of course, classical music. Among academic intellectuals polka music has suffered from a bad image. Most serious critics claimed, for example, that it lacked artistic quality, in large part because it had a rather unsophisticated audience.

It was charged that ethnic old-time was the musical entertainment of America's *lumpen proletariat,* that uncultured—according to its critics—blue-collar working class who frequented the corner saloons and taverns of midwestern industrial cities. The musical taste of this audience, some observers asserted, ran no higher than to Lawrence Welk and his unsophisticated "mickey-mouse" or "corn" music associated with "beer, brats, and bellies."[7]

The charge of schlock does have some validity, an image fostered inadvertently, though regrettably, by the very purveyors of ethnic old-time music. To increase the genre's popularity and heighten the enjoyment of their audience, some polka musicians, bandleaders, and broadcasters often acted as clowns in their presentations. With promoters themselves approaching polka music as "happy" music, it is understandable why very few music critics took the music seriously during its heyday and later. One occasionally sees references to the genre as "novelty" music, in the same class as the zany comic renderings of Spike Jones, the rather eccentric bandleader of the 1940s.[8]

Until the current generation, leading cultural critics have eschewed or even condemned the study of *all* popular music and in fact have seriously questioned the academic study of American popular culture as a whole. A brief review of that debate illuminates the value of examining this dimension of our mass culture and clarifies the social and cultural processes represented by old-time ethnic music.

The issue of the ominous effects of the new media-based popular culture came to a head at the end of World War II, just when polka music was most widely played and heard. The timing was important, because that mid-century moment was a significant juncture of several media, old and new, which were broadcasting entertainment more powerfully and effectively than ever. Around 1950, with the mature development of radio, films, and phonograph records, and the birth of commercial television, promoters were able to utilize these media as never before. That power to influence the public so effectively caused concern among intellectuals, who saw danger in the control of this mass communication.

Earlier, a 1930s work by the Spanish philosopher Ortega y Gasset, *The Revolt of the Masses,* had become a clarion call to combat the threat of a new mass society in which irresponsible individuals controlling the media could manipulate the masses. Ortega y Gasset's gloomy prediction that a new world society threatened the cherished Western values of individualism and creativity was apparently confirmed by the rise of totalitarian regimes in several European countries. Although the Allies defeated the most powerful of these malevolent dictators, the struggle invoked the horrendous misery of World War II, and the baneful effects and dangerous character of the new mass communications remained.

Sociologist T. W. Adorno, who had fled Nazi Germany for America and was sensitive to the dangers of modern communications of which Ortega y Gasset had warned, became outspoken in the postwar debate over the new mass society. He particularly feared the effects of commercialized radio, advancing the view that what was then being broadcast on that medium really helped debase culture. Radio promoted popular music, for example, a cultural form that Adorno viewed as pernicious to our civilization because the most successful song "hits" possessed a rigid, formulaic character that stifled creativity and weakened the appreciation of "serious" classical music.[9]

Another critic, Dwight Macdonald, also called attention to the deleterious impact of popular culture on high culture, pointing out an additional factor by which mass society weakened civilization: capitalistic values, which Macdonald believed were motivating media technicians to foster a mass middlebrow culture in America that was at best mediocre. He also suggested a remedy: the way to restore the high culture that had been a hallmark of the pre-electronic culture of the past, according to Macdonald, was to assure elite control of the media.[10]

Although critics hostile to the emerging mid-century popular culture led the debate on the subject, other observers were much less pessimistic about the results of the new technology on popular taste. Somewhat more empirical in their reasoning, they shifted attention away from the villains of popular culture—that is, the promoters and manipulators of the mass media—toward the alleged "victims" of the media, the audience. David Manning White, for example, stressed the positive and uplifting effects of the new communications technology. He felt the new media were educating the masses by exposing them to the classics more generally and more often than in previous eras. Gilbert Seldes, though he accepted Macdonald's concern with and focus on the media leaders, was much more optimistic about their performance, arguing that a democratic society had its own built-in safeguard: in a free society the audience and performers could determine the most beneficial utilization of the "public arts," as he called them, through the power of regulation.[11]

For three decades following this debate, a sociologist, Herbert Gans, took the lead in the ongoing discussion, approaching the subject from another perspective with revealing results. Gans concentrated in particular on the complex relationship between the media leaders and their audience. While not discounting the dangers seen by pessimists, Gans, always the social scientist, still criticized them for failing to offer much evidence for their assertions. His own conclusion assailed their central assumption that modern society had been characterized by "massification." The concept of one persistently homogeneous mass audience, according to Gans, was a fiction. The America that he described was a plurality of taste cultures, which he believed were based chiefly on class. Furthermore, he argued that the earlier critics had exaggerated the villainy of manipulators and underestimated the degree to which the audience has some influence over what it reads, sees, and hears. By the 1970s Gans had taken the position that popular culture was not inimical to high culture, for historically the latter had often borrowed both from the former and from folk culture. Thus, while democracy and creativity might not be perfectly compatible, they might coexist in a highly technological society. Most recent scholars have agreed with Gans's critique, especially with his trenchant notion of a complex, fragmented audience.[12]

Gans's observation that America has a *plurality* of audiences is especially significant for an analysis of popular culture. Gans and others have suggested that those audiences are, or at one time were, ethnically pluralistic. He also noted that our entire popular culture has been a dynamic one, constantly changing, and that the commercialized media, including popular music, have had a strong assimilative effect on the audience—immigrants and their children. Radio, records, films, and television, he concluded, were all involved in weakening Americans' ethnic affiliations and making them rather more class-conscious. By offering ethnic audiences a higher, non-ethnic, American taste culture, the media was helping to transform or Americanize them, a sociological process that was completed by the third or fourth generation. By identifying a shift from ethnicity to class identification, he argued that observers who claimed to find a late-twentieth-century ethnic revival in America among immigrant descendants were inaccurate:

When the immigrants and their children became upwardly mobile and wanted a taste culture of greater sophistication and higher status, they found it easier to choose from American culture than to upgrade the immigrant low culture or to import higher status cultures from their country of origin. Some Jewish taste culture was Americanized, but peasant taste cultures, for example Polish, Italian, [and] Greek, have virtually disappeared except for traditional foods and religious practices—and a few dances and songs which are performed at occasional ethnic festivals.[13]

Gans's observation is extremely important to this study, as it raises the central issue concerning the relationship between ethnicity and popular music: the assimilationist impact of modern mass-media communications technology. This relationship between ethnicity and popular music is the main question that this work will pursue. It is of course noteworthy that though Gans stressed the potent transformational impact of the media he made exceptions to the process based on the persistence of ethnic music and dance, even if these cultural marks were vestigial. He added that any visible signs of ethnic identity among post-immigrant generations were superficial and unimportant, representing what he termed a "symbolic ethnicity" among the descendants of European immigrants.[14]

It is unnecessary here to review the long debate among social observers on the assimilation process. In general it resembled the exchange over "massification" or diversity in popular culture. The dominant theories of assimilation have fluctuated between suggestions on the one hand that ethnicity is dying out and arguments on the other hand that it has persisted and will endure through immigrant and later generations. The latest theories from historians, folklorists, and sociologists stress the malleability of ethnic culture, that is, the complex ways in which it changes but basically remains durable.[15]

One particular theory of ethnic persistence and change is worth examining more closely here. It deals with the relationship of popular culture and ethnic pluralism, and it questions, as I do, Gans's perception that the taste culture of an upwardly mobile, later-generation ethnic group shifts completely away from its traditional base. Recent theorists hold that when two cultures meet, instead of the dominant culture totally assimilating the minority, both majority and minority are affected. Even a small and weak minority has some influence on the majority, even on its dominant popular culture.

As early as 1939, when most scholars accepted the assimilative impact of Anglo-American culture, Yale sociologist Maurice Davie made a highly unconventional reference at a historical convention to the powerful effect of this nation's minorities. At a panel discussion later published as an essay in a work titled *The Cultural Approach to History*, Davie, well acquainted with the enigma of our ethnic diversity, insisted that when two cultures came in contact they interacted, each affecting the other. This "syncretism," as he called it, was the outcome of a mutual modification of both majority and minority.[16]

Unfortunately, in the years immediately following the appearance of Davie's novel theory, colleagues ignored it. The conventional emphasis on a one-way impact, with the majority assimilating its minorities, predominated in such works as Gunnar Myrdal's *An American Dilemma* (1944), Lloyd Warner's *Social Systems of American Ethnic Groups* (1945), and Oscar Handlin's *The Uprooted* (1952). These authors and others apparently did not think it possible that minorities in a dynamic process helped to make the American culture.

More recently, however, a reexamination of the melting-pot hypothesis has led scholars of ethnicity to reconsider the thesis that the cultural-transformation process was one-way. At a conference in the mid-1950s held under United Nations' auspices, W. D. Borrie, a social worker, made a further contribution to the study of culture change by reminding his colleagues of their involvement for several decades with the many ethnic festivals in America. Those experiences, he argued, made it inappropriate to deny "the many gifts brought by [the immigrant] . . . the impact of his ideas, his talents, his hopes upon the community that admitted him." He went on to observe, as had Davie fifteen years before, that "each element has been changed by association with the other, without a complete loss of its own cultural identity" but "with a change in the resultant cultural amalgam or civilization."[17]

The ethnic revival of the 1970s prompted one observer, Anthony Smith, to respond directly to Gans's trivializing such a development. Smith argued that ethnicity was woven more deeply into the cultural life of America than in many other countries because of American hostility to a centralized political state, acceptance of pluralism as a positive value, and geographical dispersion of the population. Gans's concept of "symbolic ethnicity" was a deceptive description of the ethnic revival because each generation maintains its group attachments in a different manner.[18]

Some social historians have further contributed to the questioning of the homogenizing power of the dominant American culture by scrutinizing the daily lives of the nation's ethnic working class. In a recent examination of ethnic and black laborers' lives in Chicago in the 1920s, Lizabeth Cohen criticizes the conventional notion that the mass media of that decade totally assimilated the lower classes. She finds instead that these blue-collar families were able to mediate films, radio, recorded music, and even national consumption patterns in a way that enabled them to preserve some of their traditional ways of life.[19] She might have gone even further in assessing the impact of these lower-class cultures had she examined how the dominant culture itself was formed. Some scholars have suggested that part of its origins may have been in the culture of those very ethnic groups.

One historian, Lawrence Levine, observed in an authoritative work on black culture both before and after slavery that Negro entertainers who made records for American companies in the 1920s retained considerable autonomy. He suggested that because record companies allowed black singers and musicians to choose and perform their own material, perhaps the assimilative power of mass culture has been overestimated:

We have become so accustomed to what appears to be the imposition of culture upon passive people by modern media that it is difficult to perceive variations in the pattern. In the case of the blues . . . (and I suspect that subsequent studies will prove this to be true of many other categories of popular entertainment as well), the imposition of taste and standards was by no means a one-way process.[20]

Other students of American popular culture, including music critics, who are not specifically concerned with the assimilationist debate, have also arrived at the conclusion that cultural influences are exchanged. In a number of long retrospective surveys of American entertainment, they strongly support the idea that immigrants and ethnic groups were and still are heavily responsible for the distinctive character of American national culture. In an authoritative historical review of the nation's popular songs from the early Anglo-American ballads of the 1700s through Tin Pan Alley and rock down to the present, musicologist Charles Hamm concluded that America's ethnic pluralism, the many varied musical traditions brought here by foreigners, was the major if not exclusive reservoir of our popular music.[21]

According to another informed observer, Carl Scheele, what the immigrants carried here as part of their cultural heritage was important not only to American songs but also to this country's entire musical theater. "The peculiarly American quality of our entertainment," he pointed out in an introduction to a succinct history "is a product of creative contributions from the uprooted of other countries, the non-native, the off-spring of those who came from somewhere else."[22] What he considered especially noteworthy was how these cultural traditions came together and actually created our national entertainment in a process involving frequent cross-cultural borrowings, a feature that as we will see was especially important to the nationalization of ethnic old-time music.

Thus, recent critics of popular entertainment have heavily emphasized the ethnic influences on American popular culture, a syncretism that challenges Gans's conclusion about the disappearance of non-Anglo-American traditions. Admittedly, students of syncretism would have to accept that an Anglo-Americanization of some sort did occur among ethnic groups; minorities have obviously lost certain cultural traits, such as language and religion, especially among the post-immigrant generations. It was these American-born children of immigrants who more than their parents were subjected to conformity pressures, nativist demands, public education, and intermarriage. However, it does appear that with music the assimilation process seems to have worked much more slowly, for reasons that have been suggested by several specialists in music and psychology.

Music therapists, who employ music to comfort and treat people who are physically or psychologically ill, have suggested one reason for the durability of ethnic music: music in general, they observe, has a little-known but unyielding staying power as a necessary form of communication, a way of conveying sentiment that may be inexpressible through other means. One psychologist, Theodor Reik, referred to a particular type of enduring music, a "haunting melody," a tune or fragment that becomes associated with an emotion and persists in the mind. A person will retain that tune and continue to associate it with that feeling.[23] A psychiatrist acknowledged this property of music more specifically in terms of popular music, even extending the concept to include lyrics as well as the melody.[24] In this sense we might conclude that this effect of music is a partial conservative protection against cultural change—in other words, it blocks total assimilation. "In listening to music," a recent scholar observed, "we cannot leave our social biographies [and the traditional cultures in which we were raised] behind."[25]

Recognizing the value of popular-music study and the importance of ethnic music to both group members and the dominant culture, we can now indicate more precisely what this study of ethnic old-time and polka music will show. It will trace the historical origins of this musical genre from its source within the groups to its widening appeal to other groups and non-group members. A piece of music may have originated within an ethnic group among various regional communities and then may have gone in several stages beyond the group to national attention in the 1930s, 1940s, and 1950s. The particularly powerful force that moved those cultural elements outward to reach a multi- and intercultural audience was the entrepreneurial motive, the strong desire to make money. That entrepreneurial spirit pervaded all participants within and without the group, including musicians, ballroom operators, and music businessmen and women of various sorts. These people understood that they could commercialize what their audience liked; they could market their product, old-time folk and new-style folk-like compositions, for profit.

Some in-group ethnic entertainers were particularly astute as they helped enlarge their audience in several ways. In the process they were encouraging a sociological change by creating a new immigrant-group identity. One way they illuminated this new identity as *immigrants* was to remind their audience of their disparate regional origins. They ingeniously selected tunes which only particular group members from small localized districts in the old country recognized as their own. Yet by citing only *some* of those localities, they could make *all* group members more comfortable by reminding them that all immigrants shared the memory of some such village or provincial home. Each *shtetl, osada, bygdelag,* or *okolica,* while distinct, was still as a locality part of the cultural heritage of the entire immigrant group in America. And features of all the localities as emigrant-producing districts were surprisingly similar.

These entertainers helped make their audiences into a more homogeneous immigrant bloc in another manner as well, by reflecting the experience of settlement in America shared by all immigrants—the problems of social and cultural adjustment in the new land. Hence, by dwelling on both the provincial roots of their audiences and the problems of group newcomers, musicians and comic entertainers helped make their listeners think of themselves as immigrant Americans. Bavarians, for example, began to assume a cultural identity also as Germans and Americans; Poznanians, as Poles and American; "Litvaks" (Russian-Lithuanian Jews), as Jewish Americans; and the Barese, Neapolitan, even Sicilian immigrants, like national Italian Americans.

As this study will show, an important element in moving this process forward within the immigrant community was the desire for private gain. The capitalist ethic fostered ethnic music from outside the group as well promoting it within and by the late 1930s had begun to make some of our popular music notably ethnic in content. Particularly during the period from around World War I through the 1920s, non-group businesses involved in the newer technological media, first in recordings and then in radio, envisioned a potentially rich market for their wares in all ethnic colonies, even the smallest.

Entrepreneurs understood that immigrants held tenaciously to their musical traditions, particularly for ritual events, such as religious ceremonies, holidays, and weddings and the like, and they profited handsomely by recording and broadcasting the beloved old tunes, the polkas, lullabies, marches, and waltzes. Each ethnic-group market accepted recordings not only from its own musical tradition but also from other ethnic traditions that were familiar and appealing. Perhaps best of all, from an entrepreneurial perspective, the purchaser of records would also have a need for other merchandise from the seller, notably a phonograph. And finally, as an additional commercial opportunity, record salespeople were shrewd enough to realize that with a phonograph in the home the ethnic consumer would be ready to consider purchasing records of a non-ethnic nature as well, including jazz, hillbilly music, and Tin Pan Alley. The idea, of course, of executives at Victor, Columbia, and other companies, was to use ethnic music to open up a once-hesitant ethnic audience to the entire range of commercially recorded sound.

By the late 1920s and the 1930s, with the effective stoppage of European immigration, the depression, hard economic times, and the near-demise of the record industry, old-time ethnic music had, contrary to expectations, substantially broadened its appeal and in fact was on the verge of becoming an integral part of our national culture. Again, the chief causes were not simply the nostalgic yearning for familiar music but were linked strongly to the introduction of new communications technology and the ever-powerful urge to make money.

At the start of the depression, radio had replaced records as the major means of conveying commercial music to the public, and ethnic radio, programs aimed directly at particular immigrant groups, was already an important factor. These radio programs, which had first emerged in the late 1920s, featured an entirely new kind of ethnic band, which differed from earlier ethnic entertainment companies in that the new ensembles were not confined to playing for any particular group. They were in fact cross-cultural bands, regional musical aggregations eager for substantial material success. From the beginning they sought broad multigroup appeal by playing pieces from several group traditions. Radio provided an ideal mechanism for wider exposure, and it was supplemented in the 1930s by other technological developments which also helped build a wider market for ethnic music, such as the jukebox, which spurred a spectacular revival of the record industry by offering records to large audiences in public places, including restaurants and taverns. The new old-time ethnic bands could now reach audiences including all kinds of Americans, who could listen and dance to old-time ethnic music.

Demographic changes also encouraged these new multi-group bands. At the same time that new entertainers were offering music with a broader appeal, a more assimilated ethnic audience was developing, with far broader musical interests. Second- and later-generation descendants of immigrants differed of course from their immigrant elders by Americanizing their language and other cultural traits, but most of them did not quickly discard their group's musical heritage; in fact, they appeared to add to it. Cultivating their own music assumed the character of a pleasurable family activity, as both old and young came together to enjoy listening and dancing to the new ethnic bands. The social occasions in local halls, dance pavilions, and ballrooms were family affairs in other ways, too, as many of the bands were actually family ensembles.

Among the newer generation, the greatest appeal of this newer kind of ethnic old-time music was its danceability. Ballroom dancing, which had become extremely popular through the 1920s, was especially suited to the music of the various ethnic groups, for much, perhaps even most, of European peasant music had always been in fact dance music, polkas, waltzes, schottisches and the like. A revival of ethnic dancing acquired many nongroup adherents, and a new international dance community arose, a network of individuals from both ethnic and mixed American backgrounds; even the least ethnic, most assimilated Anglo-Americans engaged in learning the steps of dances that had earlier been performed in ethnic communities alone.

All these developments obviously had an effect on the American music business. The eager publishers on Tin Pan Alley, always looking for lucrative hit tunes, were not particular about the musical source or tradition from which they might find their next hoped-for golden disc. Some, probably more aware of the heightened appeal of "international" music to the dance-mad public, found ethnic tunes particularly desirable and exploitable and decided to make certain ethnic old-time pieces generally popular. These promoters did indeed occasionally find hits from the musical heritage of European immigrant groups, including "Bei Mir Bist Du Shön," a catchy tune from the American Yiddish theater that made the Andrews Sisters such a fabulous success in the late 1930s, and the "Blue Skirt Waltz," a Bohemian folk tune that a decade later propelled a Slovenian American bandleader, Frankie Yankovic, out of Cleveland into national attention in Las Vegas and Los Angeles.

For the full story of how ethnic music became part of this country's "Hit Parade" by the mid-twentieth century, we must start surprisingly early, at the beginning of the nineteenth century. Oddly enough, even at that early date an important part of American popular music came from the cultures of particular non-Anglo-American groups, especially the Germans, Czechs, and Italians, whose traditional band music would become ubiquitous in America in the 1800s and early 1900s.

1

Ethnic Music
and American Band Music

In the standard survey of the history of American popular music, Charles Hamm has identified many European, African, and Latin American origins for a large number of American songs and tunes over the last two centuries.[1] During the first half of this history, one of the most important, though little understood, vehicles for that influence was the American band and band music; in fact, band music in the 1800s, with its enormously broad appeal for Americans of virtually every class and ethnic group, was, at least arguably, *the* popular music of the era.[2] Modern audiences, accustomed to associating brass bands only with the athletic field, the parade, and the disappearing circus, may have trouble imagining how ubiquitous such bands once were for concerts.

But a close examination of the American band reveals that it provided a definite and pervasive European—and therefore ethnic—stamp on our popular music, in terms of both the pieces these bands played and the musicians who played them. Demonstrating these ethnic influences, however, is no easy task, in part because the historical literature on the American brass band is so fragmentary. Scholars have devoted almost no attention to the subject, and most of the literature that does exist concentrates on famous bandleaders and an occasional virtuoso; it does not place band music in general in a larger context.

Noting the familiar pantheon of famous band musicians does have a particular virtue: it offers a clue as to the extraordinary foreign influence on American band music. While there were a number of very good native American players in the last century, most notably the "March King" himself, John Philip Sousa, it is quite clear that most of the better musical ensembles were those with Old World members, often led by Old World conductors. This European preeminence began very early, in fact at the very birth of American brass bands, which originated among incoming German communities. Although brass bands had first become evident in western and central Europe in the 1600s, by the mid-1700s German military bands were clearly perceived as models, superior to any others.[3] The first musical ensembles in America appeared in the mid-eighteenth century, with the arrival of Moravians around Salem in North Carolina and at Bethlehem in Pennsylvania. Moravians distinctively used trombones in their musical bands, then referred to as "choirs," to accompany their hymns, funerals and other festive occasions. By the early years of the nineteenth century they had produced a significant brass-band literature of sacred musical works.[4]

Through the 1800s a variety of developments in American music history led to the increasingly ethnic character of many bands. Local brass ensembles emerged far beyond the few older, pietistic colonies and became essentially civic institutions, symbols of community identity as well as performing units. Supported both by public and private sources, including societies of many sorts, such as local industries, businesses, and lodges, by the late 1800s they were evident in nearly every town in the country. Bands accompanied patriotic observances, society picnics, and the reception and welcoming of dignitaries; probably most often, however, they simply gave public concerts for the townspeople. A town's leaders and members of the social elite welcomed these bands not simply for the entertainment and health benefits they provided by encouraging marches and processions but also for an even more important function: cultural uplift. By performing nationalistic and classical selections, bands educated the people to good music and thereby contributed much to the contemporary glorification of republicanism.[5]

In this social climate, a frenzy for establishing local resident brass bands emerged in the early 1800s, a movement that also had a favorable effect on the persistence and spread of ethnicity. The growing number of bands included a growing number of ethnic brass ensembles, partly because many of the new communities then being established, particularly in the Midwest, were in fact ethnic communities and partly because American town promoters considered foreigners the best musicians and actually recruited immigrant musicians and conductors.

Nineteenth-century bands were influenced by ethnicity in two ways: first, ethnic bands performed their own religious and secular hymns, tunes, marches, and dances, thereby maintaining group religious and cultural traditions, and second, foreign bandsmen were members of, and had an influence on, non-ethnic local ensembles. In the late nineteenth century some ensembles were nationally touring "business bands" with significant musicians and leaders who were immigrants and who gave musical expression to some of their group traditions. This chapter will look more closely at the early emergence of ethnic community bands among Germans, Czechs, Lithuanians, and Finns in American, and Chapter 2 will survey the Italians, who later in the century became intimately involved with the nationally touring business bands.

Virtually all immigrant groups, of course, bring with them musical traditions from their homelands, including both the most private and intimate family lullabys and the most public national marches and airs. In the nineteenth century it appears that central European immigrants, largely Germans and to some extent Czechs, many of whom settled in the Midwest, also carried over well-developed musical organizations, choruses and bands that were models for other performers. These groups, called Mannerchors, Liederkrantz and Liedertafels, along with notable brass and wind-band ensembles, had in Europe traditionally performed on many kinds of occasions but especially at musical festivals called *saengerfests*.[6] Although many reasons for the preeminence of Germans and Bohemians in brass-band music have been put forth, certainly the explanation involves religious, folk, and military traditions that have called for that type of instrumentation and performance ever since early modern times, particularly around the era and interests of Frederick the Great.[7] One typical early example of a German musical performing body was the band at George Rapp's well-known colony, Harmony, a pietistic community established in Indiana in 1814–1815. This musical ensemble was a brass band directed by the German-born Christoph Mueller, who played both secular and religious music, apparently both German and non-German, as his group gained some prominence by 1819.[8]

Before the Civil War the settlement of German communities and even the presence of German musical teachers and leaders assured the encouragement of bands. As the standard history observes, "Any [American] geographic region with a sizable German population seemed to develop brass bands almost automatically." In Pennsylvania, throughout the Midwest—Wisconsin, Iowa, Ohio, Michigan and Minnesota—and even in Texas, a region not well-known for its German ethnicity, such settlers and bands thrived together. The large German emigration to Texas in the 1840s (which also included some Czechs) was instrumental in the development of a strong band tradition in that state. In these areas, the band movement received a boost not only from the many "Germania" bands but also from German music teachers who introduced the art to aspiring musicians of various ethnic backgrounds.[9] By the end of the antebellum era, one of the nation's leading popular composers, Louis Moreau Gottschalk, observed, somewhat hyperbolically, that "all the musicians in the United States were German."[10]

Of course the fact that many American bands were German or the product of German instruction does not automatically mean that a great deal of the band music was ethnically German. The concert repertoire was in fact a mixture of European pieces along with indigenous American tunes composed expressly for bands, but even in the early years it included what we might call both popular and classical "international" or continental selections, such as waltzes, marches, and polkas, which had already become popular in the United States. Common items in the repertoire were German, Austrian, and other European popular and operatic selections.[11] This early international character of popular band music is especially evident in the role of the Italians, a group of phenomenal musicians who as we will see in Chapter 2 helped bring about a golden age of American bands from the 1890s to World War I. A significant part of the works normally played by American bands in the 1800s—in other words, a good deal of American popular music—originated from sources with which central and later southern European immigrants were familiar.[12]

A brief historical overview of band music in the 1800s suggests the increasing appeal of brass and wind ensembles. The best estimates of the numbers of American bands indicate that about 2,300 bands in 1872 had increased to more than 10,000 by 1890 and almost doubled again by 1908.[13] From these figures we can conclude that by the turn of the century nearly every community in the nation boasted at least one band, and many larger communities undoubtedly had several. In addition to the earlier ethnic and civic bands, many more specialized units emerged, including industrial or company bands, children's bands, Negro bands, women's bands, school bands, and many new ethnic bands reflecting the nationalities of newly arrived immigrants from eastern and southern Europe and even from Asia.[14]

When we look at specific bands in specific nineteenth-century communities, it becomes evident that the roots of twentieth-century popular music in America are heavily ethnic, even familial. Amateur organizations, often family groups of musicians, played for local ethnic observances and more general community activities, and some ensembles eventually formed the basis for professional bands that toured regionally or even nationally. Communities with especially active ethnic musical organizations, such as Cleveland and central Texas, would later become the home base for commercialized old-time ethnic music. Although Germans and Bohemians were by no means the only immigrants who contributed to American band music, their contributions were central throughout the nineteenth century.

The Rural Upper Midwest

IOWA

A general history of Iowa bands of the last century typifies the ethnic character of a state's musical groups and highlights the bearing of ethnicity on musical life. During the bands' golden age, between the Civil War and World War I, units performed for community events, held competitions, and gave regular concerts. Many bands were exclusively of one ethnic group, often German or Czech, such as the all-Bohemian bands of Cedar Rapids and Protivin, the statewide touring Kouba Band, and Strasser's German Band of Davenport.[15] It seems certain that these bands performed both for Bohemian religious and festive occasions and the usual secular community affairs. The German Brass Band of Garnaville, for example, performed in 1860 at a civic event honoring an aged pioneer of the town. Such activities undoubtedly helped to improve community relations among the various ethnic groups.[16]

MINNESOTA

It is of course no coincidence that the places of heavy German and Czech settlement in Minnesota were also the most active musical band centers. In one aptly named town, New Prague, which had been settled initially in 1854 by Czechs and later included a minority of Germans and Danes, a Bohemian ensemble was first organized in the 1870s by Albert Wencel and Joseph Smisek. A six-man band organized by John Sery became very popular around 1877, playing Sery's Czech compositions. In the early 1900s, two families in particular promoted Bohemian band music in New Prague, the Komareks and the Kovariks. Jan Komarek had played with Sery as a youth and by about 1905 began his own ethnic ensemble, the "Bohemian Brass Band," which included his sons, Paul and Charles. Joseph Kovarik's father was with a New York City orchestra, and his daughter was a music teacher and organist at the major Bohemian church in town.[17]

The major German settlement in the state, New Ulm, was also appropriately named. It, too, was richly musical and was especially important not only for its plethora of brass bands but also as the eventual birthplace of an unusually large number of widely known commercial ethnic bands and bandsmen, including "Whoopee John" Wilfahrt, one of the most popular German American musicians of all time. New Ulm produced so many polka kings that in 1954, *Collier's* magazine would call the small settlement "Oompah Town."[18]

A century earlier, in 1854, Central Europeans from the Sudetenland and southwest Bohemia had first settled the area. German musical organizations, including choral groups, sprang up almost immediately. Contributing substantially to making New Ulm a musical center were members of the secular, nationalistic Turnverein, singers who gave their early public performances at the local Turner Hall just before the Civil War. The first brass band, The Silver Cornet Band, led by Robert Nix, was organized in the mid-1870s. A number of similar German ensembles followed, such as a city band led by a B. Gruenenfelder around 1880; the Concordia Band of 1884; Eckstein's Orchestra of 1894; and the Second Regiment Band of 1902.

These and other bands often gave Sunday-evening picnic concerts of largely but not solely German music. A later wave of bands, formed in the early 1900s, played music especially for dancing. Two musicians, John Lindmeier, who had played Bohemian music in Europe, and Joseph Hofmeister, along with their families, were active into the World War I era to sustain the older type of brass ensemble.[19]

WISCONSIN

Another region of German and Bohemian settlement that would become a brass-band center and later produce much commercialized old-time music was the area between Manitowoc and Kewaunee, Wisconsin, in such towns as Kellnersville, named for a German from Bohemia, and Polivkas Corners, along the western shore of Lake Michigan above Milwaukee and Sheboygan.[20] As in Minnesota, the Czech and German pioneers entered just before the Civil War with a particular enthusiasm for preserving Old-World songs. A Freier Sangerbund in Manitowoc, purporting to be the oldest in the state, celebrated its diamond jubilee in 1925.[21] Just after the turn of the century, a Chicago newspaper asserted that Manitowoc County won so many musical awards because of the ethnic origins of its citizenry: "The fact that a large percentage of the population is naturally musical is due to so many musical families having moved here some years ago from Germany and Bohemia."[22] An unusual source documenting the many brass bands in the region is a collection of photographic scrapbooks, which records activities of scores of German and Czech ensembles as far back as the 1856 Schauer Brass Band of Tisch Mills. According to that record, the Schauer ensemble began with ten members, many of them from the same family. By 1896, a few of these musicians and later generations of the Schauer family had organized two other ensembles, earning them a dominant reputation among Bohemian brass-band musicians throughout northeast Wisconsin and the Upper Peninsula of Michigan.[23]

The first uniformed military band, under Ed Weinshank, was performing in 1875, and other groups playing at private weddings, dances, and community affairs in and around Manitowoc County before 1900 included the Joe Walecka (1893), Alois Stahl (1895), Joe Ramesh (1896), and probably the Joe Schleis and Joe Blahnik family bands. A major boost in the region's quality of musical life came in 1896 with the arrival of Carl Herman Dickelman, a certified graduate of a reputable school of music in German Pomerania. Dickelman formed the first Manitowoc City Band and played with other bands around 1900. The pride of the city was the Marine Band, which was organized at the turn of the century by the German American Fred Moser; as usual, several of its sixteen members were related to one another. This group became distinguished statewide and prospered even after Moser's death around 1910; by 1922 it had won three competitions, and it continued performing for at least half a century.[24]

Most and probably all of these bands performed both for public and private occasions, playing an eclectic repertoire that included old traditional as well as American tunes. One such occasion was the celebration of Kermiss, a weeklong harvest holiday popular among Belgians, Luxembourgers, and other west Europeans. Odd as it may appear, the Bohemian violinist, Charles Kepl, of Kewaunee County, was well known for his participation in this holiday in the early 1900s.[25]

Another center of Bohemian bands was around Yuba near southwest Wisconsin's Czech concentration in La Crosse. Yuba's musical history began in 1868, and later in the century much of the community's musical life was promoted by the Rott and Stanek families.[26] In northern Wisconsin, at the town of Ashland on Lake Superior, an observer noted the importance of the Bohemian Hall, along with the bands of families and neighbors as focal points for both Czechs and non-Czechs to carry on their traditional songs and especially dances in the early 1900s.[27]

The Plains, Southwest, and Texas

Although information about the musical activities of Bohemian and German settlers outside the upper Midwest, particularly in the Great Plains states of Nebraska, Kansas, and Oklahoma, is difficult to obtain, records are extant concerning the German-Bohemian bands of Texas.[28] That history, like the account of the early bands of the western Great Lakes, is significant because Texas, too, would provide a matrix for very active, commercialized, old-time ethnic dance bands later in the twentieth century. And there, too, the growth of this musical genre was closely tied to the role of families in music, in this case the Bača clan of Fayetteville.

The Lone Star state was the destination of a significant number of central European immigrants; by 1900 Texas had 160,000 German speakers and by 1910 possibly 40,000 Czech speakers.[29] As in the upper Midwest, Germans first arrived in Texas in the 1830s, settling in rural districts, chiefly in the area of eastern Texas bounded by Houston, Austin, and San Antonio, with a few settlements scattered toward the northwest, near Dallas. But in Texas Germans and Czechs were probably more rural, dispersed, and isolated than their counterparts near the Great Lakes. Certainly they were distinctive in that more of the Czechs were from Moravia than Bohemia, and according to one folklorist they played their traditional dulcimer with their brass instruments.[30]

According to the standard accounts, the Germans arrived first, in the 1830s, with the Czech pioneers coming a little later, in the 1840s and 1850s. The two groups settled in such communities as New Braunfels, High Hill, Industry, Cat Spring, Bluff, Schulenberg, and Fayetteville. The Czechs especially concentrated in Fayette and Austin counties as well as in the larger cities mentioned above. As elsewhere, they and the Germans brought with them a strong affection for music and dancing, and therefore for bands, at private affairs such as picnics and weddings as well as at public occasions.[31] In the 1850s, still quite early in their settlement, Texas Germans organized singing societies, Liederkrantz bodies, and Gesangvereine, musical groups that participated often in parades and open competitions, the *saengerfests*.[32] In response to the listening and dancing desires of their neighbors, and simply for the love of music, local groups and especially families also formed instrumental ensembles.[33]

Even a small sampling of the region's bands amounts to a long list. In the early 1900s, the small community of Cat Spring, for example, had at least three brass bands, the Loesscher, Dittert, and Prause family brass contingents.[34] The Old Moravian Brass Band was organized in Hallettsville, probably before 1899; the Knape Brass Band of Schulenberg was composed of both Germans and Czechs before 1902; three Kossa family members helped start an Ammansville brass ensemble, probably prior to 1903; and around this time John Schindler was the bandmaster and musical family head of the regionally familiar Weimar, Texas, brass band.[35]

As in the upper Midwest, Texas's Czech and German bands used Old-World brass instrumentation, were ethnic in membership, with many members from the same families, and performed a mixed civic and ethnic folk repertoire that was both European and American.[36] Finally, as of the turn of the century all the bands appeared in their performances to be more for listening than dancing.

Among these musical ensembles, the most famous was the Bača Family Band of Fayetteville, a family unit with a history transcending several generations, through a half-century marked by transition from the earlier marching-concert band to the more modern dancing, commercial type. The Bačas resided in Fayetteville, a community that, though first settled by Anglo-Americans and a few Germans, had become known in the late 1800s as the focal point for arriving Czechs, both Moravian and Catholic.[37] A brass band was formed there in the early 1880s, but it was in 1892 that the founder of the famous Bača musical dynasty, Frank Bača, started what would become the city's best known musical ensemble.[38]

Joseph Bača had brought his family to Fayetteville from Moravia in 1860. Frank, one of Joseph's two sons, had come from Europe as an infant; Frank became devoted to music as a youth and joined a local Czech orchestra as a trumpeter. He soon made a name for himself as a talented musician and composer. He married and produced a family of thirteen children, all of whom he trained as musicians, thereby forming the Bača Family Band in 1892.[39] Appearing at a large variety of local celebrations, both public and private, at weddings, parades, and picnics in both the Czech and German communities, with father Frank as leader, the Bača ensemble earned a high reputation even beyond the state. By the end of the century it was attracting musicians from all over the country. Frank Bača's death in 1907 ended preparations he was making to have his band become a nationally touring business ensemble.[40]

Cleveland, Ohio

Cleveland resembled other regions of Czech and to some extent German musical activity in America in that it would develop in the modern era as a major old-time ethnic center, but as a much larger urban center Cleveland also reveals the influence of a culturally diverse city with a population that was more varied, more concentrated, and more working class than the rural towns of the upper Midwest and the Southwest. The most obvious difference was that Cleveland's ethnic musical centers were saloons and haⅼls that were not as group-exclusive as in the rural towns and were more open to outsiders. Nevertheless, Cleveland's early musical organizations had the same goals as those in the smaller immigrant concentrations, preserving their cultural traditions through choruses and bands. The first German singing society in the city began in 1848, and the earliest singing contests took place in 1855. The initial Czech musical group probably began in 1865, with a brass band a few years later, in 1871.[41]

Cleveland's first ethnic band, the City Grays, was organized in 1840 by an Austrian who gathered together some men who played trumpets, French horns, and the trombone. Five years later, the German Guards appeared. Bohemians probably first appeared in bands in the 1860s, but their most important musical ensemble was the Great Western Band, which a Czech reorganized in 1877 ten years after it had begun, possibly with Czech membership.[42]

Cleveland's German and Czech ethnic brass bands were similar to those elsewhere not only in the motives behind their organization but also in the family nature of their personnel. Although for most of these bands little information exists concerning membership, it is obvious that the outstanding musical aggregation was like a kinship group much like the Bačas in Texas; in Cleveland, the preeminent musical family was the Hrubys. The Hrubys succeeded in carrying out what Frank Bača had planned for his family band: they became a nationally touring musical group. Also, their musical repertoire was probably more eclectic than that of the Bačas, in that they offered not only old-time Bohemian pieces but also American and international classics.[43]

Frank Hruby was a Czech who came to Cleveland from England in 1884 with his wife and infant son, after two decades as a clarinetist in European circuses and other ensembles. Before 1890 he reorganized the Bohemian Great Western Band and with his eldest son, Frank V, and seven other offspring played at a variety of city locations, including parks and monuments. By the end of the century, Hruby's ensemble was one of three Czech Cleveland bands that had established a high reputation at both ethnic and civic functions.[44] The group played at several notable occasions, including the 1896 Republican party convention and the Harding inauguration in 1897.[45] By 1907 the band had achieved such mainstream recognition that it was giving concerts on the Lyceum and Chautauqua circuits nationwide.[46] A descendant of the Hruby founder, who is also named Frank Hruby, recently concluded that a distinctive characteristic of his city was that most of its major musicians originated from the local ethnic groups. The Hrubys themselves, he asserted, contributed substantially to the membership of the renowned Cleveland Orchestra.[47]

The clearest distinction between German and Czech music as played in Cleveland, as opposed to that played in the rural Midwest and Southwest, was the type of locations where the bands regularly played. In Cleveland, bands played in open-air beer gardens, the most popular of which, over the last half of the 1800s, was Haltnorth's Gardens, which had been started by a German immigrant saloonkeeper, hotel owner, and brewer just before the Civil War.[48] These Gardens had an Old World ambience, with wooded, open-air surroundings, and in a few years Haltnorth's became a very popular immigrant social center, the major venue for the performance of many of the city's ethnic musical organizations.[49] The most significant occasion in its history came in 1872, when the Kaiser's Imperial Band performed there on its celebrated American tour.[50]

Haltnorth's Gardens was probably not unique but was similar to other places in cities with substantial German and Bohemian concentrations. Such establishments were certainly not the low dives alleged by Anglo-American critics; rather, they were places designed for family entertainment—ornate, well-lit social centers, not bars but more like restaurants, with tables and chairs and omnipresent brass bands, which played more for listening and singing than for dancing. Although the beer gardens were social centers chiefly attracting German and other central European immigrants, they may well have appealed to a few other Americans as well.

Milwaukee

Milwaukee, for example, another concentration of German and Czech inhabitants, had a large number of such establishments, the earliest of which, Ludwig's Gardens, was opened just prior to the Civil War. The most popular of the beer gardens was Pius Dreher's, later called the Milwaukee Gardens, a huge, outdoor, tree-filled pleasure park often filled to its 10,000-seat capacity with people seeking dinner, drinking, picnics, and dramatic and musical entertainment.[51] A prominent Milwaukeean described the usual kind of musical accompaniment: "Brass bands crashed their notes into patriotic airs, *both American and German,* and also provided selections from the folk song music. The American flag would flutter freely beside or over the [German] society banners and everybody was happy to feel that he enjoyed the protection of it and at the same time grateful in the thought that he was of German origin" (emphasis mine).[52] It is very likely that beer gardens in other growing cities provided a similar function, a place where newcomers could socialize, relaxing with their families while brass bands reminded them of their familiar music.[53] Of course the bands were not permanent fixtures in these beer gardens, as musical entertainment began to change around 1900, when casual performances by local ensembles were replaced by more elaborate theatrical presentations of organized entertainment—that is, by vaudeville acts.[54]

Although much nineteenth-century band music in America was German and Czech,[55] other ethnic groups also had strong and active band organizations. Information is hard to come by, but records do exist concerning three other groups with notable band traditions: Finns, Lithuanians, and Italians. The Italian impact, which is especially important because of its close ties to American band music in general, will be the subject of Chapter 2. The folk history of Finns and Lithuanians, who also helped shape the development of American musical culture, is replete with songs, hymns, and other musical forms that everyone had sung and listened to for generations in the Old World, such as the distinctive Lithuanian piece, *daina.* While both peoples suffered under Russian domination in the 1800s, Russian rule did offer some musical advantage, including the opportunity for many Finnish and Lithuanian bandsmen to obtain musical instruction through service in the Russian military. This musical training provided skills which helped immigrants establish their ensembles here in America.

Lithuanian Bands

The Lithuanians were part of what has been termed the New Immigration, first arriving in large numbers in the 1880s, much later than the Germans and Czechs. Their major destinations were the heavy industrial centers of the East and Midwest, centering early in the coal districts of eastern Pennsylvania and later in the textile centers of New England, and the steel and meatpacking centers such as Chicago, Cleveland, and Pittsburgh. Oddly, a Lithuanian community in the small anthracite town of Shenandoah, in east-central Pennsylvania, while not the largest immigrant settlement, nonetheless became the most important Lithuanian location in the first immigrant waves. The town had almost 21,000 people in 1900, of whom perhaps as many as one-third were Lithuanians. Shenandoah was a microcosm of other immigrant industrial centers, home to people from a variety of Slavic, German, and other European nationalities.[56] With such a culturally pluralistic citizenry, it is logical that a centennial publication would claim that Shenandoah had been the home of many ethnic bands, more than any other community of its size in America—German, Lithuanian, Polish, Italian, Greek, Scotch, Welsh, and Irish bands. The Irish Elmore Band, organized in 1905, was notable; a few years after its founding it was directed by one Thomas Dorsey, Sr., whose sons, of course, became famous.[57]

The best-known Lithuanian band was the First Lithuanian Band of Shenandoah, founded in 1885 with the leadership of two families, the Navitskas brothers and the Matunis clan. During its nearly half-century of existence, it played at both private and public occasions and became highly regarded, especially after it went on tour to eastern cities during the famous anthracite labor unrest of 1902 to raise money for the striking mineworkers.[58] By that date, a second Lithuanian brass band had been organized in Shenandoah, and others were formed in nearby Mahanoy City, Pittston, and Scranton, and further afield in Chicago and Worcester, Massachusetts.[59]

One authority has indicated the stages by which Lithuanian instrumentalists formed bands by the turn of the century. The Roman Catholic parishes needed both singers and accompanists for their choirs; parents wanted their children to learn the music and play an instrument; and on occasion a latecoming immigrant familiar with Russian army band ensembles became available in the immigrant colonies to form the young peoples' ensembles that adult parishioners wanted. These early musical bodies were called *kapelijonis* and later would become more formal *benais,* with initiation fees, dues, regular meetings, and uniforms. All members were amateurs, part-time musicians whose basic occupations were as factory hands or mineworkers.[60]

Finnish Bands

The Finnish band-making experience was similar to that of the Lithuanians, but with some differences reflecting the Finns' cultural characteristics. Arriving in America at the same time as the Lithuanians, the Finns settled in a few New England, Ohio, and New York colonies, but about 70,000 Finnish Americans—roughly half the American Finnish population as of 1900—concentrated around the northern Great Lakes, as mineworkers and lumbermen in Michigan, Wisconsin, and Minnesota.[61] Later, Finns also sought similar kinds of employment in the Northwest.

The Finns in America were more fragmented than the Lithuanians, with strong contingents of religious, nationalist, temperance, and socialist adherents, all of whom had substantial musical traditions. Perhaps surprisingly, the group that promoted brass bands most enthusiastically was the temperance faction, which more often than the other groups sponsored ethnic festivals known as the *iltama*. These festivals were cultural meetings whose lengthy programs included speeches, plays, and music and usually ended with dancing accompanied by a brass band.[62] Around 1900, temperance societies, with their long history of support for brass bands, joined with the socialists in many communities to build social centers, usually called the Finn Hall, for folk-music concerts and theatrical programs.[63]

The earliest Finnish bands probably began in the 1870s in Oregon and Michigan's Upper Peninsula; much more is known, however, about an ensemble in Hancock, Michigan, which started in 1886, almost exactly the time of the founding of Shenandoah's Lithuanian band.[64] A band-organizing fever spread among the American Finns from the mid-1890s into the early 1900s, prompted by the breakup at the end of the century of the Finnish army battalions in Russia, which sent many unemployed military instrumentalists to America in search of work. The musicians found work in both American and Finnish American bands.[65]

One of these emigrant band organizers was George E. Wahlstrom, who deserves the title "Father of Finnish American Bands." A horn player in the army in Europe in 1897, he came to the United States in 1903 and proceeded to organize and energize a large number of musical groups. Over the next two decades, he directed the major Finnish ensembles, especially the best-known Humina Band founded in Ashtabula, Ohio, in 1894; the Monessen, Pennsylvania, Louhi

Band, founded in 1900; and the Imatra Band of Maynard, Massachusetts, founded in 1903.[66] Finnish American bands became common in Finnish settlements under the leadership of a number of other conductors, such as J. F. Jacobson, who headed at least six ensembles, and George Sjoblom, Wahlstrom's successor, who promoted band and choral music in Pennsylvania and New York City.[67] One estimate is that there were probably one hundred Finnish ensembles playing in America by the end of World War I, concentrated in the Finnish colonies in Michigan's Upper Peninsula.[68] Calumet, Michigan, for example had about ten bands at that time.[69]

Although the Humina Band of Ashtabula was the most successful, in several respects it was representative both of Finnish community bands in general and of the other immigrant ensembles we have examined. Their eclectic repertoire was heavily Finnish but also included material extending from classical to folk and even to contemporary American pieces. They played at civic as well as ethnic functions and were so important in community life that the city of Ashtabula sought to rename the group as the City Band, a change the Finns overruled.[70] A photograph of the Rock Springs, Wyoming, Finnish band escorting Spanish-American War volunteers behind the American flag depicted a civic role for these bands that was not an unusual occurrence.[71]

The Humina Finnish bandsmen were in fact all bands*men,* without women members, but perhaps surprisingly they were not all Finnish American. Most were local, self-taught musicians with a high esprit de corps, who earned their living as laborers unloading ore boats. What distinguished the Humina group was its high reputation; also, it was not as localized as other ensembles, for it occasionally toured some of the Finnish American colonies.[72]

Unquestionably, the Finnish American bands won the hearts of their community audiences. Their decline beginning in the late 1920s probably resulted more from the impact of newer forms of disseminating music, such as records and radio, than from rejection by an increasingly assimilated audience. Even now, at the end of the twentieth century, a few Finnish American musical ensembles remain. And the earlier bands had definitely appealed both to immigrant and American-born generations, an appeal noted by an observer of the Monessen Louhi Band: "We know how difficult it is to get our American-born youngsters to take part in our Finnish activities, which they do not understand or comprehend. Music alone they understand; it enchants and attracts them."[73]

2

Italian Bands
and American Popular Music

Like other immigrant institutions, American ethnic bands had two cultural functions: a conscious role in maintaining traditions from the old country, along with a less evident function as an Americanizing force, a community bond that helped group members feel a part of their new environment. German and Czech bands had served this dual function in early American society, and throughout the 1800s, as band music became increasingly popular in the United States, ensembles of immigrants from other ethnic traditions appeared on the American scene. To be sure, ethnic bands were not the only or even the major element in the growth of this form of public entertainment; non-ethnic bands probably predominated, especially in what is recalled as the golden era of band music, the late 1800s and early 1900s. But foreign musical groups were a significant presence in the open-air brass- and wind-band concerts typical of the turn of the century.

A particular kind of band, the "business band," became widespread during this golden age. The business band was a professional group of musicians who earned their livelihood primarily by traveling on concert tours. Although the repertoires of the business bands differed from those of the local ethnic ensembles by appealing to a broader audience, including non-ethnic and multi-ethnic Americans, both kinds of bands were influenced by ethnicity. Some of the business bands that toured cities and towns across the nation helped to define in ethnic terms the music regarded by Americans in general as their popular music. This ethnic impact on America's national band music is evident when we look at the contribution of the Italians, an immigrant group that made up a large segment of the business-band musicians and conductors.

As was the case with the Germans and Czechs, the Italians came to influence American bands and band music in part because of the extraordinary need in late-nineteenth-century America for well-trained musicians. The growing popularity of bands and their music after the Civil War created such a shortage of musical talent that American-born musicians could not meet the demand. The dearth of good instrumentalists was exacerbated by the absence of music schools and conservatories in the United States, which lacked the Old-World tradition of upper-class musical patronage. Hence, when American music lovers and leaders sought musical talent for their bands, they had to turn to European-trained immigrants, who were generally considered superior to American-born musicians.[1] Very much aware of this superiority of foreign musicians, American community leaders and band promoters competed vigorously with one another to recruit immigrant bandsmen and conductors.

In 1889 an observer bemoaned the absence of American schools for training talented native musicians. "Were it not for the 'foreign element' so largely represented in *American* bands," he noted, "the latter would be far less numerous, prosperous, and creditable" [my italics]. Among the ethnic groups he considered particularly important in the makeup of popular bands he named Germans first, followed by Italians.[2]

Probably the most significant evidence of the role of immigrants in America's leading bands of the era was the composition of the best-known ensemble, that of John Philip Sousa, the March King. Sousa's father was a Portuguese immigrant trombonist who had been invited to join the Marine Band in the mid-nineteenth century, and Sousa himself became an apprentice member of the ensemble in 1868 and its director in 1880, at the age of twenty-five. In his decade or so as conductor, he made the Marine Band into an excellent and widely known performing ensemble, a success story that was based in part on the musical ability of the band's players, many of whom were foreigners.[3] When Sousa left the Marine Band in 1892 to form an independent business band, he chose his band members carefully and included many immigrant musicians from another famous ensemble, which had just disbanded following the death of its leader,

Patrick Gilmore. Simone Mantia, the well-known Italian euphonium virtuoso, was one of about forty foreigners among the fifty performers in Sousa's new band.[4]

Practical considerations also lured European musicians across the Atlantic. The low wages of an ordinary bandsmen in the United States military service, about $20 per month in the 1890s, deterred American-born musicians but appealed to foreigners. Military commanders responsible for filling band roles hence looked for musicians where they could easily locate foreigners—at the New York immigrant depot—where they found many willing enlistees among the arriving musicians.[5]

Germans and other immigrants liked and even preferred service in a military band, despite the low salary, for they viewed such employment as an expeditious means of settling in the United States. In the 1870s one American military leader eager to build up his musical contingent said he was told that "upon the arrival of German emigrant ships . . . plenty of good musicians could be had."[6] Many nineteenth-century military musical units, especially in the West, had sizable contingents of European instrumentalists.[7]

Military commanders were not alone in perceiving that foreign musicians were superior to their American-born counterparts. Sousa himself, as we noted, reflected the general esteem for Europeans in music by including a high proportion of foreigners in both his civilian and military musical ensembles. The public regard for foreign musicians also affected Sousa in a more personal way: he once confessed that early in his career he grew a beard to make himself look exotic, in the hope of appearing better qualified for musical employment.[8]

Although the precise numbers of foreigners in American civilian and military musical units in the 1800s cannot be calculated, immigrant musicians were widespread in all regions except the South, extending far beyond centers of immigrant settlement. In fact, foreign-born instrumentalists were surprisingly important to *all* American music, both classical and popular, in the last decades of the century. The 1870 census, for example, listed more foreign- than native-born professional musicians in the United States as a whole.[9]

Italian musicians were nearly everywhere in the 1800s, beginning just after midcentury, in the earliest years of Italian immigration, and even showing up in such perhaps-unexpected areas as the far West. The experience and wide-ranging mobility of Achilles La Guardia, the father of Fiorello La Guardia, the well-known mayor of New York, was not exceptional for immigrant band players. Achilles La Guardia had been well trained and experienced as a cornetist in Europe before coming to New York in the early 1880s, accompanying a female Italian singer. In 1882, just months after Fiorello's birth, Achilles joined the Eleventh U.S. Infantry band as its leader and proceeded to the Dakotas, Arizona, and other posts in the West and South before returning to Italy in 1898, at the time of the Spanish-American War.[10] Another example of Italian musicians in western bands was in the ensemble established by a large western mining company in Butte, Montana. When first organized in 1897 the band was Cornish, but it soon became largely Italian.[11]

Foreigners, especially Germans and Italians, also helped meet the personnel needs of that ubiquitous ensemble in the late nineteenth and early twentieth centuries, the circus band. Circuses and carnivals, of course, were common throughout the country, and promoters experienced constant difficulty recruiting enough musicians to lead the parades and accompany the acts. One of the era's circus-band experts proposed that bandmasters solve their personnel problems by hiring foreign musicians:

During this period [1880–1929] there was a dearth of competent musicians in this country with the result that a great many were encouraged to come in from Germany and Italy. Not all of these were assimilated by the American concert bands. . . .Carnivals competed with circuses for the services of musicians. . . .[T]he John Robinson show and the Pawnee Bill Wild West used Italian bands exclusively[;] likewise Italian musicians furnished the perfect tempo and showmanship for the circus side shows.[12]

The general welcome, recognition, and acceptance of Europeans in American musical organizations are especially significant, as the circus observer suggested, because the foreign-born character of the bands affected their repertoire. It is no coincidence that the repertoires of many major business concert bands were heavily European, especially Italian, or that Italian overtures and arias, as we will see, became familiar to American band audiences. Understanding the musical influence of these immigrants necessitates considering the traditional importance of band music among Italians and the specific context in which immigrant musicians became involved in nineteenth-century American military and business bands.

In late-eighteenth-century Italy, German influence brought brass and percussions to the Italian wind bands, which were becoming a vital element of peasant culture.[13] Individual musicians had been present earlier, of course, but by the early 1800s demonstrations of religious fervor among the peasants and of affection for the patron saints of their villages and towns had assumed a character that involved music. In frequent outdoor celebrations, musicians led processions of townspeople, thus making instrumentalists a conspicuous feature of the local *festa* honoring a village's patron saint. The musical contingent at the *festa,* the Italian wind band, was similar to the nineteenth-century American town band in that it participated in local public events, often under the patronage of a local merchant or businessman. But the Italian band was perhaps more important to community life, because its performances had a religious as well as a secular function. These bands were certainly popular and nearly universal in Italy, where, by the end of the nineteenth century, almost five thousand bands represented nearly every community and military unit in the nation.[14]

The Old World Italian band had a distinctive character that would carry over into the New World. Its repertoire was much more lyrical than that of the military-style ensembles of the Germans and Czechs in Central Europe. The Italian bands led processions by emphasizing melody rather than precise cadence. For example a kind of ensemble known as the *Ballabe* band, which was representative of the many small, folk-like groups throughout Italy, played pieces more for dancing and singing than for formal marching.[15]

Not surprisingly, then, opera music became an important feature of the band repertoire all over Italy, especially in the Abruzzi and Apulia regions, two areas that produced many emigrants who headed for the United States.[16] The most popular band pieces were the arias and melodies of Rossini, followed closely by the works of Verdi, Bellini, and other Romantics. The audience for these selections was multi-class, including the Italian elite as well as the ordinary peasantry. The love of opera music was everywhere, in the streets as well as in the salons; opera was performed formally in the nation's many opera houses but also informally, even at marionette shows. "Opera transcriptions were played in the open air," one writer observed, "by the military bands [and also] by the barrel organs."[17]

Gioacchino Rossini's use of the folk and popular idioms led to an extraordinary popularity for his music among the Italian masses.[18] Rossini's operas were part of every Italian band's repertoire, and the composer himself was regarded as a national or ethnic hero, the object of a hero-worship similar to more recent adoration of media stars.[19] Needless to say, Italians who emigrated to America shared their compatriots' love of opera, and in fact came to associate the musical genre with their ethnic identity as Italian Americans.[20] Hence, when an American band, either with or without Italian musicians, or when an Italian business or community band in America played a selection from Rossini or another of the Italian bel canto composers of the day, the performance was doubly gratifying to Italian immigrants. The playing of the piece signified American recognition of Italian culture, and it also suggested the extent to which Italian music had become an integral part of American popular culture, standard fare in the general band repertoire.[21] Without question, Italian opera music was both ethnic and American popular music.

Through the late nineteenth and early twentieth centuries, American audiences at band concerts heard programs that included some American music but relied heavily on European music, and especially on Italian opera pieces. This ethnic slant to the repertoire in part reflected the European roots and Old World training of America's better musicians and conductors of the era. Some of these bandsmen had come to America from central Europe, but especially in the turn-of-the-century golden age of bands many of them were Italian.

As early as 1804, President Thomas Jefferson had suggested to the Marine Corps Commandant that he augment the struggling five-year-old Marine Band with musicians imported from Italy. The following year, an American naval squadron sailed to the Mediterranean and returned with enlistees from Italy.[22]

Although outnumbered by central Europeans in American bands until the end of the century, Italians were nonetheless prominent long before then in certain locales and especially at the national level. The evidence in this early period is fragmentary but suggestive. A son of Italian immigrants led the U.S. Marine Band throughout the 1810s and most of the 1820s and intermittently through the rest of the century. A Portsmouth, New Hampshire, Italian Band in 1839 offered a typically mixed repertoire of American patriotic airs and Italian opera music. Possibly the first touring band in America was a Sicilian ensemble active around 1840 and also playing a mixed repertoire of Italian and American music.[23]

The father of the American business concert band was Patrick Gilmore, himself an immigrant, though Irish rather than Italian. Gilmore started his professional touring ensemble in 1859 and became the nation's leading band conductor until Sousa assumed that title about 1890. Many of his bandsmen were Italians, and many Italian bandleaders emerged later to compete with Sousa in the band business. A review of the musical careers of these immigrants provides examples of how Italian musicians drew on their cultural inheritance in their work with American bands.

One of the earliest concert-band performers and leaders was Carlo Alberto Cappa. After a solid musical education at the Royal Academy in Asti, Italy, and a short stint as a musician with the Italian Lancers, a military unit, Cappa left for Boston in 1858 to form his own ensemble.[24] Two years later he went on to New York to join one of the nation's leading groups, the Seventh Regiment Band, then under the baton of another Italian, Claudio S. Grafulla, who himself was active in many local ethnic activities.[25] Cappa replaced Grafulla in 1881 and led the band until his death in 1893. Like his predecessor, Cappa seemed to retain an awareness of Italian culture, especially in his musical compositions, which were reminiscent of his native Sardinia and Italy, and participated occasionally in community ethnic activities. Undoubtedly, the commendation he had received from the Italian king for his musical ability must have reinforced his traditional attachments. In addition, in the many performances he gave in New York's Central Park as well as when on tour, he regularly included in the programs of his concerts the bel canto opera pieces.[26]

Another Italian immigrant bandleader who achieved national attention was Francis Maria Scala, who led the U.S. Marine Band for more than fifteen years, substantially adding to its reputation for musical quality. Scala joined the U.S. Navy in Naples in 1841 and proceeded to America shortly thereafter. By the time he retired in 1871 he had improved the performances of the Marine Band by recruiting European musicians and heavily emphasizing musical pieces from his own cultural tradition, especially opera, and especially Verdi. One of his biographers estimates that about 90 percent of Scala's concert selections were operatic: "Where music was concerned [Scala] remained an Italian through and through. Italian opera was his first love. He followed the world of opera closely and often made arrangements from new operas."[27]

Scala's successor on the Marine Band podium in the 1880s was John Philip Sousa, not an Italian but the son of a Portuguese immigrant. Sousa maintained the superior reputation of the ensemble and was himself succeeded as conductor by another Italian musician,

Francesco Fanciulli, who like the others was conspicuously ethnic in the music he conducted. Fanciulli was born in 1853 in Porte San Steno near Rome, and like most of his emigrant predecessors he had completed a formal musical education at an Italian conservatory, in his case in Florence. By the age of twenty-three, when he decided to leave for New York to try his luck as a church organist and teacher, Fanciulli had played cornet and conducted several orchestras in Italy and had also become something of a composer. While crossing the Atlantic on his way to America in 1876, he began to express his attachment for his cultural home by writing *The Voyage of Columbus,* a composition focused on the heroic Italian that would later be described by Patrick Gilmore as excellent descriptive music.[28]

Partly at Gilmore's encouragement, Fanciulli became leader of the U.S. Marine Band in 1892, after Sousa had resigned to form his own touring concert ensemble. Until 1897, when Fanciulli resigned, he presented in the Marine Band repertoire a mixture of Italian and American pieces, including a number of his own compositions, one of which was entitled *From Italy to America.* He also wrote three operas, one in Italian and two in English, and he recorded a number of Italian operatic and nationalistic selections, reflecting both his native and adopted countries.[29]

By the end of the century band music was ubiquitous in America. Sousa's band toured both the United States and Europe, and tens of thousands of local community bands bands played marches, operatic selections, and other popular pieces. In addition, other ensembles crisscrossed America, bands with a distinctive presence both musically and theatrically: the Italian business bands. Italian bands stood out from the others because of their leaders who entertained audiences with eccentric, even bizarre histrionics on the podium as well as with opera selections and other Italian music. These all-Italian or nearly all-Italian ensembles were a significant part of the golden age of American bands, and among their contributions to American entertainment was education of the public to their own ethnic music.

The heyday of the traveling Italian bands began around the turn of the century and continued to their decline (though not disappearance) around 1920. Two of the leaders of the most popular of these bands were Alessandro Liberati and the best-known Italian band conductor of all, Giuseppe Creatore, whose impact on the American public was phenomenal and would become a model for ethnic entertainers around the turn of the century. Among the many

Italian touring ensembles of the era were Gregory's, Corrado's, and Gallo's Italian Bands; bands led by Marco and Orestes Vesella, Don Phillipini, and Alfred Tommasino; and the Ferulla, Satriano, Cassassa, Donatelli, Ruzzi, and Francesco Creatore Bands. Francesco and Giuseppe Creatore are likely not related.[30]

Even before the emergence of the great Giuseppe Creatore and his imitators, a few pioneering Italian ensembles had already stamped their performances with a flamboyant character and had begun to establish the popularity of a mixed American and European, but especially Italian, repertoire. One of these early groups was the Banda Rossa, conspicuous in red attire, under the direction of Eugenio Sorrentino, who came with his musicians to America in 1897, but the best known of these early bands was the band under Signor Alessandro Liberati.

Liberati was born in Italy in 1847 and before his teen years was playing his father's instrument, the bugle. He later shifted to the cornet and served as a bandmaster in his native country before arriving in the United States via Canada. In 1872 he led the National Guard Band in Detroit and then moved on to several other American ensembles, including the well-known Gilmore band, with which he played in the late 1870s and 1880s. Liberati formed his own ensemble, the Grand Military Band, in 1893, an especially successful group that featured prominent Italians as the leading musicians.[31]

The public knew Liberati not only for his competence as a bandleader but also for his unusual showmanship, such as directing his band while mounted on horseback.[32] Throughout his career he reminded audiences of his ethnic identity by performing not only selections from grand opera but even arrangements of entire acts.[33]

Unquestionably, the paramount figure among Italian band musicians and conductors during the golden age of band music was Giuseppe Creatore, that most Italian American bandsman who figured in the Broadway musical *Music Man* as the musician described by Harold Hill as a rival to the great March King himself, John Philip Sousa. Creatore possessed in abundance the flair, musicianship, and devotion to Italian opera that characterized Italian American bandsmen in general, and his career is worth examining in detail, despite the surprising absence of a comprehensive biographical source.

Creatore was born in Naples on June 21, 1871, and though little is known about his family, his parents must have encouraged him to take up an instrument because as a young boy in 1878 he was receiving a musical education, studying with a Maestro Di Nardis.[34] He later attended the Naples conservatory, where his major instrument was the trombone. He became an excellent trombonist and was also recognized by his teachers, while still a teenager, as an able conductor. He performed on tour in European capital cities when he was only fourteen years old, and in 1887, when he was just seventeen, he accepted an appointment as director of the Naples Municipal Band. The following year he organized his own musical group, which toured Italy until 1895.[35]

Unlike Cappa, Scala, Fanciulli, and other Italian musicians who preceded Creatore in America, Creatore did not emigrate on his own to join American military bands. Instead he arrived in the United States in 1899 as a member of a touring Italian musical ensemble, serving as concertmaster of the Royal Marine Band under Giorgio Minoliti.

The Royal Marine Band was not the first foreign ensemble to tour America, and though information is scanty, American tours by European bands were probably not uncommon around the turn of the century. American concert promoters, aware of the public's high regard for European musicians, must have been eager to arrange tours of foreign bands.[36] For example, the 1884 tour of a thirty-two-man Czech group under Vojtech Holecek proved highly profitable. The band's inaugural concert drew an audience of ten thousand to Philadelphia's Ridgeway Park on May 11; obviously, not all the concert-goers were Czechs.[37]

While it is unclear who sponsored the Italian Royal Marine Band's enormously popular American tour that began in New York in 1899, within a few years a host of other Italian bands came to America. Undoubtedly, the American triumph of the Royal Marine Band was largely the work of Creatore, who took over as conductor when bandleader Minoliti fell ill in Philadelphia in August 1900. Creatore's showmanship and musical leadership created a sensation.[38]

When he assumed the baton, the Italian band was filling a three-month engagement at one of the nation's major band concert centers, Willow Grove Park in Philadelphia. Creatore did not simply lead his players with his baton; he inspired them to do their best by flailing his arms and even descending from the podium to exhort his musicians individually at their seats. These histrionics were unconventional, but they were apparently effective, eliciting extremely positive reviews. The reviewer for the *New York World,* for example, wrote of "inspired performances" led by a conductor who was the "sensation of the century."[39] Over the next few decades, on tours throughout the United States and Canada, Creatore's distinctive sweeping gestures, along with his flowing black hair and "formidable" moustache, earned him such sobriquets as "Svengali of the Baton" and "Toscanini of Band Music".[40]

With Creatore's great triumph in Philadelphia, some members of the Royal Marine Band decided to leave Minoliti entirely and join the eccentric trombonist in a new ensemble. In the spring of 1901, Creatore's new group performed at the Steel Pier in Atlantic City and then set off on a five-thousand-mile tour of America, all of which was a great success. When Creatore saw a need to recruit more band members he did not, of course, seek out musicians in America, where everyone knew that talent was in short supply, but returned to Italy, where the reservoir of musicianship was larger and of better quality. He was back in New York in 1902, this time with a sixty-man ensemble.[41]

Creatore's return to his homeland paid off immediately with a highly successful premier concert at the famous Hammerstein Roof Garden in New York. Over the next twenty years Creatore became a legend among band-music lovers, continuing to tour nationally and further adding to his popularity by making records. He produced an immense number of records, probably as many as 145.[42] Beginning in 1910, Creatore and his band also spent six years on the famous Chautauqua circuit. Perhaps the most successful of all their appearances was their engagement at the 1915 Panama-Pacific Exposition in San Francisco.[43]

Ironically, the growth of the record industry in the early years of the century both boosted Creatore's popularity and led to the decline in concert performances that ruined his and so many other business-band ensembles around World War I. The wind and brass bands now had to compete with a new musical craze that was sweeping the country, jazz. As jazz music and the new dance bands that played it became more popular, the public's appetite for the older kinds of band music was dampened. Creatore and all his Italian and American band colleagues began to lose favor with the general public, except with that segment of the audience, which included some immigrants and some upper-class native-born Americans, that retained an interest in opera. Creatore had always included his people's bel canto arias and overtures as a part of his band repertoire, and until the end of his musical career in the 1930s, his programs usually included lengthy arrangements of operatic works.[44]

For example, in his band concerts at Willow Grove Park in 1902, 1903, and 1911, and in his band's early recordings for Gramofono and Edison from 1911 to 1918, he demonstrated a particular devotion to the works of Verdi and Rossini.[45] It has been estimated that between one-third and one-half of his entire repertoire consisted of opera and operetta.[46] One authority calls him a "salesman of the Italianate style" who often played Italian folk tunes and patriotic pieces along with opera and "reflected his heritage to a degree unparalleled by any other Italian bandsmen."[47]

Around World War I, as band music began to decline, Creatore decided to form his own opera companies. His early attempts failed, but in 1918 he succeeded in starting a company that flourished for five years.[48]

Creatore's career, then, is instructive, showing how Italian musicians helped to make their ethnic music part of American popular music and culture. Even the repertoires of non-Italian bands included much Italian bel canto; for example, of two hundred concert programs performed around the turn of the century by John Philip Sousa's band, the nation's most popular ensemble, more than one-third of the selections in those programs were opera music.[49] Lawrence Levine, a distinguished historian of American popular culture has observed that in the late nineteenth century, romantic opera appealed to music lovers of every class; no distinction between high and low culture had yet emerged. The audience for bel canto included virtually the entire public, both the most and least sophisticated, native-born and immigrant. The same Americans who bought the sheet music of Stephen Foster might also buy sheet music of Rossini.[50] While Levine argues that the tastes of the American public began to diverge at the turn of the century, the experience of Italian bandsmen and the explosion in popularity of band music in general suggest a date closer to the onset of World War I.

Italian Americans may never have drawn a line between high and low culture. The proliferation of local Italian American bands reflected the appeal of Italian classical music across class lines. And with so many Italian musicians in mainstream American bands, Italian romantic opera exerted a strong influence on American popular music across the board.

As we have seen, bands had been important in European village life, and like immigrants from other parts of Europe, Italian Americans were interested in retaining their traditional culture. No doubt the notable success of the Italian business bands that were traversing the country in the 1890s and afterward was a further stimulant to the creation and continuance of local ensembles. These amateur musical groups numbered in the hundreds by 1900 and continued to flourish long after American professional bands had declined following World War I. The general popularity of the operatic repertoire of Italian bands may help account for the persistence of these local groups, as their music and performances including bel canto appealed to more than just their own ethnic community and even provided a basis for good intergroup relations in many areas: "These [amateur ethnic] bands not only provided diversion for the Italian sections of various communities, but [they] also are credited with helping establish goodwill between immigrants and their American neighbors."[51]

The Italian community ensembles usually originated for traditional observances that called for music, such as religious or funeral processions. Not surprisingly, one of the earliest Italian American centers of musical activity was New Orleans, the home of both jazz and the marching band. In fact, the Italian brass-band tradition there helped to produce some leading jazz musicians with Italian ethnic backgrounds. As a distinctively cosmopolitan port city in the nineteenth century, New Orleans was the setting for many marching brass bands. Musical processions of various ethnic groups, European and African, were a common sight any season or any time of day.[52] The city's Italian community started very early; by 1850, almost one thousand Italian immigrants had settled there, more than in New York. The influx grew in the 1880s with the arrival of boatloads of Sicilian agricultural workers, and by the mid-1920s the city was home to nearly 300,000 Italians, mostly Sicilians.[53] By the time Italians began to settle in the city, audiences in New Orleans were already familiar with their music; the first Italian opera performance was in 1836, by which date Italian musicians were giving concerts there. Although it is difficult to state precisely when the Italian community in New Orleans first established its own bands, at least two well-known ensembles were active before the 1910s. The Contessa Entellina Society Band was made up of a particularly distinctive group of Albanians who had settled in Sicily in the Middle Ages; about

3,000 Sicilian Albanians eventually immigrated to New Orleans, where they set up the Contessa Entellina mutual aid society in 1886. Generally prosperous as retail merchants, these *arbushi,* as they were known, decided to form a band chiefly to help celebrate their annual feast day. The musical ensemble continued for more than three-quarters of a century, until 1961, and played on numerous occasions, both Italian and American.[54]

In this musically rich urban and ethnic environment emerged some of the major Italian American jazz musicians, including Domenic James "Nick" La Rocca, organizer of the Original Dixieland Jazz Band; Joseph "Wingy" Manone; "Papa Jac" Jacinto Assunto and his sons, Fred and Frank, of the Dukes of Dixieland; Philip Zito; and the Primas, Leon and especially his better-known brother, Louis, who will be discussed below. Hearing and seeing the many ethnic marching bands in the city, particularly the Italian ones, motivated many of the city's leading jazz musicians, some of whom, such as Irving Fasola, actually played in them.[55]

In cities where local conditions did not favor musical development quite so strongly, Italians began forming community bands a few years later than in New Orleans, generally around the time of World War I. Although we cannot estimate the total number of these amateur ensembles, they were undoubtedly widespread, for they met a compelling psychological need of immigrants to retain their group identity in a distant land and alien environment. Bands were especially important at community and family events, including traditional public affairs such as church *festas* on saint days; more personal occasions, such as weddings and funerals; and new patriotic holidays, such as Columbus Day, the observance of which became widespread in several states in the 1900s.

In 1893, in the small Italian community of Ybor City in Tampa, Florida, in 1893, a casket was "carried by four large men with uplifted hats, followed by a brass band, then an empty hearse and carriage."[56] Around the turn of the century, one of the earliest elaborate band parades took place in the nation's largest Italian community, Little Italy on New York's famous Lower East Side. A number of bands from Italian communities of New York and New Jersey assembled in Little Italy to help celebrate a national holiday, the Invasion of Rome, which had helped free the country from the influence of the Vatican.[57]

The several Italian colonies in western Pennsylvania, chiefly in coal and steel towns, were especially rich in amateur community brass bands in the first half of the twentieth century. The earliest of these musical groups were probably formed in the 1880s in the coal-mining regions of Lawrence and Beaver Counties. Detailed information is available on these bands which suggests that in addition to the usual desire to continue traditional music some of these bands aspired to surprisingly high musical standards, with the encouragement and direction of European-trained musicians, often Italians who had come to town to establish a local music school. The first of these western Pennsylvania bands was probably started at New Castle in 1898, when Feliciano De Santis, a recently arrived music instructor, set up the Duke of Abruzzi Band at his school. The ensemble gave its first formal concert in 1904, at an ethnic procession. It became known later as La Banda Rossa, the Red Coat Band, because of its uniforms. Italian railroad workers started a second band in the area before World War I, and a third band, the Musical Political Italian Club Band, was formed at Woodlawn (Aliquippa), Pennsylvania, in 1917 or 1918, made up chiefly of farmers and shepherds from Patrica in Italy. As one might imagine, the repertoire of all these ensembles was a mixture of folk, opera, patriotic, and American popular selections.[58]

Among the better-known organizers and conductors of Italian community bands was Loreto Marsella, who initiated or helped to develop at least three musical ensembles in Rhode Island and Pennsylvania. Born in Italy in 1874, he may have received some musical training before emigrating to Rhode Island in 1895 to work in a weaving factory. He soon established the Crescent Park Concert Orchestra and then the Duke of Abruzzi Band in Providence. In 1908 he moved to Philadelphia, where he set up a music school and became known for his compositions, his conservatory, and still another Italian band, the Verdi Band of Norristown, which he founded around 1920 at the request of parishioners at Holy Saviors Church and continued to direct for the next forty years.[59]

Two leading community bands in Chicago also suggest the success over time of Italian bands and the importance of their individual founders. Domenico Filacchione, who probably had some Old World musical training before he arrived in Chicago in 1918, formed a band in 1920 that became a common sight at religious and ethnic festas for the next forty years. A second bandleader, Raffaele Strocchia, emigrated from Naples around 1925 and started a musical group soon after, which quickly gained a wide reputation among Chicago's Italians, particularly for its huge Italian and American repertoire. Its high point was a performance at the Chicago World's Fair in 1933, but it continued performing until the mid-1960s.[60]

The small industrial city of Watertown in upstate New York experienced an influx of Italian immigrants around the turn of the century that included a young music teacher from the province of Salerno named Jimmy Marra. Marra, who had graduated from the Royal Conservatory of Music in Naples, arrived in Waterbury in 1904 at the age of twenty and organized a band in 1911. This band, though it became known for performances at the many tourist areas in the vicinity rather than at ethnic festivals, consisted entirely of railroad workers, many of whom were Italian, and four of whom were Marra's brothers. The mixed repertoire of Marra's band concentrated, as might be expected, on opera arias and overtures.[61]

Thus, over the entire nineteenth and early twentieth centuries Italian bandsmen added their cultural talents to New World music—to the cultural life of their own ethnic community but also to that of the non-Italian majority. As professional musicians in military and business bands, music instructors, and ordinary citizens active in community ensembles, these cornetists, trombonists, clarinetists, and other instrumentalists brought their own ethnic music—chiefly opera—to American audiences. The arias and overtures featured in the repertoires of every Italian band became popular fare for *all* American bands. Although opera music reached America through a variety of channels, certainly much of it arrived within the immigrants themselves, as part of the cultural traditions that they would sustain in the New World and that would flourish in the wider community here at least through World War I and often beyond.

The music the Italians played changed American culture. But this culture was changing in other ways, too, during these years, notably with respect to the commercialization of popular entertainment. Ethnic entrepreneurs and their allies, the American phonograph companies, had begun to transform American music.

3

The Rise of the Ethnic Music Business, 1900-1920

In the opening years of the twentieth century, as the popularity of the brass band in America was peaking and ensembles led by Sousa and Creatore were touring the nation, a new type of individual appeared on the scene, the ethnic music entrepreneur. For the next half-century, commercial activity related to ethnic music would have an important impact both on ethnic culture and on mainstream American society. Although the many ethnic musicians active before 1900, both professionals and amateurs, certainly required support services to supply sheet music and instruments and to keep instruments in good repair, most of the nineteenth-century music firms in America were non-ethnic in nature. The Czech, German, Italian and other ethnic bandsmen had to resort to noncommercial sources, especially for sheet music, because the music they needed was little known to non-ethnic Americans and thus generally could not be obtained from American music publishers or stores. Ethnic instrumentalists may have purchased publications from their European homelands, but more likely they kept expenses to a minimum by simply relying on memory. Such sheet music as was available to a local ensemble was probably not printed but copied out by hand by a member of the band.[1] There simply was no music industry serving the needs of immigrant musicians in America before this century, certainly no industry that was national in scope.

With the new century the situation was to change.[2] A huge demand for ethnic music was emerging, a lucrative new commercial market that immigrant entrepreneurs were eager to tap. Fueling the new demand was the immense increase in the number of immigrants in America from southern and eastern Europe, especially after the 1880s. Millions of Slavs, Italians, and Jews brought with them a desire to perpetuate their cultures, their arts and music, both individually and institutionally; the new peoples wanted the old music they had known in their homelands. They sought musical accompaniment especially for happy times, particularly for weddings, and also for a variety of rituals and public observances.

The first entrepreneurs to realize that immigrants' cultural interests might prove economically valuable were fellow immigrants, ethnic businesspeople who started new retail businesses within the ethnic communities to cater to the demand. Those emerging book and music stores affected the various ethnic communities into the 1920s and had an impact on Americans in general in the 1930s and beyond. The commercialization of immigrant culture helped to unify ethnic communities in America, reshaping initially fragmented groups into relatively homogeneous and cohesive ethnic markets. As the ethnic retailers began to succeed in forging new markets, mainstream businesses started paying attention to ethnic culture as a consumer demand that might be exploited for their own benefit.

The first outsiders aware of the new ethnic market, in the years just before World War I, were American record companies. By the 1930s other media businesses saw advantage in exploiting the ethnic market, including the owners of radio stations and the music publishers of New York's Tin Pan Alley. Eventually, individuals in those media recognized another profit-making opportunity: they could promote ethnic music not only for an ethnic market but for the *general American market*. By the 1930s non-ethnic businesses who first saw money-making opportunities in supplying ethnic items to immigrants now saw that the mainstream market wanted ethnic music as well. Hence, by the middle of the century, a part of *American* popular music was ethnic.

A critical factor in this commercialization of the ethnic market, acting as a magnet and facilitator for the American media, was the ethnic music firm. This institution not only responded to the musical demands of immigrants but also, to a large extent, helped to *make* the immigrant ethnic culture in America. Very little biographical information exists about these businessmen. Likely, very few seemed to be ethnic business*women*, but because these music entrepreneurs were prominent in their communities, some details of their experience are known. Although the number of individuals who established such music enterprises in the early 1900s, when millions of eastern and southern Europeans were arriving in America, cannot be figured precisely, it must have been large. These entrepreneurs and their firms knew what their customers wanted and would eventually play leading commercial roles in the musical life of their ethnic communities. While motivated by the capitalist ethic, the ethnic music businesspeople were also interested in the music itself and eager to promote widespread interest in the cultural traditions of their homelands. They published books and sheet music, not all of which was precisely the same as what the immigrants had known in the old country; some of the traditional music had been purely oral or folk and had to be "arranged" for new American musical instrumentalists, and some of the compositions that appealed to immigrants were in fact entirely new works emanating from the immigrant experience itself, emigration, settlement and adjustment. Still other pieces of interest to immigrant musicians came from the newly emerging American ethnic vaudeville and its theater.

By World War I commercial activity related to the ethnic music market had developed to such an extent that it might be termed the ethnic music industry. Businesspeople of one particular ethnic background became industry leaders: Czech entrepreneurs, whose firms grew to dominate the old-time ethnic music field by the time it became a multi-group genre in the 1930s. The most prominent of these Bohemian retailers were Chicagoans Joseph Jiran, Louis Vitak, and Vitak's partner Joseph P. Elsnic, and a Cleveland music publisher, Anthony Maresh. Other businessmen played important roles within their own ethnic communities, including Władysław Sajewski, who served Polish musicians in Chicago, and a number of New Yorkers, including a Ukrainian, Myron Surmach; two Italians, E. Rossi and Antonio Di Martino; and a Jew, Joseph Werbelowsky.[3]

Czech Business

The stories of Joseph Jiran and Louis Vitak, who pioneered the industry they eventually came to dominate, are revealing illustrations of the root sources of old-time ethnic music in America.

Around the time of the great immigrant waves, ethnic music was becoming commercialized in Europe, where a leading center of such music composition and publishing had developed in Prague, the Bohemian capital. Certainly the most conspicuous composer and therefore the leading Old World source of American old-time music was the famous Bohemian March King, František Kmoch, whose publisher was the Prague firm of Urbanek and Sons, founded by František Augustin. Kmoch's major promoter was his son Mojmir, who helped make the March King one of the most popular composers in Europe, with a genius for expressing the important relationship between band and polka music. The transition reflected in Kmoch's music would provide the basis for old-time ethnic music in America.

The actual beginning of the polka is obscure, but a popular legend credits its origin around 1830 to a young peasant girl from Bohemia. It is certain that polka music originated in that Czech province and was introduced as sheet music in Prague in 1837.[4] A Bohemian military band brought the polka to Vienna, and a polka mania quickly began to spread throughout central Europe. In the late 1830s and early 1840s the polka became immensely popular among the upper classes, entering the salons of the aristocracy in Saint Petersburg, Paris, and London.[5] It reached the United States by the mid-1840s. Ironically, the first American audience for polka was among the elite; its mass popularity in central Europe would not cross the Atlantic until the masses of peasants themselves immigrated here toward the end of the century.[6]

Of course the peasants carried with them other dance forms as well, such as the waltz and its ethnic variations, the German *laendler* and the Czech *sousedská*. But the preferred musical genre among the rural masses was the polka, and those composers who used the polka's two-step style found a mass market for their works. Music writers for band ensembles found that the dance could be readily incorporated into band arrangements because the polka two-step was very similar to the military-march tempo, which had become widely appealing as a reflection of nineteenth-century nationalism throughout the continent. This mixture of polka and march music, relying heavily on folk rather than military themes, accounts for the fabulous popular success of František Kmoch.

Kmoch was born in the Kolin district of Bohemia in 1848, the son of a clarinetist who is known to have had a deep love for folk music. In such a household it was not surprising that young František received instruction from a music teacher and obtained a music education early. Around 1871, when he was in his early twenties, he formed a band of his own in Kolin that was associated with the Sokols, whose liberal principles of physical culture and nationalism he favored. Kmoch became well known as a bandleader, particularly after he made a very successful Prague debut as a trumpeter and brass-band conductor in 1873.[7]

After touring Europe with his ensemble and establishing a music school in his hometown, Kmoch began to compose musical pieces for band, especially polka-marches that drew on his dual interest in folk and nationalistic tunes. As a composer, he was both popular and enormously prolific, producing approximately four hundred compositions for bands in the late nineteenth and early twentieth centuries. One observer judged that the wide popularity of his music in America rested on its derivation from the traditional music of the peasants.[8] His most familiar works reflected both rural life in Bohemia—in such compositions as "Koline, Koline," "Pode Mlejnem" (By the mill), "Muziky, Muziky," "Andulko Safarova," and "Zeleny Hajove" (Green woods)—and fervent Czech nationalism and militarism—as expressed in "Prichod Sokoliku" (Sokols are coming) and "Lvi Silou" (Lion's strength).

Around the turn of the century, many Czech immigrants to America brought along Kmoch's appealing, tuneful melodies not only in their heads but also, in many cases, in their baggage, in the form of sheet music published by the popular Prague firm of Urbanek and Sons. The firm apparently made considerable money from Kmoch's works in the early 1900s, and the growing Czech communities in America became a good market for the compositions of the Bohemian March King.[9] With their many musical societies, brass bands, and other musical and nationalistic institutions, the American Czech settlements generated a sizable demand for the marches and dance tunes of Kmoch and other Bohemian composers. Well aware of this eager audience and growing demand, astute music entrepreneurs, first Joseph Jiran in Chicago, and soon Chicagoan Louis Vitak and Cleveland's Anthony Maresh, among others, decided to capitalize on this new market.[10]

Jiran was was born around 1870 in Pilsen in southwest Bohemia, the region which sent most of the Czech emigrants to America in the era of mass migration from the 1870s to 1920, where he developed a familiarity with the kind of music the immigrants loved.

His parents apprenticed him as a youth to a manufacturer of brass instruments in Roumania, where he learned to make cornets, trombones, and the like. He came to America with his young wife in 1894 and proceeded to work for instrument manufacturers, first the Conn Company in Indianapolis and later Lyon, Healy in Chicago. In 1898, before he was thirty, he left Lyon, Healy and opened his own repair shop where he both manufactured and maintained musical instruments.[11] It is not clear exactly when Jiran turned to publishing sheet music, but in 1904 he obtained his first music copyright.[12] It is certain that in the first few years of the 1900s he was in regular communication with Kmoch's Prague publisher, Mojmir Urbanek, who sought American agents for the music he was printing in Europe. Prague was then a lively center of music publishing, with a large number of music houses, firms such as F. A. Dvorsky, J. Kovarik, A. Cejka, and Jana Hoffmann.[13]

Jiran and Urbanek developed some kind of business arrangement, the exact nature of which is unclear but which probably involved sharing the income from American sales of music published in Europe by Urbanek.[14] In 1907 Jiran took out several American copyrights on Kmoch's works.

Meanwhile, Jiran's small shop was becoming far more than just a place for Czech immigrants to get their instruments repaired and buy sheet music. The store on West 18th Street in the heart of Chicago's Pilsen district, which was known as "Little Bohemia," had developed into a sort of cultural clearinghouse for lovers of Czech music, especially for those who admired the works of Kmoch and similar Old World composers, such as Karel Hasler and Emil Stolc.[15] Among the frequent visitors to his shop were a growing number of talented Bohemian instrumentalists, including cornetist Bohumil Kryl, who had played in some of the major American business bands and was in the early 1900s forming a Czech brass band of his own with the Cimera brothers: Jerry, who would become a leading trombonist in the Chicago Symphony, and Jimmy, who joined the Ringling Brothers circus.[16]

Another important member of this Jiran circle around 1905 was Andrew Grill, a young Kmoch enthusiast who was devoted to the Bohemian March King's polka-march pieces. Grill's association with Jiran would be enormously profitable to both, as the former was to become the leading American arranger and composer of Bohemian-style old-time ethnic music. His value to the Chicago music publisher was indicated by the frequency with which his name appears as arranger and occasionally as composer in Jiran's sampler catalogue of the late 1930s. Grill is named on about two-thirds of the almost two hundred pieces listed, and his name is also prominent in Louis Vitak's published offerings of 1942.[17] Grill's arrangements of Bohemian popular and folk tunes and his own compositions made up a large part of the old-time ethnic repertoire, and the story of his musical career demonstrates the formative influence of Kmoch's polka-march style.

Grill, born in 1869 in the Budejovic district, was from the same region of Bohemia as Jiran and most of the Czech immigrants who came to America.[18] He joined an Austro-Hungarian military unit and learned to play several instruments, especially the cornet and violin; his later compositions would reveal the impact of his military experience. He soon made his way to America, where in 1903 he joined his brother, who had already settled in Chicago. Although the reason for his emigration is unclear, likely it was related to a search for better opportunity as a musician. The first work he could find was manual labor, working in a bottle plant. But he probably played music in his spare time, especially the military pieces of Kmoch, which he rewrote for himself and possibly for others, and he became friendly with Joseph Jiran. Sometime in the early 1900s he tried unsuccessfully to obtain a position in the American military as a band conductor, and around 1905, Jiran let him set up a violin school in rented space in his shop. Grill later added cornet teaching to his activities.

He stayed with Jiran until 1921, when he established a fully independent studio. In the middle of the decade he formed his own band, probably with his students, and made a number of Bohemian music records for Columbia and Victor, the major labels of the day. He continued his music teaching through the depression until his death in 1943.

Throughout his career, Grill's reputation in the Chicago Czech community was that of a hard taskmaster, probably reflecting his military experience, bearing, and musical interest. Like Kmoch, he was a supporter of the Sokols, and he admired Kmoch's compositions—which he often performed and used for instruction—because of their strongly nationalistic character. From 1909 Grill regularly appeared as the band conductor at the American Sokol congresses, called *Slets*.[19] But he is best remembered as the leading soldier-arranger of the most popular pieces of old-time music. He continued to write for Jiran, especially in the 1920s when the latter became involved in the selling of piano rolls and expanded his publishing of Bohemian and old-time music.[20] Grill's compositions and arrangements helped establish Jiran as the first leading publisher of old-time music.

The firm most important overall in promotion of the genre, however, was the business begun by Louis Vitak, known as Georgi and Vitak until the mid-1920s, when it became the Vitak and Elsnic Company. Vitak was certainly of Czech ancestry, but his origins remain obscure, and it is not known whether he was an immigrant himself or the American-born child of immigrants. The roots of his interest in music in general and ethnic old-time music in particular are unknown.[21] He spent his youth in the 1890s in Akron, Ohio, and opened a music store in Cincinnati around 1895.[22] Possibly in search of a larger clientele, he moved his business to Chicago about 1902 and decided to expand his firm, adding music publication to his retail-instrument business. Vitak began to compose pieces himself before 1903 (the date of his first copyrighted dance tune), and by 1909 he had added a partner to help produce and sell his works and those of other Czechs. This partner, Georgi, was a local German bandleader who himself had operated a music store specializing in concertinas.[23]

Vitak was determined to dominate old-time ethnic music publication, and he achieved his goal by World War I, both by composing original pieces and by arranging many of the popular Old World Bohemian tunes. Like Jiran, he apparently had an agreement with Urbanek, permitting him to issue works of Kmoch and other European composers in America.[24] Vitak also employed his own American arrangers of old-time pieces, including Andrew Grill, so that by 1920 the firm of Georgi and Vitak had turned out scores of polkas, marches, and waltzes and was becoming the genre's leading American publisher.

Beginning probably in 1913, Vitak's firm began putting out albums—entire collections and sets of collections of old-time ethnic works. The earliest of these volumes was likely the *Bohemian Dance Album (Česka Tanečni Album) No. 1,* which appeared in 1913 and sold for 50 cents; within the next two years, at least five more such albums were released.[25]

The Georgi and Vitak Company was prosperous and widely known by the end of World War I, but only in part because of Vitak's energy in producing more pieces than anyone else. Probably more important was the design of the music, especially the arrangements, which fed the growing dance mania in America of that time. Vitak and his arrangers, Grill and later Karol Echtner, deliberately revised the traditional music to suit that frenzy for hall and ballroom dancing.[26]

A final ingredient in Vitak's achievement was his firm's new marketing strategy to go beyond its traditional Bohemian audience, beginning in the 1920s, and issue sheet music and albums for other ethnic groups from central and eastern Europe. The new marketing policy, which Vitak pursued actively, might have been the reason for his falling-out with his old German partner, Georgi. Whatever the reason, at the beginning of the 1920s, Vitak brought his nephew, Joseph P. Elsnic, into the firm as an employee. Elsnic was a versatile and talented musician who also had good marketing skills, and he would play a major role in the continued growth of the business.

As a child in a musical family in Baltimore in the first years of the century, Elsnic learned to play the violin and then later the piano, the accordion, and especially brass instruments, including the tuba and Sousaphone. He was so proficient on the Sousaphone that when he entered military service in 1918, he was sent directly to the Great Lakes Naval Training Station as a member of the world-renowned Sousa Band.[27] After his discharge, his uncle Louis Vitak invited him to join him in the music business, perhaps already with the idea that Elsnic might replace Georgi as partner and even someday take over the business. In 1924 the firm changed its name to Vitak and Elsnic, with the latter now as part-owner. In 1926 Vitak retired, leaving his nephew as sole proprietor.[28]

The business continued to prosper, issuing new multi-ethnic dance collections throughout the 1920s, no longer directed toward an audience of Czechs only but including tunes of Germans, Poles, and Lithuanians. Between 1923 and 1930 the firm published at least nine collections of Polish dances, with about twenty-five to thirty pieces in each volume. At least one Lithuanian work was issued, with a 1923 copyright date.[29]

These new publications attracted new composers, who were now eager to have Vitak and Elsnic put out their works. The result was an enormous increase in the number of pieces appearing under the firm imprint. Their catalogs indicate that the firm added about 140 selections to one list and over 100 to another in the 1920s.[30]

The third major pioneering Czech music firm was in Cleveland, an active center of band music and, not surprisingly, a city with one of the nation's largest immigrant populations. Cleveland's music entrepreneur, Anthony Maresh, had been closely associated with the Bohemian brass-band tradition in the last years of the 1800s, a tradition that survived into the twentieth century and undoubtedly was a reason for his business success. Maresh was the son of Czech immigrant parents who likely had a great interest in music. He must have received instruction, either from his parents or from an outside teacher, for by the age of sixteen, in 1893, he had already begun composing music. The following year he led the city's major ethnic ensemble, the Great Western Band, in a performance of one of his works.

In 1896, before he was twenty, he began a music store, the Maresh Music Company, which sold both instruments and European sheet music. For his first ten years in the music business he lacked sufficient capital to buy or rent a store and had to locate his business in his parent's East 55th Street home.[31] In 1906 Maresh was able to move the firm to a separate location under a new name, the Maresh and Son Piano Company. Maresh had already prospered, not only as the owner of the business but also as a composer and arranger of hundreds of pieces of Bohemian popular music. The most popular of his works were probably his arrangement of a polka, "Na Marjance," and his own million-selling waltz, "Life Is but a Dream," both dating from about 1903.[32] Two years later he issued what was probably his first collection of old-time Czech songs.[33] Maresh became an influential citizen in Cleveland, where by World War I his store had become not only a leading Czech ethnic-music center but also a political clearinghouse.[34] Maresh was prominent on a 1907 committee that hosted a reception for the Hruby family band before one of its extended tours.

By 1920 a Czech music industry centered in two cities, Chicago and Cleveland, had emerged and begun to prosper. In addition to the industry's entrepreneurial pioneers, a number of other Czech music businessmen were active, including A. J. Turek, Jaroslav Stanek, and A. Geringer in Chicago and F. Karasek in Columbus, Ohio. The Czech entrepreneurs developed marketing strategy for meeting the demands of a growing music- and dance-hungry ethnic clientele, and in other immigrant ethnic communities new music businessmen would also emerge to supply music and services to their countrymen in America.

Polish Business

The leading and likely the first Polish music business in America was founded by Władysław Sajewski, who began his enterprise around the turn of the century in America's major center of Polish immigration, Chicago. According to his son, he initially sold general merchandise and moved into the music business in response to the demands of his customers.[35] That Polish immigrants would demand musical merchandise is understandable in light of the vital musical and dance traditions that had long been a part of Polish ethnic culture. The thirty-eight volumes of Polish folk music collected and published by Oskar Kolberg in *Dzieła Wszystkie* in 1875 testify to the richness of that tradition. As with other European peoples, the sources of Polish traditional melodies originated in a variety of secular and religious activities, such as regional holidays, band processions during the autumn religious pilgrimages to the Black Madonna shrine at Częstochowa, and family celebrations and observances, especially weddings and funerals. Like their East European and Slavic neighbors, the Polish peasants cultivated their own styles of dances enthusiastically, such as the *mazurka, oberek* (similar to a square dance), *kujawiak,* and of course the polka and waltz.[36]

Regional differences within Polish folk music make it difficult to characterize the music on a national basis. The most conspicuous Polish subgroup are the *gorali,* the mountaineers from the Tatras, whose music retains ancient and unusual harmonies.[37] Another distinction among Polish bands in both the Old World and the New involved the dichotomy between a relatively polished urban style and the more rural style called *wiejska.* However, *gorali, wiejska,* and urban bands generally share a heavy dependence on stringed instruments, the violin and bass, a feature that distinguishes Polish bands from the brass bands of the Bohemians and the Germans.[38]

Thus, when Polish immigrants began arriving in America in the 1860s and 1870s, they organized musical bodies, such as the Polish Singers Alliance founded in Chicago in 1888, centered especially at the parish church and normally under the leadership of the church organist.[39] Immigration slowed after the Panic of 1893 and ensuing depression, but as the economy recovered in the late 1890s Polish immigrants began to pour into the United States and especially Chicago, the nation's boom city of the time. Old parishes grew, and many new ones were formed, placing an enormous strain on Chicago's Polish religious and cultural institutions. The Polish immigrant population almost doubled in the 1890s, reaching about 150,000, and twenty-four new Polish churches sprang up between 1890 and 1914. With such growth the demand for instructional materials of all types, religious, cultural, and musical, was quite high.[40] Seeing the burgeoning population and responding to the urging of his wife, Władysław Sajewski decided to start his own business supplying some of the cultural goods that these newly-arrived masses were asking for. The Sajewskis rented space in 1897 in the center of the city's largest Polish concentration on the near northwest side and opened the Columbia Supply Store.[41]

At first the Sajewskis offered notions, dry goods, candy, toys, and a few religious and cultural items, such as phonograph records. Their strategy of sending out catalogues proved beneficial, quickly resulting in wide publicity for the store. The Columbia Supply Store became more than a place for Polish immigrants to shop; the newcomers transformed the establishment into a neighborhood cultural and social center, a place where immigrants could find both good merchandise and good fellowship.[42]

Władysław was especially sensitive to the musical requests of his customers and Chicago's Polish parishes because he himself had been a musician in Warsaw, a pianist and violinist.[43] He soon began to supply cultural merchandise, especially playbooks and sheet music. The more he specialized in musical articles, the more his customers asked him for, so that by 1910 his firm was exclusively selling musical goods: records, phonographs, musical instruments, and sheet music. Like the Czechs, Jiran and Vitak, he even began publishing musical works himself, employing Frank Przybylski, a trained musician, composer, and local bandleader to arrange the familiar Polish folk songs. An early collection was *Album Tańców Polskich;* volume 1 was published in 1912, and the series continued through volume 11, which appeared in 1934.[44]

But unlike his Czech colleagues, Władysław and his son Alvin, who had joined the firm in 1914 as a boy, became especially interested in the new technology for disseminating music, and they began to make and sell phonograph records and later piano rolls. In fact, music reproduction was to be a significant part of their business, from before World War I until after Wladyslaw's death in 1948. Throughout its history the Sajewski firm remained a wellspring of

Polish culture, publishing a variety of printed materials promoting folk and popular arts, skits, plays, and dances.

Of course the Sajewskis were far from the only Polish music publishers of their time. Probably before 1920 and certainly prior to the middle of the decade, F. C. and H. Schunke of Buffalo, Joseph Krygier of Philadelphia, and E. Casey Trojanowski of Dickson City, Pennsylvania, all had issued Polish dance collections for ethnic musicians.[45] By the late 1920s thirty commercial stores in Chicago carried an inventory of Polish music valued at about $250,000.[46]

The activities of Czech and Polish music businessmen were centered in Chicago, but entrepreneurs from other ethnic groups established businesses to service the cultural needs of immigrant communities in New York. In Manhattan's teeming Lower East Side, eastern European Jews, Ukrainians, and Italians were congregated, and ethnic businessmen were quick to respond to their demands for traditional music.

Jewish Business

The history of Jewish book- and sheet-music publishing in America is, as might be expected in view of the high literacy of Jewish immigrants, an especially rich topic that cannot be treated in detail here. However, it is essential to review the musical traditions of the Yiddish-speaking Jews who poured into America from Russia and neighboring lands between 1880 and 1920, for the immigrants brought with them a treasured musical heritage that came from diverse sources.

Although small numbers of western European Jews had settled in America as early as the mid-seventeenth century, the turn-of-the-century Jewish immigrants were much more numerous and much less assimilated into modern cultural and economic life. They arrived with few economic resources and a relatively unwesternized religious orientation, Orthodox Judaism, which was rooted in the isolated urban ghettos and rural *shtetls* of eastern Europe. Their culture was also relatively unassimilated, including their music, which came from a variety of Hebraic-Talmudic and cantorial traditions with strong admixtures of the mystical Hasidic influence of the seventeenth century. One result of the latter was the distinctive prominence of East

European folk musicians known as *klezmer* instrumentalists, from the Hebrew word for conveyors of music.[47] Like the Ukrainian, Roumanian, and to some extent Gypsy ensembles with whom they shared instrumentation and dances, the klezmer bands at first mainly included stringed instruments, such as the violin and cembalo. Later, in the late nineteenth century, especially in America, the ensembles featured the clarinet. Klezmer instrumentalists appeared most often at happy occasions, particularly weddings, where they played *freilichs*. At such family get-togethers, another folk figure would appear to add his original contributions to the musical repertoire, the *badkhn*, whose task was to oversee the ceremonies and through song, dance, poetry, and general merrymaking help the bride adjust to her forthcoming married life.[48]

Another encouragement to maintain and again to enhance traditional Jewish music, song, and dance was the well-known Yiddish theater. First established in Roumania in 1876 by Abraham Goldfadden, who was a musician as well as a playwright, the Yiddish theater grew out of the *Purimspiel,* a traditional dramatization of the biblical story of Queen Esther.[49] In the New World, probably more than for any other immigrant community with a dramatic tradition, the Yiddish theater provided an extremely important vehicle for conveying music and song, both folk and popular. The performances were far more than simply spoken theatricals; most included music and song as well.

The plays presented were ones that ordinary people could appreciate and understand, and frequently the lower classes figured in the plots. Whatever the presentation, comedy or tragedy, musical or melodrama, and whatever the audience, whether Old World or New, the Yiddish theater always struck, as one writer put it, "close to the nerve of folk sentiment."[50] Although the plays generally mirrored the lives of the masses, they varied widely in quality and were often condemned by intellectuals for their hackneyed plots and general lack of sophistication. Especially in America, intellectuals tended to dismiss them as *shund* (trash). But the Yiddish-speaking masses, seeking entertainment rather than uplift, loved even the most mediocre of the plays, with their simplistic themes of sentimentality, melodrama, and romance. As foreigners in an alien land, the audience found in these dramas a much-needed emotional anchor, and the Yiddish theater prospered in the New World.

Anti-Semitism in the Old World—specifically, a Russian ban on

Jewish theatricals in 1883—forced many Jewish writers, actors, and composers, including Goldfadden, to flee to the New World, where they established the American Yiddish theater, which thrived until World War I and beyond.[51] The figure most responsible for introducing and promoting the Yiddish musicals in America was Boris Thomashevsky, actor, playwright, composer, and impresario, who led the first theater presentation in New York in 1882 while he was still a teenager and a newcomer to the United States. Thomashevsky would become the very personification of the Yiddish theater in the following decades, as he delighted in appearing onstage in colored tights, which added to his sex appeal and showed off his muscular physique. It is no wonder that he remained a matinee idol long into the 1900s.

Another beloved popularizer of the music, comedy, and *shund* plays of the Yiddish theater was the comedian-singer-composer Zelig Mogulesco. In the pre–World War I era, two playwrights who provided much of the material for Thomashevsky and his players were Joseph Lateiner, who began his career with his characteristic 1884 offering "The Emigration to America," and "Professor" Moyshe Hurwitz. Other dramatists from the 1890s, such as Jacob Gordon and Jacob Adler, struggled against these *shund* writers to reform and elevate the theater with the classics, but theirs was always an uphill battle, never totally successful.[52]

Music contributed significantly to the wide appeal of the Yiddish theater. In 1910 the roughly one-half-million Jews clustered on the Lower East Side accounted for about two million annual admissions to view the light musicals and sentimental tearjerkers in which Thomashevsky and others thrived.[53] By winning such massive popularity for himself and his theater, this king of *shund* was able in 1912 to open his own National Theatre, a magnificent playhouse that quickly became one of the decade's leading Yiddish theatrical centers.[54]

One final spur to the preservation and popularity of old and new Yiddish music was the neighborhood cafe so characteristic of the Lower East Side. These cafes, less formal gathering places than the theater, were centers for relaxation, conversation, and occasional musical performance, much like the German and Czech beer gardens in midwestern cities and similar to institutions serving Italian and other immigrants that had also settled on the Lower East Side. But certainly the Jewish cafes were significant for their sociability, as settings for talk about intellectual and practical matters, and in the

early years many cafes were associated with particular regional subgroups of Jewish immigrants. Moscowitz's Wine Cellar on Division
Street, for example, catered especially to the Yiddish-speaking working class from Roumania and featured Roumanian-Gypsy music and
performers.[55]

With so many centers presenting Yiddish music, song, and dance,
it is obvious that by 1900 a demand for the dissemination and commercialization of musical materials would grow. The printing and
sale of folk and popular songs, especially collections of pieces, would
provide a needed sense of continuity and identity for foreigners in
a strange land. One of the earliest entrepreneurs to respond to the
emerging market, certainly the most successful, was Joseph Werbelowsky, who had come to America from Russia as a teenager in 1872.
By the end of the century he had formed the firm of Rosenbaum
and Werbelowsky to sell Hebrew books. Soon he began to consider
expanding his business into the publication of Yiddish music, quite
likely influenced by the growing success of an earlier publisher, Je-
huda Katzenellenbogen, who had pioneered putting out traditional
Jewish folk songs in the late 1880s as a means for immigrant en-
lightenment.[56] In 1901 Werbelowsky, his son David, and two other
booksellers formed a partnership to start the Hebrew Publishing
Company, which issued songbooks and sheet music of the most
popular tunes of Yiddish musicals and composers.[57] One particular
bestseller was the collection of the folk songs of the world's leading
badkhn, Eliakum Zunser (1836–1913).[58] Another reason for the
company's success was its policy of selling its publications at low
prices, while paying little or nothing to composers.[59]

The years before World War I were the start of a golden age of
Yiddish song composition and publication. Werbelowsky and others
not only issued the beloved old tunes, especially the romantic ones
from Europe, but also published new ones that spoke directly to the
immigrant condition. Some of the latter songs lamented life in
America, and others extolled it. A sampling includes "Di Goldene
Medina" (1901); "Ir Zayt a Griner" (You are a greenhorn) (1910);
"Elis Aylend" (1914); "Der Litvak und der Galitzyaner" (1914, on
the immigrants' regional differences); "Lebn Zol Columbus" (Long
live Columbus) (1915); and "Fifti-Fifti" (1917, concerning worker
exploitation).[60] Of course these types of published songs did not
exhaust the kinds of Yiddish tunes that the musicmen published;
some were simply taken directly from popular Anglo-American
melodies.[61]

By 1920 there were more than twenty functioning Yiddish theaters in the New York area, offering musicals containing the songs
both of older lyricists and composers such as Lateiner, Thomashevsky, Joseph Rumshinsky, Herman Wohl, Sholom Perlmutter, and
Louis Friedsell, and of younger ones such as Sholem Secunda and
Alexander Oshanetsky.[62] Other Yiddish music publishers had appeared by 1914, including small firms run by Albert Teres and S.
Schenker, but in the prewar years they competed unsuccessfully with
the Hebrew Publishing Company.[63] Although all these composers
and publishers produced and sold Yiddish music, their melodies and
instrumentation were not unique or even original; many pieces were
closely related to the music of other eastern European peoples, particularly the Gypsies, the Roumanians, with whom Jews shared the
distinctive *doina* form, and the Ukrainians. In fact, it is likely that
some of the Yiddish music companies had many non-Jewish customers.

Ukrainian Business

One example of Jewish-Ukrainian contact involves H.
Smolensky, a Jew who from 1905 to 1918 was probably the first
supplier of Ukrainian printed music in America and who helped
launch the major Ukrainian music entrepreneur, Myron Surmach.[64]
The Ukrainian folk culture, like that of the other ethnic groups,
included distinctive music played at particular times of religious and
secular observance and was also marked by regional variations. The
first immigrants to America originated from the western sections of
the homeland, known as Ruthenia, in Galicia, which was part of
Austria-Hungary in the late nineteenth century. They settled and
later concentrated in the East, in Pennsylvania, New York, and New
Jersey, working chiefly in the mines and industries of the area. They
brought with them their characteristic instrument ensemble, the *troy-
isti muzyky,* which was similar to the small country bands of their
European neighbors, the Jews and the Poles.[65] The instruments used
in the Ukrainian folk band included a fiddle, hand drums, a hammered dulcimer called the *tsymbaly,* frequently a flute, and a string
bass. Many of their dances resembled those of the Poles, but the
more distinctive and very popular *kolomyika* had a 2/4 meter like

the polka. Other Ukrainian dances included the *hutsulka,* a variant of the *kolomyika,* and the exuberant Cossack dance, the *kozak.*

Surmach, who like Werbelowski entered the music business without training in music but with a love of books and traditional ethnic literature, well understood the immigrants' desire to hold on to their music and dance after coming to America.[66] Born in 1893, he had grown up in Ruthenia and had already developed an interest in books before he left for America in 1910 with his grandmother to join his brother in Wilkes-Barre, Pennsylvania. He worked in the mines at first, supplementing his income by buying and selling Ukrainian books. Probably realizing the greater commercial opportunity in a larger immigrant center, he moved to New York City and in 1916 opened a clothing store there with the help of friends.[67]

He finally opened a bookstore of his own in 1918, on East 7th Street on the Lower East Side, where he offered many of the works he had known and sold back in Wilkes-Barre. He also sold sheet music, supplied to him at first by the Jewish retailer, Smolensky. Soon, Surmach was specializing in Ukrainian music in all its forms, including records, piano rolls, and musical instruction. His business prospered, especially as he encouraged public interest in Ukrainian music by sponsoring and producing concerts, records and eventually radio performances. He continued in the trade for almost seventy years.[68]

Italian Business

Another major group of immigrants flooding the Lower East Side in the two decades before World War I were the Italians. They, too, produced a small number of music businessmen who saw the exploding immigrant demand for ethnic music materials and sought to capitalize on it.

Like the immigrant Jews, the new Italian Americans were not a homogeneous group; a small number of relatively well-off northern Italians had come to America first, just after the mid-nineteenth century, followed by hundreds of thousands of poorer, less literate southern Italians who arrived beginning in the 1890s. Like the Jews and Ukrainians, Italian immigrants clustered chiefly along the East

Coast, from Boston south to Baltimore. Their largest concentrations were in New York state, particularly in New York City, which had 250,000 Italian immigrants in 1900. Within the city, of course, the largest Italian community was on the Lower East Side where, around 1900, Italians developed active musical organizations and hence where major music entrepreneurs located their businesses.

The Italian tradition of band and opera music, which had already made an impact on American music, produced a significant retail market for potential ethnic entrepreneurs. On the Lower East Side Italian immigrants formed amateur brass and wind ensembles and also developed another institution that helped perpetuate old-time Italian music and song, the *caffe concerto,* or *caffe chantant,* immigrant gathering places with, as their names suggest, a decidedly musical character. These social centers were like those of other groups in the neighborhood, places of entertainment frequented on Sundays or in the evenings by ordinary working-class immigrants, which offered food, wine, and vaudeville performances. These cafes were overwhelmingly popular among the Italians, perhaps even more popular than the similar institutions serving immigrants from other lands.[69] But as in other ethnic communities, the Italian cafes functioned to help create a demand for commercialized Italian music.[70]

The *caffe chantant* was important not only in Little Italy on Manhattan's Lower East Side but throughout America, wherever Italians had settled. Its form differed slightly in different cities, where various cafes might more closely resemble saloons, restaurants, or music halls, specializing variously in drink, food, or entertainment, but music, especially performances that were regionally based, was a feature common to them all. Brooklyn had at least three cafes around 1900; in Philadelphia, the best known was the Verdi Hall; Cleveland had a Teatro Garibaldi; and numerous smaller saloons and cafes existed in other East Coast Little Italies, in New Jersey, in Connecticut and throughout New England generally, and very conspicuously in San Francisco on the West Coast.[71]

In New York's Little Italy, the larger Italian immigrant cafes were all generally similar, specializing in entertainment characteristic of particular regions in the old country. The three major cafes, all of which opened in the years just prior to 1900, were Ferrando's Music Hall, the Villa Penza, and, the most popular of all, the Villa Vittorio Emanuele III, at the very center of the colony on Mulberry Street.[72] Like the Jewish cafes in the vicinity, the Italian cafes appealed primarily to an unskilled, lower-class clientele that was still identified with and interested in entertainment from particular regions of the homeland. The Villa Vittorio Emanuele III cafe, for example, often had acts and musicians that were Neapolitan; Ferrando's, on the other hand, was somewhat exceptional in offering northern Italian music, which reflected the background only of a small part of the Italian population.[73] But no matter what provincial identification a cafe might maintain, its patrons loved to go there. Amidst a haze of tobacco smoke, visitors ate, drank wine, and socialized, all the while watching and listening to performers who were singing, dancing, and playing the familiar ethnic instruments, such as the mandolin and accordion. The entertainers often performed skits, usually comic, from a tradition that dated back to the sixteenth century.

Cafe owners were fortunate around 1900 because suitable performers were inexpensive to hire and easy to find. Most were amateurs, willing to perform for token fees from the owner or for whatever they could collect by passing the hat among the audience.[74] A cafe proprietor who wanted more elaborate and professional entertainment could find that in the neighborhood, too, by the late 1890s, the period when the Italian *filodrammatico* companies were emerging. One of the earliest such troupes was La Compagnia Comico-Drammatica, which had been started in Brooklyn in 1889 by Guglielmo Ricciardi and moved to Manhattan in 1900, where it performed in the cafes.[75] Ricciardi's group was representative of many.[76]

Ricciardi and his company essentially performed Italian ethnic vaudeville. They drew on rich Italian folk material and music—for example, regional clown traditions, such as the *stenterello* from Tuscany and the *pulcinello* from Naples.[77] One popular act was the *machietta,* a familiar musical playlet—really a comic skit in song—about the lives of ordinary people. An American company might slightly alter the traditional script by including musical-comic vignettes of immigrant life, so-called *machiette coloniale.* The brilliant master of this genre in the immigrant generation was Eduardo Migliaccio.[78]

What occurred between the acts or after the show was as important to the maintenance of Italian traditional music as the formal performance itself. The entertainment would continue even without the stage performers, as the musicians played on for the audience to sing and dance. Thus the patrons not only observed ethnic entertainment in these cafes and music halls but also actively and personally cultivated the old Neapolitan and Sicilian melodies.[79]

In this musical atmosphere in Italian immigrant neighborhoods nationwide, the community developed a commercial music market in the early 1900s. Although details of the early music business among Italians remain obscure, trade in printed ethnic music apparently began with booksellers, and the leading music retailers became established in the heart of Little Italy, in and around Mulberry Street. Possibly the first Italian music-selling business was started by a Mr. Mongello, who supplied sheet music to musicians, troubadours, and other entertainers throughout the New York metropolitan area, including Long Island and New Jersey. Significantly, Mongello's trade was multi-regional; he sold the folk and popular sheet music of several Italian provinces, thus educating his customers with respect to the variety of Italian subcultures. Such an awareness was a step toward the homogenization of Italian American immigrants.[80]

A larger seller of music materials about this time was Ernesto Rossi, a Neapolitan, who had come to America as a young man and opened a general store offering novelties and books just after the turn of the century. Also locating his shop on Mulberry Street about 1910, Rossi, like the Czech merchants Jiran and Vitak, hired an arranger, an L. Conaro, to assist in revising the best-known ethnic pieces. Conaro later helped Rossi in the manufacture of Italian piano rolls.[81]

Probably the largest Italian music business in America before World War I, certainly the largest postwar concern, was the Italian Book Company, located a few doors down Mulberry Street from E. Rossi and Company. Its leader and the architect of the firm's commercial supremacy was Antonio Di Martino.[82] Di Martino was essentially an imaginative and aggressive entrepreneur rather than a musician or bibliophile, but he was clearly a patron of the arts, both Italian folk and classical literature. Born in Naples in 1876, he had a modest education, probably of a technical sort, before he accompanied his mother to New York in 1902, where his grandmother lived.[83] Two years later he was hired as a bookkeeper by a company offering general merchandise, probably mostly books, but after a dispute with the owners he started his own competing firm directly across the street. His former employers eventually relented and took in Di Martino as a third partner in a new venture, the Societa Libraria Italiana.[84]

As firm secretary, Di Martino was undoubtedly the major influence in the Societa as it became the nation's major Italian book and music firm by 1921, when its capitalization was $100,000 and it was listed in Dun and Bradstreet.[85] One fruitful strategy involved fostering good community relations, helping newly arrived immigrants find work, learn English, and otherwise get established. Grateful immigrants often responded by giving the business their power of attorney.[86] Many of the company's publications, such as its letter writer and Italian American grammar, also furthered the goal of immigrant adjustment, and the firm acquired a reputation for assisting newcomers.

Another helpful factor in the early years was a marketing emphasis on musical materials. Even before 1910, when the firm assumed its English name, the Italian Book Company, Di Martino and his partners were deeply engaged in publishing sheet music and selling gramophones, records, pianos, guitars, mandolins, violins, and other Italian instruments. Music, especially folk and popular music, was their basic offering. By the early 1920s the firm owned a large five-story building (valued at about $3 million by 1960), in the upper floors of which they manufactured their own piano rolls, "Italian Style." The rolls sold for about $1 each in the 1920s.[87] The firm also obtained a huge number of very lucrative copyrights for music compositions by both Italian and Italian American songwriters and entertainers, especially during and after World War I. Among the bestsellers were compositions by the popular Italian nationalist E. A. Mario, whose most famous work in 1918 was "La Leggenda del Piave" (The Legend of the Piave River), which recounted the famous World War I battle with the Austrians and became the Italian national anthem.[88]

A final reason for the company's prosperity was its ties with other Italian music companies elsewhere in America. The network of distributors included the Bonaldi company in Detroit, Nuovo Italia in San Francisco, and Martignoni, a religious bookseller in New York.[89]

Whether for nostalgic reasons or business purposes, Di Martino returned to Naples in 1922, setting up another publishing company there and leaving most of the New York firm's operations to others. While abroad, he certainly retained his interest in the Italian Book Company and even began to buy out his partners, eventually assuming sole ownership. The company continued to prosper, as highlighted by the extraordinary success of its "La Luna Mezzo Mare" in 1928 and the continuing popularity of Italian American vaudeville in the late 1920s, particularly in the New York area. By 1927, for example, Brooklyn and New York each claimed at least fifteen Italian comedy theaters, admission to which was inexpensive enough even for the pocketbook of immigrant families; tickets cost 10–30 cents for men, with women admitted free.[90] The Italian Book Company was the major beneficiary of this thriving immigrant theater in the late 1920s, and when Di Martino returned in 1934 to the United States to take over sole ownership, the firm prospered hugely even into the Depression. In the midst of those hard times it employed about thirty-five people and had an inventory of over 60,000 books and 50,000 records.[91]

During the first three decades of the twentieth century, popular music was making many entrepreneurs very wealthy. The rise of Tin Pan Alley, the emergence of "hillbilly" or country-western music, and the explosive popularity of jazz all made fortunes for music publishers and retailers—and not only for American, Negro, and southern firms but for those with Czech, Polish, Ukrainian, Yiddish, and Italian-speaking clientele. The list of successful ethnic music entrepreneurs is not limited to the individuals or immigrant groups discussed above; a host of smaller European and even Asian music stores and publishers appeared in America in those years to sustain the musical traditions of their peoples.[92] The market served by the new entrepreneurs was in fact a new market, reflecting an enormous willingness among a large audience—a high percentage of the American population still consisted of immigrants by 1930—to pay for traditional music, or for what might be better termed traditional and traditionally styled music. Needless to say, once shrewd ethnic entrepreneurs had discovered and developed this market, outsiders—Anglo-American music capitalists, and in particular American phonograph record companies—began to see potential profit in it. The ethnic music market was far too lucrative to leave to ethnics, and American record companies became eager to fashion the new immigrants into a commercial market.

4

Record Companies Discover the Ethnic Groups, 1900-1930

At first glance one might surmise that the recording industry, to the extent that it had any effect at all on the persistence or assimilation of minority cultures in America, would have increased the pressure for assimilation. Phonograph executives presumably would have wanted to do away with or weaken the many ethnic enclaves, in the hope of creating a large national market for their product. In the early 1900s, furthermore, the industry leaders were virtually all Anglo-Americans, members of the majority, and as hard-headed entrepreneurs their goal clearly was large profits, not the preservation of Polish, Bohemian, Finnish, or Russian traditional music.

But the actual story of the impact of the phonograph industry on American ethnic groups is quite different, for very early, even before World War I, the policy of the major record companies was to cater to the various musical demands of ethnic immigrants. Oddly enough, corporate decisions to help preserve those minority cultures reflected not sentimentality but practical business sense.

Until about 1905, though record companies already offered a varied list of European musical selections, there was little corporate recognition of the American ethnic audiences. Industry leaders apparently felt that any record-buying customer would purchase recorded music simply because he or she liked the pieces. The companies recorded Bohemian marches, Irish airs, and German-Viennese waltzes, only because they believed such selections would sell as *generally* popular recordings. But by 1910, American record executives began to consider their immigrant customers more designedly. From then until about 1930, when the depression began to devastate the industry, the major companies adopted a new policy of marketing records consciously and specifically for ethnic groups.

By the early years of the twentieth century, at the time when millions of foreigners were pouring into America, record company executives were well aware that a buyer of a cylinder or disc, whether immigrant or native, was also a potential buyer of a record-playing machine and ultimately of more records. Meanwhile, as we have seen, the immigrant communities themselves had developed to such an extent that they were supporting their own music businesses. It was clear, too, that the newcomers were good record-buying customers, and the three national companies that dominated the record industry, Victor, Columbia, and Edison, all wanted a share of the immigrant trade. Businesspeople understood that foreigners wanted their own music; it would not take much effort to turn that craving into record-buying.[1]

When Edison invented the phonograph in 1877, he originally conceived of his instrument as a device to record speech; it took a while before he and other promoters thought of the "gramophone," as it came to be called, as a means of preserving music. When the decision was made to reproduce music as well as speech, whether on the original cylinder or on the new disc invented by Emile Berliner in 1888, any observer could perceive that the new industry would help preserve ethnic cultures. Recordings were almost immediately multinational, produced both in Europe and America by artists who performed the most popular pieces in their countries, to be sold anywhere there was a market. Thus, as early as 1889, the Edison Company, for example, had made two-minute cylinders of Tyrolean airs sung by Henry Giese.[2] By 1894, one of the leading national ensembles, the U.S. Marine Band, began turning out a large number of recordings of Old World music, especially German and Italian polkas, marches, and schottisches, and patriotic, folk, and operatic pieces, for the Columbia Phonograph Company of Washington, D.C.[3] As early as 1895, the Berliner Company was issuing Hebrew songs, along with the music of other ethnic groups.[4]

In the new century, the growth of the record industry led to expansion in the reproduction of immigrant and ethnic music. By

1901, when the Victor Talking Machine Company was founded, Berliner, Columbia, and Edison, the major producers, had issued catalogues containing a great variety of Polish, Irish, Hebrew, Italian, Spanish, and other ethnic music, recorded in Europe and America.[5] Nonetheless, it is difficult to say just how conscious the industry really was of the *ethnic* market for these pieces. Much of what they recorded was for general music lovers; one need not have been Irish to purchase a disc of Irish airs or Italian to buy bel canto arias. Yet even without the industry's conscious promotion of such works among foreigners, undoubtedly the immigrants were part of the consuming public even prior to 1900, especially since the cost of records and phonographs was modest, about 50 cents for an Edison cylinder in 1898 and $20 or even less for a standard Edison or Columbia home-playing machine. One must also remember that by the first years of the century, phonograph recordings were the major medium for home entertainment.[6]

Some time early in the new century, the record companies became aware of the enormous potential of the immigrant market and decided to make records for and direct advertising at the foreign-speaking newcomers. One catalyst for the new marketing was probably the rise of the new ethnic music-store owners who would sell the records. Another spur to change may have been the start of a few *ethnic* record-makers, which of course signaled to the likes of Victor and Columbia that the immigrant communities had significant record-buying potential.

Probably the first American record producer to make and offer a music recording aimed directly at immigrants was a Czech, E. Jedlicka, in 1903. The several pieces he recorded on brown, two-minute cylinders included, as one might imagine, some of Kmoch's compositions, particularly the well-known Sokol march "Lvi Silou."[7] By 1912 certainly, and perhaps earlier, Joseph Jiran of Chicago, the leading Czech music publisher of the time, had also decided to make records, drawing on his coterie of musicians and arrangers, such as Bohumil Kryl and Anton Grill, and his mailing list of thousands of potential Czech customers. His first label, Favorite, appeared before 1912, followed by a second one, Jiran.[8]

Two marketing trends also drew the attention of national record companies to the potential of the foreign consumers: immigrants' substantial purchases of Old World discs by European artists from their ethnic traditions and the extraordinary popularity of the few classical-style ethnic singers who were then making records in America. These latter performers were basically fine-art singers who were well known before 1910 among both ethnic and non-ethnic audiences, such as the Italian Enrico Caruso, the Welshman Evan Williams, and John McCormack, widely known for his Irish airs. A standard biographer of Caruso recalled the pride invoked in his fellow immigrants who listened to the great Italian tenor on records: "To New York's Little Italy, [Caruso] was a symbol of hope and laughter in adversity. They identified fiercely, patriotically with the chubby little man who had escaped from a Neapolitan slum to win storybook success on alien soil but still spoke [accented] English and remained . . . Italian."[9] As early as 1903, Caruso had his first million-selling disc, "Vesti La Giubba." The record companies, however, used their best ethnic recording stars to cut folk songs aimed at the lower-class immigrants as well as opera for the upper class.[10]

By about 1905 the record companies had jumped into the new ethnic market with enthusiasm. Of the three major firms, Columbia, which usually ranked second in sales performance and was generally interested in marketing innovations, seemed the most eager to sell directly to foreign newcomers. Columbia was probably the first national American firm to consciously aim an elaborate ethnic catalogue at its foreign customers. Its 1906 catalogue offered musical records in twelve languages, and within three years the company had issued two additional sets of catalogues for immigrant audiences.[11]

A Columbia publication of 1909 outlined for company distributors a commercial policy that the entire industry was to follow for a quarter-century:

Remember that in all large cities and most towns, there are sections where people of one nationality or another congregate in "colonies." Most of these . . . keep up the habits and prefer to speak the language of the old country. Speak to them in their own tongue if you can, and see their faces light up with a smile that linger[s] and hear the streak of language they will give you in reply. To these people RECORDS IN THEIR OWN LANGUAGE have an irresistible attraction and they will buy them readily.[12]

Within a year Columbia was urging its sales representatives to focus their attention more on foreigners than on the native-born, because the former would purchase their offerings much more readily than the latter. Even before 1912 both Columbia and Victor were issuing records even for very small groups of immigrants, such as Greeks and Finns.[13]

Probably in 1912 Columbia, which had maintained its lead in cultivating the commercial immigrant market, organized its foreign recordings into a new international division, with Anton Heindl at the head. In May 1914 a flyer for distributors discussed the consumer-potential of the immigrant population at length, under the headline, "Energetic Dealers Find Alien Trade Profitable, Active, and Easily Acquired." Record salesmen need not be fearful of selling to immigrants, the flyer stated, and need not even know the languages of their foreign customers; selling could be accomplished by gesture, and buyers need only point to the catalogue item wanted. Agents were reminded that a customer who bought a record was a future customer for a phonograph player, at even greater profit to the salesman. The immigrants were said to be long-term customers, "starving for amusements."[14]

One Victor Company sales agent, Billy Fitzgerald of the Eastern Talking Machine Company, received permission in mid-1915 from William Wilson, U.S. Secretary of Labor, to donate a Victor phonograph to the federal immigration receiving station in Boston. The authorities "highly approved" of this gift to keep the strangers happy as they were being processed.[15] Victor issued sales directives similar to Columbia's, reminding dealers of immigrants' unshakable tie to their traditional culture: "No matter how loyal [an immigrant] may be to America . . . the call of the homeland is at all times still within him."[16]

The outbreak of war in Europe in the summer of 1914 put an end to the practice of recording foreign music in the old country and forced Columbia and the other major record companies to make still closer contact with their new ethnic audience, relying on immigrants not only as customers but as musical talent.[17] But the American recording companies, unfamiliar with immigrant musicians, needed help in identifying the most popular Polish, Jewish, and Italian musicians in American. They turned to the ethnic music businesspeople, who were already well established in their communities as vendors of sheet music, instruments, and piano rolls and were familiar with the musical talent in their neighborhoods.

Columbia, again, led the major firms in contacting and using immigrant music-store owners as recruiting agents, a practice that outlasted World War I and continued into the twenties and beyond. The head of Columbia's international division, Anton Heindl, took the initiative. Charged with recording non-art pieces of European music, chiefly folk and popular songs, Heindl had actually begun using American immigrant musicians as early as 1911, occasionally bringing them to New York for recording sessions. In the spring of 1915, with the supply of European musicians cut off by the war, he identified Chicago, with its vast numbers of central and eastern European newcomers, as a potentially rich reservoir of musical talent and made a recruiting trip there, frequenting the many immigrant cafes, halls, and beer gardens to select potential recording stars. He arranged for the necessary recording equipment to be shipped to Chicago and in the summer of 1915 set up a studio there with a Columbia technician, W. F. Freiberg, which cut a number of records of local ethnic performers.[18] A trade publication described in a glowing report a new age for the industry based on Heindl's extraordinarily rich discoveries: "Although [the war failed] to bring Europe to America in a musical sense, as a result of Mr. Heindl's exhaustive study and marked initiative, the Columbia Co. is . . . developing *the Europe that is within us*" [my emphasis].[19]

There was no doubt that Heindl was pleased with the number and quality of the ethnic musicians he was able to locate and put on disc that summer. The *Talking Machine World* prophesied that Christmas of 1915 would "certainly be a happy [holiday] season for the foreign born people in the United States so far as the contributions of the Columbia Co. is concerned."[20]

It is likely that two of Chicago's major music businessmen, the Pole Władysław Sajewski and and the Bohemian Joseph Jiran, worked closely with Heindl in locating talented folk musicians for their respective groups. The most outstanding discoveries were František Przybylski and his Polish village (*wiejska*) orchestra and Anton Brousek and his Bohemian military brass ensemble.[21] Przybylski, who had done some arranging for Sajewski's sheet music, cut Columbia's first Polish record, a piece entitled "Dziadunio," later better known as "The Clarinet Polka." This disc, an early example of Columbia's huge green-label ethnic series, bore Sajewski's name but identified the instrumentalists only as "Orkiestra Columbia."[22] Actually, Sajewski and his son Alvin were talent scouts for several record companies and represented many musicians in negotiations for recording contracts, such as comedian-accordionists Bruno Rudzynski and Władysław Polak.[23]

Heindl's other major "find" for Columbia that year was Anton Brousek, whose large band was probably brought to Heindl's attention by Joseph Jiran. Brousek had served as a musician in the American army some time before World War I and had won a huge Bohemian following with his bright, military–folk-style marches and polkas. He and his thirty-five-man brass ensemble were certainly the most popular Czech band in Chicago around and after 1920.[24] They made their first twelve cuts at Heindl's laboratory that summer of 1915, recording traditional Czech brass-band selections along with some choral works by Vitak and Tryner and new compositions by Brousek himself. The band was to make many more records for Columbia, Victor, and other companies in the next decade.[25]

The World War I era, then, represented a critical period in the development of recorded old-time ethnic music, as record companies accepted and even sought out ethnic Americans as both entertainers and audience. Records had become the dominant form of public and home entertainment, and the commercial goals of record companies had meshed with the immigrants' goals of preserving both their traditional music and the new musical creations of their communities' ethnic musicians. By giving the ethnic public the recorded music it wanted, the major American record companies had learned how to win the immigrants' dollar.

Between 1914 and 1917, the old record patents held by the major companies expired, and the record business was suddenly open to all comers. About seventy new manufacturing companies, both ethnic and nonethnic, joined the big three in the competition for the record-hungry immigrant market. The two new firms that competed most energetically for ethnic audiences were Brunswick and the Aeolian Company's Vocalion label, both of which sought out and recorded ethnic artists. By 1919 the number of phonograph manufacturers had grown enormously, to 200, and the number of record companies had reached about 150. Ethnic record labels also proliferated.[26] In 1920 a German firm, Odeon, joined the already-crowded American immigrant market with its Okeh line of discs.[27] The number of records sold and the income for the industry reached a peak in 1921 that would not be equaled for two decades; one estimate put sales at 140 million discs, for an income of $106 million.[28] The number of phonograph players was high and growing fast; it was estimated that 2.25 million machines were produced in 1919, almost five times as many as in 1914.[29]

There was no doubt that ethnic recordings had been a significant factor in the growth of the record industry. Although no figures are available concerning the number of ethnic records produced during the era, the total was considerable; in the early 1920s both Victor, the industry leader, and Columbia offered more ethnic than domestic selections. Columbia's list, which was typical, included records made for thirty-three different ethnic groups.[30]

The price of a 78-rpm disc record remained modest, just 75 cents, well within the budget of many immigrant families. The newer national labels of Okeh, Brunswick, Vocalion, and others followed the lead of the old big-three companies in relying on ethnic music-store owners as talent agents and record promoters. For example, just after World War I Greek immigrants formed two record companies, the Panhellenion Phonograph Company of New York and the Greek Record Company of Chicago. The latter was the result of the efforts of two Greek businessman-musicians, violinist George Grachis and cymbalist Spyros Stamos.[31] By 1922 a music store in Chicago, Wallin's Music Shop, had begun issuing Scandinavian records under two labels, Wallin's Svenska and Autograph.[32]

The massive effort by the enlarged record industry in the 1920s to feed the foreign-born their music is especially significant as it is contrary to the era's general hostility toward all non–Anglo American cultures—immigration restriction had replaced the open door, and an atmosphere of intolerance toward both white and non-white minorities was developing, marked by increasing anti-Catholicism and anti-Semitism and a growing general distaste for cultural differences. Southern and eastern European immigrants, despite being under suspicion as being less "American," still were able to achieve from phonograph companies the commercialization of their musical culture. To make money, Anglo-American entrepreneurs were flying in the face of assimilation pressures. Whatever the reasons, a detailed examination of the specific kinds of music that were recorded and a look at the star ethnic performers may help us determine the relationship between ethnic entertainment and the adjustment of immigrants and their families to the American environment.

The different musical genres in the ethnic market in the 1920s are difficult to categorize, and much of what was cut on record was as rich and complex as the traditional culture that inspired it. Among the many genres, one of the most popular consisted of music with traditional roots that was newly composed in America. Most ethnic pieces, whatever their background, probably did not appear on record in strictly traditional form. Some were entirely new compositions in the traditional style; others were older pieces arranged for new instrumentation. New themes for lyrics were common, such as patriotic or nationalistic themes reflecting World War I or heavily sentimental lyrics about leaving the rural life of the old country or about family breakups resulting when children emigrated to the New World. Other typical themes of ethnic songs involved the reenactment of old-country rituals, especially weddings, or the entirely new experience of American settlement and adjustment problems—language difficulties, exploitation, and the other obstacles of an alien environment. Recorded ethnic music, then, really supplied a kind of solace or mediating mechanism for many years, even beyond the 1920s, helping the immigrants to become comfortable in the new land.

Two of the leading ethnic recording artists of the 1920s were musicians who were already prominent in the previous age of the concert band, the Bohemian Bohumil Kryl and the Italian Giuseppe Creatore. Both performers had initially became well known in brass and wind ensembles popular among the general American public, but by the 1920s they were recording more strictly ethnic selections aimed particularly at audiences who shared their ethnic roots. Thus these musicians transcended the two periods before and after World War I, as did recorded music as a whole, by shifting their focus from a general audience to a more specifically ethnic audience.

Bohumil Kryl had been born near Prague in 1875, the son of an artist who presumably saw to it that he began his music education early. By the age of ten he was studying the violin. He played for a time in a circus, as both a violinist and cornetist. Arriving in America in 1889, he soon established himself as a trumpet virtuoso, engaged by Sousa and especially Frederick Innes in 1902, with whom he established his brilliance by playing about six hundred solos and became known as the "Caruso" of the cornet.[33] Around this time, as we have seen, he became acquainted with Joseph Jiran at his Chicago store, and in 1910 he formed his own ensemble, Kryl's Bohemian Band, playing more strictly Bohemian selections. Following military service during the war, he devoted himself again to Bohemian music, this time taking advantage of the recording industry's new interest in the ethnic audience. He issued cuts for Columbia, Zonophone, and especially Victor, whose Czech catalogue of 1924 lists seventeen Kryl selections, of which three were composed by Kmoch and others by Šmetana, Dvorak, and Safranek.[34]

Kryl is distinctive as one of the few musicians who was able to shift successfully from the concert-band era to the ethnic-music period, a transition that he probably accomplished with the guidance and assistance of Jiran, the music businessman he knew well. Jiran also helped other Czech bandleaders become well known through their recordings, such as Anton Brousek, who achieved the greatest popularity of all the Czechs after Heindl discovered him in 1915. Brousek had made more than thirty cuts for Columbia by 1924 and many more by 1928. Anton Grill made at least twenty-eight recordings of Czech tunes between 1924 and 1927, and the prolific Vaclav Albrecht began his record-making in 1922.[35] It is not surprising, then, that Jiran and his music store were prospering enormously in the later 1920s from this enlarged Bohemian record-making and sales.[36]

Kryl's old concert-band colleague, Giuseppe Creatore, took the same route as the Bohemian, heading up a long list of Italian recording artists who all told produced the most recorded ethnic music of any group in the twenties. And while it is unclear if this "Svengali of the Baton" had obtained help in cutting discs from any of the Italian music companies, as so many other musicians did, certainly the Italian Book Company promoted his ethnic recordings.

Creatore seemed to dominate the Italian records made in the post–World War I era. Although in performances he had stressed Italian opera, on records his band cut selections that, while still intended chiefly for Italians, included songs that were nationalistic-patriotic, folk, and generally romantic. Between 1916 and 1918 he made forty sides for Edison, chiefly opera and nationalist marches; in 1920–21, he cut sixteen for Paramount, and from 1925 through 1933 he cut about ninety for Victor. Of his Victor recordings, sales were generally small except for thirty thousand for a hymn to Garibaldi ("Inno di Garibaldi") of April 6, 1927.[37] Other Italian bandsmen who recorded specifically ethnic selections during this era were Salvatore Minichini for Victor, Columbia, and Okeh; Paolo Bolognese for Emerson; Gerardo Iasilli for Gennett and Victor; and Enrico Rossi of Banda Rossi for Victor and Okeh. The Italian lists in the record company catalogues of the era illustrate the comprehensive range of ethnic offerings directed at foreign-born customers, such as Columbia's 1930 lists, which included not only the recordings of the bandleaders mentioned above but also ballads, folk tunes, dances, comic selections, arias, and regional selections.[38] Record contracts in the files of the Italian Book Company suggest its role in promoting Italian ethnic recordings for such composers as Giovanni De Rosalia, Aristede Sigismondi, Gennaro Amato, and Joseph De Laurentis, who normally sold all rights to their individual works outright.[39]

The Poles, too, created an extensive list of recorded ethnic music in the decade, again with the involvement of both national and ethnic music firms. In Chicago, music businessman Sajewski had worked with Columbia in 1915 to get Przybylski to record some old Polish selections. In the ensuing years, new artists began to alter traditional Polish music, shifting away from the old emphasis on strings toward more reliance on the accordion and winds. A leading innovator was Jan Wanat, whose virtuosity and rhythmic bass led his audience away from Przybylski's traditional *wiejska* style. Wanat, who began recording for Victor in October 1917, made over one hundred cuts with that company through 1933, including the typical polka, waltz, and oberek, along with some vocal selections and a few comedy numbers, such as one of his last pieces, "Going to the Old Country for a Vacation" (1933).[40]

Another popular Polish musician on record in the 1920s was Frantiszek Dukla, a well-known leader of a traditionally styled Polish string-based orchestra.[41] One of his popular recordings, "Wedding from Wojtowy" (1928), is an example of use of the new medium to preserve an old tradition. Another popular recording artist, Jozef Kmiec, had a similar piece, "Party Before the Wedding" (1928). A Polish singer from Cleveland, Paul (Pawel) Faut, became famous for his "Polish Eagles" (1926), the best-selling (100,000 copies) Polish record of the decade, which told of two countrymen who failed in an attempt to fly across the Atlantic. Other notable musicians were Leon Witkowski, the leading Polish clarinetist before his death in 1923, and Karol Stoch, a violinist who recorded distinctive *gorali* regional selections.[42]

Exactly how the American record companies, especially Victor and Columbia, located and recruited so many ethnic performers remains unclear. Certainly the ethnic music firms were involved, at least in some cases, but the musicians themselves were also beginning to organize for commercial purposes, as suggested by the experience of Poles in Philadelphia and Greeks in New York City, who had started associations of ethnic musicians.

Around 1912 a few Polish musicians in Philadelphia decided they needed an organization to improve their employment opportunities. A meeting in a local Polish tavern in 1915 attracted sixteen musicians, too few to start an organization, but early the following year the Society of Polish American Musicians (Stowarzenia Polsko-Amerykanskich Muzykantów) was formally established. In its early years the group included the well-recorded accordionist, Jan Wanat, as well as a music-store owner, Ignacy Podgorski, who later developed close ties with the Victor Company in nearby Camden, New Jersey.[43] Because the association prospered through the 1920s, it is likely that Victor relied on the group, as well as on Podgorski himself, to locate some of its ethnic performers. Podgorski, a prolific arranger, music publisher, and composer probably acted as a promoter, helping to recruit Polish musicians for recordings as Sajewski had for Columbia in Chicago.[44]

Another example of an important organization of ethnic musicians was the Greek Musicians' Union of America, founded in New York in 1921 to preserve the Greek musical heritage. It undoubtedly played a role, along with the Greek record companies in New York and Chicago, in encouraging recordings.[45]

Unlike the ethnic groups discussed above, whose musical talent was eagerly recruited by the record companies, Slovenian Americans, despite a rich musical tradition, had to take the initiative in approaching the companies to assure that their music was preserved on disc. The major American center of Slovenian settlement was Cleveland, a city with such an active ethnic musical life that it would have been surprising if the Slovenians had *not* developed a vibrant musical community in the New World. Slovenians arrived to find much German and Czech band music in the city, and they brought with them a village tradition that included many religious and secular choruses as well as marching and folk bands. In the twentieth century they would become leaders in the promotion of old-time music as a whole.

Slovenians came to Cleveland in the mid-1880s, chiefly for economic reasons. They found jobs in the expanding industries of this burgeoning Great Lakes metropolis, making it their largest settlement by the early 1890s, and founded several Roman Catholic parishes, numerous singing societies, brass and wind bands, and social and cultural centers at particular taverns and halls, the most popular of which was Knaus Hall, which opened in 1903 on the main thoroughfare of the Slovenian neighborhood, St. Clair Avenue. By 1910 the 15,000 Slovenians living in Cleveland constituted the third largest Slovenian community in the world.[46]

The greatest individual stimulus to the playing and performance of Slovenian music in the city was undoubtedly Anton Mervar, an immigrant who had arrived in Cleveland in 1913, at the age of twenty-seven. Forced to work as an ordinary laborer to support his wife and child, who had emigrated with him, he nevertheless did have a valuable skill. In his Austrian home province of Styria, Mervar had learned the craft of making button accordions, and upon his arrival in Cleveland he used his spare time to continue making and repairing the instruments for customers. By 1921, he had saved enough money to set himself up in a music shop he built on St. Clair Avenue, selling not only records but also a variety of musical instruments, including violins, mandolins, guitars, and especially accordions, which he both manufactured and repaired. Accordions were then a popular instrument among Slovenians, available for the relatively modest price of about $60.[47]

Mervar became widely known for the high quality of his work, and his store, like Jiran's among the Czechs in Chicago, became a major musical exchange. A number of Cleveland ethnic bandsmen, not all of them Slovenian, frequented the shop, making it a musician's social and professional center.[48] Among the figures who undoubtedly knew Mervar and visited his store were John Ivanusch, who had studied music with Franz Lehar in Austria before coming to Cleveland in 1919 to teach and direct the group's leading singing society; pianist John Zorman, another music teacher; bandleaders such as Victor Lisjak; and above all, the best-known button-box musician, Matt Arko Hoyer.[49]

By 1919 Hoyer had emerged as the most popular folk musician in the city, known not only for his playing but for his infectious sense of humor and warm personality, which eased the cultural adjustment for his immigrant audience.[50] He had come to Cleveland in 1911, with a European background like Mervar's as a craftsman of accordions, and was a frequent visitor at Mervar's St. Clair Avenue store in the post–World War I years. Mervar helped Hoyer's ensemble, first a duo and later a trio, by facilitating their appearance on records.

As Mervar was well aware, the efforts of the leading record companies to put ethnic music on disc had not extended to the Slovenians, except for a single vocal artist in New York, Augusta Danilova, who had recorded Slovenian songs in 1917. Mervar, believing that the industry should do much more, contacted several firms and convinced Victor to record the Hoyer trio in 1919–1920. Okeh recorded ten more Hoyer cuts by 1921, and by 1930 Victor, Okeh, and Columbia had recorded more than one hundred Slovenian selections performed by Hoyer's band. Their most popular pieces were the many Old Country tunes, especially "Dunaj Ostane Dunaj" (1927), better known as "Vienna Forever."[51]

Another Slovenian individual who may have known Mervar and who contributed to Cleveland's emergence as a nationally important capital of ethnic music was a musically trained dentist, William Lausche. Although Lausche was prominent in Cleveland's Slovenian community in the 1920s, his compositions and influence so differed from those of the more traditional musicians that he must be viewed as an inaugurator of the next, multiethnic stage of old-time music. His career will be discussed in detail in Chapter 8.

The music of another ethnic group, the Irish, was also put on disc in the post–World War I era, again with a prominent assist from ethnic music businesspeople. But the story of Irish music in America is distinctive because the old Irish ethnic music had virtually died out by World War I but was revived, oddly enough, when several Irish instrumentalists appeared in America just after the war to make *American* records and thereby restore those traditional pieces. We have then the anomaly of an American commercial activity literally causing a revival of a cultural form among an immigrant ethnic group.

The Irish, of course, had begun coming to America quite early, a few in the eighteenth century and many more in the early nineteenth century. Irish music, with its reels and jigs played on old-time instruments, such as the uilleann pipes and fiddles from the 1830s and 1840s, appealed to the non-Irish as well. To the end of the century, Irish musicians and dancers found willing audiences both at group and non-group affairs.[52]

Parallel with Irish traditional music were related genres, including the popular romantic songs rendered around the turn of the century by such singers as John McCormack and the stock stage-Irish pieces in vaudeville.[53] But the traditional music reached its peak in America with its appearance in performance at the Columbian Exposition of 1893 and the field research and folk-music publications of the well-known Chicago police superintendent, Francis O'Neill, beginning about ten years later.[54] By 1910 many Irish Americans had lost interest in their traditional music, but ironically, the record companies were just then beginning to think of marketing it. The companies looked to that group's ethnic music business to identify Irish musical talent, and those businesspeople recruited some performers living in America and also encouraged home-country musicians to emigrate from Ireland. Three of the latter were flutist John McKenna and fiddlers James Morrison and Michael Coleman.

A few recordings of Irish music had appeared before World War I, in 1903 and again in 1908, performed by a German American accordionist, John Kimmel. But around 1915 a New York Irish music-store owner, Ellen O'Byrne DeWitt, decided to do something about the many requests she was receiving from her patrons for old favorite tunes. She sent her son to consult two Irish musicians she knew in the Bronx to see if they would be willing to make records. When they agreed, she entered extended negotiations with Columbia and eventually made a contract; the record sold out quickly.[55] Driven in part by the rising Irish American nationalism and expanded sense of Irish identity from the formation of the Irish Free State, a growing demand for Irish music was evident after the war. In 1922 Okeh became the first company to issue an Irish traditional series, followed by Columbia and Gennett in 1925, by which date Irish Americans themselves had formed two ethnic recording companies, the M. & C. New Republic Irish Recording Company in 1921, specializing in patriotic and nationalistic pieces, and the Gaelic Phonograph Company, which began the following year.[56]

By this time an Irish musical literature on record had begun; the all-around ethnic artists who appeared on the growing number of discs were performers such as "Patsy" Touhey, who made several records for Victor before his death in 1923; the versatile "Patrol-man" Frank Quinn and P. J. Conlon, who recorded for Gaelic; John Griffin, Pat White, the Flanagan Brothers, and Dan Sullivan's Shamrock Band.[57] The Columbia label, as usual, took the lead in making Irish records, offering more than six hundred selections by 1931.[58]

The Irish recordings of the 1920s, though they represented the same commercial strategies as those of the other groups, differed in terms of the backgrounds of many of the recording artists, who actually emigrated from Ireland in the 1920s specifically to make records of old-time traditional Irish music. To understand the musical revival sparked by their recordings we shall review the careers of a few of those old-country artists.

It is no coincidence that the leading traditionalists came from one localized area, the counties Sligo and Leitrim. By the late 1800s that region had become known for its unique fiddling and flute-playing style, particularly as performed in the popular night-long rural house dances. The region was the matrix for the most popular old-time artist in Ireland and America, Michael Coleman. Born in 1891, the son of a fiddler who had made the family home into a musical center widely known as Coleman's Cross, Coleman took to the violin as a child.[59] The motives and even the date of his emigration to America are unclear, but he was in this country by about 1913, working from the start as a musician. After a vaudeville tour, he settled in New York in 1917 and made a few traditional recordings for an ethnic label, Shannon, in 1920. Almost immediately his virtuosity, ornamentation, and genius for improvisation attracted such wide acclaim that the major labels sought his services; over the next decade and a half, Victor, Columbia, Vocalion, and Decca employed him to make more than 150 cuts of jigs, reels, and hornpipes.[60]

James Morrison, whose career was only slightly less distinguished than Coleman's and which followed extraordinarily similar contours, was another fiddler from the traditional-music fraternity in the Sligo area, where he in fact had come to know Coleman. Morrison came to America in 1915, at the age of twenty-two.[61] He settled in New York in 1918 and found a job with the Morningside Music Company, which may have helped him make contact with record companies. Like Coleman, he made his first discs with an ethnic firm, New Republic, and later recorded with the nationals, including Columbia, Vocalion, Gennett, and Okeh by 1924. Prolific on record, with almost fifty discs to his credit into the 1930s, he drew heavily on the well-known Francis O'Neill collection of Irish folk tunes. He often recorded duets with other Irish musicians, such as James McKenna, the outstanding Irish traditional flutist.

McKenna, born in Ireland in 1880, grew up in County Lietrim, an area adjacent to the musically distinguished County Sligo, and which itself already had a reputation for excellent traditional flute playing.[62] He arrived in New York in 1911 and joined the city fire department, playing the flute in his spare time, and he began recording in 1921, first with New Republic and later with other labels, including the O'Byrne DeWitt Company. McKenna recorded sixty cuts over the years through 1937, becoming extremely popular among both the Irish and Irish Americans because of his bouyant optimism and a driving rhythm conducive to active dancing. He was especially known for his polkas and for his influence on younger flutists, and his memory is still revered today in his hometown.[63]

In the case of the Irish, it is clear that by 1930 the major American record companies, along with Irish American music firms, had exposed the world to a vital resuscitation of old-time Irish music. The discs of these artists clearly became musical artifacts that not only resisted Americanization but educated record buyers to the traditional culture from the Emerald Isle.

Another ethnic group that went through the experience of becoming reacquainted via phonograph in the 1920s with its traditional musical culture was the Ukrainians. Like the other ethnic communities, Ukrainian Americans were pleased to be able to obtain copies of their old songs and dances at their local record stores. But that group's preserved music also differed from the others in the widespread, multi-ethnic appeal of the major Ukrainian American artist, Pawlo Humeniuk.

Myron Surmach, the Ukrainian music-store owner who had been his group's cultural leader around World War I, played a significant role in getting Ukrainian music on wax, which would eventually result in the most popular ethnic disc of the era. Sometime around 1925 a Victor agent persuaded him to sell Victor records in his bookstore in lower Manhattan; Surmach established close ties with that recording firm and others, especially Columbia and Okeh.[64] Although it is unclear whether the idea to make the first Ukrainian record originated with Surmach, the company, or the artist, Pawlo Humeniuk, whom Surmach knew, it appears that Surmach facilitated the arrangements to get the popular Ukrainian fiddler on disc.[65] In 1925 he persuaded Okeh to let Humeniuk make test recordings, which succeeded in convincing the company to have the musician make two ten-inch records of the popular *kolomijka* dance for the company.[66] The next year, Surmach helped Humeniuk obtain a multi-year contract with Columbia to make twenty-four records per year, which proved so popular that he eventually made eighty-three records for Columbia and others for Victor through the 1930s, more than one hundred in all.[67]

One of Humeniuk's recordings, "Ukrainske Wesilie" (Ukrainian wedding), one of his first cuts for Columbia in 1926, was likely the most popular ethnic recording in the decade, selling at least 125,000 copies in a short time and perhaps 150,000 copies or more overall.[68] One explanation for the record's extraordinary appeal is Humeniuk's brilliant virtuosity and faithful folk renditions. Reminiscing a half-century after the artist's popularity, Surmach described Humeniuk's significance for his customers:

He made it like [a] village song, just folk, really what they play . . . in the villages . . . without looking [at] notes. He [would] usually close his eyes [as he played]. And when he made . . . records, I put [them] on the phonograph and people [said], "Oh, that's exactly how they play[ed] in my village." And they [would] stop to buy. And I couldn't get enough of those records.[69]

Humeniuk had begun learning the violin in 1890, as a boy of six in the Austro-Hungarian province of Galicia, the western Ukrainian region with a rich tradition of mountain folk dance and music. He came to New York around 1902 and continued his musical studies with a well-educated Russian violin teacher, while earning his living as a tanner. He became famous locally for his performances at public and private Ukrainian functions, including weddings. His promoter, Myron Surmach, was perceptive enough to understand the immigrants' love of weddings, their eagerness to relive the joys of the traditional Old World wedding ceremony. Most likely, it was Surmach who suggested recording not only of the songs of the occasion but the entire affair, resulting in "Ukrainian Wedding," a two-sided 12-inch record dramatizing with music the event in full, from family preparations to ceremony to concluding festivities. It was also Surmach who knew and selected the two other performers who appeared with Humeniuk on the record, popular comedians Rosa Krasnowska and Ewgen Zukowsky. They and other entertainers discovered by Surmach went on to make many Ukrainian recordings for national labels.[70]

The success of Humeniuk's wedding record also reflected its appeal to ethnic groups besides the Ukrainians, especially to Poles and eastern European Jews. The majority of Humeniuk's non-Ukrainian audience were Poles, who had a similar rural instrumental tradition, particularly the Gorali, who had lived with the western Ukrainians in the Galician mountains.[71] Russian Jews also were attracted to Ukrainian music and in fact shared elements of the Ukrainian musical culture. Many Jews had emigrated to America with Ukrainians and were aware of a cultural affinity with their neighboring Slavs. In fact, at least one Jewish traditional singer who made records in the 1920s, David Medoff, worked in both the Yiddish and the Ukrainian traditions.[72] The record companies, aware of the extent to which Humeniuk's audience included Jews and Poles, sought to capitalize on the multiethnic appeal of the Ukrainian fiddler by having him record additional selections intended specifically for other East European groups.[73]

The motives of the record companies that recorded ethnic music beginning around World War I were fundamentally entrepreneurial, to make profits. Ironically, however, the marketing strategy that engaged the firms in learning about and preserving immigrants' foreign musical heritage was at odds with the nativism that characterized the era politically and socially and produced the anti-foreign hysteria of the Red Scare, Prohibition, and a new federal immigration policy hostile to immigration. Columbia, Victor, and the many other recording companies from the 1910s into the 1930s were catering to the wishes of their foreigner consumers, producing an extraordinary wealth of immigrant music, song, and dance. The 1920s may have been an era of rampant intolerance, anti-Catholicism, anti-Semitism, and racism, but it was also a time when American corporations produced ethnic material that preserved and even promoted ethnic cultures. In this instance of politics and commerce working at cross purposes, the outcome is clear: music and commercial activity were triumphant.

In serving the ethnic audience, a segment of American business was responding to market demand even in the face of conflict with the general political and social atmosphere. In fact, the powerful external pressures to assimilate the immigrants may well have been the cause of an increasing nostalgia among the immigrant communities and hence an even greater demand for old-time music. Whatever the exact cause, record companies simply decided to produce more examples of ethnic culture, engaging in an industrial and commercial process that continued into the depression in the early 1930s, when nearly the entire record industry collapsed.

The demand for old-time music must have been related to social and psychological needs of its audience. Immigrants from virtually every group wanted to be able to listen to the familiar Old World tunes. In the distinctive case of the Irish, who had arrived earlier and whose assimilated tunes were part of American popular music, Irish Americans nonetheless wanted to hear the old traditional music played by traditional artists. Ethnic Americans of all nationalities yearned to hear again those homeland tunes that reminded them of their native region, their historical roots, and especially their intimate life-cycle events, such as weddings. A 1914 publication from Columbia, the record company most responsive to the immigrant market, described that longing of ethnic members very sensitively:

With from five to eight thousand miles between them and the land of their birth, in a country of strange speech and customs, the 35,000,000 foreigners making their home here are keenly on the alert for anything . . . which will keep alive the memories of their fatherland. . . .They are literally starving for amusements.[74]

While the immigrants certainly were aware of their desire for tangible evidence of their life in the old country, they were probably less conscious of another need, to understand and develop a new identity as immigrants in a strange land. In America, they were dealing with new experiences that required understanding, problems of language and family, along with other social problems, such as meeting strange people, both other group members and outsiders with whom they now associated at home, work, church, school, or on the street. One of the sources to which they turned for help in explaining their new environment was their own entertainment, which supplied both cultural continuity with the past and, as we shall see, a highly creative and comedic approach to coping with the new challenges of the present.

5

Immigrant Entertainers
Fashion Their Audience

Recorded ethnic music was not the only cultural ac-
complishment of immigrant Americans during the 1920s; the decade
was also an era, in fact a golden age, of onstage immigrant entertainment. Exceptionally talented individuals arose in many of the
immigrant communities to become widely known vaudeville stars,
popular and influential in important ways. Their music and comic
material helped to transform their community, to bring together
disparate elements of their ethnic group and thereby forge a new
and larger audience. In the process these entertainers also aided in
establishing a common and more secure identity for their patrons,
developing bonds that were both localized and more broadly ethnic.

By World War I the major immigrant communities had established
formal and informal centers of socialization and recreation, such as
the Italians' cafe chantant, the Jews' Yiddish theater, and the Germans' and Czechs' beer gardens. Most of these places, however,
attracted only a limited segment of an ethnic group, with the limits
generally reflecting provincial or regional distinctions of the old
country. Like the neighborhoods themselves, these recreational centers were highly localized, fragmenting ethnic groups into regionally
based subgroups. Immigrants frequented the cafes and entertainment halls as provincials, as Sicilians or Neapolitans, Polish or Roumanian or Russian Jews, Ruthenians, Bavarians, or Bohemians—not
simply as Italians, Jews, Ukrainians, Germans, or Czechs. While
many immigrants experienced a transformation to a broader con-

sciousness for many reasons, an examination of how their entertainment contributed to this process suggests that they retained some kind of local regional tie along with the larger ethnic one.[1]

Old World village attachments did not disappear upon the newcomers' arrival. Immigrants sought to hold on—in part through their music and entertainment—to a psychological sense either of their own particular provincial home in the Old World or of any European locality similar to or associated with their own. In other words, the music and song they heard enabled them to retain a degree of continuity with the past by invoking memories and ties to a *generic* village or region, regardless of whether it was the real one.

Perhaps because of continuing discomfort with life in the New World, many immigrants clung to old regional affiliations even after many years in America. Obviously, the break with family and friends and familiar ways in the old country stimulated feelings of guilt and insecurity, even among immigrants whose departure had been precipitated by oppression, such as the eastern European Jews. Adjusting to life in America certainly was not easy, involving daily problems with an unfamiliar language and culture, as well as the long-term challenges of accepting different social values and coming to terms with new technological developments.

Of course the immigrants established community institutions to deal with the problem of adjustment, building religious, fraternal, and cultural organizations to maintain psychic continuity and thereby ease the pain of being an alien. Certainly, too, in the early 1900s, the 1910s and especially the 1920s, commercialized recordings of familiar traditional music also helped the newcomers make the transition. Another significant but still little-known mediator for the foreigner was the immigrant entertainer, especially the comic performer. This figure on stage and on record provided much-needed emotional comfort, and the artistry of the very best of these entertainers helped build a more homogeneous ethnic community for the future.

These singers and actors in cafes, coffeehouses, and theaters were an integral part of the evolving immigrant and ethnic culture. The handful who distinguished themselves as the most successful were outstanding not only because of their exceptional talent as performers but also because of their originality and creativity. Many composed their entire presentation or a good part of it. But while they were distinctive in their success, they were also representative in the content of their material, for upon close examination these comic figures appear remarkably similar to one another.

Virtually all of them, for example, dealt in their performances with the life experiences of a simple, rural individual. Unprepossessing, they drew their stage characters close to their audience. Under the facade of a country bumpkin, these comic entertainers would review and satirize the experiences of a rustic who had left his peasant village for a modern urban-industrial environment—the very transit of many of the patrons in the audience. But the depiction of these naive and uneducated characters was not demeaning; the characters were actually attractive, lovable, even clever. In fact, the monologues and skits in which they appeared often demonstrated how unsophisticated rustics could overcome or at least deal with the obstacles in a complex environment.

Seeing these rustics on stage must have helped members of the audience gain perspective on problems of adjustment and even gain more consciously a bond of common experience with fellow theatergoers. A new identity as an immigrant began to emerge. All of the theatergoers felt nostalgic about their old home, their village, their Polish *okolica* or Norwegian *bydelag*. Thus, to be an Italian, Jew, Pole, or German in America required a larger ethnic identification as well as a smaller, localized regional attachment—a dual identity that entertainers both played on and helped to define.

Paradoxically, by recognizing the great variety of local and regional origins of their audience beginning in the 1910s, the entertainers were building a homogeneous immigrant clientele that may have been fictional. When these comic entertainers performed, the audience warmed to the their provincial characterizations *whether or not they themselves came from those areas.* As two folk researchers have demonstrated in studies of Hungarian newcomers in the 1920s, American immigrants felt a psychic need for *any* local, regional home, however idealized and romanticized. In the case of the Hungarians, homesickness and promotion of the Hungarian state together fashioned a stereotyped and somewhat fictionalized picture of Hungarian peasant life in the immigrant mind. The image was not entirely fictional; it was based on an actual regional celebration, a wine harvest festival held by peasants in certain areas in the late 1890s. Immigrants in America, with the assistance of the Hungarian authorities, conveyed the ritual to the New World in the form of a folk-style musical called *nepszinmu,* a performance-celebration that included dancing, gypsy-type music, song, and traditional foods.[2]

Talented vaudeville performers essentially designed such a past for their immigrant audiences, as we will see below in an examination of some of the most popular acts.

One of the first comic acts to build a sizable ethnic following with routines that compared the simple life in the Old Country with the strange and more complex life in America was the Olson sisters.[3] Curiously, unlike most immigrant entertainers Ethel and Eleonora Olson were American-born, the daughters of Norwegians who had settled in Chicago. But the Olson sisters were well schooled in their provincial family origins and had an intimate understanding of the concerns of the Norwegian American community.[4]

Ethel and Eleonora had apparently obtained their extraordinary knowledge of emigrant life from their mother, Johanna, who had also inspired in them an interest in the stage. Johanna was from Haslo Indre in the Sogne district of Norway and had emigrated with her parents in 1860, when she was fourteen. The family first settled in Wisconsin, but Johanna married in Chicago in 1865 and raised her family in the large Norwegian community there.[5] She instilled in her daughters a love of music, both folk and classical, as well as a sense of humor and a great affection for her Sogne home district in Norway. Ethel, born in 1870, was nineteen years older than Eleonora, and at first the sisters pursued separate stage careers. Neither intended initially to become a comedienne; they appeared on the Norwegian stage in Chicago's Logan Square area as serious dramatic and musical artists.[6]

As performers, they complemented each other well. Ethel, who had been on stage since childhood, was the better actor of the two and an accomplished pianist. Eleonora was the better singer and had had voice training and experience with a Norwegian concert company beginning in 1905. They teamed up in 1909, when Ethel was just under forty and Eleonora was twenty.

At first their act included serious music—opera and Norwegian folk pieces—interspersed with comic monologues and songs, but it was their humor that earned them most of their popularity and made them well known in the 1910s and early 1920s, chiefly in Norwegian areas of the Midwest. They became national ethnic stars after 1915, when they received wider exposure by joining the Chautauqua circuit. The records they made for Edison, Victor, and Brunswick added to their success, even after they stopped performing on stage when Ethel married in 1923.

Their humor was based heavily on use of Norwegian dialects, especially the dialect of their mother's district, Sogne. Although they made both English and Norwegian records, even their English discs included some foreign-language segments. Probably their most famous monologue was their early "Sogne Kjerring," the Old Sogning Woman, recorded in two parts by Victor. In the monologue Eleonora, in her mother's vernacular, speaks as an immigrant wife who bewails her adjustment difficulties in the move to an American city.[7] In the stage version, the sisters would dress the part, in peasant dress with shawl and kerchief.[8] The climax of the old woman's tale of woe involves a visit to a doctor about an illness she has contracted on moving into the city, a Yankee doctor who obviously knows nothing about Norwegians because he prescribes giving up coffee. And coffee, the Sogne woman concludes, as any Norwegian would know, "is all dat holds life in me."[9]

Other anecdotes have similar themes. "The Baseball Game," for example, illustrates the confusion of a newcomer, in this case a foreign-born woman, about the peculiar language of the sport, such words as "fly," "foul" (fowl?), and "slide." "The Norwegian Girl at the Photographer" involves a dilemma concerning what pose to strike for a picture to send home to an old-country beau. Should the girl appear happy in the photo, so as to look her best, or sad, so as to convey how much she misses her sweetheart? She decides on the latter and concludes that looking miserable before the camera was "de hardest vork I ever did."[10]

Hjalmar Peterson adopted a similar approach with his Swedish American audience. Peterson's success and popularity were extraordinary, much greater than that of the Norwegian Olson sisters—and in fact among his fans were many Norwegians and Danes. Hjalmar's appeal drew on a Scandinavian comic tradition, as he assumed the persona of "Olle i Skratthult" (Olle from Laughterville), and he became director of an entire company of actors and musicians that remained popular for two decades, from World War I into the Great Depression.

As an immigrant himself, who came to America in 1906, Peterson brought with him a late-nineteenth-century Swedish tradition of the *bondkomik,* a rural peasant comic. That theatrical image of a simple rustic had already entered Swedish culture as a response to the increasing urbanization, industrialization, and modernization of Swedish life. By the time that Peterson left for America, a Swedish journalist and writer, Magnus Elmblad, had already created a classic rustic clod named Petter Jonsson, a throwback to the nation's rural past.[11] Elmblad depicted Jonsson as a confused young oaf who wore ill-fitting farmer's homespun, chewed a wad of tobacco, and generally carried himself awkwardly.[12] In America, Peterson would combine Elmblad's familiar stereotype with musical material modeled after the work of Gustaf Froding, a Swedish songwriter who used dialect in his tunes.[13]

As a cultural descendant of Elmblad and Froding, Peterson arrived with his brothers in Minneapolis in 1906, leaving behind his home in Munkfors, Varmland province, in west-central Sweden.[14] Initially, he worked as a farmhand and bricklayer, also appearing as a solo entertainer, and as an actor at a well-known performance at a 1909 county fair. In late 1909 he returned to the Old Country with a Swedish American quartet and toured there until 1911. While in Sweden he became better acquainted with the bondkomiks, especially Kalle Namdeman. Peterson's Olle i Skratthult was a comic character fashioned in the tradition of Namdeman, Elmblad, and Froding.[15]

Soon after he returned from Sweden, Peterson set up his entertainment troupe and quickly dominated what can be called the Swedish American vaudeville stage. Certainly a major boost to his popularity was his neighborhood in the Cedar Avenue section of Minneapolis, the major Swedish American cultural center and site of many cafes, hotels, food stores, and halls. In the Mozart, Dania, Eagles, and other halls, Peterson's company offered full theatrical productions evoking old-time Swedish rural life. The female star was Olga Lindgren, whose lovely singing voice Peterson had noted in 1914 and who joined the troupe shortly after it was formed in 1916. Lindgren and Peterson soon married.[16]

The performances of this company soon attracted packed houses, as many as twelve thousand at a Saturday-night show in Minneapolis and often more than one thousand in houses on the road during annual tours of Swedish American communities.[17] The huge audiences were interested mainly in theatrical productions dealing with Swedish country and emigrant life, such as the well-known musical "Varmlanningarna" (The people of Varmland). This six-act melodrama, written in 1846 and set in Peterson's home district, was a love story about a young peasant couple who, with considerable difficulty, overcame hostile parents and local convention. Audiences identified closely with the hero and heroine, seeing in the plot the sorts of difficulties familiar in their own lives.[18]

Peterson made an enormously popular record on the same theme, "Nicolina," first cut for Columbia in 1915 and later for Victor and Bluebird, which is estimated to have sold about 100,000 copies by 1930. It was so widely popular that several non-Swedish Scandinavian versions were also recorded. "Nicolina," too, is the story of rustic lovers who must wait for a father's passing to fulfill their romantic longings.[19] From World War I to the early years of the depression, the Olle i Skratthult troupe clearly dominated Swedish American vaudeville with its Old World, rural-based entertainment. Normally the company would spend the winter in the Twin Cities, go on tour in the fall and spring, and spend most of the late summer in a northern retreat reworking their program for the succeeding months. The group consisted of twenty to twenty-five performers who usually traveled in three autos to Swedish settlements all over the country, from Worcester, Massachusetts, and Jamestown, New York, to Chicago and Rockford, Illinois, to San Francisco and Seattle.[20]

A typical program of the Olle i Skratthult company at the height of its popularity in the mid- and late 1920s was much more than a musical play. In true *bondkomik* tradition, Peterson would appear in front of the curtain between acts of the play for a brief monologue called an *olio*. The audience would notice his entrance immediately, because he lumbered onto the stage with a staff in his hand, stumbling on the long scarf he wore around his neck. He was dressed in poor homespun clothes and squeaky boots, with a cap that was topped by a red rose that did not quite hide a straw-colored wig. He completed his attire with an alarm clock at his hip. His smile before he spoke revealed a conspicuously missing (blackened) front tooth and an upper lip stuffed with tobacco.[21] The audience would of course immediately break into peals of laughter, Peterson having won them to his peasant comedy even before he began his act, singing "Nicolina" or a similar rustic tune. The troupe would then resume the main drama of the evening, sustaining the theme of rural traditions, and even after the end of the play the entertainment would go on, with a *dans efter programmet*, a session of audience dancing and often singing, to the accompaniment of an accordion band. Chairs would be pushed aside, the playhouse would be transformed from a theater to a dance hall, and the scene was set for old-time *gammaldans*—polkas, schottisches, waltzes, and the like.[22]

The impact of the Olle i Skratthult company on its patrons was extraordinary, maintaining the newcomers' old-country memories and helping them achieve perspective on their alien status in America. Swedish immigrants and their families, children as well as parents, eagerly looked forward to the Olle i Skratthult season. "When Olle's group came through the Dakotas in the spring," reported one observer, "the farm work would suffer, for the young people would come from a hundred miles around to watch the zany Olle."[23] In the late 1920s Peterson was said to be "almost as famous among Swedish Americans as Charles Lindbergh."[24]

In February 1925 the Tacoma *Svenska Posten* said Peterson could be called "the greatest comedian of Swedish America, a superb artist," and in 1924 the Worcester *Svea* commended Olle for his shrewd judgments of immigrant life. So Olle was far more than a naive rustic; he was also a profound satirist.[25]

Like the Olson sisters, Peterson universalized the experience of his audience: Norway's Sogne and Sweden's Varmland became everyone's home. But Peterson's appeal went much further than that of the Olsons, drawing from all classes, at all stages of assimilation, and even from all Scandinavian backgrounds, Norwegians and Danes as well as Swedes. What he offered his clientele was an immigrant identity that was both securely local and broadly ethnic. Olle's comedy was forging a Scandinavian American audience and identity.[26]

The Italian American equivalent of the Olson Sisters and Olle i Skratthult was Eduardo Migliaccio, better known as Farfariello, whose talent for impersonations developed into a highly imaginative series of vignettes of many different rural characters. Migliaccio became the star Italian American vaudevillian for four decades, appealing to Italian immigrants from all regions and backgrounds, even though throughout his career he relied on the dialect of his own Neapolitan background.[27]

Like Peterson, Migliaccio brought with him to America some of the dramatic traditions of his region and homeland. Part of that background was the drama of Pulcinello, a comic-character skit originally derived from Neapolitan scenarios of the Commedia del l'Arte of the 1500s. Another beloved figure often found on the Italian popular stage was Stenterello, a good-hearted simpleton very similar to the Swedish *bondkomik*.[28] Migliaccio was also familiar with a theatrical form popular in the Naples of his youth called the *machiettista,* a short comic skit as opposed to the full-length dramatic play.

Born in 1880 at Cava Dei Tireni, in Salerno province near Naples, Migliaccio grew up in a family of modest means and as a youth developed a fascination with the *machiettisti,* especially the skits of a leading comic, Nicolo Maldacea.[29] In those early years Migliaccio may well have had some formal education in drama; he certainly had received training in the technical aspects of the stage, especially makeup and costume, skills that would eventually contribute much to his comic genius. As a young teenager he attended a fine-arts school of design in Naples. He came to America in 1897, at the age of fifteen.[30] Oddly, he came as a bookkeeper rather than as an actor, for he had received business training in Naples as well as some experience on the Neapolitan stage. His father, who had preceded him to the new land, had established a bank in Hazleton, Pennsylvania, a small mining town where he put his son to work.[31]

As one might imagine, the life of a bank clerk was not attractive to a youth eager to put on greasepaint and try the stage. But distasteful or not, the work he did for his father was to prove invaluable for his later career as a comic entertainer. By servicing bank patrons, particularly his immigrant countrymen, writing letters for the newcomers and helping them adjust to a new land, Migliaccio was beginning his education in the trials and tribulations of immigrant life.

This education continued after he left Hazleton for the entertainment stage in New York. The first employment he found was as a laborer in a New York sweatshop, where he learned firsthand about the needs and hopes of ordinary Italian ex-peasant immigrants.[32] Migliaccio's privileged background had presumably given him little understanding of the lives of ordinary Italians, but he would eventually become known for his great empathy for and pragmatic philosophy about his immigrant countrymen. In a bank and a sweatshop, he was acquainting himself in particular with the various characters who made up the immigrant's life in America—the basis of his comedy skits—including the greenhorn, the organ grinder, the rag-picker, the ditch-digger, and the iceman, among others.[33]

Fortunately Migliaccio did not have to stay long in the sweatshop; his good singing voice and knowledge of Neapolitan songs led to many bookings, at first for private performances at the homes of friends in the city and later for public engagements at the many

Lower East Side coffeehouses of the working-class Italian Americans. One early engagement, in 1901, was at Pennachio's, a *caffe chantant,* for about $3 per week.[34]

Migliaccio's big break came about 1904, with the help of a fellow Neapolitan and fervent promoter of Italian theater, Antonietta Pisanelli Alessandro, who helped arrange for Migliaccio to perform at a Mulberry Street theater in the heart of the Italian Lower East Side. He also obtained a booking at the well-known Villa Vittorio Emanuele III cafe, where he would establish his reputation as a comic. Migliaccio's theatrical ambitions were serious: the Italian people of New York, he believed, were an "admirable element" for whom theater should be both "entertaining and useful." He hoped that through comedy he might help audiences "open their minds" and thereby better understand their new lives.[35] The whole idea, he once explained, was that the "humor of the theatrical creation . . . relieves . . . the tragic drama [of the person] in exile, uprooted from his land and thrown [into] work . . . [I do] battle for the reeducation of the national mass in simple and fervent Neapolitan verse."[36]

Assuming the stage name of Farfariello, Migliaccio created playlets that became known as *machietta coloniale,* featuring characters who would make Italian audiences laugh during a career lasting forty years, until his death in 1946. He performed chiefly on stage but also made records and did radio broadcasts.

Farfariello's characterizations differed, of course, from the Norwegian Sogne woman of the Olsons and the Swedish or Scandinavian Olle, as Italian traditions differ generally from those of Scandinavia. Nonetheless, the similarities are much more striking.[37] Despite Migliaccio's usual delivery in his own Neapolitan provincial dialect, with occasional English words, he played for and was in the process of forging an audience of *all* Italian immigrants, which suggests that they, like Scandinavian Americans, sought *any* reminder of old-country life, even if that reminder was not of their own home province. In addition to encouraging an immigrant consciousness through language, he helped forge that new sense of community through his characterizations, which were satirical profiles of the different personal types that his audience knew well. The most important of Migliaccio's many characters was a simple, naive type—familiar in Italian popular theater—called the *cafone.* Migliaccio, then, had combined two Italian theatrical devices, the *stenterello* (Tuscan clown) and the *cafone* (poor simple worker), to fashion many of his comic figures, who resembled in many ways the Scandinavian *bondkomik*.

Migliaccio's impersonations were immensely successful over his entire career. In 1909, an Italian theater-owner on the Lower East Side engaged him for six months at a weekly salary of $65.[38] By 1917 he already had his own troupe, the Eduardo Migliaccio Vaudeville Company, with a manager, Mimi Imperato, who apparently booked the group on national tours.[39] By the end of World War I he was known among Italian Americans as "Il Re Dei Machiettisti," the King of the Machiettisti, on the immigrant musical stage. With a good eye for costume and makeup—he impersonated female as well as male characters—and with a profound understanding of the immigrant condition and good sense of commercial promotion, Migliaccio had no rival, though he did have some competitors.[40]

Understanding the reasons for his popularity requires a closer look at what Migliaccio satirized and the kind of characters he created.[41] His repertoire was enormous; during the World War I era he had about 150 skits in his collection, a number that increased to probably 400 at the height of his career in the 1920s and 1930s.[42] In these skits Migliaccio presented widely different figures—rich and poor, famous and ordinary, Italian and American—who exposed all the foibles of humanity through monologues that were both amusing and morally instructive. One of Migliaccio's themes involved the shortcomings of supposedly classless, democratic America: the yokel in America who ridiculously tries to ape the upper class by wearing a tuxedo; the up-to-date girl who knew much about jazz but nothing of her nation's history; the smug Italian woman who prided herself on her fecundity compared with her nearly barren American counterpart; the undertaker who enjoyed going to his people's banquets and feasts in the hopeful eventuality that someone would die of overeating; the immigrant who is distraught at having to reject his culture while being naturalized; the money-hungry greenhorn; the simpleton who while insisting that he had become American in truth remained very Italian; the lowly street cleaner who converses with a statue of Columbus to learn how his great discovery really benefited him; and in what was usually his concluding skit, the Barese iceman who so enthralled his customers with his singing that they forgot to empty their iceboxes.

Three of the most popular *machietti* were very much immigrant-based, carrying the same themes as those of Hjalmar Peterson. One was "Crazy Patsy," recorded in 1919, a character who viewed America as a bizarre world entirely unlike Europe, a new land where the lowliest laborer could become a professor and where freedom was too great and could lead to anarchy. Two other skits entitled "La Lingua Taliana" and "Iammo a Conailando" (Let's Go to Coney Island) drew the audience's concern to the evolving Italian American argot and the issue of change and assimilation of the traditional language.

"Il Cafone Patrioti" is of special significance because of its substantial contribution to the audience's immigrant identity, demonstrating how provincial and national ties could be compatible in making up both the Italian nation and the Italian American community. Though Italians might maintain their Genovese, Piedmontese, Neapolitan, Calabrese, Sicilian, Roman, Tuscan, and other provincial ties, "Italy, my dear sirs, many centuries and centuries before us, was like a pizza of which everyone had a slice—but it was always Italian. . . . Italy is the most beautiful country in the world."[43]

Although Migliaccio's triumph was of course originally based on his stage performances, where audiences could see his many disguises, he was able to adapt his material rather well to other entertainment media, such as phonograph records, a medium which Italian immigrants in particular cultivated.[44] As early as 1916, when recording rivals Victor and Columbia were beginning their enthusiastic embrace of ethnic artists, Migliaccio signed a contract with Victor to make discs for $50 each.[45] And the King of the Machiettisti was prolific on record—it has been estimated that he cut over 125 pieces during his career from the early 1900s to 1935. By 1920, when the Victor general catalog listed many Migliaccio cuts,[46] he had contracted with the leading Italian American music firm, the Italian Book Company, to publish many of his songs and machiettisti. By the end of the 1920s, when his reputation was at its height, he had six people in his company and typically commanded fees in the range of $1,000 for a six-week engagement, most of which went to Migliaccio personally.[47]

Toward the end of his career, from the late 1930s until his death just at the end of World War II, he continued to deliver his comic songs and skits over such New York radio stations as WAAT, which had Italian programming. For all he did to maintain the immigrants' cultural ties to Italy, it was fitting that King Victor Emmanuel III knighted Migliaccio with the Cavaliere dell'Ordine della Corona d'Italia in 1940.[48]

Among the many stars of the Jewish-Yiddish stage, one figure comparable to Peterson and Migliaccio stands out most prominently. He was Aaron Lebedeff, clearly the most popular entertainer at the height of his group's vaudeville stage in the 1920s and also the most influential with his audience. Unlike his Swedish and Italian counterparts, however, Lebedeff's popularity rested less on his characterizations than on his stage presence, which was marked by unbounded exuberance and dash. The message he conveyed, however, was similar to that of the other vaudevillians, dwelling on nostalgia for the *shtetl*, the old country village, as a generic rather than a specific locale and thereby remaking his immigrant audience into a homogeneous mass.

Lebedeff was fortunate in entering the Jewish vaudeville in 1920, when the Yiddish comedy stage was entering its era of greatest popularity, with large houses, prolific composers, and a growing demand for supporting actors and actresses. As an art form, the theater had emerged originally after the turn of the century, through the efforts of Jacob Adler, Jacob Gordon, David Kessler and others, but it did not assume its more popular character until after Gordon's death in 1910. Although a group led by Maurice Schwartz revived the more sophisticated drama in 1918, the popular theater continued to grow, attracting numerous patrons.[49] The leader of that latter genre and the major promoter of early Yiddish vaudeville was Boris Thomashevsky, who as noted above opened his magnificent National Theater on the Lower East Side, at Second Avenue and Houston Street, around World War I.

About twenty other Yiddish theaters in the city competed with the National for good acting talent, a situation to which Thomashevsky responded by becoming something of an impresario.[50] As one contemporary composer put it, the popular theater was in need of fresh faces in 1920.[51] One of Thomashevsky's "finds," arguably his greatest, was Aaron Lebedeff, a Yiddish comedian who at the end of the war was barnstorming in China.

It is not clear precisely how Thomashevsky located Lebedeff. He most likely contacted him in Asia, though he may have waited till Lebedeff arrived in New York in 1920. It is certain that before coming to America, Lebedeff already had established a solid reputation as an East European comic, the "Litvak Komiker" (the *Lithuanian* Yiddish comic)—a title given him on the basis not of his nativity (he was born in Homel, White Russia, in 1873) but his material. That distinction is important; even before Lebedeff arrived in America, he had already based his Yiddish comic material on a particular region.[52] Even in his earliest years in Russia he was devoted to a life on the boards. He loved music and often sang with the local *chazzan*, rejecting his family's plan for him either to enter their clothing business or become an apprentice to a skilled trade. As a youth, he frequently ran off to nearby cities such as Minsk to appear with small theatrical groups, but his excursions always failed, and he had to return home. Later, however, he became more successful in music and dance presentations, in operettas especially, and even opened his own dancing school and joined musical and dance groups. By 1912 he had established a reputation as the Lithuanian comic in large cities throughout the region, including Warsaw.[53] His entry into the Russian army in World War I took him further afield, to Karbin, Manchuria, where he performed for the officers. After the Russians left the Allied side in 1917 he entertained American Red Cross officials stationed there, and when the war ended he and his actress wife toured Russian Siberia and China. He was appearing in Shanghai when Thomashevsky sent him an invitation to perform in New York City; leaving his wife behind to complete their engagement, he set off for the major Jewish American city.[54]

His October 1920 debut at Thomashevsky's National Theatre was memorable—according to one member of the audience, "America [had] never seen anything better than what we saw that evening."[55] Lebedeff was an instant hit, for the same reason that he would soon become the star of Yiddish musical comedy in America: his winning, charismatic personality. He projected an extraordinary exuberance and energy, engaging his audience immediately and holding it throughout his performance. He also had a powerful singing voice, which further arrested attention and perfectly suited the acoustic demands of the theater and records. Completing Lebedeff's dramatic abilities was a remarkable zest for improvisation, as he clowned and danced his way through the performance.

By the end of the 1920s Lebedeff was not only the most popular Yiddish vaudevillian but was also composing much of his own musical material and directing stage performances. He was therefore more than an individual actor; he was in fact the leader of a troupe of Yiddish players. From the mid-1920s to the 1940s in the summer off-season, Lebedeff would regularly lead a contingent of actors and actresses to the Catskills to perfect their dramatic skills.[56]

Lebedeff's unrivaled popularity was rooted in more than his magnetic stage presence. Unlike some of his colleagues, he often performed outside New York, thereby becoming a truly national figure. He told interviewers in Chicago in 1925 and 1929 that he liked to tour as a way of keeping up with his audiences and becoming acquainted with the younger generation. By keeping his stage presentations fresh, he was able to retain the interest of Jews of both immigrant and American generations in Yiddish culture.[57]

He became well known in the Midwest, first appearing before Detroit Jewish audiences in the 1923–1924 season and returning almost annually into the 1930s. Lebedeff was said to be "always a favorite of Detroit Jewry" in that era.[58] He also played often in the major East Coast cities, including Boston and Philadelphia.[59]

His huge output of records in the 1920s, about eighty in all, mostly for Emerson, Brunswick, and Vocalion, also aided substantially in making him known nationally. Because he usually cut each record immediately after the New York performances in which a particular song was introduced, people everywhere quickly became acquainted with him and his dynamic presence.[60]

Like the entertainers from other ethnic groups, Lebedeff met a psychological need for his audience, which was ever-nostalgic about the old European homeland and yearning for a romanticized image of the place from which they had come to America. To illustrate this theme, which was developed by many Jewish entertainers besides Lebedeff, we might consider a song with which he had little connection, "Die Grine Kusine," introduced in 1922 at the Grand Street Theatre and widely featured in cafes and theaters afterward.[61] Abe Schwartz and Hyman Prizant composed the ballad, which was issued by a prominent Yiddish house, J. and J. Kammen. It related the sad tale of a naive, happy country girl with "cheeks as red as oranges, hair in golden curls, teeth like pearls, eyes like twin doves, and lips like cherries," who left home for America where she met a boy and her ruination.[62]

Lebedeff undoubtedly knew his immigrant audiences' love for the message of "Die Grine Kusine," with its evocation of the innocence of the land of origin in contrast to the complexity, anxiety, and uncertainty of America. "Liovke Maladetz," the very first comedy in which he appeared, and the one that would set his name and style, played on that theme of alienation and unease, recounting the adventures and misadventures of an unsophisticated but good-hearted rascal in Russia who encounters but eventually conquers adversity. While not about immigration per se, it did convey a certain universality. Any Italian immigrant audience watching Farfariello or Swedish audience attending an Olle i Skratthult skit would have found the concurrent Yiddish theater and even Lebedeff's role surprisingly familiar. In realizing their three similar transitions, all were clearly becoming more homogeneous. A common immigrant identity was emerging.

While not every role Lebedeff played in the Yiddish theater dwelled on the theme of European innocence and American dangers, Lebedeff became identified as a purveyor of village or small-town characters. His title as the Litvak Komiker stuck with him in the Lower East Side theaters, where entertainers often drew humor from the semi-serious conflict that had arisen between emigrants from the general area around Lithuania—the "Litvaks"—and those from the more southerly region around Polish-Ukrainian Galicia—the "Galitzyaners."[63] Throughout his career, Lebedeff almost always projected the provincial character of Yiddish-speaking Jews, as did many Jewish American composers of the era, whose music either catered to or actually inspired the audience's continuing desire to romanticize its provincial origins. One of the leading younger writers of musicals, Abraham Ellstein, probably was speaking for many of his colleagues when he expressed the view that all Jewish composers should write about their people's life in the past, whether in biblical Israel or the East European shtetl.[64] Much of the material that Lebedeff used on stage and in song, even into the 1940s, continued to carry his listeners back psychically to their home in the Old World, whether that home was Lithuania, Poland, Russia proper, or Roumania. The titles themselves of a few of Lebedeff's popular vehicles in the twenties and thirties, by such composers as Herman Wohl, Sholem Secunda, Alexander Olshanetzky, Joseph Rumshinsky, and Abraham Ellstein, suggest the pervasiveness of this nostalgic theme: "A Wedding in Odessa," "Yankel in America," "Country Boy," "A Wedding in Palestine," "Motke From Slobodke," "Caucasian Love," "Russian Love," "A Village Wedding," "An East Side Wedding," "The Roumanian Litvak," "The Roumanian Wedding" and "Der Litvisher Yankee."[65]

Of course, as the leading performer in popular Yiddish musicals Lebedeff had a formative impact on his immigrant audience, furthering their romanticized image of their origins. He also had an impact on a wider public, much larger than the audience that attended the theater. He often sang in places other than the theater, in less formal surroundings such as cafes and restaurants, at benefits, and above all on records. In rendering those popular songs, he was also rooting listeners to their provincial past and thus providing them with a new identity as Jewish Americans.

Representative of this genre of popular Yiddish ballads is "Slutzk Mein Shtele," with lyrics by Lebedeff set to music by Herman Wohl. The piece recalls one particular village, invoked as a sort of generic hometown. Lebedeff recorded it in 1925.[66] Other works exemplifying the artist's frequent regional emphasis were "A Khazendi in America" (1928), in which a Litvak, Galytzyaner, and American judge a cantor, a singer or chanter of liturgical music and prayer; "Vayt Fun Der Heym" (Far from home) (1926), an emigrant's lament; "Odesser Liedel," and "In Odessa," songs about the Black Sea port also recorded in 1926; "Petrograd" and "Roumanische Karnatzlach" (Roumanian sausage) from 1927; "Gib Mir Bessarabia," which glorified life in the province on the Russian-Roumania border; "Aheim! Aheim!" (Home! Home!) (1933), which deals explicitly with immigrant homesickness ("In the Old World on the green fields, I was never sad; but since I am here [in America], I haven't had a relaxing moment. . . . I miss my beautiful little calf . . . [and] romping with the chickens. . . . Oh! . . . send me back home!"); and "Galitzye," which told of a home province along the border of southeastern Poland and which Lebedeff often delivered at benefit performances in the late 1930s.[67]

Other songs that Lebedeff performed combined sentimentalizing of a locality with the character for which he is always remembered— the devil-may-care free spirit who loves life and all its sensual delights, as in the skit "Liovke Maladetz," the kind of person the audience itself would like to be or know. His usual costumes of Russian *rebeshko* and boots or formal attire with straw hat and cane endeared him to his audience—Molly Picon referred to him as "our George M. Cohan . . . dressed like a dandy," and others called him the Jewish Maurice Chevalier.[68] The song "Tsen Kopikes," which Lebedeff popularized in 1923, is a young swain's account of the ways he will use his money to court his sweetheart—when he finds one.[69] Other songs dwelling on love and the appetite were "Ich Hob Lieb Di Meidlach" (I love the ladies) (1929); "Hot Dogs and Knishes" (1926); and "Dudky Brat" (1923), which advises people discouraged by Prohibition to take heart—one can still get drunk.[70]

One song, however, stands out as Lebedeff's hallmark, deeply moving his Yiddish audience and exercising the exuberance and energy for which he was famous. He delivered it probably from the mid-1920s for the rest of his life, with many variations. "Rumania, Rumania" was his most popular work, and combined his charisma and glorification of the European home in the dramatic service of forging his Yiddish listeners into a cohesive audience of Jewish Americans. It was recorded in New York three times on 78-rpm discs: first on Vocalion as "Der Freilicher Roumania" in 1925, under its better-known English title for Columbia in 1941; and in a much longer two-sided version for Banner a decade later.[71]

The most complete lyrics are available on the last record, the Banner version, in which Lebedeff probably sang many of his variations. One feature of the song is that by focusing only on one source among many in the Jewish diaspora, Roumania is made to stand in for the source of all Jewish emigrants. The audience can easily extrapolate from that one region because of the multifaceted character of the song, with a Russian-born entertainer, known as the Litvak comedian, romanticizing about a land with which he was really unfamiliar. So his Roumania is everyone's home.

Lebedeff delivers the song in a gypsy-like musical style, starting slowly but gradually building in both tempo and volume to a frenetic pace and sound. He begins repeating the title often, upholding and idealizing Roumania as sweet and beautiful because of its good food and drink. While simultaneously uttering in his enthusiasm strange vocal popping noises, Lebedeff interrupts his reveries with off-color commentary: "He who has a chubby wife is much warmer in winter"; "One's own wife is good, someone else's is more exciting"; "It is good to kiss a sixteen-year-old lass [for] when one kisses an old maid, she grumbles"; and in a final gesture to enduring provincial bonds, he trumpets the verbal gymnastics of his final lyrics—"Galytzyaners make money, Litvaks make babies."[72]

Certainly it is tempting to overestimate Lebedeff's impact. He was popular for a long time as he continued to perform in revivals in the 1950s until his death in 1960.[73] But his heavy cultivation of nostalgia was not unique in the Yiddish popular theater, where audiences thrived on tales of traditional life based more on romance than reality. Overall, the Jewish popular stage in the interwar period and its musical-comedy themes led by Lebedeff and others helped their group, fragmented at first religiously, nationally, culturally, and by social class, find its way two decades later to a more homogeneous community.[74]

Both Finnish and Lithuanian immigrant life also illustrate the ameliorative and unifying role of ethnic entertainment in the 1920s based heavily on a rural past. We have already seen that both of these groups had a particularly significant musical-band tradition, and that folk and popular music was important to their culture.[75] Not surprisingly, they developed a number of active musical performers.

The Finns' entertainment came not from touring dramatic troupes such as performed for the Scandinavians, Italians, Jews, and other large ethnic groups but but from individual performers who might best be termed troubadours, in acknowledgment of their long travels to Finnish audiences from Massachusetts to Oregon. Finnish troubadors projected the familiar themes sentimentalizing life in the old country and the difficulties of settlement in the new but perhaps with less of a regional emphasis than performers from other immigrant communities. Although the singers did on occasion recall homelife in particular villages, they seemed really more eager to recognize and in fact to promote the national character of their culture.

No one performer dominated the Finnish American ethnic stage, but by the height of Finnish American entertainment in the early 1930s, three individuals stood out: Arthur Kylander, Hiski Salomaa, and Leo Kauppi. A fourth performer, accordionist Viola Turpeinen, was actually far more popular than her male counterparts, even forming a small company of her own, but though she played Finnish pieces like the others, she was an instrumentalist, not a composer or ethnic troubadour, and her audiences included more American-born descendants of Finnish immigrants and relatively fewer Finns themselves, making her story more appropriate for discussion below in the context of the next generation. Arthur Kylander was perhaps the best known and most versatile of the earlier group of performers.[76]

Arriving in America in 1914 at the age of twenty-two, Kylander became well acquainted with the lives of his working-class audience. He moved around widely, seeking the typical Finnish immigrant employment of lumberjack, woodworker, or miner wherever he could find it, in Maine, New York, Pennsylvania, Ohio, Minnesota, and finally California. Just when he started to accompany himself on the mandolin is unclear, but he began publishing sheet music in 1920 and composing his own comic songs in California in 1926, when he decided to try his hand at becoming a professional entertainer. The next year, 1927, he left the West Coast for his first tour of Finnish colonies, which perhaps was even more successful than he might have expected when, while traveling through Montana and Minnesota, he met and married his wife, a pianist who served superbly as his accompanist. By the time he reached the East Coast, he had established such a reputation that the Victor company agreed to record his first songs, twenty of them, between 1927 and 1929.[77] By that time the recording companies welcomed Finnish musicians, no doubt at least in part because the companies were aware of the Finnish Americans' devotion to the new technology of sound reproduction—the 50,000 immigrants in America by the late 1920s were buying more discs than the 3.5 million Finns in the homeland.[78] Victor took the early lead in making Finnish records, putting out its first disc in 1907, and Victor and Columbia, the label to which Kylander later switched, were greatly expanding their Finnish listings just when he was arriving in New York. The two companies made five hundred Finnish records in all between 1925 and 1935.[79]

Kylander's better-known ballads, just like those of entertainers from other immigrant communities, dealt with country life at home and immigrant life in America: "Muistojen Valssi" (Memories waltz); "The Immigrant's Waltz"; the particularly well-known "Lumber Jakki" (1927); "Talon Tytto" (1929), about a wealthy landowner's daughter from Aboe who was unaccustomed to work; "Suomalainen Ja Sauna" (The Finn and his sauna) (1929); "Nyt Mina Reissan Vanhaan Maahan" (With money made in America, I will return as a man of means, perhaps president of Finland); and "Ylioppilas Suomesta" (A university student who went to America to seek his fortune ends up digging sewers).

The tune with which Kylander is most closely associated, and the one that was most popular, is "Siirtolaisen Ensi Vastuksia" (The immigrant's first difficulties). The piece dwells on the language difficulties of a newly arrived immigrant worker, whose first English phrase is "No, sir." The phrase helps him deal with his oppressive boss, but unfortunately it is turned against him by his girlfriend.[80]

Also in the late 1920s, Hiski Salomaa was performing his ballads on stage and record. Salomaa had joined a general exodus from his

Finnish parish to America in 1909, after his mother died, and after World War I he worked as a tailor in Massachusetts and Michigan. He performed part-time and recorded eighteen pieces between 1927 and 1931. He deliberately sang for the working class, possibly with a strong political commitment.[81] Although the details of his social philosophy are uncertain, he consciously sought to appeal in his music to all Finnish Americans and to develop a single conscious identity for all of them.[82] Some of his pieces were the semi-autobiographical "Savonpojan Ameriikkaan Tulo" (A boy from Savo comes to America), about leaving his weeping mother behind; "Vanhampiian Polka" (An old maid's polka), in which a servant girl longs for wealth to go back to the old country and be her own boss; and his best known, "Lahnen Lokari" of 1928, a tale of a Finnish lumberjack who travels widely for work, even to Alaska, taking pleasure in his freedom.[83]

Not much is known about the personal life of the other popular troubadour, Leo Kauppi, two of whose songs were better hits than any by Kylander or Salomaa. "Kuuliaiset Kottilassa" (1927) treated Finnish rustic life, particularly a peasant wedding, and "Villiruusu" (Wild rose) was a European-made Columbia recording (1928) on a similar old world theme. This latter piece was a sensation for an ethnic record, selling a phenomenal 30,000 copies in a short time.[84]

It is a simple matter to identify the major Lithuanian American entertainer. Antanas Vanagaitis came to the United States with his dramatic group in 1924, already well schooled in music, which he had studied in Germany, and drama, which he had practiced for several years as an actor at the State Theatre in Kaunas just prior to his emigration. He arrived as one of four entertainers who used the name Dzimdzi-Drimdzi during their first tour of Lithuanian American colonies. The group's name identifies them regionally, referring to tired wedding musicians from the Dzukai district, one of the provinces that was a source of the American emigrants.[85] Their acts, which became extremely popular, had all the features of Olle i Skratthult and Farfariello—the comically dressed bumpkin, the variety of female and male characters, the old-country songs, and the various immigrant situations.[86]

The most important agent of the troupe's effectiveness was its recording, for which Vanagaitis himself composed hundreds of songs. One of the most popular pieces, which contributed the most to weakening the traditional Dzukai-regional emphasis of the acts, thus making audiences more cohesive as a single American ethnic community, included the songs "Daina Apie Sarkis" and "Dzazas Apie Sarkis" (Ballad and Jazz about Sharkey) on the Columbia label and "Trys Vyrukai Susistare" (Three who agreed) on Okeh.[87] The former record was cut in New York in December 1927 and quickly sold 10,000 copies.[88] These songs were a paean to the Lithuanian American boxer, Jack Sharkey, who was then a world heavyweight contender who had just fought Jack Dempsey in the best-attended match in world history. Sharkey's "ready identification with his Lithuanian background . . . made him a hero among the Lithuanian American community and in Lithuania," and the Vanagaitis ballads both reflected and secured that unifying sentiment.[89]

The 1920s, then, and possibly the early years of the 1930s, represented the golden age of immigrant entertainment, a time when vaudevillians demonstrated not only their artistry on stage but also the importance of entertainment in meeting an emotional need of their audiences. That need was to establish continuity with a past that had become romanticized by the upsetting impact of life as aliens in a new land. The skits and ballads the immigrants saw on stage certainly reminded them of their ancestral home and family far away, whether or not that reminder was accurate. The dramatized depiction was intended as a recreation of a generally happy past time and place, often a romance or a wedding, set in a time and place that, though specific and local, were nonetheless evocative of the roots of *all* immigrants, from all the villages of the lost homeland. Columbia Record Company's 1921 catalog of German records, for example, responded to just such a longing by depicting an idealized view of the Old Country on its cover. The record companies certainly understood the significance of ethnic nostalgia.[90]

When the immigrant entertainers added humorous characterizations of immigrant life to that idealized old-world setting and reflected living conditions in America, they were essentially building a new ethnic identity, fashioning a new audience. Entertainment was an important dimension of immigrant experience that helped forge an American immigrant community.

Time does change, however, and the post–World War I era was marked by an ongoing modification of ethnic music. By 1930 a number of new factors in ethnic music were appearing: radio was broadening the audience for ethnic music; a new musical instrument, the piano accordion, was dominating ethnic bands; dancing was replacing vaudeville as the most popular form of ethnic entertainment; and perhaps most important, a new, American-born generation was emerging in immigrant communities to help transform their music into an American genre. Thus, the depression became the background against which ethnic music would become popular music.

Frankie Yankovic signing photographs for fans in Woolworth's 5 & 10 store, Milwaukee, June 1948 (or possibly Boston).

Frankie Yankovic with his Yanks, after being voted "Polka King" in Milwaukee, June 1948. *Left to right:* Georgie Cook (banjo), Adolph Sernik (bass), Johnny Pecon (accordion), Yankovic, unidentified, Al Naglitch (piano).

First Czech-American Concertina Band Club, founded in Chicago, 1893. Seated fourth from left is Václav Fergl, the bandleader. The ensemble probably played at the 1893 Columbian Exposition.

Haltnorth's Gardens, Cleveland, about 1880, site of performances by many local German and Czech bands. Courtesy of the Western Reserve Historical Society, Cleveland, Ohio.

The Lithuanian band of Manchester, New Hampshire, one of many ethnic brass bands, soon after its founding in 1911.

The Italian Book Company, the largest Italian American book and music publisher, on Mulberry Street in New York's Lower East Side, 1920s. Piano rolls were manufactured on the upper floors of the building.

Interior of Edward Krolikowski's music store, Bridgeport, Connecticut, showing display cases for instruments and racks for sheet music and records.

Andrew Grill, the leading composer-arranger of polka and march music for Joseph Jiran and Vitak and Elsnic music publishers, from the 1910s through the 1940s. When this photo was taken, about 1925, he was leader of his own brass band.

A Columbia recording session in Chicago, probably of ethnic music, arranged by company agent Anton Heindl, about 1915.

	Nummer	Størrelse	Pris-fortegnelse
Norsk Kvinde i telefonen (Engelsk-Norsk dialekt) — Ethel C. Olson / En Norsk Dame ved Strandbreden (Engelsk-Norsk dialekt) — E.C. Olson	72060	10	.85
Norrönnakvædet — Erik Bye / Kongekvædet — Erik Bye	72700	10	.85
Nu takker alle Gud — Christian Mathisen / Vor Gud, han er saa fast en Borg — Christian Mathisen	69750	10	.85
Nu takker alle Gud (det engelske) — Carsten Woll / Vor Gud han er saa fast en Borg (det engelske) — Carsten Woll	72744	10	.85
Nytaarssalme (Grundtvig) — Woll / Julesang (Adolphe Adam) — Woll	65597	10	.85
Og jeg vil ha mig en Hjertenskjær / Eg giætte Tulla—Folkevise — Aalrud Tillisch	63620	10	.85
O Herre (V. Krag-Eikki Melatin) — Eleonora Olson / Blio hos mig, Mester (Henry F. Lyte) — Ethel Olson-Eleonora Olson	72323	10	.85
Overmaade fuld av Naade (Arrangert af C. Elling) — Werner / Den blide tanke (W. A. Wexels-A. P. Berggreen) — August Werner	72855	10	.85
Paa Fjellet (Louise Michaeli) — Nathalie Hansen / Liden Kirsten (Eyvind Alnaes) — Hansen	69324	10	.85
Paa Kampen—Vals — Hans Erichsen-Harry Syvertsen / Skynd Dig Reinlender — Hans Erichsen-Harry Syvertsen	72891	10	.85
Paal paa Haugen — Christian Mathisen / Aa kjöre Vatten aa kjöre Ve — Christian Mathisen	72581	10	.85
Permenions—Vals — Harry Syvertsen / Farmorlin—Reinlander — Hans Erichsen-Harry Syvertsen	72801	10	.85
Per.s Sang (Fra "Til Säters") (P. C. Riis-F. A. Reissiger) — Mathisen / Halvor.s Sang (Fra "Til Säters") (Riis-Reissiger) — Ethel Olson	69464	10	.85
Potpourri Two-Step (1) Imorgen Aften (2) Ship Ahoy — John Lager-Eric Olson / Trondhjemsvalsen — John Lager-Eric Olson	72543	10	.85
Puddefjorden—Vals (Traekspil) — Fritz Aase-Hugo Johnson / Mazurka No. 1 (Johnson) (Traekspil) — Fritz Aase-Hugo Johnson	69465	10	.85
Saa danser jeg dig imöde (Barbara Larsen) — Erik Bye / Hei husbom i hel — Erik Bye	72763	10	.85
Saeterjentens Söndag — Rören / Millom Bakkar og Berg utme Havet — Rören	63397	10	.85

Ethel Olson

Lager-Olson

	Nummer	Størrelse	Pris-fortegnelse
Saeterjentens Söndag (Ole Bull) (Violin Solo) — Arthur E. Uhe / Solveigs Sang (Edvard Grieg) — Grieg Instrumental Kvartel	72356	10	.85
Sang Til Bergen (Johan Nordahl Brun) — August Werner / Norg Du huis Mödingord (Adolpf Thomsen) — August Werner	72499	10	.85
Saeterjenten — Ester Olsen / Fisker Valsen (David Hellström) — Ester Olsen	72772	10	.85
Ship Ahoy! — Robert Sterling / Han kom aldrig igjen — Robert Sterling	69955	10	.85
Saeterjentens Söndag — Carsten Th. Woll / Til min Gyldenlak — Carsten Th. Woll	65688	10	.85
Saeterjentens Sang (Hansen) — Nathalie Hansen / Mit Hjerte og min Lyre (Moore-Kjerulf) — Nathalie Hansen	69413	10	.85
Se Norges Blomsterdal — Carsten Th. Woll / Lille Haakons Vuggesang — Carsten Th. Woll	72987	10	.85
Sidatereis (Henrik Wergeland-Eyvind Alnæs) — Rolf Hammer / Den store, hoide Flok (E. Grieg) — Rolf Hammer	68451	12	1.35
Skal vi gaa hjem til Norge — Sigvart Borgen / Lars Olsens Afsked — Sigvart Borgen	72144	10	.85
Skynd Dig Reinlender — Hans Erichsen-Harry Syvertsen / Paa Kampen—Vals — Hans Erichsen-Harry Syvertsen	72891	10	.85
Sognekjärring (Foste Part) (Deklamation) — Eleonora Olson / Sognekjärring (Anden Part) — Eleonora Olson	72183	10	.85
Solefaldssang (fra Svein Uræd) — Carsten Th. Woll / Venetiansk Serenade — Carsten Th. Woll	65686	10	.85
So lokka me over den myra (Österdalen) — Aalrud Tillisch / Kari aa Mari, slaa op nu (Österdalen) — Aalrud Tillisch	72618	10	.85
Solveigs Sang (Peer Gynt) (Grieg) — Lydia Lindgren / Synnöves Sang (Björnson-H. Kjerulf) — Lydia Lindgren	69109	10	.85
Solveigs Sang (Edvard Grieg) — Grieg Instrumental Kvartet / Saeterjentens Söndag (Ole Bull) — Arthur E. Uhe	72356	10	.85
Sönner af Norge — Rören / Det norske Flag — Rören	63396	10	.85
Sönner af Norge — Victor Orkester / Saensk Nationalsang — Victor Orkester	16596	10	.85

Hansen

A page spread from the 1921 Norwegian ethnic catalogue of the Victor Talking Machine company. Pictured at upper left is Ethel Olson, who with her sister Eleonora developed a musical-comedy routine about an old woman from the province of Sogne, their ancestral home.

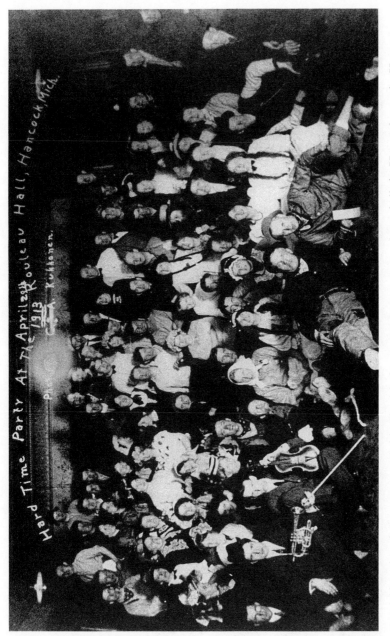

A working-class dance party, probably Finnish, in one of the numerous dance halls in Hancock, on the Upper Peninsula of Michigan, 1913.

Costume ball at South Side Auditorium, St. Paul, with some dancers in ethnic dress, about 1926. A sign on the wall announces the usual ticket price: 25 cents.

South Side Auditorium Orchestra, managed by H. J. Brunzell, St. Paul, January 1926.

Bača's Dance Pavilion outside Fayetteville, Texas, where the famous Bača band played. Window covers could be raised in warm weather.

The Olle I Skratthult troupe, the best-known Swedish American entertainers, who toured widely in the 1920s and 1930s. Photo by David Peterson, courtesy of Minnesota Historical Society.

Italian comic entertainer Farfariello (Eduardo
Migliaccio) in acting pose, probably 1920s.

Poster announcing Yiddish musical comedy "I Would If I Could," which featured the song "Bei Mir Bistu Shein," probably 1933. Photos in the poster are of singer Aaron Lebedeff and composer Sholom Secunda. Courtesy of Sheldon Secunda.

Viola Turpeinen, the famous Finnish American accordionist, soon after her arrival in New York, 1934.

Members of the Joseph Divisek School of Music, led by Frank Divisek, in concert in Boston, 1932.

Frank Gaviani (*far right*) with members of his accordion school in concert, Worcester, Massachusetts, 1939. Growing enrollments in such schools reflected the increasing popularity of the accordion.

Folk dancers sponsored by New York's Folk Festival Council, at the Astor Hotel, December 1932. Folk dancing became widely popular during the 1930s. From the Elba F. Gurzau Papers, courtesy of Balch Institute Library.

Advertisement for Krolikowski's Radio Orchestra, Bridgeport, Connecticut, 1936.

45th
Anniversary

Of

BACA'S BAND

Will Be Celebrated

Wednesday, SEPT. 8, 1937

At

K. J. T. HALL

Fayetteville, Texas

Celebration Begins At 3:00 P. M.

With Plenty Of Music

Big Supper at 5:00 P. M. Meal Tickets: 30 cents

Free Dance at Night

Plenty Refreshments

Everybody Is Cordially Invited To Attend And Help The "BOYS" To Celebrate This Big Day.

—BACA'S BAND

Advertisement for a dance celebrating the Bača Band's forty-fifth anniversary, 1937.

The Viking Accordion Band from Albert Lea, Minnesota, an early crossover band, in costume in the early 1930s. "Skipper" Berg, the band's founder, is second from left.

Bernie Whyte (Witkowski) and his Silver Bell Orchestra, a prominent Polish crossover band, at Glenwood Manor Ballroom, Brooklyn, September 1938.

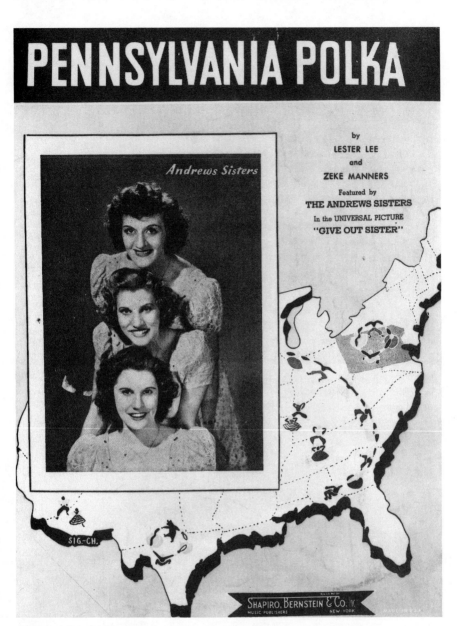

"Pennsylvania Polka" sheet-music cover, featuring the Andrews Sisters, who promoted ethnic and polka-style songs. Song by Lester Lee and Zeke Manners, © 1942 Shapiro, Bernstein & Co., Inc., New York. Renewed. Used by permission.

Romy Gosz, a prominent polka bandleader, playing at a Wisconsin dance hall, probably in the 1940s. Photo from band scrapbook, courtesy of Kewaunee Historical Society.

Lawrence Duchow leading his Red Raven Orchestra at Chicago's Trianon Ballroom in 1949, at the height of the polka craze. He is instructing dancers in folk-dance steps. Photo © 1949 BPI Communications, Inc. Used with permission from *Billboard*.

The marquee of New York's famous Roseland Ballroom, announcing Frank Wojnarowski's band, probably in 1950. Engagements of polka musicians at leading ballrooms such as the Roseland suggest the wide acceptance of polka music as an American dance form.

Poster for a show at the Polish National Home in Chicopee Falls, Massachusetts, probably in the early or mid-1950s, featuring "top headline Polish radio stars, America's number one polka stylists." The show is advertised in English, suggesting its appeal to non–Polish Americans and American-born descendants of immigrants.

6

Hard Times and Ethnic Old-Time in the Crossover Age, 1930-1940

Just about when immigrant vaudeville was widely popular, at the end of the 1920s, when record companies were issuing more ethnic discs than ever and stage performers were attracting huge audiences, the Crash came, hard times followed, and the new immigrant-entertainment industry appeared on the verge of collapse. The downturn in the economy hit foreign newcomers particularly hard, because most of them were blue-collar workers, and it began to seem likely that as families struggled to reduce their non-essential expenses, their support of the immigrant stage would weaken and immigrant musical comedy itself would soon disappear. What entertainment that remained would be for a wealthier, English-speaking audience who could better support their stage.

Another apparent threat to the continued performance of immigrant song and dance at that time was demographic. The highly restrictive immigration laws of the early 1920s had sharply reduced the influx of immigrants, especially of eastern and southern European peoples, thereby increasing the significance in immigrant ethnic communities of a new population element, the American-born generation. These youngsters growing up in the immigrant colonies had much weaker ties with the homeland and with old-time ethnic culture than their elders. The American-born generation was assimilating, argued sociologists during this era, and tension was developing between foreign-born parents and their native-born children. In the late 1930s one prominent American historian, Marcus Hansen, in a well-known talk before a Swedish society, conceptualized such conflict as a "law" of generational change: pressures toward assimilation, he said, regrettably forced the second generation to want to forget what the immigrant generation wanted to remember.[1] What was being forgotten included, of course, the old songs, dances, and skits that immigrants had loved to hear on record and see in performance over the previous decade.

Some of those parental fears were in fact true; a generational gap did indeed develop. The clash between European elders and their American offspring has been so common that it became one of the enduring, classic themes of American literature in all its forms.[2] Certainly sociologists correctly identified that family battle between foreign parents and native-born offspring as a cause of social problems, especially juvenile delinquency, in the 1920s and 1930s.[3]

Hard times also played a more direct economic role in weakening ethnic popular culture. The depression caused a drastic decline in the recording industry's output of all records, including the immigrant/ethnic catalog list. The income of the industry as a whole dropped from $75 million in 1929 to just about $6 million in 1933, and the number of records produced dropped from about 100 million in 1927 to only 6 million in 1932.[4] By the mid-1930s, so many firms had folded that only three companies were active in the industry, producing many fewer ethnic records, and even among these few most were either reissues or discs made in Europe.[5] In part because of that weakened support, one of the most successful immigrant stage companies, the Olle i Skratthult troupe, folded before the end of the 1930s.[6]

Yet astonishingly, despite all the social, economic, and apparently cultural devastation wrought by the depression, ethnic music and dance—in a new form of that genre—were in fact thriving by the end of the era. Certainly, ethnic entertainment was changing; less of it was in the form of the ethnic, foreign-language vaudeville of the 1920s, and much more of it involved a new type of ethnic-music performance, better known as ethnic "old-time" song and dance or, as some called it in the late 1930s and after, "international" music.

This new development generally originated within the immigrant communities, but it proceeded beyond those groups, gaining such outside popularity that by 1940 it had a considerable impact on and really became a new part of American *mainstream* popular culture. So in the depression while one form of ethnic entertainment, musical comedy, was in decline, a new form was appearing—and transcending the old group boundaries. The ensembles leading this new form and carrying it to the general public were called "crossover" ethnic musical ensembles, and their efforts were very effective.[7]

A concrete example of the powerful impact of immigrant music on the general musical scene was the extraordinary popularity of, even frenzy over, two ethnic pieces in 1938 and 1939: the Bohemian "Beer Barrel Polka," and the Yiddish "Bei Mir Bist Du Shön." The process by which the music of a single immigrant group became, by the end of the depression, an integral part of the nation's "hit parade" reveals the emergence of a new segment of American popular culture.

The roots of the cultural crossover of the 1930s can be identified in the immigrant entertainment of the 1920s, when stage stars such as Lebedeff and Farfariello had helped to restructure our pluralistic society, drawing together the plethora of disparate subgroups into larger ethno-national audiences. These entertainers had helped to homogenize their particular peoples into Polish, Jewish, and Italian American communities and make them conscious of their new *American* immigrant identity. Such a sociological process could make exchanges and borrowings of ethnic music and dance here easier. Cultural "crossovers" were much easier between Polish Americans and Czech Americans, for example, than between, say, Kashubes and Moravians.

Another source for closer interchange between ethnic cultures in America was the more salubrious climate of the 1930s for intercultural understanding. Unlike the dominant condemnations of group differences in the 1920s, contemporary observers of the next decade began to stress the desirability of the international or multicultural American society. At the start of the depression, intellectuals seeking a better definition of the nature of American culture noted two characteristics: the folk traditions of ordinary Americans and ethnic pluralism. Their heralding of folk origins seemed to be a reaction to an overemphasis in the previous decade on the nation's technological achievements, while the focus on pluralism arose after the passage of the immigration-restriction acts, when the pluralistic origins of American society could be explored without the fear of being inundated by newcomers. The rise of racist, totalitarian regimes in Europe caused a reaffirmation of pride in democracy, with its principle of tolerance. Thus intellectuals in particular, but the general climate as well, became relatively more favorable to ethnic diversity, although not necessarily to the notion of a *permanent* diversity.[8] As cultural manifestations of pluralism, the great outpouring of song and dance of foreign peoples found a new appreciation among *all* Americans, not just certain ethnic groups at that time. Still another aid to the acceptability, spread, and crossover of ethnic dance in particular was the growing popularity of dance itself.

The status of this activity actually began improving years before. As early as World War I, social dancing was widely practiced—in fact, some have called it a craze—though it was not until about 1930 that everyone would participate in ethnic forms of dance. Until then, the social and ethnic remained separate, with non-ethnic Americans engaging in ballroom dancing, such as the foxtrot and Charleston, while eschewing the polka, schottische, czardas, or oberek of the immigrant.[9]

There was, however, one group of Americans who as early as the beginning of the century had been promoting ethnic folk dancing for non-group members: social workers. Their campaign would become so successful by the depression era that they would help bring about an international folk-dance community and thus contribute to the success, by the World War II years, of images of American culture as multi- and even inter-ethnic.

In the early 1900s Progressive reformers such as Luther Gulick and his aide, Elizabeth Burchenal, initiated the general appreciation of immigrant cultures, particularly their folk dancing. They organized instruction for schoolchildren in ethnic dancing, justifying it in terms of its moral and physical benefits. Later, just before World War I, Edith Terry Bremer made a similar effort, establishing an International Institute within the YWCA to encourage interest in foreigners' arts and crafts and thereby convince outsiders of the value of their cultures.[10]

Bremer's idea spread quickly, and by the end of the 1920s more than fifty "Y Institutes" had been formed around the country to sponsor occasional metropolitan folk festivals, as they were called. Two huge exhibitions that became models for the others were the "Festival of America's Making," held in New York in 1921, and the "Festival of Nations," held in Cleveland in 1927.[11] These were huge and impressive affairs displaying ethnic arts and crafts and encouraging the entire citizenry to appreciate their neighbors' foreign cultures.

The hard times of the 1930s actually stimulated the spread of ethnic dance around the country and in various ways helped the growth of an international folk-dance movement. Economic pressures encouraged Americans to admire the richness and diversity of ethnic dance as an entertaining and inexpensive form of recreation. The 1930s were the heyday of the permanent metropolitan ethnic folk festival, led initially by the International Institute of St. Paul and further spread by such other organizations as the National Folk Festival Council, begun in 1934, and by a host of individual crusaders.[12] By that time a small but devoted array of ethnic-dance instructors was emerging from various ethnic groups to give lessons to the public at large, including Vytautas Beliajus of Chicago, Elba Farabegoli of New York and Philadelphia, Linnea Osman of Minneapolis–St. Paul, Alfred Sokolnicki of Milwaukee, Chester and Margaret Graham in Michigan, Michael and Mary Ann Herman of New York, and Song Chang of San Francisco.[13]

The best indications of the recognition of international folk dancing as part of our culture were the dance demonstrations by ethnic instructors at the major world's fairs of the period: Beliajus at the Chicago Century of Progress of 1933 and 1934; Chang's International Dancers at the San Francisco World's Fair in 1939–1940; and the Hermans at the New York World's Fair, for the New York Folk Festival, also in 1939–1940.[14]

In 1934 one of the Council leaders, Mary Wood Hinman, justified the international folk dance movement as appropriate for every American: "No [one ethnic group] can be considered to have a corner on folk dancing of any kind."[15] Thus, a definite sharing of formal immigrant dance forms—with the American public at large and certainly with, as shall be discussed below, the American-born children of immigrants—had taken place before World War II.

Years before, the goals of Progressive social workers in putting on the folk festivals had included the welding together of the immigrant family, parents and children. And some evidence suggests that the embarrassment and shame with which second-generation immigrant children regarded their parents was not universal. Wearing an elaborate and colorful costume while appearing before a non-ethnic audience in a tuneful and rhythmic dance may have appealed to immigrant children. Such participation in a demonstration of folk culture may in fact have caused not embarrassment or a sense of inferiority but pride. As one high school freshman who appeared in one of the early New York Festival Council pageants asserted in 1932,

"I used to feel ashamed of everything 'old country,' but we have had so much fun at the festival and it was so beautiful that now I am proud of the things my mother tells me about the old country and I love my costume."[16]

This folk-dancing enthusiasm among some may have been not only a conscious defense against external denigration but also a manifestation of a more aggressive anti-Yankee hostility among ethnic youth. The YWCA published a booklet in 1935 entitled, *What It Means to be a Second Generation Girl,* in which one essay written by an American-born Ukrainian told of her response to Anglo-American denigration of her heritage at school. In reaction, she decided to "spread as much information [about her old country] as possible" by learning about Ukrainian folk dancing, taking "much joy in the colorful costumes and whirling figures."[17] While certainly these brief statements of two ethnic youths do not disprove the rejection of their generation, they do suggest that ethnic music and dance in particular had a definite attraction for some young people at that time, one that would help another kind of ethnic art form, group band music.

There also arose in the late 1920s and early 1930s a type of ethnic dance band different than the sort that had existed before. The earlier ensembles had devoted their performance more or less exclusively to their own groups, playing at private or restricted establishments for relatively little income. In contrast, the new groups of ethnic musical instrumentalists might best be described by a title given to them later, "crossover" ensembles. Begun in part in response to the poor economic conditions and aiming to become professional dance bands, they were distinguished by much more emphasis on commercial objectives and by an awareness of and desire to appeal to outsiders as well as their own Americanized ethnic generations.[18] They also readily adapted the contemporary instrumentation of mainstream dance bands to their ethnic tunes, employing nontraditional reeds and brass in orchestral arrangements resembling those of the mainstream groups.

Other developments of the early 1930s also favored the more commercial objectives of these new bands, such as the building of new dance halls to accommodate the dance craze, a revival of the recording industry, and especially the era's technological developments, including the spread of radio and the emergence of the jukebox. As the commercial potential for ethnic dance music became apparent, even national Tin Pan Alley music publishers recognized the moneymaking possibilities of this more appealing international or ethnic music, and they began to engage these new ethnic ensembles.

The rise of these highly commercialized crossover or "territorial" ethnic bands, as they were also termed, and their appeal to the younger generation and outsiders might best be appreciated in terms of contrasts with their predecessors, the much smaller, local ensembles, often more purely monoethnic, which had typically operated only semi-commercially, working for small fees or even no fees at all. Such musicians, of course, had proliferated in ethnic communities around the country ever since the late nineteenth century or the turn of the twentieth century, either in brass concert bands or as accompanists for private family weddings, group picnics, and fraternal socials. In rural areas they played on weekends at homes or in barns for what were called house-dance parties. All of these affairs appeared to be closed to non-group members, but actually, in the 1920s especially, much evidence suggests that outsiders and relatively assimilated young people from the American-born generation also participated. A few of these ensembles were commercial enough to appear occasionally on radio, usually on Sundays, acquainting both group and non-group members with the polka, waltz, schottische, and other elements of ethnic dance music.

In Utica, New York, for example, a small industrial city populated heavily with Poles and Italians, the Polish American community had a lively group of musicians who played at various celebrations in the early 1900s. With the help of a local radio station broadcasting Polish polka and ethnic music, two second-generation musicians told folk-survey interviewers in the 1970s that in the depths of the depression they had earned good money, $8 or $9, playing weekend dates with their family's band. The folklorists concluded that local radio stations WIBX, WGAT, WRUN, and WBVM had provided multi-ethnic programming and were responsible for broadening the enthusiasm for various ethnic dance styles.[19] A contemporary examination of Slavic multi-ethnic dance contingents in the western Pennsylvania steelmaking towns around Lyndora described a similar broadening "Americanization" of the musical traditions of ethnic groups including both first- and second-generation Slovaks, Poles, Russians, and Ukrainians. One Polish American youth noted the appeal of the ethnic dances: "You had to dance when my father played the violin,

it was so rhythmic."[20] An extremely popular dance band in the community was a group that had attracted regional attention by appearing on WWSW in Pittsburgh beginning in 1934. "Mitch Rudiak
and the Ambassadors" played a variety of ethnic music and jazz and
was eclectic with respect to personnel as well as repertoire; members
included a Jew, a Hungarian, a Slovak, a Pole, and a Russian.[21]

The Slovak dance bands of Milwaukee in the late 1920s and early
1930s were far more restrictive in terms of audience and venue. They
performed only at Slovak dance halls and socials in the city, where
outsiders were not much in evidence. However, the dance tunes they
played were multi-ethnic, including the most popular contemporary
American steps. At least sixteen Slovak bands were listed in the city
directory (others came up from Chicago), and their ethnic repetoire
included pieces from both Slovak and non-Slovak traditions, featuring especially the Hungarian czardas and Bohemian waltzes. The
recreation was not limited to immigrants; the American-born Slovak
young people thoroughly enjoyed learning all the ethnic dances in
the 1920s and 1930s.[22]

Outside the big cities, immigrant communities might be expected
to embrace ethnic crossover and interaction much more slowly, for
many rural areas were settled by only one ethnic group, and acculturation proceeded far more slowly. Also, the assimilative influence
of radio might be weaker in rural areas, where a much smaller percentage of the population owned radio sets in the medium's first
decade. But such assumptions are not entirely accurate; even in
America's agricultural heartland, ethnic crossovers were common,
as indicated by the dance experience of much of the farming population in Wisconsin, Michigan, Minnesota, and Nebraska.

The typical setting for ethnic dance in these states' rural areas
were house parties, held chiefly in colder weather, and the regional
dance platforms called "boweries" in Minnesota and Wisconsin,
which were utilized in the summertime.[23] In Wisconsin, which may
have been typical of its neighboring states, the house parties of the
1920s and 1930s were gatherings in homes, barns, and schools associated with whatever nationality predominated in the district. Furniture would be cleared for dance space, a small fiddle or accordion
band called in, and people would walk or ride several miles to the
dance, spending the night and bringing along their children, who
slept at the place.[24] But although observers often referred to these
affairs as "Norwegian" house parties, because they were usually held

in places where Norwegian immigrants predominated, the dances were in fact often regional rather than purely ethnic, attended by neighbors whose background might be German, Swiss, Polish, and Bohemian. Furthermore, the music played was as often the French Canadian reel and the Irish jig as it was strictly central and northern European. The more northern lumbering regions of these states had even more ethnic interchange at these affairs.[25]

A Minnesota woman described the dances as diverse: "Some of [the dance melodies played] undoubtedly originated in Norway. I'm sure many . . . were of Swedish origin. . . . There were a lot of Swedish people in the area and also a number of Czechs and some Polish and Finnish. . . . The Czechs had a lot of musicians, especially accordion and concertina musicians . . . and there would be a mixture of tunes as well. . . . I'm sure a lot of them had German origin . . . among these so-called old time tunes."[26]

A Wisconsin woman offered a similar description of the multiethnic nature of the social gatherings in her community: "We were just neighbors, all neighbors and friends that knew everybody else."[27] Another observer in the Upper Peninsula of Michigan stated that public dances there provided an interethnic sense of the community as early as the turn of the century. Crossovers worked in both directions there: while some immigrant musicians were learning to play at square dances, non-ethnic fiddlers were playing traditional Swedish and Polish dances.[28]

All these examples suggest that from both urban and rural communities where ethnic groups had settled, a "multi-ethnic European musical form" or "international" ethnic style was arising in the 1930s.[29] In many localities local ethnic bands were playing a mixture of both old European ethnic tunes and popular American songs. Like the old community brass bands of the previous century, the new bands performed at local public events and at many private affairs. Although some were very popular locally and appeared on local radio, none really provided a sizable income for the musicians.

Among developments in the depression era that produced larger, much more commercial ensembles, who toured and made records, was the emergence of the ballroom as a site for dancing. Of course the general dance craze of the World War I era had created a role for a new kind of music businessperson, the ballroom operator. In place of the dance halls of the early years of the century, which had served primarily as drinking establishments, Prohibition created an attractive business opportunity for more widely acceptable dancing establishments that did not serve drinks.[30] New and larger dance halls arose in both the larger cities and the countryside, originally to service the majority of patrons interested in Dixieland, jazz, and general ballroom dance. The old-time ethnic bands, of course, had played in group halls in many areas and continued to do so in the 1920s, 1930s, and later. But with the growing popularity of polkas and the like among all people at this time, many non-group, commercial ballrooms welcomed ethnic bands to perform often on nights that alternated with evenings devoted to the better-known swing dance bands. Thus by the early 1930s crossover ensembles could set up regional tours in ballrooms. It is important to note that a number of these ballrooms were built as elaborate palaces, accommodating hundreds, sometimes thousands, of patrons. Obviously, when these elaborate dance houses invited polka bands they were encouraging development of a large audience for the genre.

Two of the most famous such ballroom operators were Andrew Karsas, who with his brother, William, opened the million-dollar Trianon ballroom in Chicago in 1922 and the even more expensive Aragon four years later, and Tom Archer, who began his chain of Midwest dance structures in Iowa, Missouri, South Dakota, and Nebraska in the mid-1920s.[31] By the end of the depression, the large metropolitan dance palace was a common sight around the nation.[32]

Another aid to the wider commercial scheduling of ethnic bands around 1930 was, of course, radio, which by then had replaced the phonograph as the major medium of home music entertainment. By 1931, 40 percent of American homes had receivers, and by 1938, more than 80 percent.[33] Despite its introduction just prior to hard times, that medium did so well that it was accurately called "depression-proof." Because music, including orchestras and bands, was such a major part of what was disseminated over the new medium, ethnic music was probably on the airwaves as soon as commercial radio started in the early 1920s, though regular broadcasting of ethnic music and skits did not begin until later in the decade. The leading urban centers for disseminating immigrant music were likely Cleveland, New York, and Chicago. WJAY (Cleveland) developed the most comprehensive multi-ethnic schedule, beginning with a Polish offering in 1929 and growing to twenty-two ethnic "hours" each week by 1935.[34]

By the early 1930s many stations in cities and even smaller towns issued foreign-language broadcasts on which ethnic music and bands could be heard. Ethnic musical interchange and crossovers certainly must have been fostered by the increased access radio provided for a variety of listeners to hear a variety of ethnic music. In addition, even non-ethnic stations often did remote broadcasts from dance ballrooms, providing a much larger audience for the polka bands.[35] Some non-musical programming familiarized the general public with ethnic family life and culture, such as the early soap opera "The Rise of the Goldbergs," later "The Goldbergs," an extraordinarily popular series that began in 1929 and lasted into the age of television.[36]

Still another factor was the rise in acceptance among all dancers, ethnic or not, of a relatively new musical instrument, the piano accordion. The accordion had originated in other instrumental forms as a medium for folk music in a number of regions of the world. It was not until the late nineteenth and early twentieth centuries that it developed into the instrument known today, with a righthand piano keyboard, and claimed increasing popularity as an accompaniment of both folk and popular pieces. In doing so it both reflected and widened the appeal of such music, eventually breaking out of its traditional popular-folk domain and becoming common in American dance orchestras. It even appeared in the most serious concerts. Another source for its greater acceptance around 1930 and after was the much-improved quality of both instrument manufacture and performer.

The fundamental principle of the accordion's sound, a vibrating reed, can be traced back to the ancient Chinese. Various early forms of the instrument, such as the hand-held button concertina and related button diatonic accordion, were developed in the mid-nineteenth century, chiefly for folk music. The modern piano accordion was introduced in Vienna in 1863, and it is believed to have appeared for the first time in America in San Francisco in 1909.[37]

The performer responsible for its appearance there was an Italian-born immigrant, Pietro Diero, who became not only the first American virtuoso but also the first major promoter of the instrument. He played it in the popular vaudeville theater, made many records, and later joined with an Italian American music publisher, Octave Pagani of New York, in 1918 to popularize the instrument widely.[38] The piano accordion caught on quickly in the late 1920s, often as a more full-bodied replacement for the smaller squeeze-boxes of the ethnic bands that played the old folk-type pieces. It also became a regular component of the best known jazz, sweet, and swing dance bands of the era, such as the bands led by Paul Whiteman, Richard Himber, Phil Spitalny, and Vincent Lopez.[39]

Its expansion after 1930 was phenomenal, fueled in part by the need of all dance bands, ethnic and otherwise, for more substantial instrumental accompaniment and greater volume in the large dance palaces and ballrooms of the time. The traditional emphasis on strings and especially the violin, which had characterized the older, smaller, village-style bands, especially Slavic American ensembles, yielded during the 1930s to a more prominent role for the louder reeds and the piano accordion.[40]

With the accordion's triumph, especially in the ten years after the mid-1920s, a new category of virtuosos became familiar to the ethnic- and ballroom-dancing public, performing first as soloists or with stage bands and later especially on radio. These talented instrumentalists included, in addition to the pioneering Deiro Brothers, Pietro and Guido, Charley Magnante, Frank Giviani, Pietro Frosini, Anthony Galli-Rini, Joe Biviano, and Charles Nunzio.[41] A few were non-Italians, such as Scandinavians Eric Olzen, Arvid Franzen, Edwin Jarl, Viola Turpeinen, and Chicago's Max Stelter.[42] They often held staff positions or had their own programs on radio.[43] They performed and even composed pieces that were or became a part of the old-time ethnic repertoire, especially Italian songs and dances. While further popularizing that immigrant musical genre, accordionists were also eclectic in their programming, with repertoires that included operatic and symphonic selections.[44]

By the end of the 1930s an accordion craze had taken place; the instrument achieved new heights in popularity among the entire population. It was revealed, for example, that several leading movie stars played the instrument.[45] Also, with the increased demand for sheet music, new publishers joined older ones in issuing accordion arrangements, especially for the old-time ethnic selections. Joining Vitak and Elsnic of Chicago, O. Pagani of New York, and the Scandinavian Dahlquist Company of Minneapolis, were such newer houses as the Chart Music Company and especially John Krachtus of Chicago.[46]

The accordion appealed especially to young people, and numerous schools of instruction were aimed at them. One of the earliest and largest was that of Eddie Jarl in Brooklyn in 1926; another was the 1925 Wales School of Chicago, which by 1940 had four hundred students; and probably the most highly regarded was that of Pietro Deiro in New York, founded in 1929.[47] By 1938, when a group of leading accordionists formed the national American Accordion Association in part to standardize instruction, one estimate anticipated that there would be 35,000 students in accordion schools by the end of that year. Another observer around the same time counted with satisfaction thirty-six accordion schools in sixteen states. Support for the instrument was broad-based; the schools were not established exclusively in those ethnic population centers that had traditionally used the instrument but included institutions in the South and Far West.[48] It is no wonder then that in the three years before 1937, sales of the instrument increased fivefold to about 100,000, a sum that likely grew ever larger into the 1950s.[49]

Still another development in the mid-thirties helped the spread of the new Americanized ethnic music: the revival of the phonograph industry, whose sales turned upward from a low of $7 million in 1934 to $26 million in 1938. This improvement of course affected all popular music as well as the new crossover ethnic bands.

One source of the record industry's revival was technological; radio, which early on had been a competitor to the phonograph, soon became a complement to it as disc jockeys such as Martin Block and his Make Believe Ballroom appeared on the air beginning early in 1935.[50] Another aid to the expansion of recorded music at this time in public places was the jukebox. The idea of "coin-in-the-slot" music was of course not new; a New York company had manufactured a jukebox-like machine as early as 1890, but the first electrically amplified, multi-selection phonograph was introduced only in 1927.[51] Prohibition itself boosted jukebox use, as speakeasies needed inexpensive musical entertainment. And from the late 1920s onward, many proprietors were eager to transform any public house, tavern, restaurant, or ice cream parlor into a small dance hall.[52] The cost per selection was only a nickel, certainly widely affordable, even in the depression. Because bar and restaurant owners viewed the jukebox as a recruiter of customers, it is no surprise that the number in operation multiplied quickly in the 1930s, from about 25,000 in 1934 to 350,000 in 1940. In 1939, when there were about 300,000 functioning machines offering some 13 million records, five jukebox manufacturers sold an additional 70,000 instruments. Jukebox popularity continued to grow; by 1942 about half a million were in operation, offering about 12 million records to patrons.[53]

Still another industrial change enlarging the record-buying public was the introduction of the inexpensive disc. Until the depression, the usual price of a 10-inch 78-rpm record was 75 cents, which perhaps did not limit the audiences sharply while times were good but began to seem prohibitive to the working-class public when times became hard. Within the record industry, executives began casting about for a way to issue cheaper discs. The leading label, Victor, acted first by establishing its new Bluebird series in 1933, with records priced at just 35 cents, or three for a dollar.[54]

The leader of the trend toward cheaper records for the masses was not a Victor employee, however, but the business genius Jack Kapp, founder of Decca. Kapp, the executive probably most responsible for bringing the new ethnic old-time or "international" music to national attention, had an uncanny ability to discern public taste. It was he, for example, who signed a well-known crooner, Bing Crosby, along with a number of other entertainers who would eventually become major recording stars, including Guy Lombardo and the Andrews Sisters. Part of that ability to discern hit tunes and leading performers was developed over an entire lifetime in the record business. Born in Chicago in 1902, he was the son of a Columbia record salesman who occasionally allowed him to handle his route even as a youth.[55] From his father Kapp learned the commercial part of the record business but also an endeavor that was even more important: forecasting hits.[56]

As a young man in his twenties, Jack Kapp became a talent scout for Brunswick, especially its Vocalion label, and in the late 1920s he was recruiting African American talent. This solicitation showed that he was open to music from diverse sources, so long as it promised to be appealing to middle-class taste, which in time would also include ethnic music. Kapp's continual stress on market potential rather than music quality earned him the title of a "man of no taste, [but] so corny he's good."[57]

Kapp not only had a rare nose for the hit but was also bold as a business competitor. With the collapse of the record industry in 1932, he agreed with the trend to offer cheap records but he went one better than the other major companies in feeling that low cost need not mean poor-quality performers. He fortunately had a financial backer in this strategy, E. R. Lewis. In the 1920s and early 1930s Lewis was head of the British Decca Company, and upon Kapp's request for help in 1934 he invested in his new venture, American Decca.[58] Decca's unorthodox strategy included not only concentration on cheap discs but also a focus on the jukebox as the major means to disseminate the product, an approach that the other two major labels, Victor and Columbia, had at first frowned upon.[59]

As one might imagine, Decca became a very sympathetic outlet for ethnic music, even in its more traditional forms, such as an Irish series starring Michael Coleman. The traditional recordings were of course in addition to the better-known and more widely accepted crossover ethnic music, including by 1940 "Whoopee John" Wilfahrt, "Happy Harry" Harden, and "Jolly Jack" Robel, among many others.[60]

Kapp's efforts were enormously successful. By 1938, only a few years after its formation, Decca's sales had risen to a close second place in the industry, reaching 12 million discs annually, behind Victor's 13 million. Columbia was a distant third with 7 million.[61] By 1940 Kapp had two ethnically based hits that symbolized the arrival of that type of music in the popular charts: the Andrews Sisters' renditions of "Bei Mir Bist Du Shön," and "Beer Barrel Polka," along with "Jolly Jack" Robel's instrumental version of the latter.[62] His faith in the power of these kind of works, anglicized for the mass market and delivered via the new jukebox, had been justified by 1940. By that time some felt that the jukebox was a more necessary device to make hits than radio, a position that Kapp had taken years before.[63]

Kapp was astute enough to choose two particular works which were situated in the confines of their respective communities, one from Yiddish musical comedy and the other from the Bohemian countryside, and to get them into American homes everywhere, from New York to New Orleans to Seattle by 1940. How he in particular and the American record industry in general accomplished this crossover is a significant process to trace.

The song "Bei Mir Bist Du Shön" came from the pen of Sholom Secunda, one of the leading composers of Yiddish musical comedy in the 1920s and 1930s. Born in the Ukraine just before the twentieth century and coming to America as a youth in 1907, Secunda obtained a musical education and, though he wanted to become a composer of serious music, joined the ranks of writers who supplied the burgeoning Yiddish musical stage in New York during World War I.[64] He became deeply involved in Jewish music throughout his life, and besides composing music for the Yiddish theater he played at Jewish Catskill resorts and was musical director for the major Yiddish radio station, WEVD, and critic for the Yiddish-language *Jewish Daily Forward* in the 1920s and early 1930s. He became acquainted with the Yiddish musical stars, especially Aaron Lebedeff, who asked him to write a piece for a 1933 comedy, "I Would If I Could," to be produced at a Brooklyn Yiddish theater. He apparently came up with the tune in a humming exchange with his wife in 1932, but whatever its origins he submitted it to his longtime lyricist, Jacob Jacobs, and the completed piece was given to Lebedeff, who after some resistance accepted it.

The piece was copyrighted the next year, 1933, and though the stage production lasted only one season, the song became a more lasting, but still modest, Yiddish hit, selling 10,000 copies in a short time. One reason for its success was its optimistic theme, which appealed to people experiencing hard times: in English, its title asserts that "By Me (or, As Far As I Am Concerned), You are Grand."[65]

For several years the piece was played chiefly at Jewish events, at resort hotels and private affairs such as weddings and bar mitzvahs. Either late in 1936 or early in 1937 two brothers, J. and J. Kammen, Yiddish music publishers from Brooklyn, bought the song outright from Secunda for $30.[66] Although Jewish audiences had welcomed the tune, Secunda had made little money on it and was happy to get rid of it. Unfortunately for him just as he dispensed with the song, others became interested and turned it into a gold mine.

Just a month after the transaction "Bei Mir" began to receive outside attention. A Tin Pan Alley songwriter, Sammy Cahn, had known of the song since 1935, and he joined with his lifelong friend and manager, Louis Levy, in feeling that the piece had popular potential. With another friend, lyricist Saul Caplin, in September of 1937, they went to some Harlem night club or theater to hear and see it performed—surprisingly enough, by two black entertainers who sang it in its original Yiddish![67]

Levy then began to believe that the song would be a hit, and that he knew just the performers to record it, a group of female vocalists known as the Andrews Sisters, who had recently come to New York from Minneapolis and were struggling to be recognized. Apparently it was David Kapp, the younger brother of the Decca head, who first saw and liked the group and urged Levy to contact the young women. He did, liked them also, and even had them learn some Yiddish phrases both to improve their bookings and to help them learn the song he had heard.[68] He took them to Jack Kapp to have

them record "Bei Mir." But Kapp shrewdly refused to allow the trio
to record the piece in Yiddish and, aware of the audience, insisted
that they perform it in English. That decision, of course, meant
writing new lyrics, so probably on Kapp's instructions Levy returned
to his friend Cahn, who with an associate, Saul Caplin, quickly provided the new text. Cahn's own ethnic background may have contributed to his compelling interest in the piece; a devoted Jew, he
had grown up on the Lower East Side with Cohen as the family
name and knew Yiddish.[69]

The Andrews Sisters finally recorded the song on Decca Record
1562 on November 24, 1937; a few days later Kammen sold the
music rights to the Harms Music Company. Within two months the
song was a smash hit, selling a quarter-million records and 100,000
pieces of sheet music.[70] Before the end of 1938 a number of popular
stars had performed it, adding to its mainstream legitimacy. It became an integral part of the swing repertoire when the Benny Goodman Quartet cut an extended two-sided record version of the piece
on December 21 and 29, 1937, in New York with vocalist Martha
Tilton. More significantly Ziggy Elman was featured on trumpet
with a lengthy klezmer-like solo.[71] He performed it later with Goodman at the Carnegie Hall jazz concert with Tilton on January 16,
1938.

In addition Guy Lombardo featured the work on his weekly Sunday radio program; and other stars, including Bing Crosby, Rudy
Vallee, and Al Jolson, soon came out with their own versions. Ella
Fitzgerald recorded it with what was termed a "hot" treatment. One
informed estimate was that the number of "Bei Mir" records on all
labels totaled over 2.5 million.[72]

Its popularity extended nationwide, even sweeping sections of the
country quite unfamiliar with Yiddish culture. In those areas people
were heard to demand that popular tune with the strange title, like
"Buy a Beer Mr. Shane," or "My Dear Mr. Shane," or "My Mere
Bits of Shame."[73] When Warner Brothers bought the piece for a film,
and ASCAP gave "Bei Mir" its annual award as the most popular
song of the year, it was obvious that Kapp's Decca label had scored
very well.

Of course the greatest beneficiaries were the Andrews Sisters, who
because of the song were brought out of obscurity and in fact made
into popular, and wealthy, stars.[74] Louis Levy soon became their
manager and married one of them, Maxine, in 1941.

Even more important than the rise to stardom that this Yiddish song gave to the nation's leading female group was its influence later on the Andrews Sisters' song selection. While one cannot designate any one thematic type for the thousands of cuts that produced sales totaling tens of millions of records throughout their incredible career, one can say that in this early period at least, and occasionally later, they were the leading popular vocalists to draw their works heavily from the ethnic reservoir.[75] It is difficult to say if this policy of exploiting ethnic music was a fully conscious one, but certainly Louis Levy, who was closest to them at this time and became their agent, provided a good rationale: the newer musical genres, he believed, which the major music publishers had previously avoided, provided great commercial potential.[76]

A good question is why this little-known fragment of Yiddish musical comedy achieved instant popularity. To better understand that acceptance, it is necessary to review and compare the lyrics of the Yiddish and English versions. Cahn, of course, was very familiar with Yiddish and was reasonably faithful to the original, a romantic ballad clearly in the tradition of an old-time ethnic song. The lover maintains that he is so fully in love that even if the beloved were characterized by extremely unattractive qualities, such as wooden legs or being as black as a Tartar, the romance would survive. *Even if you were a Galitzyaner,* the lover sings, "to me you are [still] the one in the world."[77] The English version presents a similar sentiment, but from a more international perspective: "I could say 'Bella, Bella,' even say *wunderbar* / Each language only helps me tell you how grand you are. . . ." Here again is an American popular song clearly taken from ethnic old-time music and made appealing in part by the cosmopolitan atmosphere of the depression.[78]

Hence, the Andrew Sisters did a great deal to bring ethnic or ethnic-styled tunes to national attention and even at times to hit status. And they continued to do so; for example, almost immediately after the "Bei Mir" smash, they went again to the Yiddish source on February 21, 1938, with "Joseph, Joseph." This record, Decca 1691, was no equivalent hit, but it did achieve modest success. A third effort based on a Jewish theme, "I Love You Too Much," was much less popular.[79] And they did not confine their ethnic crossover efforts to Yiddish culture. Another source of their repertoire, and the source of another hit record, was the music of central and eastern Europeans, specifically "The Beer Barrel Polka," which they cut, of course, for Decca as the first of several Decca polkas they were to record over the next few years. Some of the others were "The Pennsylvania Polka" (Decca 18398) and the "Strip Polka" (Decca 18470), both recorded in 1942, and the "Victory Polka," recorded with Bing Crosby the following year.[80] The singers' "Beer Barrel Polka" was as much a hit as "Bei Mir," and for many of the same reasons, but an earlier instrumental version by Will Glahe on the Victor label had prepared audiences for its appeal.

Contrary to early assumptions, "Beer Barrel Polka" was never a folk tune. Its origin goes back to about 1927, when Jaromir Vejvoda, a young Czech musician living in Zbraslav, just outside of Prague, wrote a tune called "Modranska Polka" for his father's brass-band repertoire.[81] It became locally popular and caught the attention of a leading Prague publishing house, Hoffmann and Widow, which in 1934 got Vejvoda to agree to have it brought out commercially as a song.[82] The publishers introduced him to a songwriter, Vaclav Zeman, who added lyrics and altered the title to "Skoda Laska," or "Unrequited Love." The song became popular all over Europe under many different titles; in Germany, for example, it was called "Rosamunde." Very likely, the song arrived in America after Tin Pan Alley lyricist Lew Brown heard it and joined with Vladimir Timm to give it an English title and lyrics, probably as early as its original European appearance in 1934. Timm was actually a Greek American, Tetos Demetriades, who had joined Victor Records in 1930 and later headed its International Division, interested in promoting continental-style music.[83] In any event the German musette accordion bandleader Will Glahe recorded an instrumental version of the song for Victor in Europe, probably in 1935 or 1936, using the title "The Beer Barrel Polka." Glahe's record, Victor V-710, met with good success in America, selling about a million discs by 1943.[84]

Exactly how the Andrews Sisters acquired the tune is not clear. Sheet music for it became available from the well-known Tin Pan Alley music firm of Shapiro, Bernstein, which had always been sensitive to the commercial potential of popular music about ethnic groups; its publications in the 1920s and 1930s included such titles as "Yes, We Have No Bananas" (1923), "Rose of Washington Square" (1919), "Where Do You Worka, John" (1926), and especially "Oh, Ma-Ma (Butcher Boy)" (1928, 1938), taken from the famous 1928 Italian song "La Luna Mezzo Mare." The firm maintained European contacts to locate potential American hits and had actually obtained an American copyright for the "Beer Barrel Polka" music from the Hoffman firm in Prague back in 1934, when Brown wrote his English lyrics.[85] They renewed that copyright in 1939 and issued or reissued the Brown-Timm edition, which may have been the version that the Andrews Sisters recorded on Decca 2462 on May 3, 1939.[86] Another claim, however, is that a Slovak ethnic band-leader, "Jolly Jack" Robel from Shenandoah, Pennsylvania, had been back to Europe, rearranged the piece with an eye toward recording it himself for Decca, and sold his version of the work—which the Andrews Sisters then used—for $500.[87]

Although the origin of the arrangement may be in doubt, its popularity is not. By early September, the Andrews Sisters' recording had sold more than 350,000 discs.[88]

The success of both the instrumental and vocal renditions had a great impact on the music industry. One informed observer has gone so far as to suggest that it may have been the cause of the revival of the entire record industry, giving it its best year over the entire decade.[89] Sheet music sales for the piece also skyrocketed reaching about one million copies by 1944.[90] The various forms of this "Polka" certainly became the rage that summer of 1939; by June 24, the song had reached the number-three spot on the "Hit Parade," and it remained there or higher through mid-July. Needless to say, many other mainstream recordings of "Beer Barrel Polka" quickly appeared, including versions by Sammy Kaye and Lawrence Welk on Vocalion, "Jolly Jack" Robel on Decca, Bill Gale, and a host of others.

The song repeated the success of "Bei Mir" from the previous year for much same reason, including the era's general acceptance of foreign music. Also, the song fit in with the current dance craze for lively tunes, making it especially well suited for the jukebox, which as Jack Kapp of Decca had appreciated early on, tended to favor the popularity of music suitable for public places where dancing might occur.

Testimonials to the extraordinary appeal of this new "polka" disc were widespread. Vic Schoen, the bandleader who provided the in-strumental accompaniment for the Andrews Sisters record, said he initially "hated the Beer Barrel Polka and arranged it as badly as I could," anticipating disaster. But the record "turned out to be their biggest hit."[91]

Billboard Magazine followed the progress of the tune closely. In early June 1939 it observed that it was one the three top "smashes" of the day because of Decca's one-two punch: "It's been Willie Glahe practically all the way . . . now [the] Andrews Sisters platter is helping to keep this novelty going."[92] And another observer wrote a few weeks later in the magazine's "Record Buying Guide": "Time doesn't seem to be able to dislodge this titan among contemporary [jukebox] machine successes. Each week for the past several should have seen the start of its demise, but it's apparently imperishable. There's no sense in guessing or even attempting to estimate when it should be taken out. Hold on to it until the barrel can't roll any longer. It's still Will Glahe, of course, as if you needed to be told. And for support it's still the Andrews Sisters."[93]

By later in the month jukebox operators from distant areas, not normally polka centers, were testifying to the success the disc was enjoying in jukebox play. From a New Orleans amusement company, a writer asserted that the original Glahe rendition looked like a "long lifer," and a Spokane jukebox operator called it his best money-maker: "I have been using this platter more than a month and many times it collected as many nickels as all the other records in the machine together. I have had them wear out in two days."[94]

Other observers linked the success of the new discs to three mutually reinforcing trends: a rage for the polka, an interest in the accordion as its major instrument, and an enthusiasm for jukebox play. A poll of several hundred jukebox operators in 1949 ranked the "Beer Barrel" records as ninth in popularity over the previous decade, just below "Easter Parade."[95]

In the midst of the summer of 1939 one novelty-company representative observed that the jukebox industry needed more polkas: "The trouble with the tunesmiths of today is that they don't put out enough songs which can nurse those [jukebox] nickels like the 'Beer Barrel Polka.' " The song's "outstanding popularity," he said, "has brought a good play to the other polkas," which had "been leading the field of nickel nursers . . . for more than a month now, and if the Andrew Sisters don't run out of breath, it should continue to nurse the field at least another month."[96]

On July 5, 1939, another trade publication, *Radio and TV News,* identified the Glahe–Andrews Sisters record renditions as the source of the current but still little-known ethnic-dance hysteria: "Unexpected and unpublicized, a nationwide craze for the sprightly dance melodies of Central Europe was launched almost overnight by the . . . 'Beer Barrel Polka.' " And it added, "Today's polka craze is unique . . . for while the leading dance bands blanketed the air waves with swing and 'sweet' music, coin-operated phonographs were sending the polka on its spectacular rise to fame. Soon millions were humming, whistling the sweet, sparkling melodies of Bohemian folk dance music." It concluded that the disc's popularity continually wore out the records in the jukebox.[97]

The enthusiasm for this new popular music produced a statement by a member of the accordion-music industry, which had certainly been well aware of, and constantly self-conscious about, the instrument's general acceptance. He welcomed these new lively jukebox records for their generating a popular passion for the polka which in turn made for greater recognition and wider appreciation of the instrument. "This polka rage," he said in late 1939, "which received its impetus about a year ago from a string of Victor records featuring the accordion, bids fair to make this instrument even more popular than it now is. The peculiar style of the polka is such that it is best performed by and shows off" the accordion.[98] And one writer for an accordion trade paper welcomed the craze over the new piece for its success in bringing together many different kinds of people: "Ever since the 'Beer Barrel Polka' was introduced," he said, "everyone from debutantes to trained bears has been dancing to polka."[99]

Thus, by the end of the year Jack Kapp's strategy of using the jukebox more than other media to sell his Decca records had paid off handsomely. By producing cheaper discs that featured performers who entertained the masses—including stars who offered lively and highly danceable tunes, particularly polka pieces—he had through 1939 outsold the other leading companies, Columbia and even Victor.[100] The combination of the two ethnic-style hits from the Andrews Sisters, one Yiddish-based and the other Bohemian-based, was the major source of Kapp's triumph. One observer indulged in hyperbole to evaluate the summer of polka delirium: "These nice ladies . . . have produced a series of musical slams which have driven sections of our citizenry into dementia. . . . When science . . . brought forth the coin phonograph and those diabolical instruments confined themselves exclusively to [novelties like] the 'Beer Barrel Polka' . . . the numbers of burghers leaping out of upper story windows rose to alarming proportions."[101] The Andrews Sisters continued of course to promote polka vocals and extend that genre's golden age into the war years and throughout the 1940s.[102]

The two songs that the Andrews Sisters made popular in 1938

and 1939 were significant in the history of American popular music for a number of reasons. "Bei Mir Bist Du Shön" and the "Beer Barrel Polka" were significant as crossover ethnic pieces that became a part of our national popular culture, but they also helped to establish by 1940 an entirely new popular-music category on the national charts, providing mainstream recognition at the national level for bands performing crossover music. The popular-music industry, which had already incorporated the western or country-western categories by the end of the depression, now embraced a new kind of popular music termed "international."[103] The reference itself may have been new, but it actually referred to a musical genre that had been emerging from crossover ensembles since the start of the depression.

There were in fact two subdivisions of this new "international" category—truly *international* bands, whose eclectic repertoires originated in several ethnic traditions, and more local or regional bands, with roots in a relatively monoethnic society. The best representatives of the former category, which offered a more homogeneous American and international style, were four leaders: a Ukrainian, Wasyl Gula (Bill Gale); two Jews, Harry Harden and Henri Rene; and a Slovak, "Jolly Jack" Robel. Their outstanding common characteristics were their ready adoption of the manner and instrumentation of the larger dance bands or orchestras of the time and of course their wider popularity, among both ethnic and general audiences. They were the greatest beneficiaries of the ethnic music that Tin Pan Alley popularized.

Bill Gale's enormously prolific recordings for Columbia, including the enduring "Beer Barrel," became immensely popular; unfortunately, he remains an enigmatic figure, known only as a Ukrainian musician whose repertoire was occasionally biased toward Ukrainian dances and who frequently changed the names of his several bands.[104] He was among the major promoters of the commercialized polka beginning in the 1940s.

Another leading practitioner as well as promoter of the international polka style was Henri Rene, a musette accordionist who loved the instrument as central to the new genre.[105] Rene's real name was Harold Kirchstein, and unlike Gale he came to ethnic music directly as a trained European musician, not via any American ethnic community. A native German, Kirchstein had received formal music training at the Royal Academy in Berlin.[106] Although little is known about his career in the Old World, he probably organized and led a European orchestra on tour in the mid-1920s and became familiar with American popular orchestras then, as he came here briefly to play banjo, guitar, and piano in several ensembles. He settled permanently in the United States in 1936 and soon came in contact with another promoter of the emerging ethnic-style music, Tetos Demetriades. Demetriades, who was then head of the new International division at Victor, was responsible for renaming Glahe's "Beer Barrel Polka" record and helped to make it a hit. Kirchstein joined Demetriades' staff in 1939 and under two band names, the Rene and Andre Musette Orchestras, began to cut pieces for Victor in May 1940. In two years he recorded about ninety tunes, chiefly polkas, most of which were not remade or rearranged ethnic pieces but rather originals written by him, such as "Windmill Tillie" (Victor 756), "Burning Cheeks" (V-195), "Chicken Farm" (V-794) and others with clearly American titles. All represented the new international style.[107]

Kirchstein would continue to record such works for Demetriades, even following him when the Greek American left Victor to set up his own independent Standard Record Company in the late 1940s. The bandleader left ethnic music in the fifties and went on to Hollywood, where he maintained a creative role in the industry as a Victor Artist and Repertory man.[108]

Another popular and prolific international performer was "Happy Harry" Harden, a contemporary of Kirchstein's whose life and career followed a quite similar pattern. Harden, too, was a Jew, a musette accordionist schooled in Europe with a band that owed its style to the contemporary swing and sweet orchestras of the time rather than the smaller regional ethnic bands. Like Kirchstein, he maintained his super-territorial and continental manner rather than adhering to any particular ethnic roots. He was born Daniel Stoljarovič in the Ukraine in 1901 and fled during the Russian Revolution to Roumania. He later found his way to Prague, where he studied music, and for the next twenty years, he played the piano in several European cities, including Prague, Bern, and even Moscow. He apparently wanted to maintain a cosmopolitan continental character rather than an ethnic one, for in 1932 he changed his name to Harden, made records in Europe, and came to New York just before the war broke out in 1939.[109]

His American musical career began a few months later; in March 1940, "Happy Harry" Harden's Musette Orchestra launched a prolific recording list for Decca, making forty-two cuts over the next two years. His repertoire was eclectic and "international" in the extreme: besides the well-known "Beer Barrel," recorded on March 28, 1941, his cuts included Bohemian, Italian, Latin, and some original pieces. The new compositions were designated either as "American" or "swing" polkas, again identifying the new polka style.[110]

The fourth bandleader in this set was "Jolly Jack" Robel of Shenandoah, Pennsylvania, best known for his 1939 instrumental recording of "Beer Barrel Polka," which like Harden and the Andrews Sisters he recorded for Jack Kapp's Decca label. Robel differed somewhat from the others in that he was able to perform well in two milieus, both in the Slavic American ethnic community in which he was raised and in the international or American musical setting. His success in both realms reveals much about what the regional ethnic musical environment was and how well this emerging international style was supported by the later-generation ethnic audiences in the 1930s and 1940s.

Robel was born in Austria sometime around 1900, but his parents brought him to America while he was still very young and he grew up in the New World. The family's first destination was Bethlehem in eastern Pennsylvania. Robel married a local woman and moved to Shenandoah in 1925. Shenandoah was a particularly significant town demographically, an anthracite mining community with a distinctively large variety of resident ethnic communities—a veritable laboratory of the assimilation process, with a fascinating mix of ethnic neighborhoods, citizens of western, eastern, and southern European descent, and many Protestant, Catholic, Orthodox, and Jewish religious organizations. Robel himself was active in his ethnic community, a member of the First Catholic Slovak Union and president of the Shenandoah branch of the union in 1931.[111] But his musical career was in no way ghettoized. For example, one of his first jobs, and probably the source of his interest in music in general and in the harmonica and clarinet in particular, was as a clerk in local music store. The establishment apparently had a multi-ethnic clientele.[112] He played for the major town band, the famous Elmore Band of Shenandoah, which had been founded in 1905 with Thomas Dorsey, Sr., as conductor. Dorsey, the Irish American father of the two major swing bandleaders, Jimmy and Tommy, Jr., taught Robel the clarinet, thus training a Slovak American musician to play with an Irish American family ensemble that had an German ethnic brass band tradition.[113] Robel further moved beyond his own community around 1931, when he joined a popular Polish polka ensemble from Wilkes-Barre, Brunon Kryger's Band.[114]

In the early and mid-1930s he moved back and forth between his ethnic community and the local society at large, forming his own Slovak ensemble to play both ethnic melodies and American tunes during the ethnic "hours" programmed by local radio stations WEEU in Reading and WAZL in Hazleton. His band soon became widely known in the region especially after it played for mixed audiences at the area's most popular ballrooms, on Friday nights beginning in 1937 at the Lakewood Ballroom and in 1938 at the Ritz Ballroom in Pottsville, where Robel drew crowds averaging one thousand.[115] Such ethnic and general popularity was certain to attract recording companies, and the band, which was actually an orchestra of a dozen or so musicians, started to make records in the mid-thirties. A set of eleven tunes cut in New York in September 1936 included both Slovak ethnic pieces and original tunes for Columbia, Vocalion, and Brunswick. Among the original compositions was "The Okey-Dokey Polka," which became his first widely popular piece.[116]

Among about forty cuts that Robel made for Kapp's Decca in the late thirties and early forties was "Beer Barrel Polka," recorded on March 26, 1939, just prior to the Andrews Sisters' vocal rendition of the piece.[117] The standard claim is that the disc's sales totaled $780,000, and though such sales figures are difficult to verify, certainly "Beer Barrel" became his most popular work and the source of his national reputation.[118] From then on, Robel became much more of an international orchestra leader, continuing to play on local radio and to well-filled ballrooms for the many different nationalities in the hard coal region. As the town paper observed, he differed from many swing and popular leaders because he "stuck for the most part to the kind of music the people in the coal region love—and wisely so. People everywhere love the spirited rhythms he dishes out."[119]

In the late 1940s and 1950s his popularity continued and spread widely among the general audience. The government's efforts during World War II to boost the morale of soldiers led Robel to tour hotels, nightclubs, and auditoriums, first in Cleveland, Pittsburgh, and Philadelphia, cities near his home district, and later as far south as Florida and west as Chicago. Late in the war he joined with "Happy Harry" Harden on a long-running radio series called "Polka Holiday," which was distributed to American armed forces overseas by a Decca affiliate, the World Broadcasting System. On the air, he and Harden demonstrated how far the international ethnic style had traveled, well beyond the community halls and taverns of the twenties and early thirties. The two bandleaders also had a two-year engagement at Armando's Supper Club in New York.[120] Robel's greatest mainstream recognition came in 1950, when Universal Motion Picture Corporation presented him with its Harvey Happiness Award as part of its promotional efforts on behalf of the feature film *Harvey*, which starred Jimmy Stewart as an entertainer who made people happy.[121]

Robel then was a symbolic as well as a popular ethnic bandleader, a widely popular musician in his own right but also a representative of the host of local and regional ethnic ensembles that were providing the American public with a new multi-ethnic and original dance music. By drawing on the commercial and cultural developments of the depression decade, including new ballrooms, popular local radio stations with ethnic programming, and the renewed interest of the record companies sparked by the emergence of the jukebox and the inexpensive phonograph disc, Robel showed how an ethnic orchestra could become an international one.

7

Regional Crossover Bands, I: Texas and Minnesota, 1930-1950

Our account of the triumph of ethnic-crossover music in the mainstream of American popular culture has linked it to national conditions of time and performance, but developments at the regional level were also significant. In fact, localized musical activities in the early 1930s and thereafter helped to prepare the national audience to welcome polka-type music in general and the Glahe–Andrews Sisters–Robel versions of the "Beer Barrel Polka" in particular.

Certain states, cities, and rural areas became fertile ground for the international musical style that became so dominant by 1940. The career of Jack Robel exemplifies the value of a favorable location: the Slovak bandleader's musical career had begun in a town with a rich ethnic brass-band tradition. Virtually every other popular ethnic ensemble arose similarly, in a region that had historically been a focal point for ethnic music and that, beginning in the late 1920s, was generating a new type of ethnic band, much more commercialized than the earlier musical organizations and eager to convey their music to much larger audiences. By the early thirties and on into the forties, these ethnic *crossover* bands became dominant, playing for multi-ethnic audiences.

Not surprisingly, the particular regions from which concentrations of these newer ensembles emerged were locales that had received large numbers of Slavic and central European immigrants, especially Czechs. Such areas included the largely rural areas of east

Texas; the upper Midwest from Nebraska and the Dakotas, through Minnesota, Iowa, northern Illinois, and Wisconsin; and some of the more urbanized centers of the East, such as Cleveland, the New York City area (including New Jersey and southern New England), and all of Pennsylvania.[1] To achieve success the major musical groups in those areas found that they had to synthesize the traditional pieces with American instrumentation and content, borrowing heavily from the popular mainstream bands of the time, especially the dance orchestras. The traditional tunes of the Old World were not enough to sustain a commercially oriented ensemble; to be viable, bands had to add original selections and mainstream dance music to their ethnic renditions, making for a very varied repertoire. These multi-ethnic and crossover bands at both the local and national levels became dominant into the forties.

Texas, long a meeting place of different ethnic cultures, was home to many peoples with a profound love for music, especially dance music, including blacks, Mexicans, Germans, and Slavs. A continual musical exchange existed among these groups especially in the period after 1930. This cross-cultural impact would in fact produce a new genre of American country music, a cultural hybrid that included Anglo-American music known as Western Swing.[2]

The most active group transforming the old into a new ethnic music were the Czechs, who had settled in Texas early and had been the mainstays of the pioneer ethnic brass bands. Czechs continued to cultivate the state's musical culture, especially its dancing, in the 1920s and later and undoubtedly were a model for the Germans and Poles who lived near or within the East Texas Czech settlements.

One of the reasons for the endurance and in fact expansion of Czech music in the twenties in the Lone Star State was the continuing growth of the Czech ethnic community and the relatively slow assimilation process, a reflection of the Czechs' isolation in rural communities with little contact with the culture of the Anglo-American majority. The number of foreign-born Bohemians in Texas, only about 12,000 in 1920, trebled by the end of the decade, and the total Czech community, including native-born descendants of immigrants, was sizeable by the mid-1930s, around 300,000, in fifty-four settlements clustered chiefly in Austin, Lavaca, and Washington counties.[3]

In addition to their expanding numerical growth, by the 1930s

Czech Texans had constructed facilities designed specifically to help cultivate ethnic folk- and popular-dance activity. Ever since the late nineteenth century both the Czechoslovak Benevolent Society (CSPS) and the Slavonic Benevolent Order of the State of Texas (SPJST) had been building lodge halls and pavilions to accommodate the group's passion for polkas, waltzes, and the like. One estimate was that as many as one hundred such halls were built in the nearly half-century after the late 1800s.[4] Some of the wooden pavilions were ingeniously constructed so that they could be used in any season, with large window-partitions that could be drawn up in the oppressively hot Texas summer to allow maximum ventilation and then lowered in winter to function as walls enclosing a dance area heated by a stove.[5]

One musician described a typical evening at the SPJST dance hall in the Bohemian communities of Snook and New Tabor in the mid-thirties, when, as a young teenager, he performed with the Snook Polka Boys. About 125 tickets would be sold for 50 cents each, but attendance was actually double that figure because women were allowed in free.[6] Normally, entire farm families came with their children. The dancing would go on until quite late, and the mothers would deposit their infants under the benches lining the walls, where the babies would sleep throughout the evening. Noise and rowdyism were minimized, because alcohol was not permitted inside, though the men did go outside to drink. The repertoire would include not only the more familiar Czech besedas, polkas, waltzes, and schottisches but also similar selections from the Polish and German traditions and modern dance selections as well. The musicians' pay varied, but generally it was quite good for those hard times in the thirties, $4 to $12 per night.[7]

It is unclear exactly when privately owned, commercial ballrooms similar to those in the North began to appear in southern cities, but it is known that at least one Czech American, Bill Mraz, operated an extremely successful dance palace around this time in Houston. Mraz and his family had formed their own ethnic family band and also hosted a number of outside musical groups at their dance hall. The ballroom was quite large, similar to those in the Archer network in Iowa and vicinity and the huge Aragon and Trianon structures of the Karsas Brothers in Chicago.[8]

Supplementing the dance halls as boosts to the persistence of folk-dance activity in Texas in the depression were the various expositions held in the state at that time. As elsewhere in the nation, displays of various forms of ethnic culture were quite common at these fairs, and ethnic music and song were performed at the San Antonio Bicentennial of 1931 and the Texas Centennial of 1936.[9]

Like other parts of the country by the 1930s, Texas, too, had radio programs that were broadcasting ethnic material. Czech hours appeared rather common. In the thirties, Czech Texans could listen to their music from a number of local outlets, especially around Temple, Houston, and Dallas. Out-of-state stations also broadcast Czech programming, especially from Nebraska.[10] All of this entertainment, plus the growing revival of the record industry, made the new old-time or international music and dance a permanent cultural feature of Texas society.[11]

Finding receptive audiences among both Czech and non-Czech audiences, the Bohemian musical ensembles grew rapidly. As many as one hundred Czech bands were active at the start of the depression, around 1930.[12] A few, of course, stand out, such as the several Bača Family Bands and the phenomenally famous "Adolph and the Boys," whose fabulous success was initially the result of radio. Another ensemble that helped to widen ethnic dancing was the Patek family band of Shiner, Texas, first led by John and later Joe Patek.

The Bača group, of course, was not a new family ensemble; Frank Bača and his son Joe had established their brass band before 1920 and gained a reputation throughout the state for performing excellent concert and folk-style march music. The ensemble had lost its leader, Joe, in 1920 and some may have feared that the end of the Bača era was at hand. But another Bača, John R., took up the baton and maintained the group's dominant position among performing bands, playing ethnic music throughout that decade and into the next. In fact he continued to build the Bača reputation until his death just at mid-century.[13] He did this by maintaining some of the band's old style, such as the hammered dulcimer featured as the central instrument, but including a number of new features, including selections from the mainstream American repertoire. He also saw the commercial value of exploiting the new media of radio and records, and thereby disseminating his band's tunes to reach a wide audience well beyond the old Bohemian community.

By the late 1920s the Bača Band was a much larger ensemble than ever, more like an American swing orchestra, with about fourteen musicians. It was appearing on radio, on the increasing number of Czech programs; very likely its first broadcast was on KPRC in Houston in 1926. A few years later John Bača added recording to the band's radio work, making more than forty cuts in San Antonio for Columbia, Okeh, and Brunswick between 1929 and 1935. The band put on a memorable fortieth-anniversary concert in the summer of 1932 and did other broadcasts on WOAI in San Antonio, KGKL in San Angelo, and KTRH in Houston. With all of this activity local papers gave John Bača, formerly known as the Texas March King, the multi-ethnic title of "Polka King of Texas."[14]

Sometime before 1937 the Bača dynasty changed somewhat. Two family members split away from the main ensemble and started bands of their own, which also made records and appeared on radio. The family tradition of high-quality ethnic music remained intact.[15] One of the breakaway Bača orchestras, led by I. J. Bača, inaugurated a very popular program, the Czech Melody Hour on KTEM radio in Temple on November 29, 1936, which also featured other Czech bands, including the Divis, Kostohryz, and Majek orchestras, and likely other Bača groups.[16] By the time one of the Bača bands performed on KGKL in San Angelo in 1939, the family musicians were a familiar fixture on Texas radio.[17]

Another well-known contingent with a huge heterogeneous following was a group first called "The Gold Chain Bohemians," later "Adolph and the Boys," a band that rocketed into prominence after it appeared on radio. It became as well-known in the state as Bob Wills and his Texas Playboys, the founders of Western Swing.[18] This band is noteworthy not only because of the sensation it created first on radio and then in area dance halls in the mid-1930s but also because of the prominent role of its sponsor, Universal Mills of Fort Worth, in providing much of the musicians' early momentum. Commercial considerations—a flour-milling company's interest in selling its products to German and Czech customers—helped create an enormously popular ethnic band, thus bringing ethnic music far beyond its local roots. About 1935, Universal Mills and some radio stations that had joined together in an association called the Texas Quality Network decided to hold a contest to select a band that could best sell the company's product, Gold Chain Flour.[19] The winner was a group led by Julius Pavlas, which played old Bohemian tunes. When the officials invited Pavlas and his musicians to return he was unable to obtain the same band members and had to borrow new instru-

mentalists from another bandleader he knew. After further compli-
cations, such as lack of sheet-music arrangements of Viennese
waltzes, which Pavlas ultimately obtained from Vitak and Elsnic of
Chicago, the Texas Quality Network set up a remote broadcast studio
at a relatively convenient location in Schulenburg, and the new
group, now called "Professor Adolph and the Gold Chain Bohemians," began broadcasting a fifteen-minute program at 8:15 in the
morning of November 3, 1935. The outlets were stations in Dallas,
Houston, San Antonio, and Fort Worth. The hastily assembled ensemble of ten musicians from two bands, playing hurriedly obtained
and newly arranged sheet music—a combination of European salon
music and Bohemian polkas and waltzes—surprisingly clicked with
the audience. As one listener put it: "They soon had thousands of
regular listeners, an outpouring of fan mail, and all the bookings
they could handle."[20]

A sense of showmanship enhanced the band's appeal, particularly
with the advice of the show's sponsor and its Dallas advertising
agency. On the program, frequent joking and banter went on between Pavlas and his musicians. They appeared frequently in Tyrolean costume, reflecting Pavlas's eagerness to appear multi-ethnic
rather than specifically Czech; the name change to the more generic
"Adolph and the Boys" also endeared them to their heterogeneous
audience.[21]

As an instant hit, the group was in heavy demand for personal
appearances. They purchased a bus and traveled around the state,
often playing nightly to audiences as large as one thousand.[22] They
continued on the air for nineteen months, until May 1937, but their
touring began to interfere with the broadcast schedule back in Schulenburg. As an extremely popular group, they made a number of
records for Columbia-Okeh-Vocalion, cutting twenty-seven sides in
two sessions in 1936 and 1937.[23] The records, which featured their
favorite traditional and original works, of course broadened their
popularity. The whirlwind stardom ended abruptly at the end of the
1930s, however, when they and their sponsor could not agree on
another radio contract.[24]

A third Texas crossover contingent was the Patek Band of Shiner,
which, like the Bačas and so many other ethnic ensembles, was a
family band that continually enlarged its audience through the generations by means of ballroom, radio, and record work. The father,
John, had been a bandleader in Europe in the 1890s just prior to

emigrating. Settling in Shiner and producing six sons, he decided to establish his family band in America in 1920, playing at both public and private affairs, especially in the large cities of Houston, Corpus Christi, and Fort Worth.[25]

Under John Patek the band made polka records in 1937 for Decca, and when he stepped down in 1940 his son Jim took over the group.[26] At that time only three of the nine members were outside the family. Another son, Joe, took the baton in the early 1940s, and the band became a great favorite with both Germans and Czechs, continuing their radio work, many dance-hall bookings, and a few recordings right down until the early 1980s. One of Patek's characteristically "borrowed" features as a crossover band was the employment of an electric guitar, a common element in many of the Texas ethnic bands' instrumentation.[27] Despite this innovation the younger Patek in the mid-1940s and later still sang tunes in the original Czech.[28]

Thus these three widely known ethnic bands, the Bača, Gold Chain, and Patek ensembles, along with numerous lesser-known groups playing throughout Texas, won a wide audience for continental music and dance. Many of the other groups, like the Pateks, used guitars and other contemporary instrumentation. Adolph and the Boys dispensed with the traditional accordion and relied heavily on strings, especially bass and violins, as might be considered appropriate for a band in the Southwest.

The ubiquitous Czech-led bands of the 1930s and 1940s were not the only group in Texas that was was cultivating polka music. Mexican Americans also contributed their own interpretation of the European continental genre. At least one star Mexican instrumentalist, Narciso Martinez, played for his Czech neighbors as well as for his own community.

The polka, along with the redowa, waltz, schottische, and other European dance forms, had come to Mexico early, in the middle and late 1800s, probably from European immigrants settling directly in Mexico, not from those in the United States. Monterrey, for example, had a small colony of Germans as early as 1895, who probably introduced the one-row European button accordion and German dances around the turn of the century. Other instruments used to play those dance tunes were fiddles and flutes.[29] From Monterrey the European style of dance music became known as *norteño* music and was found chiefly in working-class cantinas throughout northeast Mexico and south Texas. In these cafes an accordionist was usually accompanied by a twelve-string guitar called the *bajo sexto*. The combination of these two instruments in those locations produced what has been called *conjunto* music.

Musicians at these cantinas played in the tradition of the *baile de negotio*, public dances known to have existed in San Antonio as early as the 1870s. There, impresarios employed young women to dance with men for a few cents. With this type of commercialized entertainment, along with demands for musicians at more private functions, an opportunity developed for musicians to earn income from their playing, particularly in the 1920s when recording companies also began cutting Mexican music.

Among these cantina musicians arose Narciso Martinez, a Mexican accordionist who has been called the "father of conjunto music." Martinez's career reveals some closeness to those European Texans with whom he exchanged ethnic musical influences.[30] He was born in Reynosa, Mexico, just opposite McAllen, Texas, in 1911 and grew up in the lower Rio Grande Valley.[31] He took up the one-row button accordion and began his professional musical career as a teenager in 1927. A year later, he lived near Corpus Christi, Texas, and switched to a two-row instrument. It was there that he played at Slavic affairs, where he not only became more familiar with his hosts' music but also informed his listeners of his own. "From these Central European immigrants," it was said, Martinez "borrowed much of his repertoire" and talked "with much fondness about the Bohemians [in particular] who apparently loved Mexican music, especially waltzes and redowas. He played many dances for them and was hired without a singer—just with his accordion."[32]

While Martinez was not the only Mexican conjunto musician, he was certainly the best and most widely known. A Hispanic furniture and musical instrument dealer sponsored him to make records for Victor's Bluebird label, and his first hit was appropriately a polka, called "La Chicharronera," made in 1935 with his constant bajo sexto accompanist, Santiago Almeida.[33] Martinez's compositions, performances, and records, especially his polkas, became very popular among both Latins and Anglos. He recorded a score of titles in 1936 and others later and toured the Southwest widely. Aware of his appeal among Anglos, especially those with a strong ethnic dance tradition, the Victor company issued some of his tunes in its Polish catalog, under the pseudonym "Polish Kwartet."[34] Additionally, it appears that his work was especially popular among the Basques in America. But despite his popularity, Martinez was naive in his commercial arrangements and generally discriminated against as a Mexican, and he made little money. Through the 1930s, even when Anglos engaged him to perform at their dances they did not fraternize with him. The unusual bridge that Martinez provided was musical and cultural, not social.[35]

Of all the candidates for the title of model crossover entertainer, the musician who best synthesized European and contemporary American musical genres was Adolph Hofner of San Antonio. Hofner not only deliberately pulled together both Old and New World elements in his music but in fact produced a distinctive new American music, a segment of country music that itself was an eclectic mixture of ethnic and indigenous influences. That music is Western or Texas Swing.[36]

Hofner was born in 1916, the son of immigrants from Austria-Hungary; his father was part German and part Czech, but his mother, who was the greater influence on her son, was all Czech. They lived in Moulton, in the heart of Czech Texas, and Hofner grew up there and lived in the vicinity throughout his life. His family was so steeped in their ethnic community that the first language the young boy learned was Bohemian rather than English. In addition, because his parents loved music and dance—his mother sang and played the concertina, and his father played the harmonica—he grew up listening to and becoming acquainted with traditional polka music.[37] The parents especially liked the music of the Bača Family Band and bought its records frequently.

Adolph's taste was somewhat broader however than that of his parents'; besides the traditional pieces, he also liked listening to Hawaiian and American popular music. In the early twenties he especially loved hearing Al Jolson on the crystal set. As a teenager he and his younger brother Emil, called "Bash" because of his shyness, formed a duet called the Hawaiian Serenaders. He performed on the ukelele, while Bash played the steel guitar. The family moved several times, always staying, however, within the heavily Czech region of East Texas, until 1926, when they finally settled in San Antonio. Some of Adolph's primary education was in a Czech Catholic parochial school.

As a schoolboy Adolph really lived in two worlds, the one of his parents, who often took him to their Bohemian dances, and the other that of American popular entertainers. He had a strong desire to be a singer, and his models in the late 1920s were the crooners of the time, such as Russ Columbo, Bing Crosby, and especially a local vocalist, Milton Brown. Brown was the singer in 1930 for the future king of Western Swing, Bob Wills, who then had a group called the Fort Worth Trio.

Adolph and his brother decided to make their way in popular music, and after getting bookings around San Antonio, they struck out from home in 1936 and joined a traveling western band, Jimmie Revard and his Oklahoma Playboys. Apparently, the experience was not totally satisfactory; the boys returned home and even left music briefly the following year. They decided to try again in 1939, forming their own group, called "Adolph and All the Boys," playing western-style swing music. They recorded their first major hit, "Maria Elena" for Columbia, at that time, characteristically borrowing it from the Latin repertoire. When Bash went into the service in World War II, Adolph took the band to the West Coast, changing its name slightly to Dolph Hofner and the San Antonians to avoid the anti-German hysteria. Throughout this period the Hofner ensemble continually played, broadcast, and recorded Czech tunes as well as American ones.[38]

After the war, the band actually increased its ethnic recordings significantly.[39] Hofner made a number of Czech records on the Imperial label between 1948 and 1950, and with the sponsorship of a Texas brewery his band issued a number of popular polkas and traditionally styled pieces. Some of the better-known were "The Shiner Song," which was taken directly from an old ethnic tune, "Farewell to Prague," and "Louka Zelena" (Green meadow), which he did at San Antonio in 1948 and which he insisted was, like so many of his other pieces, brought to America by his mother.[40]

Despite his increasing interest in later years in traditionally oriented pieces, Hofner's band maintained its crossover quality. He occasionally used an accordion, but only sparingly, and his basic instrumentation relied heavily on strings.[41] Throughout his career, the sound of his work retained its European character. "Hofner's main claim to fame," noted a recent observer, "is combining the ethnic music of the large South Texas German and Czechoslovakian population with early Texas swing or jazz to create a new form of music. [As Hofner put it] 'I was about the first guy to put a country music sound to German and Czech music. That gave me a start. . . . And to this day it follows me.' "[42]

Another hotbed of ethnic crossover musical groups in the thirties and forties was the upper Midwest, especially Minnesota.[43] Minnesota, of course, was the home of American Scandinavians and was also, like Texas, the residence of many Germans and Czechs, who had produced their many brass bands. And Minnesota, too, had developed a network of rural and urban dance halls and of radio stations friendly to the new musical genre. Two major centers produced crossover bands: the Scandinavian-dominated Twin Cities and the German-Czech town of New Ulm, a community noted for what has been called "Dutchman" music. Two crossover bands outside those communities also stand out: the Czech ensemble of Jerry Dostal of Glencoe and especially Skipper Berg's Viking Accordion Band of Albert Lea.

The leading Scandinavian bandleaders of Minneapolis in the late twenties and early thirties were the Norwegian Thorstein Skarning and the Swede Ted Johnson. Both played traditional dance tunes true to their ethnic traditions, but they also performed in a manner that showed American influences. Unlike popular musicians in Scandinavia, however, these Minnesotans did not play the old-country folk tunes associated with the traditional hardanger fiddle; the traditional pieces in their repertoires included only music called "Gammaldans," the simplest, most easily learned dance pieces, similar to the waltz, schottische, and polka to which the Germans and Czechs in the vicinity danced. Hence an assimilation, an Americanization had begun. As one observer put it, the Scandinavian American musicmen "took elements of both Norwegian (and Swedish) and American cultures and synthesized them into ethnic humor and music which was different from the original Norwegian and closer to American cultures, but distinct from both. Because of the popularity of this music and its availability to all Scandinavian-Americans through recordings and radio, the 'culture within a culture' became a distinct entity. . . ." The jazz and country fiddle music of the region were cited as elements that made this ethnic music distinctive.[44] Two bands exemplifying this synthetic quality, especially the unusual admixture of hillbilly western and ethnic music, were very popular Norwegian entertainment groups, the Thorstein Skarning family band and the well-known radio personalities, Slim Jim and the Vagabond Kid of Minneapolis.

Thorstein I. Skarning was a Norwegian immigrant who formed a group in the 1920s to play Scandinavian music at traveling ethnic stage shows.[45] His was a rather musical family; his wife sang at performances, and his two sons, Thorstein B. and Osmund, were drummer and accordionist respectively, joining the group in the 1930s. Quite likely, the younger Thorstein occasionally replaced his father as leader.[46] The Skarning ensemble finally established a permanent base in the state's largest city in 1935 and became famous on radio and record, both for performing old Norwegian favorites, particularly "Farvel Min Fedreland" (Farewell my native land) and for blending them with a country-western sound. The emphasis on the latter was obvious in the name of the band—"Skarning and his Norwegian Hillbillies"—and they were well known especially for their thrice-weekly broadcasts on WDGY in Minneapolis.[47]

The younger Skarning took over the band when his father died in 1939, disbanded it during World War II when he was in the Marines, and reformed the ensemble as Skarning's Norske Orchestra in 1946. They played the same types of tunes as earlier at barn dances and on Scandinavian radio programs and toured the region extensively. Thorstein also arranged tours for other musicians and became known as "the hillbilly Hurok of the mid-continent."[48]

A similar group combining Norwegian and American western-style music were two brothers who were extremely popular in the 1930s among radio listeners in the area. Ernest and Clarence Iverson, better known as Slim Jim and the Vagabond Kid, were essentially singers who combined cowboy songs with old Norwegian folklike melodies, particularly English and Scandinavian hymns. Much of their repertoire was original.

The great-grandchildren of Norwegian immigrants, Ernest and Clarence Iverson were born in 1903 and 1905 respectively to a rural Norwegian-speaking family in Binford, North Dakota. After their mother died when both were still young boys in 1910, a housekeeper, Molly Rood, who was well acquainted with Norwegian folk music, taught them traditional songs and also taught them how to play her own instrument, the finger guitar, thus providing them with much of their later Norwegian repertoire.[49]

Ernest, who also loved playing the drums, first began performing at the age of eight. Bored with small-town life, he dropped out of high school for a job with a traveling Wild West show that was on its way to Texas. It was as a guitar-player in Texas that he decided to adopt the image of a cowboy entertainer. Being 6 feet 4 inches in height, he took the name Slim Jim. In 1927 he moved to Omaha, where he appeared full time on radio as the "Master Troubadour" and leader of a western band, The Rough Riders. After their father died that year, brother Clarence teamed up with him on a program of an Omaha radio station.

Five years later, after both Iverson boys had traveled extensively, they rejoined each other in Minneapolis on what turned out to be an immensely popular program on WGDY with a sponsor, a furniture company that prided itself on having a working-class clientele. At the height of their popularity they were receiving as many as a thousand letters per week.[50] Their success was clearly due to their rather sensitive understanding of their Midwest audience, both its ethnic background and its regional culture stressing clean, family entertainment that included some religious sentiment. They offered the most popular Norwegian tunes, especially dialect and comedy pieces, western songs, and immigrant and native hymns, a musical array with broad as well as strictly Norwegian American appeal. Ernest himself was really multi-ethnic, as his wife taught him German songs that he occasionally offered along with Scandinavian material.[51]

A list of the songs the Iversons offered on one program on WGDY, January 10, 1937, is likely typical of their many radio broadcasts. They sang "Great Judgment Day," "Bury Me Beneath the Weeping Willow," "Florella," "The Crazy Song," and the Norwegian "Moder Jag Ar Trot nu vill jag sova."[52]

Adding to their exposure through the 1930s and 1940s, the brothers appeared regularly with a western-style band in bookings around the Twin Cities and on records, especially on the Soma, Twinto, and FM labels. They offered a hybrid-crossover mixture of what was termed "Scandinavian country music."[53] Among their most popular pieces were "Scandinavian Hot Shot," "I Been a Swede from Nort' Dakota," the well-known "Nicolina," "The Little Girl Next Door to Us," and the widely known Slavic composition, "Helena Polka."[54]

Clarence interrupted their success when he went into the service in World War II. When he returned, the brothers restored their popularity with more radio work. At mid-century Clarence decided to leave the show and return to North Dakota as a nurseryman.[55]

The legacy of Slim Jim and the Vagabond Kid is both colorful and obvious. They were, as one observer put it, "the foremost exponents of the Scandinavian American hybrid style which [combined] Scandinavian lyrics with a typical Southern instrumental accompaniment."[56]

The most popular bandleader in the Twin Cities was Ted Johnson, a musician who on first impression was much more insular than the Iversons. But Johnson's ensembles were highly urban and while more heavily Swedish than Skarning or Slim Jim, he could be termed multi-ethnic also, for the way he popularized among the city population the Scandinavian American dances, the *Gammaldans,* which appealed to people in hard times. As a violinist, Johnson helped to transform traditional Old-Country, string-based ethnic dance known as *Bygdedans* to an accordion-based style similar to the old-time American polka, waltz, and the like.

Johnson, a self-taught musician, was born in 1903 and took up the violin at age six.[57] He chose that instrument in particular on the basis of his admiration for the famous Norwegian virtuoso, Ole Bull. By the mid-1920s he had organized his own eleven-piece orchestra and must have achieved some notoriety, for his group's first major engagement was at one of Minneapolis' leading hotels, Hotel Nicollet. This booking suggests that he was already seeking to go beyond his own Swedish ethnic community for a general audience.

For some reason Johnson next went back to a more ethnic repertoire in 1926. Olle i Skratthult brought him into his troupe, especially to entertain patrons at those famous post-performance dance sessions where Gammaldans was carried on. Johnson stayed with that ensemble until about 1930, when he joined another well-known and exclusively ethnic orchestra of the time, led by Oscar Danielson.[58] He finally decided to re-form his own band and got a booking at the well-known Stockholm Cafe in the heart of the Minneapolis Swedish quarter, which became his headquarters for the rest of his career, until the mid-1940s.

Although Johnson now appeared to concentrate his band's activities within the ethnic enclave, he also made some changes that appealed to a broad Scandinavian American and American clientele. He engaged a talented accordionist, Orville Lindholm, who could play the more Americanized numbers, and in the summertime he often took his musicians on tour to more openly public locations in the Midwest and Northwest states.[59] From the mid-thirties through the forties, Johnson and his orchestra played a mixed repertoire to heterogeneous audiences, especially third-generation Scandinavian Americans, at such places as the Minnesota State Fair; he performed on stations WCCO, WGDY, and WTCN in Minneapolis and KFYR in North Dakota; and he played at various Minnesota dance halls, the famous Prom Ballroom in St. Paul, and Norway Hall and the Uptown Auditorium in Minneapolis. These dance halls were nearly always full, as the cost of admission was low in the late 1930s, 25 cents before 9 p.m. and 35 cents afterward.[60] Because of his popularity, he twice cut records, in 1936 and again in 1945, for RCA Victor and Brunswick in Chicago and Fargo, North Dakota.[61]

In selecting a name for his orchestra, Johnson provided a further indication of his increasing readiness to mix his both ethnic and American pieces in his repertoire. At first he called his group the Nordvest Skandinavisk Orchestra, which he later changed to something more Anglicized: Ted Johnson and his Midnight Suns.[62]

Outside Minneapolis, another center of ethnic music in the state was a much smaller rural community to the southwest, New Ulm, which as the name implies, was German in origin and had developed the expected rich tradition of German brass bands in the late nineteenth and early twentieth centuries. That tradition would continue into the 1920s and produce an amazing proliferation of commercial German ethnic bands. The most outstanding was the "Whoopee John" ensemble, which lasted with much national notice for three decades ending in the 1960s. For its historic preoccupation with ethnic music, one journalist referred to New Ulm as "Oompah Town."[63]

The type of bands that New Ulm produced in late 1920s and after, known as "Dutchman" bands, were found elsewhere in German population centers but flourished so in New Ulm that the town could be considered the matrix of that musical genre. "Whoopee John" began in New Ulm as a regional bandleader and quickly achieved national stardom by broadening his repertoire. Another well-known local product was Harold Loeffelmacher and his "Six Fat Dutchmen." Both drew upon the musical talent of New Ulm families and the dominant "Dutchman" tradition there.

Tracing this type of music clearly suggests that while it did have a musical sound that was distinctive, it was also—like the music of Texas and Minnesota Scandinavians—a synthesis of traditional and contemporary material. Beginning in the late 1920s New Ulm German bandleaders sought to appeal to a heterogeneous audience and played both popular-American and ethnic pieces, including ethnic selections that were Slavic and Scandinavian in origin as well as their own German repertoire.

The origins of the American Dutchman style had arrived in New Ulm before 1920 from its source in southwest Bohemia. Two bandleaders especially, John Lindmeier and Joseph Hofmeister, had emphasized the marchlike military pieces with the appropriate instrumentation, the button accordion, drums, and heavy brass. An additional contributor to that style was John Fritsche, who also ran a town brass band up to and during World War I. Lindmeier, Fritsche and many of the Dutchman musicians came from the so-called "Goosetown" section of New Ulm, which was heavily Catholic, working-class, and musical. The bands of these men often consisted of related family members, and it was their sons or nephews who by 1930 had taken over the town's new generation of dance bands, more attuned to the mainstream ensembles with winds and reeds, stressing English-language songs and the more popular polkas and waltzes, often based on American experience. This mixture was the essential Dutchman genre.[64]

The sax player, Victor ("Fezz") Fritsche, for example, John's son, first played in his father's band after he finished high school in 1926 and took over the baton after his father's death in 1940. He became very successful with his familiar theme song "Tanta Anna," done in Dutchman style, along with a huge repertoire of over 150 records representing both American and ethnic music.[65]

Before Eddie Wilfahrt took over his brother John's band in 1924, when the latter went off to radio work in Minneapolis, he had already played with his cousin, Emil Domeier, a cornetist and concertina player who also struck out on his own and eventually formed a group in 1929 with *his* relatives and friends. In the following twenty-eight years Eddie Wilfahrt did not make any records but did appear on radio KYSM in Mankato and traveled extensively over a six-state region.[66] Other prominent Dutchman-style musicians and bandleaders in the period were the nine male children of Joseph Hofmeister; two sons of John Lindmeier; Ellsworth ("Babe") and Virgil ("Swede") Wagner; Emil Scheid, who was later known for his Dutchman-like "Hoolerie" Band; and the most successful of the New Ulm musicians and the foremost exponent of Dutchman music, Harold Loeffelmacher.[67]

Oddly, Loeffelmacher did not come from a family of musicians. He was born in 1905, son of a farmer who moved to New Ulm in 1922. The young Loeffelmacher first intended to be a painter, but a rural Lutheran minister who needed a violinist for church services persuaded him as a youth to take up that instrument. In high school in the mid-twenties he became more sensitive to what appealed more to his audience and switched to the brass instruments so important in German music, especially the trombone and bass horn, the latter of which would become his trademark and lead, emitting the distinctive "oompah" Dutchman sound.[68]

He played in a local military band around 1928 and hoped to become a professional musician, but he hesitated and became a salesman instead while playing part time. After a dispute with the band he was playing with, he decided to form his own ensemble, a small group that would perform a variety of popular dance pieces, not the Dutchman type but the more contemporary material.[69] To emphasize that sophisticated, mainstream approach, Loeffelmacher experimented with the band's name, at first choosing "The Broadway Band" and "The Continental Band" before finally deciding on "The Six Fat Dutchmen."[70] That final title was not quite apt; the original band of 1934 had seven musicians, and none was fat. But the inaccurate reference seemed to draw crowds; by 1938 when he began to travel beyond southern Minnesota he enlarged his ensemble to ten and occasionally twelve members.[71] Most were of German origin, including Emil Scheid and Babe Wagner, who later formed their own ensembles. And of course they played the old-time polkas, waltzes, and other dances.[72] Loeffelmacher always insisted on a heavy brass arrangement, not only to feature himself but also to generate the high volume required for the large-sized ballrooms in which he preferred to get his early bookings. The amplification in those halls was usually inadequate.[73]

Loeffelmacher certainly had a flair for promotion and showmanship, sometimes entering competitive band tournaments, called "battles," where sponsors had audiences evaluate band performances. He also recorded often, making over three hundred sides for RCA from 1945, amid a frantic travel schedule extending from Canada to Texas, often with as many as three hundred dates a year. In the late 1940s the Fat Dutchman and his crew sometimes performed on ninety consecutive nights. Traveling 125,000 miles per year, they gained a wide following of fans from many backgrounds.[74] The band was especially well-liked in Texas, where they drew as many as two thousand to a dance and in fact established a record weekly attendance at the Mraz Ballroom in Houston sometime in the 1940s.[75]

Often participating in "battles of music" with Loeffelmacher in the 1940s was Jerry Dostal, a Czech from rural Glencoe, Minnesota, who led the state's most prominent Bohemian band. Dostal, whose father had played the accordion for a family band in the early 1900s, took up the drums and got his first jobs in the early 1930s, playing mostly with Czech bands. His pay then was about $3 per night at traditional family and Bohemian community affairs, often held in barns, not ballrooms.[76]

Dostal's playing changed after his marriage in 1934, when his wife, Ethel, became his manager, and he decided to begin his own orchestra on the prevailing crossover principle of playing a mixed ethnic and mainstream repertoire. His band performed on several radio stations, first in Minneapolis, and then, in 1939, on the Iowa State University station WOI in Ames and also on one of the region's most powerful outlets, WNAX in Yankton, South Dakota. By the early 1940s his band was firmly established, playing German, Bohemian, American, and even occasionally Scandinavian selections. Like the Texas Czech bandleaders, Dostal took most of his dance tunes from the Vitak and Elsnic publications. The selections certainly appealed to Dostal's audience.[77] At this time Dostal was booked regularly in regional ballrooms such as the Woodcliff in Spencer and George's Ballroom in New Ulm, where attendance routinely averaged about one thousand. Band "battles," most often with Loeffelmacher's Six Fat Dutchmen, supplemented Dostal's income because admission to these double-header affairs was 90 cents a head, a little higher than at regular dances, generating a more lucrative gate often totaling about $1000.[78]

By 1941 Dostal and his wife decided to run their own musical enterprise and bought a pavilion at Silver Lake. They brought in both mainstream and ethnic bands—Lombardo and the Dorseys, as well as Yankovic, Welk, and "Whoopee John"—charging 75-cents admission and averaging about five hundred dancers per night. They prospered, with a ten-employee staff, but after Dostal went into the service in 1943 he turned over the management of the business to his wife. When he returned in 1946, he reassembled his band and became at least as popular as he had been before. His year-round schedule included dates at leading ballrooms in such Minnesota towns as St. Paul, Montevideo, and Austin, as well as at many places in Iowa and Wisconsin. There were so many ballrooms in the state that in 1952 Dostal and his wife organized the Minnesota Ballroom Operators Association, for which Ethel served as secretary. He also made records for Coral and Soma, beginning in 1948, somewhat late in his career.[79]

The most multi-ethnic of all the Minnesota bands and perhaps therefore the model crossover ethnic group was the Viking Accordion Band of Albert Lea, led by Leighton "Skipper" Berg. At the outset, Berg did not intend to be an ethnic bandleader; he had attended college in the late 1920s, majoring in economics and business with an eye toward entering retailing. The education would help him and his band later. As a teenager, he had learned to play the accordion and the banjo well enough that when the oncoming depression forced his boss to lay him off at a retail store in 1929, he turned to music for his income. He joined two other friends in a trio, which took bookings at local affairs, particularly house parties. By late October 1930, the small group joined four other musicians, most of them Scandinavian, to form a polka ensemble that specialized in Scandinavian music.[80] For its theme, the band used the well-known Swedish immigrant song, "Halsa Dem Dar Hemma (Greetings to Them At Home)."

Berg saw immediately that to get bookings and maximize their income the band would have to become better known, an objective for which the new medium of radio seemed ideal. He applied to several stations in the region and met with some success, chiefly because he occasionally agreed to have the band perform without pay. Between 1931 and 1932 the band became familiar to listeners in the area, performing on a number of stations, including WMT in Waterloo, Iowa; WOI in Ames, Iowa, the station on which Dostal appeared a few years later; the powerful WNAX in Yankton, South Dakota; and WDGY in St. Paul. In most cases the radio audience phoned in requests to the stations, but occasionally the band did remote broadcasts from ballrooms, such as the Electric Park dance hall at Waterloo. Traveling to a station to do a broadcast could be burdensome, especially without compensation; Ames, Iowa, for example, was a 240-mile round trip, and Yankton was much further.[81]

Nevertheless, ballroom bookings did develop, beginning in late 1930, especially after the bandsmen began to make their performances more theatrical by donning costumes and including comic skits in their repertoire. Their "Scandinavian" attire included red vests, black jackets, white shirts, and Colonial-style knee pants and socks. According to Berg the audience, even the later, non-immigrant generations, responded warmly to these presentations, and the young people became interested in ethnic cultural matters. But Berg quickly saw that to widen the audience, his Viking Accordion Band would have to appeal to more than Scandinavians. He trained the group to play a variety of music, including Bohemian, German, and even Italian and Irish ethnic selections (the latter for the area around Dubuque, Iowa). The band would also include American popular music in its repertoire, and Berg even arranged for a woman to teach him the Czech words to some of the pieces he sang. The audiences' reactions were highly enthusiastic. For example, for twenty years following the band's performance at the CSPS Hall in the heavily Czech city of Cedar Rapids, the entire band would be invited to dinner at a Bohemian home.[82]

Berg wrote, "We seemed to strike the right chord in the hearts of the various ethnic groups. We played their type of folk songs." One small-town Iowa paper expressed the reason for the delight of townspeople who went to their dance in 1932: "They particularly excel in playing Bohemian dance music. . . . Some of [our] people did not believe that an orchestra could succeed in playing both Bohemian and modern music at the same dance. They went to hear the Vikings and were convinced."[83]

Berg himself knew the source of their success as early as 1934. "Our ability to play a variety of ethnic music as well as modern was a great selling point for our band."[84] And "We could adopt our style of music to a particular community, whatever its nationality."[85] Probably because of its crossover breadth, the band decided to drop its original ethnic identification in 1939, albeit somewhat belatedly, shedding its Scandinavian costume and donning modern dress, the American band attire of the tuxedo.

Through the 1930s the Viking Accordion Band grew in popularity as it traveled widely around the region. It would appear regularly in fraternal halls and Turnvereins in nine states, from Wisconsin to Kansas and up to the Dakotas and Minnesota. Normally consisting of seven musicians who made a contemporary sound with saxophones, clarinets, trumpet, banjo, and drums, the band provided people eager to dance with just what they sought: an inexpensive form of recreation in hard times. And Berg tried various ways to have as large a crowd as possible, setting ticket prices as low as 25 cents and even allowing some patrons to get in free at times.[86] Like the other bands, they played for rural families who would come to the dance halls with their small children, whom they would bed down while they danced until early the next morning.

The repertoire of the Viking Accordion Band included an incredibly varied selection; they played pieces that were the favorites of each of the many different ethnic communities in which they appeared. Most of their pieces in the late 1930s came from the sheet music of Vitak and Elsnic, which by then had become a mixed house serving several groups. The band also exploited the publications of the Bohemian businessman Joseph Jiran; the leading Scandinavian music house of Dahlquist of St. Paul; the Sajewski music company, and the multi-nationality pieces of the Chart Music Company of Chicago; the Norwegian Dalkullan Company of the same city; and O. Pagani Brothers of New York. From O. Pagani they obtained selections for the Italian colony of Des Moines, which had an extraordinary dance interest.[87] To add to their popularity Berg also arranged for the group to make records, twenty-three in all, for a great variety of labels through the 1930s and later, including Melotone, Perfect, Brunswick, Vocalion, Decca and Columbia.[88]

Berg broke up his band in 1942 after military service claimed several of his musicians, but he restarted it with new instrumentalists in 1944, and it continued to the mid-1950s, as popular as ever. In 1954 *Billboard Magazine* voted the ensemble the fourth most popular "international" band of the Midwest behind "Whoopee John," Frankie Yankovic, and the Six Fat Dutchmen.[89]

By the early 1940s, then, Minnesota had emerged as one of the most fertile regional centers of the new "international" style, with a great variety of bands, including Scandinavian, Czech, German, and mixed groups working out of the Twin Cities and New Ulm, crisscrossing the state and region to offer a wealth of ethnic dance entertainment. The bands obviously attracted the attention of music critics—much of it unfavorable, unfortunately, because of a disdain for their mixture of comic routines and novelty songs with their better-known polkas and waltzes. At the height of this frenzy for polka music in 1943 one Minnesota social critic referred to the outlandish comic bandleader Freddie "Schnickelfritz" Fisher as typical of the successful musicians who had given Minnesota its reputation as the center of a cultural form that had no real cultural value. Although the state was the home of the admirable Minnesota Symphony and leading institutions of higher learning it was also the "birthplace of that rural bred, unbuttoned type of music known as 'corn,' " which this critic defined as the "untrammeled sounds [of] 6–7 piece bands that specialize in jerky-rhythmed unsophisticated music of hayseed heritage, featuring cowbells and other freak and pseudo-musical noises." The "heart and soul" of this " 'music' (let's call it music for lack of a better term) is blatant, old-fashioned hokum with funny hats, costumes, horseplay and noise-making hardware. The real tragedy to all of this is that some have been so successful at it." Decca, he pointed out, was the major American villain as the leading promoter of that genre, helping a non-musician like "Schnickelfritz" sell 15,000 records in two weeks and earn $1,000 per night—"not bad for a country boy." The "craze for corn and novelty is at a peak that might be even higher if the recording companies had enough shellac and manpower to feed the public demand." Among the other Minnesota culprits in that promotion of bad taste he named "Whoopee John," the Vikings of Albert Lea, Ted Johnson and his Swedish band of Minneapolis, and Pa Trister and his Screwballs from La Crosse.[90] Whatever one's evaluation of the newly emerging international style, by World War II Minnesota certainly had gained a new reputation as a home for it.

8

Regional Crossover Bands, II: Wisconsin and Cleveland, 1930-1950

The new interethnic or international style also appeared in other locations where Czechs concentrated, in east-central Wisconsin and Cleveland, places that like Texas and Minnesota had a rich tradition of ethnic brass bands around the turn of the century. The Czech colonies and band tradition in Wisconsin were largely rural and had developed chiefly from a particular farming region in the east-central part of the state, around Kewaunee and Manitowoc and the small towns of Tisch Mills and Polivka's Corners. Cleveland, on the other hand, was of course a major urban center, where Czechs but also, more importantly, Slovenians had come to dominate old-time ethnic music in the post–World War I period. Nevertheless, these two Midwest centers, rural and urban, both produced musical ensembles that contributed substantially to the regional support of the new musical style. A few of the most successful bands even brought their material into American popular music, and certainly many of these ethnic-based bands and entertainers aimed their performances beyond their own group and generation, aided by new instrumentation and facilities that had emerged particularly in the depression: ballrooms, the jukebox, and radio.

Two of the most commercially successful Wisconsin bandsmen at this time were Romy Gosz, who featured the Bohemian brass style, and Lawrence Duchow, whose performance was more in the New Ulm–style Dutchman tradition.[1] More than any of their contemporaries, Gosz and Duchow helped fashion a grass-roots audience in their region and sustained ethnic dance music. Both came from east-central Wisconsin, an area that had produced a great number of older style ethnic brass bands, including one ensemble in particular that was a model for Wisconsin bands of the depression era, the Altman-Walecka band, formed in 1910, which later became better known as the Pilsen (Wisconsin) Brass Band.[2] Their home town of Pilsen, located twenty-five miles north of Manitowoc, is in that so-called polka belt in the east-central section of the state.

This Walecka group was in actuality a transitional ensemble, a modification of the conventional marching aggregations of the previous century, playing at numerous private affairs such as weddings and also at the major, civic events in communities in the region. The Altman-Walecka ensemble consisted of six amateur instrumentalists, five farmers and a painter, all of Bohemian ancestry, who played the old traditional music on the standard ethnic instruments, alto and bass horns, clarinets, and cornets. The musicians did have some musical instruction, but they offered their repertoire from memory rather than from sheet music.[3]

These Pilsen musicians were much sought-after, playing as many as sixty dates consecutively in the immediate post–World War I era. Their income, however, like that of many of the older band ensembles, was quite modest, about $9 per night. Significantly, this group had quickly attained crossover status, featuring not only the conventional ethnic dance pieces, the polka, waltz, and schottische, but also American and German selections, the laendler, galop, reel, and two-step. In addition their audience was normally rather mixed; they played for area Germans, Poles, and Belgians as well as their own Bohemians.[4] Multi-ethnic appeal was probably characteristic of Bohemian bands then, as the Bohemian Hall of a similar ensemble, the Ashland (Wisconsin) Bohemian Brass Band, held weekend dances for the general public around World War I.[5]

At any rate, in the 1920s a new generation of Bohemian bands, with names that became familiar to people around the countryside— Zahorik, Naidl, and Urbanek—arose in the Manitowoc area. These ensembles modified traditional instrumentation to make it more acceptable to native American taste, reducing the brass and adding pianos, accordions, and drums. In addition, they sought a healthy income from their playing by appearing at commercial dance halls, which provided more compensation, about $4 per man per night at such popular places as Martin Ouher's Silver Lake Lodge. The admission charge at that and similar dance halls about 1930, 35 cents or more, was certainly within the means of working farmers and townspeople in the depression. Some places had enclosed dance floors and might charge patrons by the dance, 5 cents for a three-minute spin around the floor. The owner of the establishment would provide food and drink, mainly non-alcoholic during Prohibition. For further lures, operators would devise various come-ons to attract and keep their clientele, such as chicken raffles.[6] As in the rest of the country, a dance madness had seized the area by the 1930s, and many towns in rural Wisconsin and in the upper Midwest had at least one dance hall; by the early 1940s, twenty were operating in Manitowoc County alone.[7]

A good example of the new generation of commercially oriented ethnic bands then emerging was that of Quirin Kohlbeck of the Manitowoc County area. Kohlbeck began his career very young, joining his uncle's band as a ten-year-old drummer about 1921 and barnstorming with his own group in Michigan and Illinois in the early 1930s. He appeared regularly on Green Bay and Manitowoc radio. Other examples include Matt Kulhanek, who with his Grenadiers played chiefly in Michigan, and Jim Nejedlo, who led his Bohemian Brass Band from 1930 to 1943, when he realized that the old ethnic brass bands were obsolete and formed a more contemporary ensemble, appropriately called the Modern and Old Time Orchestra.

The most important of these transformed ethnic bands was that of Paul Gosz of Grimms, Wisconsin. Gosz had begun a group in 1921 made up of his three sons, George, Mike, and Roman, a typical family band that eventually became known as the Empire Band. The most junior Gosz, Romy, who was later to become a star polka bandleader, had started rather young in the ensemble, like Kohlbeck, as a ten-year-old instrumentalist, in his case playing piano.[8] In a few years Romy became more than just a member of the ensemble; he made his extraordinary imprint on his father's band when he was still a teenager. In the early 1920s, Paul decided to work more at his major occupation in a lime kiln, and the older brother George assumed the baton. The leadership however ultimately fell to the youngest son in 1928 when Romy was barely eighteen.[9]

With such a young musician at the helm, who was in fact still a minor and thus unable legally to manage a band and conduct its business, Romy Gosz feared that the ensemble's fortunes would suffer. To disguise his leadership, he decided for the time being to keep his father's name for the group. Hence, long after the elder Gosz had retired, Romy's band was still called the Paul Gosz (pronounced like "cross") Orchestra.[10] In fact, his father, a drummer, may have continued to play with the group occasionally until around 1930, when he was in his sixties.[11]

The junior Gosz, though facing practical problems with respect to his youth, had no hesitation concerning the direction of his ensemble. Romy had definite ideas on his group's route to success. His early strategy was to emphasize the making of records, despite the depressed character of the industry, encouraged by the proximity of a record company, one using the Broadway label in nearby Grafton. Then and throughout his career Gosz avoided radio work, as he believed his band would do better in personal appearances interacting with audiences. His assessment was probably accurate. Regular or frequent playing over the air, he felt, would cut down too heavily on his men's traveling and meeting people.[12] Thus a short time after he took over the baton, probably in October 1931, "The Paul Gosz Orchestra," came out with fourteen cuts on seven records. These were a judicious mixture of old and new pieces including some of the traditional favorites.[13] A notable example of this synthesis of old and new was the recording of the "Pilsen Polka" which became a bestseller through the decade and was the work responsible for initially popularizing the Gosz band.[14]

Gosz also stressed the more conventional Czech favorites, rather than playing a variety of ethnic dances. He always sought to retain the old brass sound of his pieces, as illustrated in how he changed his own instrument after his trumpeter had to leave early in the band's career; since no one else offered to pick up the cornet, Romy himself gave up the piano and trained himself on it. But retaining the echoes of Bohemian brass did not mean retaining all its musical tradition, and his band had crossover characteristics in both its instrumentation and its style of play. Soon Gosz added drums and saxophone and gave a definite role to the piano, making the group a contemporary ensemble. It is clear that from about the mid-1930s mainstream musical influences, such as American jazz and popular music, altered the prior reliance on march tunes.[15] As one observer put it simply, by incorporating modern influences and employing a faster tempo, he brightened the old Bohemian dances.[16]

Gosz became a common figure on records, building a rather large repertoire. His list included pieces cut on Columbia, Brunswick, Okeh, Vocalion, and Decca labels, about seventy in all in the years between 1933 and 1938.[17] His most famous were "Prune Song" (Chicago, circa 1933), "Red Handkerchief Waltz" (Chicago, November 1934), and "Picnic in the Woods" (New York, August 3, 1938), each of which, one observer claimed, sold 100,000 copies.[18] He continued to emphasize recordings even after the war, contracting with Mercury, Universal, and others so that by the time he died in 1966, he had cut a huge number of songs, about 170 sides in all.[19]

By playing in the ethnic vein but also catering to the taste of his *general* Wisconsin audience Gosz's band had become broadly popular in the region by 1940. For example, in 1934 the Wisconsin American Legion convention adopted his "Prune Song" as its theme. During the war he received about twenty-five letters per week from servicemen asking for his records, and in the war years his band was in such great demand that he would occasionally get bookings that would occupy his ensemble for as many as fifty consecutive nights. The band's slogan at this time declared "Jump and Toss with Romy Gosz." Around 1940 one Sheboygan radio station polled its listeners asking them to name their favorite bandleader; Gosz placed first by a substantial margin over the well-known western bandleader-singer Gene Autry.[20] It was common for Gosz to attract crowds of sixteen hundred people each night at the Bluestone Park Ballroom near Green Bay and one thousand at the Theresa, Wisconsin, dance hall, numbers that clearly showed the band was a favorite with Dutch, German, Polish, and Belgian peoples in the region as well as with the Czechs.[21] A typical evening at the Bluestone revealed a rather enthusiastic audience. The band would schedule seven fast-paced dances in an hour, a pace that would tire ordinary patrons. But the crowded 125-by-75-foot dance floor was always full, with a sea of people moving like waves. "When the music [would stop], the crowd [would go] wild with cheers and whistles."[22]

The music the Gosz band played appealed not only across ethnic groups but also across generations. Despite the continued occasional use of lyrics in the foreign language, young people still enjoyed the dancing associated with it. As one observer noted in 1945, "[Gosz] keeps up with the young folks, or maybe you'd say the young folk keep up with him. In this part of the country, everyone seven [years of age] on up dances the polka. Even the bobby soxers love the old rhythms."[23]

The national press by that time, including *Billboard* and *Time* magazine, regarded the Gosz band as having a large and devoted following in the upper Midwest and considered Gosz's musicianship substantially responsible for maintaining the polka craze there.[24] In anointing Gosz as "Polka King" in 1945, *Time* referred to his multi-ethnic following as devoted "polka addicts."[25] His reputation became legendary, and at his funeral at Kellnersville in 1966, an enormous crowd came to pay its respects—twenty-three hundred people filed by his casket in one day.[26] Soon after his passing, his son Tony decided to continue the orchestra, playing and recording some of his father's old favorites beloved by so many.[27] A quarter-century after Gosz' death, a survey found him to still be a model even for contemporary bands in the region.[28]

The other outstanding regional bandleader in Wisconsin was Lawrence Duchow of Hilbert, who was best known for his direction of the Red Raven Band. Unlike Romy Gosz, Duchow played in a style more in the Dutchman tradition, but this ethnic style was less marked by a Bohemian character. Also Duchow's instrumentation was much closer to the mainstream; his music sounded like that of the common bands of the time. In fact, Duchow's heavy use of the piano accordion, which he himself played, was his only concession to being an ethnic band. Normally, his ensemble consisted of a judicious mixture of reeds, winds, and a little brass, accompanied by string bass and a piano. He did not retain or attempt to modernize much German material; most of his selections had English titles and were original compositions. Duchow was much more of an entrepreneur than Gosz; he utilized all the media, including radio, and was more of a showman, trading especially on his weight and his large size. He was, therefore, much closer than Gosz to the sweet dance band genre then being projected by their national contemporary, Lawrence Welk.

Duchow was born in 1914 near Potter, Wisconsin, not far from Gosz's hometown, in a heavily musical environment, where the performance of ethnic music and dance in local social centers was quite common. One local observer identified a school band director who worked near Potter in the 1930s as largely responsible for the regional popularity of band music among school-age students.[29] Little is known about Duchow's parents, except that they were American-born of German background and apparently encouraged their sons with their music; young Duchow took up the accordion when just a boy, and his older brother Reuben played the alto saxophone.[30]

In 1932, at the age of seventeen, Duchow had the entrepreneurial incentive to form a typical ethnic family band consisting of four men, Reuben and himself and another set of brothers, two neighbor boys. They called themselves "Hal's Bluebirds of Chilton" and got their first regular booking in a dance hall near Potter.[31] The following year the band enlarged to seven members and adopted the name of the Red Raven Orchestra, a title that Duchow undoubtedly felt was more appealing. He formally became the group's manager, and he had his sidemen dress appropriately in red silk shirts.[32] Besides quickly obtaining bookings at local dance halls in Brillion and Appleton, Duchow also got his ensemble to appear on radio, on stations WHBY in Green Bay and later WTAQ in Appleton.[33]

Unlike Gosz in his early career, Duchow became quickly popular with both older and younger generations. This wide popularity was based on the distinctive sound of his band, probably its unique synthesis of old-time dance and modern American ballroom music.[34] He soon realized that to become truly successful his group would have to win a much wider audience beyond east-central Wisconsin, so in the mid-1930s he decided to get out-of-state ballroom bookings, traveling to Iowa, Illinois, and Michigan (but not to Minnesota, which had many Dutchman competitors). He also opened his own Red Raven Inn in Hilbert in March 1938, to assure an added income for himself and his ensemble. And he began to make records, obtaining contracts in 1938 with Victor and in 1940 with Decca, two labels that as we have seen favored Duchow's kind of music. The Red Raven Orchestra cut fourteen pieces for Victor in Chicago in December 1939 and made others for Decca in mid-1940. These selections, such as the familiar "The Jolly Coppersmith," "Green Grove Polka," and the "Clarinet Joy Laendler," were largely taken from the Vitak and Elsnic publications, the major source of the emerging international style. A few were original, such as the "Red Raven Polka."[35]

Those records were actually made by a completely new ensemble, as his old musicians had left him by 1939. His band was not entirely professional; the players probably had other full-time jobs and balked at Duchow's insistence upon extended touring.[36] At any rate, Duchow had little time with his new contingent before he had to interrupt his own career in 1942 and enter the service.[37] When he was discharged in 1945, he knew that if he wished to have more than a local band and reach the largest possible audience, he would have to continue recording, do more extensive touring, and play at the leading ballrooms.[38] He was able to reach his objective, and by the late 1940s he had come close to becoming a national star.

One great boost to his career was getting a regular Wednesday night booking for his reconstituted band between 1947 and 1949 at the famous Trianon Ballroom of the Karsas brothers in Chicago. He was also able to broadcast from there over a major station, WGN, between 1947 and 1949.[39] Another enormously favorable factor was his scoring almost immediately with a hit record, the "Swiss Boy" waltz, which was his own composition in Dutchman style. A newspaper headline told the full story of the piece, "Larry Never Saw the Alps, Doesn't Yodel Well, But His 'Swiss Boy' Wow's 'Em."[40]

The piece was an instantaneous success. One Wausau, Wisconsin, music store reported that it sold 3,000 records of the piece in less than ten days. In New York City, a place the Red Ravens had never visited, fans bought 200,000 copies in one summer month.[41] Duchow also increased his support at home, regularly drawing over two thousand ethnic dancers three nights per week in the late forties at the Appleton (Wisconsin) Cinderella Ballroom.[42]

The peak of the band's success was in 1949, after a huge recorded repertoire of three hundred tunes.[43] A caption to the January 15, 1949, *Billboard Magazine* cover photo of the Red Ravens playing at the Trianon Ballroom in Chicago relayed the stature of both the band and its leader. Duchow was called a "veritable one-man music industry," the "backbone of the music business in the Middle West, though unknown to aficionados of Tommy Dorsey or [swing bands]." It relayed the action in the photo, stating, "Here . . . Duchow and the Red Ravens are moving a long string of players through a folk dance . . . where he introduced Old Timer dances every Wednesday night."[44]

Later that year *Cash Box Music* magazine took a poll to identify the nation's most popular contemporary orchestras, and Duchow ranked rather well. Vaughn Monroe came in first, but Duchow was fifteenth, just behind Spike Jones.[45] A leading popular band critic summed up Duchow's group's role in the continuing craze for ethnic music: "If the current trend to old time dancing continues, it will be spearheaded by the bands of the caliber of Lawrence Duchow and his Red Raven Orchestra."[46] By this time, Duchow's band was a large ensemble similar to the swing and sweet bands, featuring three saxophones, two trumpets, a bass, tuba, drums, piano, and two accordions. Their repertoire was clearly a mix, emphasizing pieces of the international genre, two-steps, polkas and schottisches, but also the leading romantic Tin Pan Alley ballads.[47]

Another localized hotbed of ethnic music in America in the 1930s and 1940s was Cleveland, Ohio, which, like Texas and the upper Midwest, had been a magnet for Central Europeans, especially Czechs and Slovenians, and as noted above had been an early center of brass and concert bands. In the 1920s, even after the larger waves of immigration during the previous decade, Cleveland continued to attract immigrants to its Slavic and German ethnic neighborhoods, and by 1930 the city's various ethnic groups were surprisingly well balanced in population, each numbering between 20,000 and 40,000. These communities were therefore large enough in size to make what sociologists called institutionally complete communities, with churches, volunteer associations of various sorts, newspapers and fraternal associations. They were of course varied in content, including Czechs, Poles, Yugoslavs, Italians, Hungarians, Germans and quite likely Jews and Slovaks.[48] Cleveland's leaders were certainly conscious of this diversity in the ethnic festivals held in the late 1920s, often referring to their city proudly as a highly cosmopolitan community.

This wide variety of substantial ethnic communities was reflected in the area's radio programming, for by 1930 there was considerable nationality broadcasting. The dissemination of many different ethnic cultures over the air obviously promoted those groups' traditional music, but it also may have modified those cultures, for the listening audiences cannot have been totally discrete. Undoubtedly at least a few Czechs must have also tuned into Polish hours and vice versa, and Hungarian to German, Slovak to Slovenian, and so on. The ethnic radio audiences in the 1930s may not have been aware of this interchange, but certainly what began to emerge around 1940 was an indigenous type of ethnic music, a Cleveland style to polka music, which would help make for a new polka craze in America after the first led by the "Beer Barrel Polka" in the late 1930s. This new postwar enthusiasm would be led by Cleveland's own polka bandleader, Frankie Yankovic.

The outstanding contributors to popularizing ethnic music widely over radio in the thirties in Cleveland were two promoters, a Pole,

John Lewandowski, and a Czech, Fred Wolf, along with Czech, Slovenian, and Croatian musicians. Lewandowski, a native of the city, was born there in 1890 and had over the years by 1930 acquired a rather large following among the just over 35,000 Polish foreign-born and other Polish Americans in the ethnic community. This was largely because he often served public and semi-public roles in the city even in his occupations, from streetcar conductor to policeman to real estate operator to city councilman by the mid-1930s.[49] When one adds to this a certain personal charisma he had among his countrymen it is not surprising that he was successful in putting on the first local program of Polish music on WJAY in 1927. And it is understandable that the station urged him to conduct a regular program for his group in 1931. He would continue as a radio host for over two more decades.

By the mid-thirties, several other ethnic radio emcees appeared, so that in the midst of the depression Cleveland probably had the most comprehensive ethnic programming of any locality in the country. With considerable pride in 1935, one newspaper reporter pointed to the twenty-two different language programs carried weekly on three radio stations, mainly WJAY.[50] These programs were all distinguished by the airing of a great deal of ethnic popular music, along with some semi-classical and classical selections. Besides the several programs Lewandowski ran, one of which, the oldest, had run continuously for five years, there was a popular German program that featured all types of that group's music, particularly yodeling; a Slovenian presentation that had been started by host John Grdina in 1931; two programs in Czech by Fred Wolf, one of which featured a ten-piece orchestra; two in Slovak; four in Hungarian; and others in Italian, Croatian, Greek and Yiddish.[51]

Another enormously energetic promoter of Polish ethnic programming in the city was the European-born actor, Paul Faut. He was a trained dramatic artist-singer of several entertainment areas, who switched his attention from drama, which declined in the depression, to music. He cut about one hundred Polish records for Victor in the 1930s and promoted nationality programming in Cleveland and Akron in the 1930s and 1940s. Like Lewandowski, Faut was devoted to Polish culture at several levels, featuring both the folk works, such as polkas and obereks, as well as the more "serious" works.[52]

Ethnic broadcasting in the city by the mid-1930s was probably well organized, not the fragmented activity one might guess from the many distinctive groups. A Nationality Broadcasting Association existed, with Lewandowski as president and Fred Wolf as secretary at that time, and the body offered an award to ethnic broadcasters to assure the quality of the programming. A Slovenian on WGAR won it in 1937.[53] In Cleveland, certainly, ethnic bands had a good opportunity to disseminate their music among their own audience and even outsiders, and with a multi-ethnic radio association, some interethnic influences were certain to have developed between the various programs and music.

The music of two of Cleveland's immigrant groups, the Czechs and the Slovenians, dominated all others in popularity around the 1930s and 1940s. The person most responsible for Bohemian musical leadership was the Czech bandleader and composer, Jerry Mazanec; the individual who was the major creator of Slovenian compositions was Dr. William Lausche.

Mazanec does not quite fit the Robel model of a new-generation ethnic bandleader who borrows heavily from outside the group or uses non-group sources for his compositions. He is not a crossover musician in the sense of so many others in this period. But while he did play only Czech pieces, he did so in a highly original and distinctive manner. By that reputation Mazanec won not only a large Bohemian American audience but a following among non-group members as well—he was a Czech-American or American bandleader, certainly not just a Czech one. Little is known directly of his aims as an ethnic musician, but the few biographical facts available suggest that he aimed his performances at his fellow ethnic-group members. He obtained a position about 1933 in the music department of the Ptak Furniture Company, a Czech enterprise located in the major Bohemian section of the city. He remained there for almost the next forty years, most of his adult life.[54] Mazanec's love, however, was more to play Czech music than to sell it, and about 1934 he organized an ensemble of eight men.

The band grew to be enormously successful, playing first on Sundays at Czech picnics, regularly for eight years on Fred Wolf's Czech radio hour into the early 1940s, and also in person six nights a week at a nightclub, the Golden Goose. By the time Mazanec made records in 1941, the group had taken to calling itself the Golden Goose Orchestra. The band appealed to dancers in particular for its distinctive performances, playing polkas in an unusual staccato style.

The ensemble became so much in demand that at the height of its popularity the advance bookings were several years in length.[55] One can learn what pieces the men played by reviewing the large number of records they made, just over sixty in all, with major labels, first with Columbia in 1941 and 1942 and later with Continental.[56] All of the Columbia cuts were in the Bohemian language.[57] But despite Mazanec's concentration on his own group's musical material, he still was well known beyond the confines of his ethnic community. When his admirers held a day of recognition for him just before his death in September 1982, the Mayor formally proclaimed that day as one all Clevelanders should observe.[58]

The single group that did the most by far to alter Old World music to make it more palatable not only for their own group in America but for Americans in general was the Slovenes. And they did it in their American cultural capital, Cleveland, a city that as we have seen had developed conditions making it particularly fertile ground for a number of well-known regional and occasionally national ethnic bands, specifically Slovenian ensembles. One Slovenian individual stands out in terms of leadership that helped establish Cleveland as a leading American old-time ethnic music center: the composer William Lausche.

The Lausche name is well known to Ohioans, as William's brother, Frank Lausche, became a very popular governor and senator in the post–World War II era. But it was William—Dr. Bill, as he was called—who created much of the musical repertoire that numerous successful polka bands used to make Cleveland a polka capital, including the leading American polka ensemble by mid-century, Frankie Yankovic and his Yanks. Surprisingly, Dr. Bill was not a professional musician; he was by profession a dentist, who simply had a profound attachment for both traditional Slovenian folk songs and contemporary American jazz. He put them together in the late twenties and early thirties, thereby creating the so-called Slovenian (American) style ethnic music.

Until the first years of the 1920s, it did not look like Lausche would become a significant musical figure. His parents, Louis and Marie, were not particularly gifted musically; they both had come to Cleveland as teenagers around 1890, and Louis soon found a job as a sheet-metal worker. Although he died in 1908, when his son William was just ten, he did pass along a manner of living that the latter would follow in his musical activities: an awareness of being ethnic in America, living in two cultures, a traditional and a contemporary one. Louis was a model for his children in the way he functioned as an intermediary and interpreter for the Slovenian immigrants who continued to pour into Cleveland, trying to help them participate in American life as quickly as possible. By the turn of the century the Lausches were providing their countrymen with extensive legal, religious, and social assistance.[59] The family prospered and later put up a building that housed facilities for the immigrants, including a restaurant and newspaper.[60] From his earliest years, William learned about *both* the Slovenian and American worlds, since these were areas in which his parents regularly worked.

As so often was the case, it was William's mother who encouraged her ten children in music. It is not surprising then that the surviving six were musicians.[61] William began taking lessons on the piano in 1908 at age ten and by 1920 had acquired a sound musical education in the Cleveland Slovenian community's rich musical environment. William, however, decided not to become a professional musician, opting for a more stable income; he completed his dental training in 1922.[62]

His greater love was music, however, and he would perform on the piano when he could. He got bookings at nightclubs in and around the city and even assisted, as one might expect, in supporting the city's Dental Society Orchestra. But more significant than his playing was his composing, which combined his knowledge of Slovenian folk music with his passion for the contemporary American idioms, ragtime piano and jazz. The result was that from the mid-twenties on to World War II his enormous number of arrangements and compositions reflected both European and American genres. These Lausche works were really the source of what has been termed the Cleveland "sound," a type of ethnically based music that included sophisticated harmonies, an accelerated tempo, syncopation, and the banjo.[63]

Of course Lausche was not solely responsible for the spread of the new ethnic music in the twenties; Matt Hoyer and others had already been performing and making Slovenian records. Dr. Bill, however, was most responsible for modifying or Americanizing the old Slovenian polka.[64] He became well known not only as a songwriter but also from his instrumental work on radio and record. His major means of disseminating his material was by way of numerous recordings, including many discs on which he provided piano accompaniment for his sister Josephine, who with her friend Mary Udovich did the vocals on Slovenian songs.

The earliest record he made was for Victor late in 1924, immediately after the opening of his group's major cultural center in Cleveland, the Slovenian National Home, an event at which Dr. Bill, Josephine, and her friend performed and later cut four pieces from that presentation. These were Lausche's modernized arrangements of several group songs, among which were "Sirota" (Orphan), and "Na Strunam" (To the Keys).[65] Three years later Columbia called him to New York to record more of his arrangements. Over nine sessions from 1927 to 1932, he cut about sixty pieces with his sister's duet and a New York orchestra.[66] Lausche was extremely prolific, continuing to compose and record, especially for Continental Records in the early 1940s. He wrote his last piece, a waltz, in 1967, the year of his death.[67]

Lausche also appeared often on radio. He and his sister were well-known participants on John Grdina's Slovenian hour from 1932, and in the late 1930s he occasionally led small combos on other ethnic programs on WGAR.[68] His most popular arrangements and compositions were his theme song, "Ko Pridem Skozi Log" (Walking in the Valley), "Na Gremko Domov" (We Won't Go Home Polka), which was later recorded as "Sondra's Polka," "Ljubca" (My Sweetheart Polka), "Snowflake Polka," written about 1930, "Greenleaf Polka," "Johnny Cake (or Slovene) Polka" (circa 1942), "The Hunter," and his two original and most popular hits, "Cleveland, the Polka Town," and "The Girl I Left Behind" (Nebom Se Mosila).[69] These pieces really constituted the core of the Slovenian American ethnic repertoire.

Lausche's legacy was even more significant than might be suggested by his imaginative style or the large number of his compositions. As the popularity of his work among Slovenian musicians suggests, he had a formative influence on others, especially the several important Slovenian American bandleaders who in the years up to and following World War II constituted a major part of the Cleveland polka community. These musicians included Johnny Vadnal, Lou Trebar, Eddie Habat, Pete Sokach, the Croatian Kenny Bass, Frankie Yankovic, and above all the bandleader the city respected and loved the most, accordionist Johnny Pecon.[70]

Pecon developed as a musician directly under Lausche's tutelage.

Like his mentor and other crossover leaders of his day, he pulled together traditional ethnic and contemporary American characteristics, joining the traditional melodies with the ragtime-jazz idiom. Pecon's association with Lausche began early and continued throughout the latter's life. The families had probably known one another even before Pecon was born in 1915.[71] Pecon's father had been a musician, a chromatic accordionist, and before he died in 1933 the youngster had spent much time at the Lausche home, learning Dr. Bill's compositions, which he undoubtedly played at various private affairs.

By the late 1930s Pecon had formed his own band and also played often with his friend Lou Trebar and Trebar's ensemble, in East Cleveland locations, at Tino's Bar and the Twilight Ballroom, both in the Slovenian Saint Clair Avenue district in northeast Cleveland. Trebar too had been associated with the famous dentist-composer, playing with him on Slovenian Hours on WJAY in 1929. He had been a part of the famous Hoyer Trio in the early 1930s and was again on radio from about 1934 to 1939 on Antoncic's Slovenian Hour on WGAR.[72] He probably did some of the latter appearances with Pecon.

When Lausche obtained a new recording contract with Continental in 1941 or 1942 for an instrumental trio, he featured Pecon as accordionist.[73] Just about then, a Slovenian radio personality introduced Pecon to Joe Sodja, who like him was broadening Lausche's music with a distinctive virtuosity on the banjo.[74] Although Pecon had to suspend his professional career for four years beginning in 1942, when he left for service as a Seabee in the U.S. Navy, soon after he returned he experienced a surge in his reputation and income, becoming a national star working at first with Yankovic and later making his own hit recordings, as will be discussed below.

Johnny Vadnal, another well-known musician whose style was similar to Pecon's, also synthesized Slovenian-based music with the contemporary American genres and appealed in particular to the same audience that Pecon did, young people in their late teens and early twenties.[75] Vadnal's mother, Anna, as so often is the case, was responsible for the formation of a family quartet in 1935. She encouraged the eldest of her four sons, Tony, the seventeen-year-old violinist who served as leader of the group, and John, the youngest at twelve, the accordionist. The size of the band fluctuated over the next few years from a quintet to a trio.[76] When two of the brothers joined the service, Johnny Vadnal formed his own ensemble, which became a hit just after the war, especially after making records for RCA Victor. He cut about one hundred 78s with them up to the early fifties, including some of Lausche's compositions and his popular theme, "Wayside Polka." Other popular discs were "Slap Happy Polka" and his biggest seller, "Yes Dear Waltz," which it was claimed sold 50,000 in the first week.[77] From the nearly universal use of English language titles of the pieces he played, the large numbers he drew to personal performances—often as many as fifteen hundred at the Bowl Ballroom on the city's south side in the late 1940s—his popular radio work over the Mutual network, his being named Cleveland polka king in 1949 and Midwest champion at a 1953 Grand Rapids, Michigan, contest, and above all his particular appeal to teenagers, Vadnal was indeed a leading crossover bandleader, popular among a variety of fans, old and young Slovenians as well as polka enthusiasts in general.[78]

Another important polka music maker of the time was Kenny Bass, a bandleader and well-known radio and television disc jockey, whose impact extended beyond performing for the local polka audience into an important role in the communications media. Bass, whose real name was Peter Bastasic, was of Croatian rather than Slovenian descent. He grew up in the late 1920s in the Collinwood section of the city, which was the training ground for so many of Cleveland's ethnic bandleaders, where he was a relatively unknown guitar player in the years prior to World War II. He became prominent after he changed his instrument to string bass and joined the well-known Eddie Habat–Pete Sokach "Tune Mixers" when they began early in 1948. Habat, also a Collinwood product indebted musically to Lausche, maintained a two-year association with Sokach that was best known for their hit Decca records, "Socialaires Polka" and "Blue Skirt Waltz," on which Bass was the bass player.[79] During this time, Bass, who was well aware of the large number of other eastern and southern Europeans in Cleveland, was encouraged by a Croatian friend in the music business to broaden his audience. He anglicized his name, became a leading polka disc jockey over station WSRS, and formed his own general ethnic band, the Polka Poppers, all by the end of 1950. He also formed his own music publishing company and made records of a multi-ethnic or generalized American character.[80] Like Vadnal, Bass's multi-ethnic appeal and crossover character were rather obvious. He also was named Midwest

Polka King in 1951, and the hundreds of polka-style records he made for Coral, Decca, and Roulette labels then and later indicated a wide multi- or even non-ethnic following. In fact, his most popular discs were the generalized American ethnic polka hits, "My Polka Lovin' Gal" and "Lake Erie Polka."[81]

In addition to the statistics and other details that confirm the broad appeal of these polka bands in the years just prior to, during and after World War II, fragmentary evidence suggests that in Cleveland both the older and younger generations were polka enthusiasts. One observer described the extraordinary effect of Johnny Pecon's music on dancers, in words that must certainly apply to the audiences of Sodja, Vadnal, Habat, Bass, and the others as well. Recalling those years from his vantage point in 1973, the writer suggests the psychological exhilaration that polka music in general and Pecon's band in particular produced among listeners and dancers of all ages: "As a child . . . I remember the fascination with which I and perhaps my playmates would listen and be thrilled by the accordionist playing at some festive occasion, a wedding or maybe a christening to which our parents took us. . . . The beauty of the bass [notes] produced a heady intoxication, accentuated by the rhythmic sagging of the wooden floor of some little hall rented for the occasion, as the dancers twirling and stomping gave flesh and blood to the music." He added that the melodies affected listeners especially deeply, "so melodious that we could hardly contain ourselves. Such are the fantasies conjured up in my mind as I listen today to a Johnny Pecon record."

The writer went on to indicate how Pecon's music reminded them of the beauty of the Old Country and thereby pulled the generations together:

The music of Pecon brings me to the rolling hills . . . of Slovenia. The country music of Slovenes is outdoors music, striving for distant echoes among the hills and valleys. Certainly this is music from the soil emerging as with a kind of love affair with the Slovenian planincas going back centuries. To a [serious non-Slovenian music lover], this music is perhaps trivial . . . in a Bach-Wagnerian context more like yodeling is to singing. But an Alpine soul surely stirred by a beautiful rendering of a mountain song ingenuously trilled with a yodel or a soft-as-rain voice from . . . far off—and Beethoven must wait a bit . . . at those all-Slovenian dances and picnics or an old fashioned wedding.

And he concluded: "The accordion player inspired by the ambience of gaiety . . . reaches newly created heights of euphoria, so that some dancing swain is transcended to vriskat[,] that special cock-crowing hoot that can come out only when one is possessed by a demon of pleasure. [When one plays Pecon records, one finds] in that music for that moment [that] there is pleasure enough. Play that muska Krajnska[,] Johnny! Play, Play, Play and may you live forever."[82]

Illustrating the increasingly multi-ethnic character of polka music in Cleveland during these years is a 1969 statement by Jerry Bukac, a prominent Bohemian polka musician and radio disc jockey.[83] Bukac, known as "Mr. Bohemian," offered fervent support and enthusiasm for the music of other groups, undoubtedly expressing the sentiments of many other polka-lovers and revealing the existence of a multi- or inter-ethnic audience for local ethnic music from whatever group it came. Bukac spoke, appropriately enough, at a Czech festival held at a Slovenian National Home in the metropolitan area:

I love all music whether it's Polish, Slovenian, German, Ukrainian—it makes no difference. I love all the nationality bands and I think they're all tremendous. I always said a lot of times on my program, why can't we get united and have more of these affairs? What's the difference if you're Bohemian or Polish or Rushian [*sic*] or Italian? If we were all the same and liked one kind of polka, that wouldn't be any fun! It takes *all* the nationality polkas to love. And when I'd say there's gonna be an affair and somebody says, "Are you goin' Jer?" I'd say "sure." "But that's so-and-so language," and I'd say, "I don't care! It's music that I *love* and I *will* be there!"[84]

9

Americanized Scandinavian and Polish Bands: New York and the East, 1930-1960

The third major area of considerable ethnic musical activity in the quarter-century after the depression was the northeastern United States, the region extending from Philadelphia and eastern Pennsylvania through New York City and on into New England. The prominent ethnic bands from this area tended naturally to reflect the people who had settled in this highly culturally diverse region. Although a comprehensive survey of ethnic bands there is impossible, two nationalities stand out as having produced and commercialized a substantial amount of their music in the three decades before 1960. Those groups are the Scandinavians and the Poles.

This commercialization involved a change in their music, the nature and impetus of which might be termed Americanization. Because ethnic populations in the Northeast were much larger and more concentrated than elsewhere into nearly self-sufficient communities, ethnic musical ensembles tended to be more group-centered. Hence, there appeared to be fewer crossover bands than in the Midwest or Texas. One would be unlikely, for example, to find a group of musicians in the New York metropolitan area in the thirties and forties like the highly versatile Viking Accordion Band of Albert Lea, Minnesota, playing a combination of Italian, Irish, Slavic, and German selections.

But even though leading ethnic bands of the Northeast may not have borrowed music from other groups, they nonetheless did not retain totally traditional repertoires. Scandinavian and Polish musicians produced many new and original works, some based on the group members' American experience but all still related more or less to traditional musical forms. Another form of Americanization was related to the way in which that music was played, which adopted a performance and instrumentation model based on American mainstream dance bands. In fact, little difference existed between the typical American ensembles in the area hotels and ballrooms and the various Polish and Scandinavian musical bodies.[1]

Among the many reasons for the particular attractiveness of modern band instrumentation probably the most significant was the distinctive pervasiveness of mass communication in this most highly urbanized region. Radio coverage was particularly thorough in the New York metropolitan area in the thirties and forties, and the region was also the center of the nation's radio and record industries. The national media's promotion of mainstream orchestras undoubtedly helped to transform and assimilate at least in part the small, folk ethnic ensembles that had typified so much ethnic music around World War I. There was a new generation of ethnic bands emerging in the 1920s, many more and different instrumentalists, developing roles for the more modern reed and brass instruments and more conspicuous places for drums and piano. The piano accordion was becoming more important than the button box-concertina or button accordion of the past.

Ethnic radio was an important catalyst helping to stamp ethnic music with mainstream musical influences and to widely disseminate that new kind of music. More outlets offering ethnic material probably existed in this region than anywhere else, and from the very beginning of the depression such nationality material on the air was widespread and easily accessible. A few stations actually specialized in ethnic broadcasting, of which ethnic music was a significant part of the programming. After the collapse of the recording industry in the early thirties, radio replaced phonograph records as the major disseminator of music, ethnic music included.[2] The number of area stations broadcasting ethnic music, news, and entertainment grew throughout the 1930s and became widely accessible as sales of radio sets continued; by 1938, about 82 percent of the nation's families had radios.[3]

Of the earliest stations to broadcast in a foreign language, certainly the best known was WEVD in New York City, begun in 1927 by Yiddish Socialists. Like several others later it proclaimed itself "the station that speaks your language."[4] WOV, also in New York, was established a year earlier and by the mid-1930s was offering programs in the Italian language only.[5] WHOM was begun in 1920 in Jersey City as a station that "specialized" in foreign language programming. Although it is unclear just when WBNX in the Bronx adopted its slogan similar to WEVD, "The Radio That Speaks Your Language," and WFAB in New York its motto, "The Voice of the Foreign Languages," the stations went on the air in 1927 and 1930 respectively and likely followed that policy soon after those dates.[6] WBNX stands out in particular, for by the start of World War II if not earlier, one could describe it as essentially a multi-ethnic station. It had a rather strong signal for a radio outlet of its sort then, around 5,000 watts, with a great variety of programs of ethnic music, news, and entertainment presented by a host of different ethnic announcers—Ukrainian, Lithuanian, Armenian, Italian, and Polish, among others. A Polish musician played ethnic music as its staff accordionist in the early 1940s.[7]

Like Lewandowski in Cleveland, New York had its dean of Polish radiomen as well. He was Michael Kecki, who with his wife, Natalie, worked on several stations and promoted Polish music, which for more than half a century beginning in 1933 they and their guests often played live. Kecki's early work was over WWRL on Long Island, and then for 15 years until 1949 he broadcast over WHOM. Later he and his wife ran their "Voice of Polonia" on WHLD and WWOL (Manhattan, later called WLIB).[8] The Keckis, of course, were hardly unique as ethnic broadcasters; it is quite likely and can be assumed that all the stations they worked for offered programming for other nationalities as well.

In Pennsylvania ethnic programming was also quite common prior to World War II. It began in Philadelphia with occasional programming before 1930 and regular daily programs after that date, over WRAX in Italian, German, Yiddish, and Polish.[9] By 1939 other stations in the city, WDAS and WPEN in particular, announced in the major trade publication that they either issued or solicited ethnic material.[10] A Wilkes-Barre outlet, WBRE, followed the same policy at the time, with a special interest in Polish and Italian material. One of the strongest stations in the northeast part of Pennsylvania was WSCR in Scranton, which accepted ethnic programs.[11] It in fact had an Italian couple on its staff, Angelo and Rose Fiorani, who produced Italian programs that were aired there and on WBRE and WEEU, Reading, and possibly at other stations in the mid-thirties.[12]

New England also had stations which broadcast in foreign languages from the start of the depression. WCOP and WHDH in Boston offered Italian programming and probably other group fare as early as 1932, and WUNR had a Polish half-hour as early as 1936 and has continued to broadcast polka and popular music along with community news down to the present.[13] In Connecticut in 1939 three outlets listed themselves as welcoming "foreign accounts": WTHT, Hartford, which was broadcasting a regular Polish program, WELI, which was offering some of its fare in Italian and Polish, and WBRY, Waterbury–New Haven.[14]

With good radio programming and wide geographic coverage in the 1930s in the Northeast, the dissemination of ethnic music was further served with records by 1940 and especially afterward. As noted, Decca and jukeboxes did a great deal to resuscitate music on discs in the 1930s, and sales for the industry quadrupled to $26 million in the four years before 1938. The major labels, Victor and Columbia, began again to issue ethnic musical records in good number. However, these labels did so reluctantly, and much of the music on their ethnic lists consisted of reissues of older records; by the mid-forties these major companies were no longer cutting much new ethnic material, though they readily offered contracts to the more highly Americanized ethnic bands, as noted in the case of Romy Gosz on Mercury, Duchow on Victor, Pecon on Capitol, and many others on the persistent Decca.[15] By 1952 Columbia and Victor gave up on their ethnic series entirely.[16]

Despite the waning interest of the major labels, beginning in the mid-1940s the Northeast and the nation were well served by new recording companies issuing ethnic material. A host of new smaller record firms concentrated around New York, each of them usually focusing on the music of a single ethnic group. They still catered to ethnic demands and numbered in the hundreds, thereby extending opportunities to eastern musicians in particular. One incomplete list cited about 150 ethnic labels, about one-fifth in the metropolitan New York area, especially the larger ones, such as Balkan, Continental, Scandinavia, Standard, Harmonia, Banner, and Dana.[17] A few of these labels, including Continental and Dana, also tried with occasional success to compete in the general popular market as well. Leaders of this new rank of recording companies helped substantially—in fact were critical—in making and keeping ethnic music popular among both group and non-group members.

The founder of Continental had the insight into popular music that Jack Kapp did a decade earlier. Donald Gabor had come from Hungary in 1938 and got a job with RCA Victor, working his way up to a position as manager in the vast foreign-language department under Tetos Demetriades, a Greek who had made ethnic records earlier for the company. Noting Victor's flagging interest in the genre but also realizing the continuing demand for all types of ethnic music, especially the six hundred radio stations seeking foreign music records, he decided to begin a company to satisfy that demand. He also saw a need for an inexpensive label for light classics and semi-classical works. In 1946, he purchased Continental with a loan from Demetriades, and he later established a second label, Remington in 1950, to bring out inexpensive editions of the classics. The result was a highly successful enterprise by mid-century.[18] Apparently as a result of his own interest in the field and seeing his protege's achievement, Demetriades decided to strike out for himself and begin a recording firm in the mid-forties.[19] He founded still another new label, Standard International, a firm that offered an enormously varied musical list from seventeen ethnic groups, especially Scandinavian, Slavic, and German music.[20]

A third and possibly even more successful example of the new postwar ethnic recording companies was the Dana label. Walter Dana like Gabor had spent most of his early career in Europe, in his case in Poland, as a trained pianist, composer, and impresario of a singing group, Chor Dana, which toured the U.S. in 1936. He settled here permanently just after the war broke out in 1940 and did radio work in Detroit, reestablishing his chorus, who sang and even recorded a variety of Polish popular and art songs for Harmonia and Victor. Late in 1945, apparently sensing the same need that Gabor did, he started his company and began recording mostly Polish musicians and singers. But he also cut other international-style records and even contracted popular artists such as Larry Clinton and Ray Bloch. By 1952 *Billboard* magazine ranked his company third in income just behind the majors, Victor and Columbia.[21]

These various new labels, then, were meeting a felt demand among a large segment of the mid-century American audience. But more precisely how they prospered and helped to popularize New York ethnic entertainers can best be seen by looking at some of the leading musicians in two of the more active ethnic communities, the Scandinavians and the Poles.

One of the earliest popular Swedish instrumentalists was Eric Olzen, a composer-accordionist who while spending much time in

Europe switched to a more American instrument when he settled here.[22] Born in Sweden in 1895, as a boy he learned to play the chromatic accordion. He came to America as a teenager and soon decided on a musical career, at first as chiefly a classical musician with his ten-man orchestra. Just before World War I he shifted to playing the piano accordion. After returning to Sweden he came back to America in the mid-1920s, switched more to popular pieces, opened a music school for his instrument in Brooklyn in 1926, which became one of the largest in the country, and began publishing his own sheet music in the early 1930s, with such compositions as "In the Hay Loft," "Koster Waltz," and "Sunbeam Polka." He was well known among local Scandinavians in the mid-1930s for his Saturday morning radio show on WBBC in New York.[23] He made around two hundred records of various genres for the leading labels in the twenty years following World War I.[24]

A similar entertainer, though younger and more Americanized and hence more popular by the late 1930s, was Eddie Jahrl. He, too, was a Swedish accordionist who settled with his family in Hartford as a teenager in 1916. He moved to New York soon after, when he realized that he would have greater opportunities there as a musician. After touring with vaudeville for a while, he switched to folk and popular recording and performance of polkas, waltzes, and schottisches particularly, at the urging of the head of the foreign department of Columbia Records.[25] He recorded fifty records for that label by 1934, one of which, "Gukvalsen" (Cuckoos' Waltz), sold an estimated 100,000 copies.[26] He later won a contract with Victor, opened a music business in 1937, the Scandinavian Music House, and in World War II moved to Manhattan and joined in the new wave of ethnic recording companies. His two ventures, Scandinavia and Cordion, offered pieces by Olzen and other group musicians. He was especially popular in the 1940s, as he often appeared on two New York stations, WBBC and WBYN.

Jahrl's orchestra, the North Capers, was rather distinctive and ethnically synthetic in its offerings. The ensemble was composed of a mixture of modern and traditional instruments. Even when rendering ethnic music, Jahrl used a guitar, xylophone, and tuba along with the traditional violin and accordion.[27] Certainly, the sounds offered by Olzen and Jahrl from the mid-1930s were closer to the swing bands of the era than to the older compositions of the Olle i Skratthult troupe, which was breaking up just about that time.

Far and away the most popular Scandinavian performer of this era was located in New York; that was the female Finnish American accordionist, Viola Turpeinen, whose major career spanned the thirties and forties. On the surface she was like the many other specifically ethnic performers of the previous era, such as Olle i Skratthult, Eduardo Migliaccio, and Aaron Lebedeff, restricting her playing to works from her own Finnish traditions. Like her fellow Finnish entertainer, Arthur Kylander, she played works that certainly forged her listeners into a more homogeneous ethnic community. Working mostly out of New York but touring major Finnish colonies from Fitchburg, Massachusetts, to Astoria, Oregon, she certainly won an enormously enthusiastic following from her countrymen, who loved to listen to and especially dance at her performances. Yet Turpeinen was also a crossover musician, a characteristic which made her stand out distinctively from the many other Finnish American performers. One must remember that she was basically a dance musician, not a singer, so it was less necessary for her audience to understand her music linguistically. Her fans based their support on her accordion playing, not only as a virtuoso but also as an instrumentalist with a phenomenal ability to convey the spirit of her dance pieces, the polkas, waltzes and schottisches.

To be sure, all Finnish Americans knew and loved her music, but what is probably less known is the great impact she had on both her own cohort of American-born Finns and Americans who were not of Finnish descent. This broader appeal far beyond the traditional immigrant audience was due to what she played. Again, she stood out from her group contemporaries, such as Kylander and Salomaa, for her appeal was not for her songs or ballads but simply her playing for dancing. Her audience did not need to know the foreign language. Although she played exclusively in Finn Halls in the major Finnish American mining, lumber, and farm communities of the Upper Peninsula of Michigan, Wisconsin, and Minnesota, it is plausible to assume that Italians, Slavs, and other Americans from those areas, passionate for dancing, attended her performances. Hence, in the Finnish American regions she was likely as popular with non-Finns as she was with Finnish Americans![28]

Hence Turpeinen was much more of a crossover musician than her contemporaries—not in borrowing from others but in encouraging her multi- and non-ethnic American-born audience in their enthusiasm for the international ethnic dance music in the thirties and beyond. It certainly is ironic that while some Finnish Americans remember Turpeinen for providing them with an American ethnic identity she was also Americanizing them less self-consciously by popularizing the nation's pastime of international ethnic dance. Obviously, environmental and historical factors, her family and musical colleagues as well as her innate talent, all helped make her legendary reputation.[29]

Turpeinen was born November 15, 1909, and grew up in Champion, Michigan, in the heavily Finnish region of the Upper Peninsula—at the right time and place, certainly, for her later career.[30] She was the eldest of three daughters of an immigrant father. They moved shortly afterward to another heavily ethnic community, Iron River. The timing of her arrival was fortuitous, for it came near the start of the golden age of Finnish American music, the period just prior to and following World War I, an era of a large number of ethnic bands, a plethora of ethnic recordings, and the common construction and use of group halls around the country for musical entertainment. Turpeinen's own parents and other relatives were definite contributors to that era, as a number of them were highly musical, especially on the button accordion. The young Viola particularly admired one of her uncles, who was boarding with the family and whom she loved to hear play.[31] Seeing their daughter's interest and recognizing her talent, the parents arranged that she be given lessons by a number of local Italian instructors. This was the start of the Turpeinen's long association with Italian teachers whom she realized were masters of the piano accordion, the instrument she became devoted to. By the early twenties, as a young teenager, Turpeinen was already playing in public at *both* the local Finnish and Italian halls.[32]

Having been taught by Italians and playing at that group's major entertainment center, the young musician easily acquired fans among that group as well as her own. Certainly her love of Italian music was no secret. She occasionally would even play works from Italian opera along with popular Finnish tunes.[33] In the mid-twenties she gained a promoter, John Rosendahl, a Finnish comic-violinist-entertainer, and with a third musician, Antti (Andrew) Kosola, they moved to Chicago and toured the upper Midwest. But soon wishing to become totally professional by playing to a larger local Finnish audience, the small company transferred to New York City in 1927. There they found more opportunities, and Turpeinen was also able to further develop her talent at the nation's leading accordion school,

Pietro Deiro's Excelsior academy, where she became associated with the leading instrumentalists in the country, including the great Deiro himself, Frank Gaviani, Arvid Franzen, and the other Scandinavian and Italian virtuosi in the city. Turpeinen's most famous photograph was made at this time, showing her promoting an Excelsior accordion, the manufacturer with which her mentor, Deiro, was also associated.

While Turpeinen was furthering her art professionally, John Rosendahl was able to obtain many lucrative bookings for the trio. As was so often the case with this new generation of ethnic entertainers, even in the depths of the depression the troupe prospered. Even Rosendahl's premature accidental death in 1933 did not diminish the fortunes of the Turpeinen ensemble. Other talented musicians had more than filled his place. Another female musician from the Upper Peninsula, Sylvia Polso, had joined them in New York even before Rosendahl's passing. She became popular also, given the nickname, the "Greta Garbo of the Accordion."[34] Another associate was the imaginative William Syrala, a popular drummer and cornetist who was also a composer. He married Viola in 1933 in an elaborate musical ceremony attended by many accordion virtuosos.

When Turpeinen and Rosendahl first arrived in Harlem in 1927 because of Rosendahl's efforts, the group's performances included occasional comic skits. Later they dropped the dramatic presentations and simply gave dance performances. They were able to obtain many and even regular bookings at a number of leading numerous Finnish halls in the metropolitan area, including the Raivaaja, the Ribaya, and the largest one in America, the Labor Temple at Fifth Avenue and 126th Street, along with other houses in Brooklyn and Jersey City.[35] Again it is likely that the troupe played for some non-Finns as well as their own, since they also got bookings at non-group locations, including the Metropolitan Ballroom and the Polish Hall in Manhattan in the 1930s.[36]

Beside their success at these numerous in-person performances, the Turpeinen ensemble also won a larger audience immediately by cutting records—especially for the major labels, Victor and Columbia. She recorded over one hundred tunes in all, continually from the late 1920s through the 1930s; she cut about half of her entire recorded material for about ten years after 1946 with Tetos Demetriades's Standard International.[37]

Turpeinen and Rosendahl cut six pieces for Victor in January

1928, which showed her virtuosity. These works, including "Kau-haven Polka" and "Emma Valssi," helped substantially in making her famous.[38] Over the next three years the ensemble recorded thir-teen records for Columbia and Victor, all Finnish pieces, some of which were Turpeinen solos and others with Polso. Turpeinen oddly did not obtain a regular radio program of her own, although given her popularity similar to other ethnic stars, she certainly could have. Still, she did make a highly successful appearance in reaching a Fin-nish American audience on a major program of the decade, Major Bowes' Amateur Hour in April 1936.[39]

Her major medium, however, was appearing in person locally, nationally, and internationally on tour. After a highly successful trip to Finland and Scandinavia, setting attendance records there in the early thirties, another boost to Turpeinen's legendary status among Finnish Americans was her touring Finnish American colonies coast to coast for most of her career, even into the 1950s, after she moved to Florida. The typical itinerary would begin on July 4 in Fitchburg, Massachusetts; then on to Ohio; to Turpeinen's home region, the Upper Peninsula and the upper Midwest; to Red Lodge and Butte, Montana; to Washington and occasionally California, even Los An-geles; and finally home to northern New Jersey.[40] The Finns, of course, especially those associated with temperance and socialist movements, had built community recreational structures, where Tur-peinen was booked, such as the Hancock, Michigan, Labor Hall; Unity Hall in Escanaba; the People's Hall in Bessemer; and the Lib-erty Hall in Marquette. Most of her performances were for dancing, and the admission in the thirties was normally what the patrons, virtually all working-class farmers, lumbermen, and mineworkers, could afford, usually 50 cents for men and 25 cents for women. The dancing would usually begin about 8 P.M.[41]

According to two testimonials, Turpeinen's troupe's annual visits were events to which children as well as adults looked forward. As a Newberry, Michigan, enthusiast described it, despite the formal community policy against dancing, dances would be held weekly at the local Finn Hall with a local accordionist playing the usual polkas and waltzes in front of the stage. It was there at the dance that children learned the steps, girls with greater enthusiasm than boys. In any event the hall's stage was always "reserved for celebrities such as Viola Turpeinen," who came by on tour.[42] A woman who grew up in the Finnish colony at Hubbardstown, Massachusetts, remembered the large crowds that Saturday night dances attracted in the early thirties in the region as each of the neighboring Finnish towns alternated holding the event. Parents always brought their children with them to the dance hall, known in Hubbardstown as Farmer's Hall, thereby exciting all generations. Turpeinen's annual July visit and performance was the major social event of the year.[43]

Perhaps the best proof of the extraordinary effect of Turpeinen's playing on audiences of all ages is the fact that another well-known Finnish American entertainer cut a record about one of her dance-hall performances. The piece is entitled "Tanssit Kiipilla," recorded by Antti Syrjaniemi in 1928 on Victor V-4040, about Turpeinen's playing at Cape Ann, Massachusetts. As Syrjaniemi described the event, the dancers became so exhilarated from the way they moved their feet that many thought it was a wonder they survived the occasion at all. The effect on people of all ages was magical. Grandparents became limber, and young and old became delirious. Seldom had anyone seen such a joyous occasion. The piece concluded, "And the girl played like a heavenly bell."[44] Her audience regarded her as a cherished visitor, as she often stopped at private homes for a sauna or other form of ethnic hospitality.[45] As one observer summed up, she was "*the* dance musician of her ethnic community."[46] Her fans nearly deified her—some Finnish Americans felt she gave them a new sense of themselves—and the saying went, while the old country may have its Sibelius, "we have our Viola Turpeinen."[47]

Certainly Viola Turpeinen was not the only popular Finnish American entertainer of her time; there were others such as Hannes Laine, another popular accordionist and Walter Toppila, a xylophonist, who also made records, filled dance halls, and generally appealed to all generations.[48] But what made her career outstanding was that from her New York headquarters in the depression, Turpeinen was able to widen the appeal of her ethnic music among not only a variety of Finnish-Americans but also all Americans.

Polish American musicians in the greater New York metropolitan area were bringing about a similar form of Americanization in this period from about 1930 to mid-century. Certainly a much larger number of them than Scandinavians had settled in that region, which extended from eastern Pennsylvania into southern New England. Estimates of their communities in the 1920s show about one-quarter million in New York City and Philadelphia and many more in outlying areas. They were of the blue-collar class in the interwar period, miners and laborers in the anthracite fields of Scranton, Wilkes-Barre, and Hazleton, textile and refinery workers of Paterson, Passaic, and Bayonne, slaughterhouse workers in Brooklyn, unskilled and semi-skilled operatives of the many factory towns of Connecticut, Rhode Island, and western Massachusetts, such as Bridgeport, New Britain, Waterbury, Springfield, and Chicopee, and truck farmers of western Long Island and the Connecticut River valley and around Deerfield and Sunderland, Massachusetts. Like many other groups, such as the Finns, by 1930 these immigrants had centered much of their social and recreational life around their fraternal halls, often called Dom Polski, their Polish National Homes, although they also attended their dances in more public, commercial ballrooms as well.

And indeed like the Midwestern Germans and Czechs, Polish Americans, too, had a vital place in their lives for music and dance, especially the polka, waltz, and oberek. Thus in their Polonia settlements, they supported a large number of their own musicians, individually and organized in local bands. But support was unusually imbalanced: despite the fact that most Polish Americans lived in the Midwest, from Buffalo and Pittsburgh westward through Cleveland, Detroit, Chicago, Milwaukee, and Omaha, most major Polonia orchestras and their distinctive musical idiom emerged from the Northeast, the Middle Atlantic region in the 1930s and 1940s. That type of music is known as the eastern style of Polish "polka" music.

One will recall that up to the mid-1920s, it had been the *wiejska* (village-style) music that dominated Polonia, a music that featured violin and bass playing in compositions of a generally slow tempo. This type of music was very close to the traditional folk music that had been promoted by the Chicago Sajewski firm, recorded in the earliest records, and encouraged by musicians such as Dukla around World War I. Some Chicago Polish musicians would continue to appear on record later, but clearly none was as significant as the eastern-style bandleaders in the thirties, forties, and fifties.[49] A modification of that earlier village style would reappear from Chicago-style roots at mid-century and later, with the dramatic emergence of "L'il Wally" (Władziu Jagiello) and his more traditional, folklike vocals and simpler instrumentation.

Still, for the quarter-century after the depression the popular music that captivated Polish America was that played by the several leading eastern bands. These were such figures as Brunon Kryger and Ignacy Podgorski of eastern Pennsylvania; Ed Krolikowski, Walt Solek, and above all Frank Wojnarowski of Connecticut, Jan Robak and Jozef Lazarz of Massachusetts, and Bernie Witkowski and Ted Maksymowicz of the New York City area. Their advantage over their western colleagues in dominating Polonia music was in part due to their being located near New York, the city that then had much control of the national media, both print and electronic.

These men played a music that was particularly Polish American, tunes in both English and the ancestral language with instrumentation similar to non-Polish bands. Such a repertoire obviously would appeal to a more Americanized clientele, an audience that was increasingly American born and more familiar with mainstream popular music. As with the newer German, Czech, and Scandinavian American entertainers discussed previously, these more recent Polish American bands of the east sounded very much like the contemporary ballroom bands of their day. They were usually larger than the previous generation of ethnic bands, numbering around ten members or more, and they heavily favored the instruments of greater volume, such as the virtuoso clarinet, accordion, drums, and brass, instead of the formerly dominant strings. Their music also contained considerably more improvisation, with more vocals and original composition. Finally, they commonly used English in titles and heavily in the text of their pieces.[50] It is also important to understand that most of these eastern bandleaders were not amateur folk musicians but had been well-schooled in their art in America, if not Europe. Thus, they were likely aware of their modification and alteration of traditional tunes.

Like so many other immigrant entertainers, many of these bandsmen wrote entirely original pieces based on their listeners' own American experience. Thus it is not surprising that this new eastern style would appeal in particular to the younger generation of Polish Americans, those born in the United States after World War I. While this type of music had roots in the keyboard polka of European urban centers, its reflection of features from popular contemporary American music earns it consideration as a sort of crossover cultural phenomenon. Some non-Polish Americans undoubtedly knew of these easterners because they played often, though not exclusively, in public theaters and ballrooms outside their own community. But wherever they performed, they certainly helped their audience accept and support all kinds of polka music as mainstream popular music.[51]

Probably the pioneer and founder of this more assimilated eastern style was Edward Krolikowski. Regardless of his strong Polish ancestry and ethnic identity—he was in fact a local Polonia leader—he was no ghetto individual. He was also familiar and dealt with the dominant Anglo-American culture throughout his life. He was not only an ethnic musician and bandleader but also a shrewd businessman who in those hard times of the thirties understood the practical value of building an audience wider than his own people. He knew the benefits of dealing with the entire multi-cultural population of his hometown, Bridgeport, Connecticut. More than his Polish musical colleagues, Krolikowski dealt directly and intimately with both the American and ethnic non-Polish communities.

Krolikowski was a second-generation Polish American, born of immigrant parents in the heavily industrial and highly diverse ethnic city of Bridgeport, in either 1892 or 1893.[52] His mother and father were both musically inclined, and when they decided to return to Poland in 1903, Krolikowski entered the Warsaw Conservatory to become a concert violinist. His early education also included learning six languages and, like that of "Skipper" Berg of the Viking Accordion Band, considerable business training. His background in both languages and commerce would be of great help to him when he later set up his own firm.[53] When the family returned to the United States in 1908, settling at first in New York, the young man first tried a religious vocation but quickly took up music, playing in several musical ensembles.

In his early twenties Krolikowski finally decided to strike off on his own by forming a band and going far out of town, traveling with his musical group through the American South. It is important to understand that in these years around World War I, the young bandleader was obviously learning about American culture visiting areas unfamiliar to Slavic Americans and playing popular contemporary music, jazz, and the like. He returned to Bridgeport in 1920 and with his mother's help opened a music store a year later. His merchandise consisted of both various ethnic and contemporary American sheet music, piano rolls, records, and phonographs. The venture turned out rather well in a short time, in large part because of Krolikowski's fluency in six languages.[54] His stock in the late thirties was the largest of any music store in the state.[55]

Krolikowski formed his first band in the early 1920s, but it was not an ethnic ensemble. He played at vaudeville theaters and private affairs and played little if any ethnic music until 1928, when, with the prospect of a large family to support and thus a need for an assured income, he decided to form a polka band.[56] His initial prospects were promising, and he was able to get his men onto radio the next year on WICC. As a businessman running a growing music store, he was able to get good support and the sponsorship of other local Polish businessmen.[57]

Eventually he and his band appeared on the local station weekly until 1938, when they transferred to WELI, a New Haven outlet. His band was called Ed Krolikowski and His Radio Orchestra, and with frequent radio work, the ensemble prospered.[58] The band broadcast remotes from his music store, performances that became so popular locally that traffic jams occurred just before program time. He also sought to widen his audience in other ways, adopting a popular playing style similar to that of non-ethnic contemporary dance ensembles.

From his many years as a non-ethnic musician, like Lausche, he had grown to love the contemporary jazz music. He played traditional ethnic dance pieces with an obviously strong Dixieland and swing influence. With this distinct style, he sought to appeal not only to Poles but also to other Slavs and Americans who loved dancing the variety of ethnic dance steps, polkas, waltzes, and obereks. He undoubtedly liked the nickname the "Polish Paul Whiteman," but it really was inaccurate; he should have been called the "Polka Paul Whiteman."[59] Another factor in Krolikowski's assimilative role as a musician was his employment of non-Polish musicians in his ten-piece band, instrumentalists who were familiar with American popular music and the contemporary character of the band itself, usually trombone, trumpet, clarinet, violin, piano, string bass, and drums.[60]

Krolikowski was quite willing to make records as another way of widening his audience. He cut a total of fifty-eight in all, the first few with Victor and later the bulk with Columbia in the two decades before mid-century. Columbia's manufacturing plant was in Bridgeport, which must have helped the Polish bandsman contact that company's ethnic promoter, Sandor Porges.

Some of Krolikowski's best-selling polkas were the most familiar Polish and Czech selections from the Vitak and Elsnic catalog, such as "Baruska Polka" for Victor in 1929 and "Dziadunio" (Clarinet Polka) and "Helena Polka" for Columbia in 1940. Ironically, this last work, a Bohemian piece by Elsnic, was his biggest hit, allegedly selling one-quarter million soon after it appeared.[61]

Probably the most important factor in Krolikowski's efforts to win a general audience for his big-band style polka music was his scheduling of frequent ballroom engagements, particularly at Bridgeport's leading commercial dance palace, the Ritz. The Ritz, which had been refurbished and much enlarged in 1923, had become one of the leading ballrooms in the country, impressing visitors with its elegant crystal chandeliers and its immense size, the length of an airport runway.[62] It obviously was the city's answer to accommodate the major dance bands' engagements. Opening day had Vincent Lopez's Orchestra, with an admission charge of 65 cents. Throughout its history down to the 1950s other big bands visited regularly, including the Dorseys, Rudy Vallee, Larry Clinton, Artie Shaw, and Vaughn Monroe. They drew anywhere from a typical 1,000 patrons to just under 4,000. At its height in the late 1930s the Ritz operated four nights per week, with swing and sweet bands on weekends, square dancing on Thursdays, and polkas on Wednesdays.[63] For these evenings people would come from as far away as New York and Springfield, Massachusetts.[64] Another dance center in town that was only slightly less popular was the Pleasure Beach Park Ballroom.

Krolikowski was able to book his band into both dance halls. He played at Pleasure Beach weekly in the thirties, where the cost of admission was 50 cents and he and his band were able to draw about 1,000 on "polka" nights.[65] One way he maximized his attendance in the mid-thirties was to hold the local Miss Poland of Connecticut contest at his performance. The competition took place there over six years after 1933.[66] Announcing his performances at the Ritz, where he would usually play to 1,000 to 1,500, the newspaper notices typically read like the one for November 29, 1939, which stated that Krolikowski's Band would hold a masquerade ball with an admission charge of 40 cents. Both polkas and swing dances would be played and cash prizes would be offered.[67]

With all of Krolikowski's efforts to attract non-Poles to his music store and band performances, it is clear that he considered himself both Polish and American. He headed the local Polish Businessmen's association for a time, was a member of other Polish fraternal bodies, and served on a committee of the local Lions order. Clearly he contributed locally to popularizing ethnic music among a variety of Americans.[68]

Brunon Kryger of Wilkes-Barre and Ignacy Podgorski of Philadelphia were contemporaries of Krolikowski and also transcended their group in their areas—the two Pennsylvanians were friends and associates and as much American as they were Polish. However, they expressed their crossover character somewhat differently as both were prolific composers who concentrated on their own and their audience's American experience.

Kryger like Krolikowski had had a formal musical education. Born in the western Polish territories at the turn of the century, he very much wanted to be an entertainer and studied voice at the Poznan Conservatory after World War I. He appeared in Philadelphia in 1925, following a childhood sweetheart to America. His destination was a fortuitous one for his later musical career, as the Victor Recording studios in Camden were nearby and he made friends with the major Polish American music figure in the city, the very active music businessman Ignacy Podgorski. The latter apparently admired Kryger's fine tenor voice and likely helped him record a number of traditional Polish folk songs. Together, they also put ethnic comic material on disc. Kryger remained in Philadelphia until 1930, when he assumed a position as musical director at a church in Shenandoah, Pennsylvania. There, he formed his own International Orchestra, which toured the United States. Kryger finally settled in Wilkes-Barre in 1936, opening a music store and school and organizing a modern musical ensemble. The band consisted of brass, wind, and strings; it was an eight-man group that eventually included his three sons.[69]

Kryger appeared often on radio, especially in Shenandoah and Wilkes-Barre over WEEU, Reading, WAZL, Hazleton, and WBRE and WILK, Wilkes-Barre. But it was his record-making that made his name in the region, as he cut more than two hundred pieces for Victor and later for Harmonia.[70] Kryger, like Krolikowski, rarely traveled out of his state and booked often in the anthracite-area ballrooms, such as the Sans Souci Park and Granada dance halls in his hometown.

While he played the standard popular Polish pieces, he was probably most remembered for his original compositions, many of which reflected the lives of his audience. These were recorded for Victor, as "Shenandoska Polka," "Dziś w Ameryce Smutno Nam" (Sad Life in America), "Dzień Polska w Ameryce" (Polish Day in America), all in 1932; "Mainer Lebra Poszukuje" (A Miner Looks for a Helper), in 1933; and "Polka Z Majnerska" (Miner's Polka) and

"Wujo Sam" (Uncle Sam), both in 1941. He also recorded a number of works with English titles, such as "Accordion" and "Rocky Glen Polka," in 1941.[71] He was obviously aiming much of his music at multi-generational listeners, both immigrant and American-born. That he was able to appeal to that larger audience was shown by formal popular recognition near the end of his career. He toured western Pennsylvania often and was voted King of the Polkas, the best in a 1947 competition of 14 polka bands held in the Pittsburgh Arena.[72]

Kryger's friend Ignacy Podgorski was more important as a contributor to the eastern style than as a performer, though he did play the violin and produced a large number of records. He arrived in America with his wife in 1906 at the age of twenty, a devoted student of Polish folk music. Although he did organize his own orchestra and appear on radio and record for the leading labels, his major interest was in music publishing. He put out a huge number of traditional ethnic selections, arranging about fourteen hundred old folk tunes and dances, to be played by modern Polish American orchestras, especially for the new instruments he used.[73] Podgorski was also involved in other ethnic music promotions, initiating the Polish Hour in Philadelphia over station WTEL in the early 1930s. He apparently ceased his regular personal appearances as a band-leader-performer early in 1937, though he did record more pieces for Harmonia just after the end of the war. Along with the Society of Polish Musicians mentioned earlier, with which he was associated, Podgorski was responsible for making Philadelphia a center of Polish music activity.[74] Other local musicians involved were Jan Wanat until about 1930, Joseph Krygier, who like Podgorski ran a music store and published ethnic music, and band leaders Walter Ossowski, Walt Leopold (Podoszek), and Walter Dombkowski, just before, during, and after World War II. The Polish American string band that became a part of the city's famous Mummers parades about then was further evidence of the music enthusiasm in Philadelphia's Polonia.[75]

Krolikowski, Kryger, and Podgorski were in effect the major early promoters of the Polish urban musical style. Others, slightly younger, also contributed to the predominance of the eastern genre somewhat later, into mid-century, including Jozef Lazarz, Jan Robak, Walt Solek, and the most popular bandleaders, Bernie Witkowski, and Frank Wojnarowski.

Jozef Lazarz was somewhat exceptional in that he was not a polished musician but more of a fiddler who kept much of his music closer to the folk idiom. But his orchestra was similar to the others along the Atlantic. He was a violinist who arrived as a teenager in 1913 at Indian Orchard, near Chicopee in western Massachusetts. His success as a musician came late, as he spent much of his early life working at unskilled jobs and performing only in his free time at private affairs. His fiddling virtuosity was "discovered" when he was thirty-three at a sensational 1928 public performance in Holyoke.[76] Victor offered him a contract quickly, and he recorded about eighty pieces for them and later for other labels, such as Columbia and especially Demetriades's Standard International.

Lazarz was very much in demand locally and was one of the eastern bandleaders who traveled with his ensemble widely, around that region and into Ohio and western New York.[77] His distinctive appeal was based heavily on his many compositions, a very large number in English. His more popular compositions featured vocal duets, especially Julia and Henry Wegiel, who were superb harmonizers.[78] Lazarz's most popular hit was one of the compositions he modernized from an old folk tune, the sprightly stringed "Pizzicato Polka," recorded for Victor in 1940.[79] Despite the centrality of the violin in many of his performances, his band clearly had adopted the mainstream American big-band sound.[80] Lazarz died in 1982, when he was in his nineties.

A local friend of Lazarz and fellow violinist whose band was not as well known was Jan Robak of Chicopee, who was born in 1890 and probably formed a band in the early 1920s that was similar to the rural-style bands of Chicago, consisting mainly of strings.[81] As a fiddler—the quintessential traditional Polish musician—Robak would frequently be called, perhaps along with another stringed instrumentalist, such as a bass player, to accompany Polish home celebrations of various types, especially, as one might imagine, weddings. These engagements were known locally as "Kitchen Rackets," gigs in homes similar to the "house parties" of the Midwest Norwegians where, after the residents cleared away the table, chairs, and other furnishings, dancing would be held in the kitchen. In those early days such festivities would continue for two, even three days. The pay for the musicians would be 25 cents a tune, with paper money usually placed in the sound hole of the stringed bass.[82]

Thus Robak started out playing traditionally styled pieces, often his own compositions in the old manner, of which there were many.

In fact his first records, which he made for Columbia in 1930 and 1931, were cut under the title, the "Wiejska Orkiestra."[83] He had joined with Wladyslaw Fronc in 1931 to form the small four-piece Robak-Fronc Orchestra. Soon, however, whether because Robak sensed the desire from his audience for added instrumentation or because he needed more volume to play in the larger halls of Worcester (White City), Springfield (Joyland), Palmer (Forest Lake), and West Holyoke (Hampden Rapids), he had to add other pieces, including drums, piano, and banjo. Those new instruments made his group sound more like the larger American swing bands. By the mid-thirties the Robak-Fronc ensemble was really an ethnic dance band, mixing polkas and foxtrots in the major regional ballrooms and the Polish fraternal halls, especially the National Home at Windsor Locks, Connecticut.[84]

Another Connecticut Polish musician, Walt Solek, went even further in changing ethnic music in an American direction. He had no choice in this regard, because his musical instrument was not a traditional one like the violin but rather, the drums. Solek was much younger than Lazarz and Robak, born almost twenty years after them, and in America, not Poland. His father and brother Henry were both musicians, and he joined the latter to form the Krakowska Orchestra in the mid-1930s.[85] Solek decided to stress his own style by the late 1930s by developing a comic repertoire. He soon became known as the "Polish Spike Jones," obviously a strategy that stressed the contemporary over the traditional.[86] He formed a band in 1939 and made some records with Victor but had to enter the Navy, after which he restarted his ensemble and expanded it to ten pieces. His first major hit was a polka for Columbia, "My Girl Friend Julayda," given humorously in English in either 1940 or 1946.[87] Solek played and recorded many pieces, but his other best-known recording was for Dana, "Who Stole the Keeshka?"[88] Solek frequently translated Polish lyrics into English, a strategy that probably represented his effort to retain the support of the younger American-born Poles. He certainly acquired numerous fans for his music, traveling widely out west well beyond his group centers.[89] Closer to home, he was able to draw large crowds; in 1950, for example, he was booked for the thirty-first anniversary of New York's famous Roseland ballroom, and even in later years when polka music was declining in popularity he could still draw an unusually large audience of 3,000 at a dance hall in Barnesville, Pennsylvania.[90]

Two bandleaders were even more successful in attracting fans, especially youthful ones, in the golden age of polka music in the forties and early fifties: Bernie Witkowski, a clarinetist, and Frank Wojnarowski, an accordionist. These musicians, clearly the leading popularizers of polka music, had somewhat different styles. Witkowski was an artist-improviser who leaned more toward American jazz, while Wojnarowski had a larger band and remained somewhat more ethnic in his selections.

The quality of Witkowski's artistry was almost preordained. He was from a family of musicians, mostly clarinetists like him. His father, Bernard, Sr., was a clarinetist who came to America from Prussian Poland around 1890 with his two brothers, Leon, also a clarinetist, and Ignacy, a violinist. The family settled in Brooklyn. Leon was clearly the dominant one of the siblings, a virtuoso player classically trained in Europe, a figure to whom a musically conditioned nephew could look up. Between 1915 and his death in 1934, the years when Bernard Witkowski was growing up, his uncle Leon was a leading recording artist for Victor's many Polish ethnic discs, a bandmaster of a large American band at Luna Park, Coney Island, an occasional soloist with a major symphony orchestra, and and a Carnegie Hall concert artist.[91] With such a brilliant career, he was obviously a model for and a great influence on his young nephew, whose standards of playing were to be equally high.[92] Young Bernie was surrounded by music and musicians throughout his childhood—his brother played for Paul Whiteman, and two of his cousins were musicians as well, including one who was a violinist known as "King" Anthony Witkowski and who competed with Bernie as a popular Polish musician.[93]

In such a milieu it was not surprising that the young Bernie would begin getting bookings at the age of twelve, and by 1932, when he was sixteen, he was playing on radio on WWRL, Long Island, in a Polish ensemble known as the Orzeł Biały (White Eagle) Orchestra. It was in this period of the early 1930s that Witkowski's career pattern of improvisational artist, record maker, and radio personality was established.

In part because of his musical ability, Witkowski led a dissenting group of White Eagles in 1932 to form another ensemble, Srebny Dzwony, the Silver Bell Orchestra, which he and a sideman, Edward Bebko, got on a local ethnic radio station, WHOM.[94] Witkowski and Bebko also formed a smaller group, "Trzy Galgany" (Three

Ragamuffins), and the two Witkowski ensembles also began making records in 1934 for Victor's International Division. They next obtained radio work with Bebko's help, as he was familiar with the medium from his employment as a radio organist before he joined the Silver Bells. About 1938, Bebko was able to get Witkowski himself appointed staff musician on WBNX in the Bronx, one of the more powerful New York City stations that promoted ethnic broadcasting. The bandleader benefited greatly professionally in that position, which he held for number of years. On the air he would play not only Polish pieces but the tunes of many nationalities.[95]

All during this time Witkowski and his ensembles were appearing at local nightclubs and halls. A frequent engagement in the late thirties was at the Glenwood Manor in Queens, which catered to younger Polish and likely other polka enthusiasts on Thursdays.[96] Another regular gig was at the Arcadia Ballroom on Broadway in Manhattan.[97] Witkowski also played in New Jersey, especially during the years 1940 through 1960, when he was often booked at the Belmont Ballroom in Garfield. At all these places and at area Polish Homes, such as the one in Harrison, New Jersey, Witkowski's typical attendance was large, from 800 to 1,000 people.[98]

Witkowski's compositions and arrangements were certainly part of the eastern polka style, reflecting his love of jazz. It was this taste that differentiated him from his uncle, who was of an older generation closer to traditional folk music. The younger Witkowski did continue to play some of the old-time ethnic music, including the polka, oberek, and waltz, but he was more devoted to modern American jazz, with its characteristic improvisation and syncopation. As he matured, he switched his musical allegiance from his uncle to a new musician, Benny Goodman. And with his eagerness to master his instrument, he studied with a first clarinetist from the New York Philharmonic, even studied at Juilliard and obtained a master's degree in music from New York University.[99]

While Witkowski was one of the leaders of the eastern style, playing at fast tempo with instruments similar to a swing band, his own imprint was quite discernible. He not only added jazz elements to his huge record production but he also synthesized other contemporary themes into his compositions. One of his well-known musicological inventions was incorporating in his polkas in the later 1950s a Latin influence. One result was characteristic of his unusual compositions, a polka conga.[100]

The extent of Witkowski's modification of the two step polka was extraordinary. Some of his best jazz works were "Fire Polka" (1936), "Clarinet Polka" (1939), and "Na Około Czarny Las" (In the Dark Forest) (1939).[101] He also recorded polka-like material under the name of Bernardo Blanco (for Bernie Whyte, another of his stage names).

Another illustration of Witkowski's imaginative playing was his use of the polka idiom to provide unusual sounds to express non-musical settings. The best examples were the very popular pieces, "Locomotywa Polka" (1935), one of his first, and "Fire Polka" (1936), where he integrated into the piece the sounds of fire-engine paraphernalia. Between 1937 and 1941 he wrote many other polkas with sound effects, including works dealing with Coney Island, the World's Fair, an airplane, a music box, squeaky shoes, a canary, a parrot, and a horse.[102]

The volume of his recorded works was enormous. He made at least one hundred pieces for Victor from 1935 to 1942, moved to Standard International to cut discs for Demetriades from around 1946 to 1950, and appeared on the Dana label for the first years of the 1950s, all before starting his own company about 1953.[103]

Whatever the cause, Witkowski's clarinet virtuosity, his improvisation or simply his high standards as a bandleader, he had a large following up to 1960 and later. One of the leading female polka singers, Teresa Zapolska, ascribed her inspiration to become a vocalist to hearing Witkowski over WBNX and his music on Kecki's Polish program on WLIB around 1950.[104] The leading critic of Polish polka music writing in the mid-1980s ranked him just as highly: "Bernie Witkowski set the standard for eastern style performance. Although some have lived up to his standards, his performances have never been surpassed in technical brilliance or creative flair."[105]

Witkowski did have a competitor. Frank Wojnarowski was the other leading exponent of the music that dominated Polonia around mid-century. He differed from Witkowski in that he had two enormously popular hit tunes, "Jedzie Boat" and "Matka," which recording company executive Walter Dana helped popularize. Wojnarowski was less the artist, more a band leader, and he aimed his music more directly at Polish Americans. He also did far more traveling, and he did not achieve stardom until a little later, around the late 1940s. But as with Witkowski, the route of Wojnarowski to popular success was based on his success in modifying traditional ethnic music. In his case, too, it was as a proponent of the eastern style.

Wojnarowski began his musical career with many disadvantages, although his one major boost to stardom was his fortuitous association with the consummate music businessman, Walt Dana, just after World War II. As a teenager, he had come to the United States from Poland at a bad time, 1929, on the threshold of the depression. Wojnarowski had had a few lessons on the violin in the old country, and when the family moved from Pennsylvania to Bridgeport in 1930, his mother was able to pay for additional music instruction. The expense paid off, because a short time later the family lost its savings in a bank failure and had to go on relief, forcing young Frank to begin a small four-man band about 1932 to earn income.[106] While he did get the standard private bookings for weddings, christenings, and other occasions, he played both Polish and American dance tunes. Like Krolikowski, he considered ethnic music a bit "corny" and thought of making his band entirely into an American dance band. Very likely, since the majority of his band members in those early years of the thirties were themselves not Polish (most were Italian), they urged him to change his own name and that of his band to Frank Wayne and his Orchestra.[107] But apparently he decided to continue with ethnic music. Probably with the help of Krolikowski, whom he knew, he was able to get bookings for his ensemble at the two major ballrooms, Pleasure Park and the Ritz. These bookings were apparently insufficient, and since he found little radio work and had no real Bridgeport anchor, Wojnarowski decided on a strategy of performance that eventually would make him a dominant regional, if not national figure. He decided to travel, to bring his music, which was essentially the eastern style, personally out to the west.[108]

His first goal was to break into the New York area, and he was able to do so in the mid-thirties with a first booking at the Polish Home in Jamaica. A short time later he got an engagement at the famous Roseland Ballroom in Manhattan, probably the first Polish polka bandleader to do so.[109] He also went much further afield, to western Pennsylvania, where he had discovered an extremely heavy and unfilled demand for good polka dance bands. In a short time Wojnarowski had set up a schedule that would continue for most of his career, playing part of the year at home and touring the rest of the time, in New York, western Pennsylvania, Michigan, and Ohio, both in the larger cities and in any of the small towns where he could get a booking. He kept up a hectic schedule, spending as much as two months on the road with only a two-week break.[110]

Throughout the postwar years, Wojnarowski attracted huge crowds. He was a frequent visitor not just to the major New York ballrooms, such as Roseland, but also to the Trianon in Toledo, where he once drew a record 4,000, and Westview Park in Pittsburgh. More than 1,500 came to see him at the Aragon in Cleveland, 3,000 at Erie, and as many as 6,000 heard him in Detroit.[111]

As the first major eastern polka band to tour the Midwest, Wojnarowski and his bandsmen profited much. They did not do as well with records. Wojnarowski made two discs with Harmonia about 1946, but they did not sell well, and when he noticed Dana had just started a recording company office in New York at that time, he contacted him and found him to be most encouraging. In 1948 Wojnarowski showed him a piece he had composed along with Slovak and Italian cowriters. Dana recognized it as a potential hit, and helped the bandleader record it. The result was Wojnarowski's first major success, "Jedzie Boat" (Ferryboat Polka), which had appeal not only for Polish but also a general American audience.[112] Wojnarowski's reputation as a bandleader went beyond Polish Americans. He had never restricted his sidemen to being Polish, and by mid-century he was paying them more than some of the leading American dance bands.[113]

Wojnarowski scored even better in sales at the end of the polka era, again with a million-selling hit for Dana. That was "Matka" (1961), a sentimental waltz in Polish that swept Polonia, although curiously, despite a larger sale than "Jedzie Boat," its audience was probably more exclusively Polish American.[114]

The success of the three major Polish bandleaders in promoting the new eastern style must be viewed in its context; although in this book we cannot examine in detail the careers of all these musicians, by mid-century there were many such entertainers, especially around New York City. Other individuals assisted in the spread of the eastern style in specific ways. Dana, certainly, recorded most, really almost all, of these musicians and must be considered *most* responsible for the dominance of the eastern style in the late forties. Some of his more distinctive artists were the Polish American tenor, Staś Jaworski, who sang with the reformed Chor Dana before the war and added his vocals to various eastern bands after; another instrumentalist-singer, Regina Kujawa, the major female vocalist of that time who recorded with many of those Dana ensembles; and still another band-leader, Ted Maksymowicz.[115] Maksymowicz's role was particularly significant, for he, too, brought the eastern style to a new type of American audience, the upper classes. From the mid-thirties to the mid-fifties he sought to make his ensemble one of the fine society dance bands, but one heavily emphasizing polkas and other ethnic dance music. He, too, played often at the city's major ballrooms; he was probably at Roseland more often than his colleagues, regularly for seven years after 1949.[116] And it was Maksymowicz who intro-duced the polka to the famous Harvest Moon Ball, the annual event held in Madison Square Garden.[117] Obviously Maksymowicz brought that ethnic musical genre to dancing Americans whatever their background—some of whom might have avoided polka music without him.[118]

A particularly happy gathering took place in early March of 1951, which symbolized the dominance of this Polish eastern style not only in ethnic music but to some extent in American popular music in general. The ostensible reason for the meeting was the wish of New York–area Polish musicians to thank Michael Kecki as the dean of local Polish American broadcasters for his promotion of his group's music. The occasion was in fact the coming together of all the leading eastern style bandleaders. Present, too, was the other figure most responsible for the success of that genre, Walter Dana. Besides these two media men, Kecki and Dana, the gathering in-cluded all the leading New York Polish music people, the Witkows-kis, Bernie and Antoni, Wojnarowski, Maksymowicz, Kujawa, Ja-worski, Victor Zembruski, Eddie Gronet, Gene Wisniewski, Terry Zapolska, Freddie Yarosz, and Joe Kurat.[119] These people had indeed popularized their music nationally and particularly among the younger generation. An unusually perceptive observer just after mid-century who was recounting immigrant contributions went far be-yond the usual litany of athletic and military heroes to cite in the Polish case their two most successful musical figures:

The performers who recently have exercised the greatest influence—among the jukebox set at any rate—are the leaders of Polka Bands. For many years while such groups provided Polish language programs with traditional ma-zurkas, polkas, and obereks, they attracted only a Polish audience. Then they changed their style, added a batch of hot licks, put in a Gene Krupa beat (He, too, is a Pole), translated old lyrics into English and wrote a batch of lovely new ones. . . . Suddenly low-power stations found themselves capturing network audiences as millions of high school live wires began arguing the . . . merits of Frank Wojnarowski's pressing of Broke But Happy Polka versus Bernie Witkowski's recording of Wha' He say Mambo. In Chicago recently one disc jockey asked his listeners to name their favorite Polka band. Within 3 days he had received more than 22,000 postcards.[120]

10

Ethnic Music Becomes
Popular Music, 1940-1960

As we have seen, the depression era brought many so-
cial forces to bear on ethnic music, creating the scene for the eventual
triumph of the Polish eastern style in the ethnic music community.
The public's need for inexpensive entertainment, the introduction
of new mass media, especially the jukebox and radio, and the ethnic
musicians' adoption of the mainstream form and style of the big
band all had popularized the international style of the late thirties
along with the many regional ethnic bands, including Scandinavian,
Czech, and German ensembles in addition to the Polish. But it was
the historical conditions of the next era, the 1940s, dominated of
course by the nation's involvement in World War II, that changed
social life in major ways contributing to the continued spread of
polka music. America's entrance into the armed conflict affected
regional ethnic bands, like Vadnal's of Cleveland and Duchow's of
Wisconsin, whose leaders found renewed interest in ethnic music
and dance that reinvigorated their bands after the war, and it also
transformed some regional musicians, raising them into national
entertainers. These new stars began as local musicians and may not
even have traveled outside their regions, but they still became widely
known as notable American performers far beyond their home districts in the decade and a half after 1945.

What had happened was that the war brought on a second craze
for ethnic music. The first had arisen among a recreation-starved,
dance-mad public in the mid- and late thirties, with the "Beer Barrel

Polka," and "Bei Mir Bist Du Shön." The second passion for polka arose in the late 1940s, especially around 1950, with the appearance of a new group of nationally known ethnic entertainers and bandleaders, including the immensely popular Italian troubadour, Nicola Paone; the widely-known Czech-German Minnesotans, "Whoopee John" Wilfahrt and the Plehal Brothers; a new and very successful bandleader, Lawrence Welk; and above all, the man who more than any other popularized and nationalized old-time ethnic music, Frankie Yankovic.

The war itself helped produce these ethnic music stars. Historians have already cited the role of World War II in diversifying our popular music, which also broadened the appeal of polka music.[1] The conflict brought with it much social change, especially a shifting of population, both military and civilian, for new jobs and wartime necessity: southerners moved to the North, northerners moved to the South, easterners met westerners and vice-versa, and the troops overseas were exposed to European life, creating much new cultural interaction among Americans at home and abroad and much more familiarity among Americans of various localities and traditions with other ways of life about which they had previously been ignorant. This social mixing inevitably contributed to the intermingling of different musical genres. In the military service especially, in private and public situations, records, radio, and the stage all broadcast more widely than ever the musical preferences of some to others. Country music devotees, for example, grew in number, as did polka enthusiasts.[2]

In addition, changing conditions in the music industry furthered the breakdown of the traditionally dominant musical style, Tin Pan Alley, and provided openings for new genres, thereby making our popular music more complex. Around 1940 the new radio broadcasters' association, Broadcast Music Inc., broke the monopolistic hold of ASCAP (the Association of Composers, Authors, and Publishers) over what was played over the air. The resulting competition led to the appearance of new kinds of music, alternatives to Tin Pan Alley, which thereafter had a better chance of being aired over the networks.

Another liberating force in America's popular music was the outcome of the well-known strike of musicians from 1942 to 1944. When the major record companies each settled individually to end the dispute, even greater decentralization of the industry resulted, with many new firms enhancing competition. New companies like Capitol, anxious for quick security in the music market and profits, were eager to accept previously marginal genres, such as country-western and ethnic music.

A final boon to new kinds of popular music was the general affluence of the time. The inexhaustible manpower need of the war virtually eliminated the unemployment of the thirties, and the blue-collar working class, including the white and even non-white minorities, acquired new wealth. Although scarcity of consumer goods made it difficult for Americans to fully spend their new-found riches during the war, they could do so at the end of the conflict. Hence, while popular music of the thirties still reflected chiefly the taste of the white middle class, that of the forties became more the music of the minorities, including blacks, Mexicans, Jews, and Catholics.[3]

The character of that new nationalized ethnic music continued to change in the new decade. It became more commercialized than ever, no longer chiefly the music of adult immigrants for weddings and group occasions. Rather, these tunes of the forties were an Americanized genre suitable for both dancing and singing, which appealed now as much to the younger generation as the older, of whatever background, ethnic or not.

The experience of one little-known polka band, Shep Wolan's ensemble from the Boston area, illustrates the great boost the war gave to the spreading of polka music among all Americans who served in the armed services. Wolan was not a national star; he made very few records, and he sharply limited his performances to eastern New England, chiefly Massachusetts and Rhode Island. Yet while continuing to restrict his travels to his region, he was still able to place himself in an unusual position of disseminating his music much more widely by broadcasting to troops overseas, thus acquainting a wide array of Americans from all over the country with his kind of music.

Like so many other leaders, Wolan was a second-generation Polish American, born in 1904 in one of New England's Puritan centers, Salem.[4] And like other band musicians, he came from a musical family; his father, who had entered the United States in 1895 as a musician, composer, and bandleader, often played for local weddings. Shep (Sylvester) soon joined his father in his music shop, where the elder Wolan made and repaired string instruments. Some of his customers were members of the Boston Symphony, who instructed Shep in the violin.[5] Wolan formed a band of his own in 1928, and like other eastern-style ensembles he played a variety of Polish and American dance music, both semi-classical and popular at area hotels, ballrooms, ethnic churches and halls, and nightclubs. He became well liked, especially after his recording with RCA Victor and his radio work, mostly on WLAW, Lawrence, but also on six other stations in greater Boston area. His theme was based on a well-known Polish tune, "Under the Warsaw Bridge."[6]

His distinctive legacy, however, was what he and his band did during the war. After playing on short-wave radio as an experiment, he transmitted his music regularly to Europe and the Allied theater. For this he received much mail from American and other Allied troops.[7] Undoubtedly, Wolan was one of the leading educators of the soldiers to the beauties of polka music.

While Wolan and others were further popularizing their music from the ethnic communities, the nation's leading entertainers, such as the Andrews Sisters, were simultaneously doing the same with more general polka tunes, such as the "Pennsylvania" and "Victory" polkas. By the end of the war, the nation appeared quite ready once again to welcome ethnic music as a part of the national entertainment. That readiness helped a particular group of entertainers, Italian Americans, move into the national spotlight. Except for opera, Italian American musical culture had been rather segregated from most Americans, despite its very rich tradition of music and entertainment, which had produced an enormous number of ethnic recordings on all the leading labels in the 1920s and 1930s. Their best known entertainer, Eduardo Migliaccio, "Farfariello," had been an immensely imaginative comedian, but unfortunately for a rather limited audience. He had performed only in Italian for Italian Americans.

After World War II, a new creative genius, Nicola Paone, had appeared to take Migliaccio's place. Paone, however, differed from his predecessor by winning a larger audience, not just those who understood Italian. By his originality he achieved national stardom, contributing a few of his selections to American popular music and culture. His impact was of such significance that it also helped convince another well-known American entertainer, jazz musician Louis Prima, to perform similar Italian-styled material.

Paone's career trajectory was complex. He continued the tradition of the older group performers, composing many pieces in Italian, which sensitively reflected immigrant and ethnic life. Like Migliaccio, he had the ability to both understand and convey in his art the soul of ordinary Italian Americans. His most popular piece "Uei Paesano," mobilized his ethnic audience to think of their common national identity as overseas Italians. But Paone was also able to reach and win non-Italian Americans, with songs that he wrote in English, mostly comic novelties about Italian American concerns, but subjects that anyone could understand and empathize with. Paone's universal, multi-ethnic appeal as both a composer and entertainer is suggested by estimates of the sales of his records, which certainly numbered in the tens of millions.[8]

Paone's mother was the first source of his interest in Italian songs and ballads. Living in Spangler, a coal-mining town in western Pennsylvania, where Nicola was born in 1915, she soon recognized that her son had a warm and talented singing voice and encouraged him to learn the traditional Italian tunes.[9] His father, who had been a mineworker since the turn of the century, decided in 1923 to return with the family to Sicily, where his wife died and the family was forced to remain in the old country. The young Paone got some musical education in Sicily, but the family was quite poor; partly to distract himself from their troubles, the boy would compose "little melodies of [his] own."[10]

By 1930, believing better opportunities were back in America, Nicola went to live with his sister in the Bronx, New York. The next few years he became well-acquainted with the unskilled labor typical of the Italian immigrant experience, which he would later express in song. In the early 1930s, he worked as a shoe-shine boy, a hat blocker, and a busboy at an Italian restaurant.[11] Dutifully, he sent money home to his family in Sicily, but his major interest was in singing, and with a considerable vocal talent, he decided to try to enter opera. He won some amateur contests in local theaters and on radio in Philadelphia and New York, especially on WOV which was broadcasting a large number of Italian programs.

At first Paone earnestly wished to become an opera star and started taking formal voice lessons. To earn the money for such instruction, he decided to learn the jewelry trade. He never made it to grand opera, however, because he chafed at the strict regimen of instruction and identified strongly with lower-class Italian immigrant life and especially with the folk and popular music of his community. A newspaper account of his career explained that "he . . . decline[d] . . . an operatic career because he believe[d] that the popoular [*sic*] and characteristic song best expresses the love of music for all nationalities."[12] Paone himself later recalled that by eschewing opera for music that was popular, he could "sing for everybody, all the people, close to their hearts."[13]

By 1940 he had begun singing popular Italian folk music, stornelli and canzoni, for Italian American audiences.[14] But because he could not earn a living entirely from his music, Paone opened a jewelry store in New York about 1942 and began to compose and perform on the side, writing sensitive compositions in Italian about the experience and lives of his Italian American audience. After several recording firms rejected his proposals to cut such material on disc, he decided to set up his own firm, which he called Etna, a name, of course, reflecting the well-known landmark of Sicily.[15]

Whatever the prospects for Paone's venture, the very first record he made on his label quickly became a hit. "U' Sciccaredu" (The Little Donkey) (Etna 1-A) produced an overwhelming response, reflecting Paone's uncanny ability to express the sentiments of his ethnic audience. The song was a brief comic tale about the value and demise of the peasant immigrants' most beloved animal, the people's beast of burden. The piece also signified Paone's gradual move away from the old folk tunes he previously sang to original popular music. Toward the end of the war, Paone began to write and record works for a larger audience, including material in English for Americans as a whole. He also began to get bookings in nightclubs where non-Italians could hear him and started performing on radio, including WHOM and the powerful WBNX.[16] His beautiful voice, his warm sensitivity toward his listeners, and the growing evidence of a devoted following eventually persuaded a major label, Columbia Records, that it had erred in refusing him earlier. Columbia finally signed him to a contract, probably sometime in 1946. But Paone as both a composer and performer could not accept certain restrictions that the company had placed on his art and soon ended his association with Columbia.

Still making his own records on Etna, Paone saw his career soar in 1947 and 1948 as he continued to compose songs about what he knew, the simple feelings and dilemmas of his now several audiences, his Italian, Italian American, and non-Italian listeners. He soon scored again with an even more popular record, "The Telephone No Ring," a disc that was ultimately to sell about five million, according to the composer.[17] This was another comic piece that appealed to ordinary listeners, especially Italian Americans and other ethnic Americans. It is the story of a frustrated foreigner who is trying unsuccessfully to cope with an officious telephone operator and the complexities of modern communications technology.

With two golden records to his name, Paone, as one might imagine, attracted the attention of major music publishers as well as record companies. Elliot Shapiro, head of Shapiro, Bernstein and Company, a major Tin Pan Alley firm that had already demonstrated much support for ethnic-based music, contacted the new Italian troubadour and developed a close working relationship with him, putting "Telephone No Ring" into print in 1947.[18]

A further boost to Paone's rise to stardom at this time was his association with Sandor Porges, a Columbia Records "A and R man" (Artist and Repertory). Porges, a Hungarian immigrant, was extremely important to the rise of ethnic music, assisting a number of ethnic entertainers, particularly after he moved to the new Capitol Records firm established by Johnny Mercer. He signed Paone to a second record contract, which proved far more to the Italian American's liking than the first.[19] Paone later added to his wider audience exposure and his role on the popular American music scene by making records for other companies, including Victor, Capitol, and ABC Paramount. He also replaced crooner Julius La Rosa on the Cadence label.[20]

A close look at a few of Paone's many compositions suggests his skill in constructing a repertoire for his several constituencies. His total output numbered about 175 compositions in Italian and English, most of them dealing with the simple but universal activities of everyday life familiar not only to working-class Italian Americans but to all ordinary people.[21] A bias toward the concerns of the lower social class is evident from the titles of Paone's many English tunes written and recorded around 1950, such as "Tony the Iceman," "The Peanut (Vendor) Song," "The Popcorn Man," "The Subway Song," and "Show Me How You Milk the Cow." Other titles dealt with universal subject matter: rejected love in "Eleanore (Please Open The Door)" and newlywed life in "What You Gonna Do?"[22]

Representative of this awareness of and sensitivity to everyday human concerns is "Yakity, Yak," about a nagging wife:

If Tony comes from work with a big smile and feeling gay,
"Where have you been all day?"
But if he's feeling sad and tired, then she'll say, "I see,
Outside you have good times and home you'll come cry to me."
Yakity, Yak, bla, bla, bla, bla.

Yakity, Yak, bla, bla, bla, bla.

That's all you'll hear all day.
If Tony tells his wife, "I'll take you out," she'll say, "What for?
I think you just don't like to stay with me at home no more."
But if she likes to go some place, and he don't want to go,
She cries, "You never take me anywhere, you so and so!"
Yakity, Yak, bla, bla, bla, bla.
Yakity, Yak, bla, bla, bla, bla.[23]

Another of his songs, "The Big Professor," is a gentle satire on speaking with an accent:

Oh, I am the bigga professor, don't think that I'm a fool.
I am the bigga professor, and I never went to school.
I come to theesa country when the people ask for me,
To teach the broken English at the university.
My grandfather went to college, he had a lotsa degree.
He had a dozen titles, and he gave them all to me.
So I don't have to study, my grandpa know ev'rything.
He left me his diplomas, and I got the right to sing . . .
Oh I am the beega professor, it's my family tree,
So I teach the broken English at the university.
If you wanna be a barber, or a waiter in this land,
You gotta speak the English that's hard to understand . . .
If you wanna gooda job, don't forget to come to me.
I teach you broken English and you'll make lotsa money . . .
I work for two months for one university,
Then I lost my job when they come to tella me
That their chief professor, he putta bigga squawk,
Because all the teachers there start to speak the way I talk.[24]

These tunes were of course only a fraction of Paone's compositions, which included many other sentimental and comic ballads referring especially to immigrant life.

Paone, however, still sought more than group recognition at this time. Besides his English pieces he appeared in a number of leading night clubs in New York, Philadelphia, Rochester, Pittsburgh, Buffalo, Chicago, Toronto, and elsewhere to large, appreciative audiences.[25] In March 1948, one columnist announced that this "Italian Bing Crosby" was opening at the Iceland Restaurant "for a limited engagement" that turned out in fact to be a lengthy engagement. In the fall Paone was pictured showing his millionth recording of " 'Telephone No Ring' to Ann Jeffreys of 'My Romance,' " while breaking attendance records at that same restaurant.[26]

An account of a 1950 booking in Rochester, New York, illustrates Paone's appeal to his audience. On an April Sunday afternoon a "goodly crowd" of 1,800, "mostly Italian" but not exclusively so, had gathered to hear him at the city auditorium. The audience became so enthusiastic over the "extraordinary entertainer" that the two-hour show lasted more than three hours. Paone's several million records apparently had prepared his listeners for the happy occasion. As a result of the warm reception, the promoter, one Vincent Faga, decided to hold a second show the following month.[27]

That Paone by mid-century had achieved national stardom is indicated by his engagement at the New York's RKO Palace Theatre in the fall of 1951. Paone headlined the vaudeville bill of ten acts and a film and drew a capacity audience. Two reviews concluded that the performance of this "Italian troubadour," who offered renditions of his best-known ballads, was a great success. Both reviewers praised him for his personal warmth and showmanship, though they disagreed on the quality of his voice.[28]

In 1953, yet another hit song further enhanced Paone's popularity nationally and internationally. "Uei Paesano" (My Countryman), written in Italian, again reflected the singer's sensitive comprehension of the emigrant soul. He wrote it following the warm hospitality some friends and fans in Syracuse, New York, offered him on one of his tours.[29] The song advocates a spirit of commonality among all Italian emigrants far from home, overriding even strong regional ties that might tend to divide the community. This was a sentiment that Paone's predecessor Farfariello had fostered, albeit not so self-consciously. By the time he wrote the tune, Paone was already a star internationally among Italians worldwide, and in fact he first performed "Uei Paesano" in Buenos Aires, where he had been invited to perform by Argentinian Italians. The performance was such a sensation it nearly caused a riot.[30] The record of "Uei Paesano" ultimately sold better than any other Paone made, partly, no doubt, because its lyrics represent the quintessential emigrant lament, a theme Paone used a number of times in other compositions.[31]

The song begins by justifying emigration; Italy unfortunately sends her people abroad because it cannot support them at home. Yet while an emigrant overseas "gains bread," an Italian far from home "loses happiness." An emigrant must keep family ties, and must especially write home to mother. But when mother dies back home, and the emigrant feels the frustration of separation, the best source of consolation is in friendship with another Italian emigrant, who shares similar distress and thus makes the tragedy seem more tolerable.

Paone concludes with an impassioned plea:

> But [whether] you are Piedmontese, Lombardo, or Genovese . . .
> Venetian or Giuliano, Tridentino or Emiliano, from the Marche or
>   Tuscan, maybe Umbrian, my paesano,
> From the Abruzzi or the mother, Eternal Rome.
> Are you from Napoli, Pugliese, maybe Sardo or Calbrese, Lucano or
>   Siciliano? It doesn't matter, you are Italian.
> And if you're Italian that is enough because all of Italy is beautiful.
> This is the truth—give your hand . . . come here and say "Uei
>   Paesano!" "Uei Paesano!"[32]

The song was a far greater hit with Italians than with Paone's non-Italian audience, but it did have some effect on American popular music. With record sales in the millions, Shapiro, Bernstein arranged with Paone to have their lyricist write English lyrics.[33] Thus "Way, Paesano," became a part of our popular music literature in the early 1950s. It was recorded in English by Art Mooney on MGM records, although it was not the hit that it was in Italian or as commercially successful as its composer or publisher had hoped. Paone further influenced American popular music in a way that unfortunately would bring an end to his professional singing career: through his association with the well-known jazz musician, Louis Prima.

Prima's musical career of course, differed from Paone's, especially during the years before World War II. Born in New Orleans, Prima had established himself among aficionados during the depression as a potentially good, young jazz trumpeter in his early twenties. Jazz enthusiasts also considered him highly as a composer. His most famous pieces were the well-known "Sing, Sing, Sing" (1936), followed by "Robin Hood" (1944). But regardless of their artistic quality, these compositions were not financial successes, thus leading Prima around the end of World War II to look around for commercial hits. He found them in Italian American novelties for both Italians and Americans.

In performance, Prima had always been something of a showman before crowds, and as such he probably became aware of the great financial potential in novelty Italian dialect and comic material. Paone's success undoubtedly reinforced that idea. In fact, even during the years when he was strictly a jazz musician Prima had written at least two works of the new genre, "Please No Squeeza da Banana" (1944) and "Felicia" (1945). But it was likely a performance at Rochester, New York, at the war's end that convinced the jazz musician to emphasize these pieces, when it became clear to him that they had great appeal among the younger Italian American generation.[34]

To the great dismay of his former jazz fans, in about 1946 Prima almost entirely forsook his previous work and began performing the new genre. The results were Prima records around mid-century very similar to Paone's, such as, "Luigi" (released 1953), about a neighborhood numbers racketeer; "Baciagaloop (Makes Love on Da Stoop)" (1947), a tale about the lack of privacy in an urban Little Italy; "Angelina" (1945), his mother's name; "Felicia No Capecia"; "Josephina, Please No Leana on the Bell"; and even Paone's own composition, "Eleanore (Open the Door)" (1951).[35]

When Prima recorded "The Little Donkey" for Victor, a work with music that was the same as Paone's first hit for his own label, the two entertainers nearly became involved in a lawsuit. Paone contemplated a suit for copyright violation, but their representatives arranged to settle out of court, in an agreement that Paone later felt Prima violated. The incident disillusioned Paone, and despite his many later successes, he ultimately became convinced by similar losses and disappointments to retire from the entertainment business in his mid-fifties. He decided to take up the more satisfying creative profession of cook and restaurateur, an interest he had had since his work as a youth in a New York restaurant.[36] Nonetheless, as Paone's millions of records found their way into the hands of both Italian and non-Italian Americans, his influence was undoubtedly significant. It demonstrated to Prima and others in mid-century the enormous commercial potential of the ethnic music market.[37]

Another ethnic musician benefiting from the wider postwar acquaintance and acceptance of ethnic music was a Bohemian concertina player from New Ulm, Minnesota, "Whoopee John" Wilfahrt. Like Prima, Wilfahrt had a musical career that extended over several phases, though he assumed newer and higher levels in ethnic music rather than entering the new genre from elsewhere. Wilfahrt first played for the local Czech and German societies of his hometown, later became a regional bandleader, and finally in the 1940s achieved national recognition. Wilfahrt accomplished this last phase by cutting a huge number of records. He did not travel outside the upper Midwest but nevertheless obtained a national audience by the 1950s. While Wilfahrt did much radio work, he became a nationally known star largely through the medium of the phonograph—especially with the help of that record company executive chiefly responsible for the dominant international style, Jack Kapp of Decca.

The first stage of Wilfahrt's career terminated in the mid-1920s, when he was about thirty. By then, with his mother's encouragement, he had first organized a trio with his clarinet-playing brother Eddie. Wilfahrt had recruited his sibling and a neighbor to play what was basically Czech music at house parties and other small gigs around New Ulm. That ensemble enlarged to about eight by the early 1920s and became known as "Hans Wilfahrt and his Concertina Orchestra."[38]

The group's fortunes took a decided turn for the better in 1924, when the band began to gain a wider hearing. They started to commute to the Twin Cities to play on the air for WLAG (presently WCCO).[39] Two critical steps in the group's rise occurred in 1926 when the band began recording, cutting nineteen songs for Okeh, and in 1929, when they stopped commuting and resettled in the Twin Cities.[40] Wilfahrt's new plan was to eschew the ethnic ghetto and aim his music at a much larger audience, even anglicizing the name of the ensemble in 1928 to John Wilfahrt's Concertina Orchestra. By 1931 the band had assumed its essentially permanent character, similar to the contemporary American dance band. It had nine instrumentalists: two saxophones, two trumpets, a slide trombone, tuba, piano, drums, and of course a concertina.[41]

In the early days of the depression, as with many other ethnic bands, the hard times seemed inconsequential to Wilfahrt's musicmen, who were busy touring hotels and ballrooms from Wisconsin to Nebraska, playing weekly at their permanent location, the Deutsches Haus in St. Paul and the Marigold Ballroom in Minneapolis, and continuing on radio, WDGY and KSTP, as well as WCCO. Most important, however, were their records. They would cut a huge number of tunes through the decade and beyond, and while no specific evidence exists, it is plausible to assume that that medium was more likely than in-person performances or radio work to acquaint the public outside the upper Midwest with their playing.

Wilfahrt had the good fortune of working as early as 1930 for Brunswick and its agents, David and Jack Kapp. The Kapp brothers knew the enormous potential of the band's audience and in July 1930 were anxious to have them record as much additional work as possible.[42] When the Kapps started Decca in 1934, one of the brothers, David, tried hard to bring Wilfahrt under contract. He wrote the bandleader earnestly in a communication that illustrated the Kapps' aggressive recruitment: "Our records are just going on sale and, as I told you the last time I saw you, it looks sensational. We have signed up some of the biggest of all the automatic [juke box] operators. I still think it would do you a lot of good to be under the Decca label."[43]

Wilfahrt, however, was then and for a few years later recording for Vocalion, but he finally did yield to the Kapps' entreaties, and in January 1938 he began cutting a long list of tunes. Among those first pieces was the well-known Polish "Clarinet Polka," which would become a golden record and a hit. He had at least three million-sellers, including his theme, the "Mariechen Waltz," "When the Sun Comes Over the Brewery," and "When Otto Plays the Polka."[44]

The first market reaction to his Decca work was encouraging. Wilfahrt wrote Jack Kapp in late March, 1938: "To my great delight . . . two of the four records my orchestra made for your good company are already on the market and in great demand . . . [V]arious music houses in town . . . report a gratifying demand for these records."[45]

It is difficult to estimate just how many discs Wilfahrt cut, but there were a great many, most of them in the quarter-century before he retired in 1960 with the Kapps' Decca label. They were certainly compatible with that company's commitment to popular jukebox music—particularly polka music. One estimate is that the ensemble cut about two hundred pieces for Decca in the 1930s, 1940s, and 1950s and perhaps as many as three hundred in all for all labels, including Okeh, Vocalion, and Brunswick.[46] Whatever the precise figures, it is certain that by 1941 his music was very well known in his region, and because he recorded for national labels, especially Decca, people beyond the upper Midwest would have heard of his selections as well. One claim is that he ranked third behind Bing Crosby and the Andrews Sisters in total record sales for Decca.[47]

Just as important as the huge disc repertoire in establishing the band nationally was the type of music Wilfahrt played, which has been described as in the "Dutchman" style.[48] The music is characterized by heavy brass instrumentation with a frequent marchlike melody punctuated with drums and concertina—the famous oompah beat. "Whoopee John" was always aware of projecting that character in his performances. By the late 1930s he would commonly appear with German lederhosen, Jaeger Alpine hat, and other Bavarian attire. His appearance was clownlike and ethnic, characterized by frequent vocal "whoops" and pronounced corpulence.[49]

This "Dutchman" character was really a projected image, as the music itself was far more popular than ethnic or traditional. The band was highly commercial, seeking to appeal to the widest possible audience. "Whoopee John's" performances were eclectic—while the instrumentation did have a certain German flavor, the band often, after the late 1930s, played dance tunes that were not Central European in origin, including British, Scandinavian, and Slavic tunes, along with occasional renderings of foxtrots and jazz.[50] The person most responsible for that "big band," rather non-ethnic, sound was the group's arranger, "Red" MacLeod, who began a long association with the group about 1938.[51]

For their basic repertoire, the group had depended heavily on the publications of Vitak and Elsnic, which at that time was branching out and including a variety of the dance tunes of several ethnic groups. That breadth of repertoire was of course good business and necessary, for the group traveled to different ethnic communities. In a 1946 statement reminiscent of Berg and his Viking Accordion Band, Wilfahrt explained how ethnicity could be flexible: "We have music from just about every European country which we play. We have some modern dance music, but mostly the crowds want the old-time things. In Swedish communities we have to go heavy on the Swedish tunes. Around New Ulm and Mankato, it's German and Austrian music they want. At Green Isle we play them Irish tunes and up around Cumberland, Wisconsin, we play Italian music."[52]

By 1940, Wilfahrt was very popular in the upper Midwest. A poll of Twin Cities radio listeners named him as the third most popular entertainment artist.[53] With the onset of the war, the musical group was at its peak of regional popularity, and by mid-century it had achieved national recognition.

But early in World War II the band's Germanic projection appeared likely to cause problems, as rumors spread that "Whoopee John" and his musicians might be disloyal. It was even said that the bandleader's son, Pat Wilfahrt, was actually pounding out Morse

Code on his drums, revealing troop movements to Nazi agents dancing in the audience! Some jukebox operators apparently believed
such allegations, or believed that their patrons believed them, and
withdrew some of the band's records from their machines.[54] But the
general public stood by the band, and "Whoopee John" achieved
national popularity toward the end of the war and in following years.
In the next two decades the band averaged about three hundred
booking dates annually. The Kapp Brothers were so sure of Wilfahrt's
wide national appeal during the war that they tried unsuccessfully
to get the ensemble in a Hollywood film. Apparently, the plan fell
through because of wartime rules forbidding the filming of German-
led ensembles.[55]

By the fifties, the band was never busier on the broadcast media.
It performed almost every day, with four live weekly radio shows
and TV appearances each Sunday afternoon.[56] There were other indications that "Whoopee John" was known and loved far and wide,
such as a brief letter in 1946 from a New York Decca agent, who
complimented the Minnesotan on being a national star, as evidenced
by a recent Hooper rating that he said tied Wilfahrt with Carmen
Cavallaro as one of the nation's leading bands.[57] In 1956, *Down Beat
Magazine* announced at an annual convention of the National Ballroom Operators that based on a two-year poll, "Whoopee John's"
band was the most popular polka aggregation in the country.[58]

The band's appeal proved durable even after "Whoopee John's"
death in 1961, when his son Pat took over the ensemble and continued it for nearly a decade thereafter until he, too, died. Still another revival of the group in the mid-1970s was able to get about
one hundred bookings per year.[59]

A group of performers whose careers closely resembled that of
"Whoopee John" and in fact appeared with him on occasion were
the two Plehal Brothers, Tom and Eddie, who were also of Bohemian
descent.[60] Their popularity was much briefer than that of their fellow
Minnesotan, but their rise was actually more meteoric. The Plehals
traveled more extensively and to more distant audiences. They grew
up just west of the Twin Cities and became known for their harmonica playing over WCCO during the 1930s. Their repertoire was
like Wilfahrt's, old-time ethnic music from the same variety of ethnic
groups, but they tended to mix Western swing with their polkas and
waltzes. Just prior to the war, they went off to Hollywood to become
national stars, and they played on national network shows there and

in Chicago. As one might guess, the Kapps of Decca signed them, too.[61] The war began just at the peak of their career, and they both entered the military service. They returned to WCCO, where the Purina Mills program they were on was distributed around the country, and then appeared with both Wilfahrt and on the nationally known Eddie Arnold (country-western) program before ending their public performances about 1949.[62]

One can describe Wilfahrt and the Plehals as nationally-known ethnic musicians in mid-century who helped acquaint the general public to group-based dance music. Another bandleader who contributed to that widespread acceptance is the currently well-known popular bandleader, Lawrence Welk. Welk is much better known for his immensely successful programs over television, which began in the early fifties *after* the era of ethnic music acceptance. However, the public should know that he was an important entertainer before that decade, making his own distinctive contribution to getting the public to support polka music. In the thirties and forties Welk uniquely integrated polkas and polka-style waltzes into the standard dance band repertoire. While it can be said that Wilfahrt was an ethnic bandleader making "Dutchman" music popular throughout America, Welk was essentially an American bandleader of "sweet" music who encouraged the public to consider all polka music as part of the dance band repertoire.

The source of Welk's aim to reform American dance music goes back to the early years of his career, when he idolized the big bands. As he grew up, he fashioned his own ensemble like them, but along with his standard dance band pieces, the foxtrots and rhumbas, he included multi-ethnic European tunes—those that he grew up with in the upper Midwest and those from other ethnic people had known in the East. That strategy, along with a quality of showmanship he learned from three mentors—an itinerant Irish American entertainer, George Kelly; a Midwest ballroom entrepreneur, Tom Archer; and the Chicago Greek American showman, Andrew Karsas—helped Welk gain an astounding durability as a popular entertainer. He was able to last far beyond the close of ethnic music's golden age—into the sixties and seventies, the era of rock. Besides getting good advice from others, as with the other ethnic musicians, Welk's wartime experience was very beneficial, allowing him to make a special appeal to young people, particularly servicemen and their families. At the outset of his career Welk appeared to emerge as the typical regional ethnic music man. But once he became fully professional, he veered into a more distinctive career as a mainstream bandsman with a decidedly ethnic character.

His parents, youth, and early music performance were most assuredly within a particular ethnic community. Welk's mother and father were Russian German immigrants who had come from the Ukraine in 1892. They settled in a German-speaking farming area near Strasburg, North Dakota, where they had relatives.[63] The Welks were a particularly musical family. Welk's father, Ludwig, was a blacksmith who played Old Country tunes, and when Lawrence (born in 1903) was a child his mother taught him to dance to much of the German folk and popular music.[64] The family would often sing and dance in the evenings while the father played the pump organ and the instrument he would later teach Lawrence to play, the accordion. As a young boy, Lawrence loved playing music, especially as he hated farm work and sought an escape from it. When he soon began to perform at barn dances and at weddings at the local German church, Ludwig became increasingly critical, for he did not want his son to become a professional musician. The tension between the elder and younger Welks mounted until 1924, when Lawrence left home to play in a nearby band. He occasionally did return home but by then the young accordionist essentially had committed himself to become a professional musician. He was now playing at *non-ethnic* engagements. In 1927 he teamed up with George Kelly, who led a group called the Peerless Entertainers and taught the budding German American entertainer the rudiments of stage presence.[65]

Welk certainly needed such advice from the more experienced entertainer, for he apparently suffered from a personal dilemma affecting his performance. His goal was then to play for an English-speaking audience, but he did not know the language well. Welk had grown up with little formal schooling and had always used German as his basic language. In fact, he would not learn English well until the late 1920s, and he continued to be reluctant to speak at length to his audience. That hesitancy was to continue for another twenty years, until Welk was well into his forties.

Fortunately reticence did not make him timid as a musician. By 1927, for example, he already viewed himself as a bandleader and was willing to travel far out of his region, going to Texas for a short time to direct a contemporary dance band provided for him there.

When he returned to the Dakotas, Kelly had decided to retire, so Welk struck out on his own entirely, forming his first musical ensemble, a four-piece band. A powerful radio station in Yankton, South Dakota, WNAX, had just been bought by a large seed company and needed a new music director; Welk canceled a trip he had planned to the South and remained at that outlet with his band for nine years, until 1936. During that period he and his ensemble toured the area regularly and became much better known in the region.

In these years, however, it was becoming clear that Welk did not want his band, first known as his "Novelty Orchestra" and later as the "Hotsy Totsy Boys," to be a typical ethnic polka ensemble. He had always admired the emerging swing and sweet bands of the 1920s and 1930s, such as Paul Whiteman's, and the Dixieland groups, such as Red Nichols and his Five Pennies, and certainly by the early thirties he hoped that his men could compete with those American dance ensembles.[66] For example, the very first records he made for Gennett in November 1928 and for Broadway, Lyric, and Vocalion in 1931 were not ethnic pieces but standard contemporary popular tunes. Welk did not record his first polka until 1939.[67]

Welk's bands—he had several during his years with WNAX, because of difficulties with his musicians—were not even the major polka ensemble on that station. That was John Matuska's Bohemian men, who played pieces from the publications of Vitak and Elsnic. Welk and his group, on the other hand, usually performed the more contemporary marches and foxtrots; the polka and waltz were exceptional in their repertoire.[68]

Certainly with the extraordinary power of WNAX's signal, broadcasts of the various Welk bands developed a large audience for him, and invitations for bookings began to come in from all over the upper Midwest listening area. There is some discrepancy as to just how well Welk was doing at this time, around 1930; he apparently had difficulty in maintaining a band and may have left music entirely. But it is also clear that he had many engagements in both the Midwest and beyond, many of them arranged with the help of Tom Archer, owner of a leading network of ballrooms, who like Kelly was an adviser to Welk, instructing the young bandleader on how to put on a successful dance engagement.[69]

By 1936 Welk had been fairly successful as leader of a midwestern territorial band and was beginning to work toward his goal of leading a national dance band like Jan Garber.[70] He quite nearly attained that objective quickly, with bookings in 1937 in major hotels in St. Paul; around New Year's Eve, 1938, at the William Penn Hotel in Pittsburgh, where he first used the "Champagne Music" term to describe his music; and in 1939 at the famous Edgewater Beach Hotel in Chicago, where other nationally known dance bands had played.

His repertoire indicated his musical philosophy about what he played and for whom. His music was chiefly for dancing, and the tunes were the standards played with a smooth and bouncing style. This did not exclude ethnic music, waltzes and polkas, but the objective was to play what was familiar to the masses, catering to what people knew rather than introducing them to new works, a conservative philosophy that aroused the hostility of music critics, who referred to Welk's material as "mickey mouse" and "corn." As a leading reviewer put it later, he satisfied "those who are looking for nice, clean, Rotarian entertainment."[71] Welk himself put it succinctly in a brief comment in *Billboard* Magazine in 1939: "Primarily we try to please all customers."[72]

It was clear then in the late 1930s that Welk wanted his ensemble to be an American dance band that occasionally played ethnic-styled selections. A photograph of his band at Pittsburgh's William Penn Hotel in late 1938 shows them not in lederhosen like Wilfahrt's band or in folk costume like the Viking Accordion Band or Adolph and the Boys of Texas, but in formal attire. They wore white ties, tuxedos, and tails, as befitting the standard hotel dance orchestra.[73] Welk's program from an Edgewater Beach Hotel engagement in mid-September 1939 also showed his eclecticism. He opened with his theme, "Bubbles in the Wine," done in an "unusually tuneful arrangement," followed by "The Beer Barrel Polka," and a novelty song, "Bulldog and Bullfrog," then "When My Baby Smiles at Me," "Ragtime Cowboy Joe," and a vocal, "Old Man Mose."[74] This combination of old favorites with a popular polka such as "Beer Barrel" or "Clarinet Polka," which usually closed his performance in the 1940s, made up his typical presentation, one that made him commercially successful even before his appearance on television.

During the World War II era, with the success of the international-style polka music already noted and its growing commercial potential, Welk began to include more of that genre in his offerings and proceeded to record those selections. Thus came the "Beer Barrel

Polka," for example, for Vocalion in April 1939, the "Clarinet Polka" for Decca in early 1941, and the "Barbara" and "Pennsylvania" polkas a year later for the same label, among many others.[75]

One further booking contributed substantially to Welk's wish to be a nationally known bandleader—his engagement at Andrew Karsas's palatial Trianon Ballroom. In the summer of 1940 he signed a contract with Karsas to play regularly at his ballroom, probably one of the largest in the country.[76] Karsas also included remote radio broadcasts from his establishment, on WGN, one of the leading Midwest outlets.

Karsas was a superb businessman, probably the most successful dance-hall operator in America, and like Kelly and Archer he furthered Welk's education on how to win an audience. He quickly sensed that Welk's reluctance to socialize with the dancers was a problem, no doubt related to his difficulty in speaking English. But he worked on that and made it into a virtue later with the help of a Milwaukee promoter.[77] "The kids who come in here to dance will go home and tell their friends the next day that they got your autograph," Karsas advised, as Welk recalled in his autobiography. "You can establish more goodwill and build up your band more quickly by spending a little more time out there autographing and talking with your audience than you can in any other way."[78]

Welk's engagement at the Trianon was generally successful, and he stayed there for nearly a decade, throughout the forties, appearing also at other Chicago locations, particularly the city's other major dance palace run by the Karsas Brothers, the Aragon. In addition, Welk continued to go on tours to the East. The war itself had a favorable effect on his popularity despite an occasional bad booking. He also authored music albums, the first of which, Leeds Music Corporation's 1942 *Lawrence Welk's Polka Folio,* edited by Harry Harden, identified him as leader of the "most important polka band in America according to popularity polls." Although this estimate may have been an exaggeration, it did indicate that by then he was widely known.[79]

In addition, Welk played at many of the military installations in the Chicago area. He scheduled his own performances for servicemen and also filled in when other entertainers were unable to appear. One visit to a service hospital with his Champagne Lady of the time, Jayne Walton, was recalled as especially welcomed and satisfying.[80] Whether the bandleader realized it or not such performances did a great deal then and later for his goodwill. It is likely his generosity was later rewarded as he familiarized the young servicemen from outside the region with his music and made some of them his fans.

In addition to his work in Chicago, Welk continued during the war to tour extensively. One extended itinerary in the spring of 1942 took him to various locations in the East and Midwest, where he had engagements from the Ritz Ballroom in Bridgeport, Connecticut, to Pennsylvania, Michigan, Iowa, and Kansas City. Not all of his engagements were entirely successful, but he certainly was promoting ethnic music as general dance music. A particularly fortunate booking was at the Capitol Theatre in New York in 1943. The Capitol had engaged the top-named ensembles, and Welk was flattered to be considered one of them.[81]

Probably the major test of the acceptance of Welk's synthesizing old American favorites and ethnic dance pieces, his "Champagne Music," was his first foray to the West Coast in 1945, where he feared that a booking in San Francisco might prove disastrous. The city was full of servicemen returning from the war, and of women who had gone to meet them. What was scheduled as a six-week engagement lasted six months, and Welk then went on to Los Angeles to greet still other enthusiastic crowds.[82] After the death of Andrew Karsas and a disagreement over salary with his brother William, Welk returned to the Aragon Ballroom in Los Angeles in 1951.

In 1953 Welk began his fabulously successful television programming. TV did not make him a star—he had already enjoyed years of national prominence with his "Champagne Music"—but it did bring the North Dakota farm boy a salary of $2 million a year and lasting recognition on the entertainment scene.[83] As early as the late 1930s Welk had devised his repertoire, an unusual mixture of both old ethnic dances and old American standards characterized mainly by their danceability. All along, he had turned his back on the critics, arguing that all he was offering was what his dancers wanted. A *Look* Magazine article put Welk's position succinctly: "Nobody likes him but the people."[84]

Welk's entire career was based on getting to know his audience intimately, and as he did over the years they responded enthusiastically and supportively. The North Dakota bandleader described a typical reaction among the Trianon patrons sometime during the 1940s, an audience on this occasion made up chiefly of young Polish Americans who simply sought to enjoy themselves in a short period of dancing pleasure, which they knew that Welk could provide. They all did the polkas and schottisches in unison, bouncing up and down together as if in a directed unit:

It was the custom . . . for groups of boys and girls to come separately, as well as on dates, and many a lifetime romance began with a tag dance at the Trianon. Some nights we had a predominantly Polish audience, and how that big room would come to life then! The Polish polka is very fast, very quick, and requires tremendous endurance. Watching from the stage as the dancers bobbed up and down, it used to look to me as if the whole floor was on springs.[85]

11

Frankie Yankovic: The Polka King When Polka Was King

On the evening of June 9, 1948, in the City Auditorium in Milwaukee, Wisconsin, an eager crowd of over eight thousand fans had gathered for what they considered a momentous occasion. Aware that the city was possibly *the* American capital of ethnic music, a local impresario had decided to produce a competition to determine the nation's king of polka music.[1]

Such coronations of musical royalty had of course taken place before in other ballrooms in other cities, and they would continue in the future. The polka-mad public loved such contests, as did promoters who saw in them attractive financial rewards. Jerry Dostal of Minnesota, for example, while an active polka music man also played the role of a promoter, holding band "battles" around his state with a fellow bandleader, Harold Loeffelmacher and his Six Fat Dutchmen; in 1947, Brunon Krygier had been involved in a similar naming in Pittsburgh, competing successfully for the crown against fourteen local bands; and fans of the eastern strain of Polish polka music sometimes referred to their own musical kings, Dana recording stars Frank Wojnarowski and Bernie Witkowski.

But the contest in Milwaukee was different; it could actually make a valid claim to status as the nation's most authoritative coronation. Milwaukee was centrally located in the polka belt, which extended from Connecticut to Nebraska and from Texas up to Minnesota and the Dakotas—generally in a large southern arc around the Great Lakes. And while the largest Wisconsin city may not have been the home of a large number of nationally famous bandleaders, it was surrounded by many active German, Czech, and Polish musical communities. In addition, Milwaukee was a leading center of the polka's best instrumental ally, the accordion. In the late 1940s about eight thousand students were enrolled in Milwaukee's accordion schools, a figure cited by the major trade journal as making the Wisconsin metropolis "the best accordion city in the whole country."[2]

Location was not the only significant factor; the timing of this event was critical. Mid-1948 was near the very peak of that second national rage for polka music, when a number of ethnic polkas had finally made it as American hit music. In that year, high on the popular charts was the "Too Fat Polka," sung for Columbia records by the nation's leading radio and TV personality, Arthur Godfrey. It was a novelty number, to be sure, a comic piece rather than a sentimental one, but still a tune that the public undoubtedly loved and accepted widely. This record by Godfrey provided a particular satisfaction to more traditional ethnic-music lovers because its melody was in fact originally an old Bohemian American tune, made over later by English-language arrangers. "Too Fat" was a 1903 tune called "Na Marjance," written by Anthony Maresh, which was recorded in 1906 on Victor E3322. If that hit was insufficient to indicate polkas as popularly American, a number of other contemporary polka or polka-styled tunes of that year were also on the charts, including an old hillbilly country-western tune rearranged into a polka piece, "Just Because," which was selling very well nationally during the Milwaukee festival. "Just Because" had been rewritten by one of Frankie Yankovic's Yanks, Johnny Pecon, and was on its way to golden status, and the Yanks were contestants in the great band battle in Milwaukee. In addition, another widely popular American tune at that time was the Swiss piece, "Toolie Oolie Doolie" (The Yodel Polka), which had been copyrighted in Zurich in 1946 and in the United States two years later by C. K. Harris. Finally, still another polka success in 1948 was the best-known hit of the popular Polish American polka bandleader, Walt Solek, "My Girl Friend Julayda."[3]

In addition to these ethnic-styled tunes sweeping the country, the polka had gained even further recognition in 1948 in the nation's popular-music capital, New York City. When the widely known Guy Lombardo, the man who played "the Sweetest Music This Side of Heaven," took a leave from the Taft Grill of the Roosevelt Hotel, the owners chose to replace this enduring American musical institution with a dance-band leader who was promoting polkas, Law-rence Welk. This temporary substitution of Welk, whose home base was Chicago's Trianon Ballroom, certainly added to his and ethnic music's national stature.[4]

Thus choosing a polka king in Milwaukee was an event that, ac-cording to newspaper reports, assembled thousands of people who were not "jitterbugs" but "polka-bugs."[5] The royal title to be gained there then was undoubtedly important on a nationwide level, and those seeking the honor were all highly regarded by the public. This then was to be a battle of titans.[6] All the musicians present had produced popular hits and in the process had amassed a devoted fan following. The Milwaukee Slovenian, Louis Bashell, for example, had just scored with his "Silk Umbrella Polka," which he claimed had sold 200,000 copies. Romy Gosz, the well-known German-Bohemian musician from upstate Wisconsin with his mellow trum-pet, was another pretender to the title with many enthusiastic sup-porters. Also contending were Harold Loeffelmacher, who with his Six Fat Dutchmen was, along with "Whoopee John," the leading "Dutchman" music interpreter, and Lawrence Duchow and his Red Ravens, who had just made "Swiss Boy Polka" the previous year with an astounding total sales, according to reports, of nearly half a mil-lion records.[7]

The winner by clear majority of votes was Frankie Yankovic, the Cleveland bandleader-accordionist. He with his Yanks had so moved the crowd that at their turn on the stage the band had difficulty stepping down. The dancers refused to let them retire, insisting they be given more than their allotted time.

Yankovic's crowning was not only recognition of his leading place among polka bandleaders but was also symbolic of the transfor-mation of ethnic music over the previous century. As ethnic music and bands changed from the military and concert bands of the nine-teenth century to the specifically ethnic and then commercialized popular ensembles of the twentieth, Yankovic himself went through all those stages and actively helped create the culminating era of ethnic music in the late 1940s and early 1950s.

The polka king's route to national stardom went from the Col-linwood section of Cleveland in the 1910s to Hollywood, Las Vegas, and New York in the 1950s.[8] Like so many other ethnic bandleaders, including Welk, Paone, Witkowski, and Wilfahrt, Yankovic was the son of immigrant parents, yet another refutation of the idea that the American-born generation rejected traditional ethnic culture. Yankovic's parents were both Slovenian newcomers who had gone separately to Davis, West Virginia, in 1903 to work in a lumber camp. The father, a blacksmith, and the mother, a cook for the workers, met and married there.[9] Young Frank was born in Davis in 1915, but almost immediately the family moved to the Collinwood area of Cleveland, where they had relatives and could feel particularly at home in the southern part of the neighborhood, one of the most Slovenian of all American neighborhoods. Many of the immigrants found work in the heavy industry that was located nearby, especially the railroad yards and a large Fisher Body assembly plant.[10]

Yankovic's boyhood was steeped in the Slovenian American cultural milieu. The ethnic language was spoken at home, and his parents often took him to Slovenian cultural events where music was especially prominent. Yankovic recalled that the fraternal lodges, for example, often had old-time brass bands playing at their social functions, particularly for parades, which fascinated the young musician-to-be.[11] Band concerts were of course quite common in American cities in the early 1900s, especially, as we have seen, in Cleveland, which had a plethora of ethnic groups and was a fortunate environment for a future musician such as Yankovic.

For the young Yankovic, even more significant than the musical life of the city at large was what was going on at home. The Yankovic residence was something of a social center for the Slovenian neighborhood. To help with living expenses his mother took in boarders, some of whom were musicians and singers of Slovenian folk tunes. One of the men impressed the young boy in particular. He was Max Zelodec, who apparently taught his eager admirer Slovenian songs on his button box. With the encouragement of his parents, who bought him a three-row German instrument in 1924 when he was only nine years old, Frankie was delighted to play it. As he later recalled his homelife at this time, "We couldn't afford lessons but we took in [Slovenian] boarders at our house and they used to sing all the time. I listened and accompanied them by ear."[12]

As a teenager in the late 1920s and into the depression, Yankovic's musical experience followed the pattern typical of many ethnic musicians. He worked at various jobs for the local Slovenian community, at weddings and other ceremonies, especially at the large Slovenian National Home. Besides being able to get dates from his ethnic neighbors who were eager to dance, he had the support of his parents, especially his mother, who despite the hard times of the depression prevailed over his father's initial opposition to buying him an expensive $500 piano accordion, the instrument to which Yankovic switched in 1931. The high status of such a musician in Slovenian American society likely made the family willing to make the sacrifice.

Another boost to his career was his association with Joe Trolli the following year. Trolli was an arranger-composer of Italian American background with whom Yankovic would have a long and fruitful relationship lasting most of his life. He would work with the accordionist in modifying the many ethnic, especially Slovenian, tunes with which Yankovic was familiar.[13] Also helpful at this early stage of his career was his first band, a trio of accordion, banjo, and drums, an instrumentation characteristic of the Slovenian music then played in Cleveland, particularly the many Lausche pieces that Yankovic knew.[14] Lausche was of course Yankovic's dentist as well as to some extent his musical mentor.

Yankovic's ensembles over the years were always small; he never sought a large dance orchestra like the ones led by Welk and Wilfahrt. His musical "sound" would not change significantly, though in 1938 he did add a few pieces, such as a piano and stringed bass, that enhanced that sound rather than changing it. Still later he added a solovox and/or a second accordion, chiefly to increase volume while retaining the intimacy of a small ensemble.

Radio and recordings assisted Yankovic in the depression as they had for so many other ethnic bands. The Slovenian Sunday program in the ethnic series promoted by the Polish American John Lewandowski over WJAY gave Yankovic his first broadcasting opportunity in 1932. He would play regularly on radio programs for the rest of his career. For example, in 1938 the major Slovenian radio impresario, "Heinie" Martin Antoncic, put the young accordionist on his show on WGAR, and Yankovic profited much from that association.[15] By then Yankovic felt that he and his men were ready to make records, and he went to both Columbia and Victor for contracts. Both firms, however, turned him down, Columbia because of its own internal structural problems and Victor because it simply did not want to expand its ethnic offerings.[16] Probably because of this rejection, Yankovic turned to his friend Antoncic and a Czech promoter, Fred Wolf, head of the Cleveland Recording Company, both of whom were happy to help him make records on his own.[17] The band then recorded Yankovic's first two records in 1938 under the Yankee label—three polkas and a waltz medley, all of them Slovenian.[18] Four more Slovenian pieces done by the "Joliet Jolly Jugoslavs" appeared under the Joliet label the following year.[19] Both runs, totaling about 6,000 records, sold out immediately with the help of the distribution of Anton Mervar's music firm.[20]

Yankovic was tiring of working in factories and playing music only as an avocation, so he joined with a few others and opened a bar late in 1941. The tavern soon became a center of polka musicians. Besides attracting the notable young ethnic musicians and bandleaders of the time, such as Kenny Bass, Johnny Vadnal, and Eddie Habat, Yankovic's cafe also drew frequent visits from his fellow accordionist Johnny Pecon, who would later substantially help Yankovic's rise to national visibility. But America quickly entered the war and complicated Yankovic's musical career; he was in his mid-twenties, and in 1943 he decided to enter the army by requesting induction.

At first it appeared to many, including Yankovic himself, that because of the war, he would have to suspend his drive to gain recognition as a polka bandleader. Yet in a number of ways, the future polka king profited greatly from being in the service. The demand, of course, for recorded ethnic dance music mounted through the war, and Yankovic returned home on leave a few times to supply that demand. He continued his association with Fred Wolf, recording more tunes on the new Jolly label and cutting discs for the new Continental company, which as we have seen was anxious to promote ethnic music. Between 1942 and 1945 Yankovic recorded about fifty pieces in all.[21]

With polka popularity soaring in the postwar era, opportunities expanded for musicians such as Lawrence Duchow, Johnny Vadnal, and Yankovic. In February 1946, Columbia eagerly engaged Yankovic.[22] The arrangement helped substantially in making him into a national star, and he continued with that label for about a quarter-century, during which time he made about two hundred recorded pieces. His band's disc sales were in the millions.[23]

The new attention from the recording industry led Yankovic to reconsider his philosophy. He decided to play not just for Slovenians but for the public in general, especially, as he stated, for the working classes. Almost from the time he finished high school until he went off to war, Yankovic himself worked at blue-collar jobs, mainly as a patternmaker in a foundry and at the familiar Fisher Body plant in his Collinwood neighborhood. Especially in the immediate postwar era, this ethnic bandleader sought to find a common denominator in the musical taste of the ordinary American. His motivation was not only class- and ethnic-based, of course, but highly practical as well; he knew he could make more money by appealing to a multi-ethnic, American audience. He put his idea simply and candidly at the very beginning of his autobiography: "Although there are . . . doctors, lawyers and architects in our audiences, I like to think of myself as the blue collar worker's musician. I'm proud of that. After all, this country was built on the blood and sweat and guts of the blue collar man. . . . I'm a blue collar guy and so was my father. So were most of the people I've been close to." And he concluded with an insight into his own ability in music: "I'm just an average guy who is lucky enough to understand what a lot of average guys in the country like to hear."[24]

Yankovic's new-found aim to be more ecumenical, eclectic, and commercial in his repertoire came largely, if not totally, from his military experience in the war. While he was still in Europe after seeing action at the Battle of the Bulge in 1945 he met Sidney Mills, his sergeant, who offered him a new performing philosophy. Mills was a nephew of Irving Mills, who ran the famous Mills Music Publishing Company in New York. The younger Mills urged Yankovic to consider that larger American mass audience and reach them by hooking up with his uncle's firm. It was advice that the Slovenian American took to heart and acted upon when the opportunity presented itself. And it did so quickly when he joined with Johnny Pecon. Together, they helped make Yankovic's Yanks one of the nation's most popular *American,* not just ethnic, bands.

Before entering this new recording phase of his new universalist career, Yankovic had to rebuild his band, stressing the full sound he was perfecting just before his induction into the service. In 1946 he again based his instrumentation on a solovox (electric organ) along with an additional accordionist. Fortunately, he was able to obtain the latter in Johnny Pecon. Pecon had known Yankovic before the war, had frequented Yankovic's bar, and above all was a superb musician. One will recall, too, that he was a protege of Dr. William Lausche. He became a business partner of Yankovic's when he and several others joined with the bandleader to open a second bar, which again became the major center of the Cleveland ethnic and polka musical community.

Yankovic, with his band and business reestablished and his association resumed with arranger-composer Joe Trolli, embarked in 1946 on an immensely prolific period of composition and performance. Now he, Trolli, and Pecon worked together to update—one could say "Americanize"—some of the old Slovenian folk and Slovenian American popular tunes. As Yankovic recalled their work, they would spend much time in the basement of Yankovic's bar poring over their compositions. "Joe Trolli, my old accordion teacher, Pecon and I would take old Slovenian folk tunes that had been around for hundreds of years, put new piano and accordion arrangements to them and add American titles."[25]

This composing trio was now creating music that one might term crossover, tunes that the many crossover ethnic bands of the day had been performing since the thirties. The products of this Yankovic-Pecon-Trolli collaboration were hardly sectarian. They got their material from wherever they could find a likely hit, including other ethnic traditions. For example, Trolli exploited his own Italian background in composing the popular "Tic Toc Polka," and from the German tradition they obtained the "Rosalinda Waltz." The Mills Company willingly published the first of many folios of these new eclectic Yankovic pieces about 1947.[26]

In the immediate postwar period Yankovic not only drew readily from a varied ethnic background for his pieces but he also designed his Yanks' repertoire as a melding of many group and American musical traditions. Of course such a strategy would not only produce new tunes but also be good business, as it would enlarge his audience considerably. And it would pull together many different Americans. Thus, Yankovic was really continuing what the "international" polka style had begun ten years earlier. "I always figured if I aimed my music toward only one nationality, I would be cutting down on the market," he admitted in his 1977 autobiography. "So I tried to develop a sound that *all* nationalities could identity with."[27] He reiterated that objective in a 1980 interview: he "worked for a sound that would appeal to everybody, not to maybe just Yugoslavs or to the Polish people or to the German people or to the Czech people . . . [one that] appealed to all the different ethnic groups [as] one specific nationality."[28] Yankovic's two back-to-back major hits, "Just Because" in 1947–48 and "Blue Skirt Waltz" of 1948–49 had just that assimilative impact—really forging an *American* polka. These hits came at the height of polka acceptance in the nation, and Yankovic was both the major promoter and the major beneficiary.

It was Pecon who brought "Just Because" to Yankovic's attention, in a way that again shows the formative influence of World War II in broadening musical taste.[29] As a protege of William Lausche in the thirties, Pecon had already been involved in ethnic polka music and had frequently visited, and sometimes played at, the various polka bars and dance halls, including the Twilight Ballroom, Tino's Bar, the Metropole Cafe, and just before Pearl Harbor, Yankovic's new tavern.[30] In 1942 he enlisted in the service, in his case the Navy Seabees, and he was shipped to New Guinea in the South Pacific. While there, the Slovenian American accordionist did on occasion perform, and in the process he exchanged pieces with musicmen of differing backgrounds.[31] One guitarist played a country-western tune, called "Just Because," which was written by the Shelton Brothers, Bob and Joe, and Joe Robin around 1936 and had been recorded on Decca about then.[32] The piece affected Pecon, and he took it with him back to Cleveland, where with Yankovic's encouragement he reworked it as a polka tune after he joined the Yanks in 1946.[33] Because Columbia feared a recording industry strike about that time and wanted to build a large inventory of discs to be released, they called Yankovic to New York late in the year to cut a number of tunes, one of which was their made-over "hillbilly" piece on a second side.[34]

The result was unexpected by both Yankovic and Columbia, as the tune scored in places not known as centers of polka enthusiasm. Somewhere around 20,000 to 30,000 records of "Just Because" were sold immediately in Boston during the early weeks of January 1948, and Columbia sent Yankovic there to encourage more sales.[35] In a few months, "Just Because" became the Yanks' first golden record, selling about a million. *Billboard* Magazine rated it thirty-fifth of the year's most-played jukebox selections.[36]

Another hit record, "Blue Skirt Waltz," followed in 1949 on the heels of "Just Because" to push the Yankovic quintet by 1950 into the position of one of the nation's most popular vocal bands. The source of this second triumph was rather distant from the country-western tradition; it came from Czech popular music. In addition it was Yankovic's music publisher, Jack Mills, who made the initial suggestion to record the work, not the bandleader or any of his men.

Probably sometime in 1948 Mills sent Yankovic a list of Bohemian tunes for possible recording.[37] One of the pieces, entitled "Sukynka (Cervena)" or "Red Skirt Waltz," had been composed by Vaclav Blaha probably in 1944 and published in Prague in 1948. It was particularly appealing to the Yanks' bandleader, who urged Mills to get someone to write English lyrics for it. Mills complied, recruiting Mitchell Parish, who had written such successful lyrics for "Stardust," among other pieces. In the meantime, Yankovic got Columbia to arrange to record it. Because the song's lyrics required female vocalists, the record executives contracted with a relatively unknown duet, the Marlin Sisters, to accompany the Yanks. The women had had no popular hits and had never done any polka-styled material. Their major experience had been rendering Jewish songs in and around the New York City area. In any event this odd ethnic mixture of a Bohemian tune, Slovenian musicians, and Jewish vocalists clicked, and upon its release January 17, 1949, it turned out to be an even greater hit than "Just Because."[38]

Just why "Blue Skirt" did so well is open to speculation. Certainly there were several contributing factors, perhaps mainly related to the special appeal of the "sound" that Yankovic wanted to make his distinctive trademark, the sound of a small ensemble of banjo, solovox, and accordions, similar to the Cleveland-style polka bands.[39] Another factor, of course, was the historical moment in which it appeared, when so many other popular pieces were ethnic-based polkas and waltzes. In fact, another Cleveland ethnic band had put out "The Blue Skirt Waltz" with Parish's English lyrics just before Columbia released the Yankovic version, and it too had been a hit, selling only slightly fewer than its later competing disc.[40]

An additional contribution were the English lyrics, a major improvement over the originals, telling a story much more acceptable to American audiences. Both versions concentrated on color, but the English lyrics chose blue, which made for a more romantic and sentimental ballad than the original red. The Czech narrative is simple and direct, that of a woman who states that the dress she will wear to greet her lover will have the same hue as a cherished one she wore as a young schoolgirl:

> When I was a little girl attending school,
> My mother always dressed me in my little dress,
> It had to be a red skirt, otherwise I would not go.
> Today I have such a skirt which I love best, a little red skirt I love best
>   of all.
> This evening I will put it on when you come
> The little skirt, nicely hemmed, decorated by folds,
> Like our love, it will be forever.[41]

Parish's English version is more complex, a male/female dialogue using blue more symbolically. Perhaps it was fitting that Yankovic and Johnny Pecon did the male vocal response on the record:[42]

[*Female*] I wandered alone one night till I heard an orchestra play
I met you when lights were bright, and people were carefree and gay.
I was a beautiful lady in blue, I was in heaven just waltzing with you,
You thrilled me with strange delight, then softly you stole away.

[*Male*] I dreamed of that night with you, lady, when first we met.
We danced in a world of blue, how can my heart forget.
Blue were the skies and blue were your eyes, just like the blue skirt she
    wore.
Come back, blue lady, come back, don't be blue anymore.[43]

Exactly how well this second Yankovic hit sold is difficult to state.
It is generally accepted that it, too, was a golden disc, reaching
fourteenth on the popular charts. Certainly it was a best-seller for
about six months.[44] It turned out to be the second most popular
record in 1949 for Columbia, after its leading cut, Gene Autry's
hugely successful "Rudolph the Red Nosed Reindeer."[45] But statistics are less important than its general impact along with "Just Because" from the previous year. The two recordings had certainly
heightened the public's enthusiasm for records of polka-type bands.

Because that Milwaukee polka festival of June 1948 took place
between the two hits, it is easy to understand why the thousands
attending chose Yankovic as king by a wide margin, nearly eight to
one. The selection not only identified a leader of polka music but
also reflected the general rage for that new musical genre among all
generations, both young and old. "Teenagers are jumping from jit-
terbugging to polka dancing," observed the local reporter covering
the event. "This latest trend of the younger set was inescapable at
the Auditorium . . . when . . . students of the 'jump and toss' school
of dance gathered to crown the Polka King." The reporter said he
was informed that dancing schools were "swamped by requests from
high school kids who want polka lessons," and that a band booker
had told of "women in their seventies so crippled with rheumatism
they could hardly negotiate the stairs . . . frolicking around like
young fillies after the music started."

Record-company representatives also reported that the polka craze
had assumed truly national proportions, equaling if not outstripping
the appeal of big swing bands. As an RCA supplier covering Wisconsin and Michigan put it: "Without even hearing them, our record
dealers would place orders of 2,000 copies of the latest releases of
Duchow and the Dutchmen. . . . That's twice as much as any name
band—including Tommy Dorsey—can attract." A recording-industry

executive from New York said that midwestern polka bands were getting such a response in Texas, Oklahoma, and elsewhere that "we can't fill orders." Phil Spitalny, the New York bandleader well known for his female orchestra, told the Milwaukee festival promoter that "people all over the country are going crazy over polkas and [similar] folk music."[46]

It is certain that these Milwaukee observations were not just a local response to a local polka festival. Yankovic's ensuing tour of the entire country was highly successful. His ensemble both capitalized on the mounting polka dance enthusiasm and further stimulated it, before and especially after the release of his "Blue Skirt Waltz." Early in 1949, right after Columbia released the piece, *Billboard* Magazine found in a survey that the Yanks had vaulted quickly from obscurity into thirteenth place among the nation's bands most played on jukeboxes.[47]

The impact was far more than the appearance of a new popular band; it was the appearance of a new popular music. A newspaper critic in 1949 identified the deeper significance of Yankovic's "Just Because" when he asserted, "Yankovic took an old Hill-Billy tune and started a national polka craze."[48] Later that year one of the local polka bandleaders promoted another band competition in Milwaukee, this time a battle of different musical genres, polka versus jazz. Before another large crowd, the Yanks and some other ethnic ensembles competed with Duke Ellington and his band, with the prize once again going to the Slovenian American.[49]

For the next few years, until the mid-fifties at least, the Yanks toured the nation as one of the leading popular *American* bands. They ran an incredibly full schedule in 1949, apparently appearing on 275 nights at ballrooms and dance halls, even outdrawing in small and large towns the much better-known commercial bands of Guy Lombardo and Vaughn Monroe, according to *Time* Magazine.[50]

If their gig at the Chicago Sokol Hall in November of 1949 is any indication of the kind of music they played, it was a judicious mixture of ethnic and contemporary American dance tunes. Yankovic himself sang these pieces in many languages, including English, German, Bohemian, Polish, and of course his own Slovenian.[51] Whatever the repertoire and the music variety, this polka band achieved what had eluded other ethnic ensembles. They even won bookings in the more sophisticated nightclubs of the nation's entertainment capitals, in New York, Hollywood, and Las Vegas. At these centers they introduced what had been an ethnic and working-class musical form to the American upper classes. For example in 1949 the Yanks found a warm reception for their ethnic music for two months among patrons at the Village Barn in New York City.[52] And over the next two years, 1950 and 1951, they were often on the West Coast in Hollywood and on the Las Vegas strip performing at the famous clubs there. They played at Los Angeles's Aragon Ballroom for six weeks and while in the area made a number of five-minute movie shorts for Universal, especially of their twin hits.[53]

The major nightclub the Yanks appeared at was the famous Mocambo's in Hollywood, where they played an eight-week engagement on Monday and Thursday nights in the summer of 1950. There the Yanks instructed many of the major stars in the new fad.[54] The society section of the local Los Angeles newspaper listed the well-known personalities trying their hand at the new steps, such as Jane Wyman with Sir Cedric Hardwicke, Betty Hutton with Pat De Cicco, Diana Lynn and John Lindsey, Rosalind Russell and Freddie Brisson, Spike and Helen Jones, Lorraine Cugat and Virgil Moore, along with others, including Ann Sheridan and Gale Storm.[55]

They first had a little difficulty mastering the quick two-step as they "panted and puffed around the dance floor."[56] But with the Yanks' strategy of slow pieces first and quicker tunes later, the exclusive audience of Hollywood society persisted and ultimately did master the polka. The entire experience was obviously highly satisfying to the Cleveland bandleader, who noted the newly elevated status of his music, formerly a maligned lower-class dance. Yankovic observed with satisfaction that now that polka music was sweeping the country, he and his Yanks "had [the movie stars] in the palms of our hands."[57]

Yankovic had clearly arrived as a major national bandleader, helped, of course, by the promotional efforts of his record company. One promotional gimmick was to push polka dot dresses with department stores. With such aids but more likely because of the continuing appeal of that ethnic music, the Ohio Slovenian continued to find a ready acceptance and a good audience nearly everywhere, especially in the nation's entertainment capitals and with the media generally. He recorded at least three songs, for example, with Doris Day in 1950, and in either late 1950 or early 1951 he won first place on the nationally known radio program, "Arthur Godfrey's Talent Scouts."[58] A photograph of him with Bob Hope and Marilyn Maxwell in 1951 suggests that the Yanks were back at the Mocambo a second time.[59]

Yankovic also appeared at the Golden Nugget at Las Vegas about then, where his polkas were so popular that they motivated his audience to violate club rules. His booking was in the Nugget's cocktail lounge, where dancing was not permitted, but when the Yanks played, the patrons left their tables and did the steps anyway, in any available space.[60] He found a similar enthusiasm in 1952, when he and his men were paid $2,500 to play at Lake Tahoe's Wagon Wheel during the World Olympics.[61] Throughout the fifties, Yankovic continued his extended national touring and made appearances on many of the major television variety shows.[62]

Yankovic and his Yanks, of course, were not the only and perhaps not even the most popular ensemble playing polka-ethnic music. Lawrence Welk's appeal during the Slovenians' heyday around the early 1950s was at least equal to if not greater than that of the five touring musicmen from Cleveland. But the two bandleaders differed: Welk was leading a big band that played essentially all-time favorites, some of which were ethnic polkas, while Yankovic was basically an ethnic musician who by his musical arrangements and performance transformed that kind of music so it would appeal to all Americans.[63]

Epilogue

Any discussion of a peak of popular interest inevitably must deal with its decline. The national love affair with polkas came to an end. Yet that decline of mass enthusiasm meant not the demise of old-time ethnic music but rather its transformation and change after midcentury and even, recently, a modest revival.

Certainly no one can doubt that polka music suffered a weakening of popularity in the late 1950s, for which observers have offered several explanations. For one, all popular music was undergoing a revolutionary change at that time, and what people had liked up to 1960 was increasingly rejected afterward. Another genre—rock and roll, of course—was the dynamic new attraction in music. When the bulk of the consumers of popular music began rejecting the older song stylings of Tin Pan Alley, with its big bands and crooners, ethnic music also suffered. Music publishers like Shapiro, Bernstein and Mills Music Company had so closely tied polkas to that kind of "sweet" music that when many in the audience started to reject the traditional pieces they also started to reject the old ethnic music.

There were other reasons for the decline of polka and ethnic music's popularity in the 1960s. One was the greater hostility of many intellectuals and upper-class Americans to what those tunes represented, a socially and culturally pluralistic society. For these people the melting pot had always been a much-desired social and cultural objective, and ethnic music, which had always labored under the burden of low artistic status, was further condemned for its association with an unassimilated, boorish lower class, the ethnic *lumpen proletariat*.[1] More than ever, the American elite in the 1950s and 1960s regarded polkas and like music as part of the mediocre, distasteful culture of beer-drinking, half-literate, white working class clods—people like "Ignatz Dombrowski, 274 pounds, 5-foot-4," who "got his education by writing into a firm on a matchbook cover."[2]

In addition, new recreational forms undercut the older enthusiasm for ballroom dancing, which of course damaged the advocacy for polkas, waltzes, and foxtrots. New steps attracting the public, especially the younger generation, were those associated with newer music and newer dances. By 1960 the big-band age was over, and many of the old, palatial ballrooms that had catered to those ensembles *in tandem with* polka bands had either closed or were used for other activities.

Those large dance structures and halls became uneconomical in addition as many of the public turned away from dancing entirely for their recreation. Instead, they engaged in more passive forms of leisure fostered by the new major entertainment medium of the 1950s and 1960s, television. The former type of ethnic dancing simply could not adapt to the emerging dominant visual technology.

One polka-styled band did survive and in fact thrive in the new era, but only because it altered its format. Lawrence Welk's surprising ability to hold the general public's support all through this era was a result of his showmanship and his willingness in the new television age to adapt his performance to sight as well as sound. He gave his audience something new in the 1960s, called "visual vaudeville," song and dance acts. The North Dakota accordionist was no longer leading a band that played polkas, waltzes, and foxtrots for dancers. His listeners now were far more watchers than participants.

A particular event of the 1960s illustrated just how dated the old polka music was. In 1963 a Milwaukee ethnic composer-promoter, Bob Kames, remembering the boisterous festival of fifteen years earlier, organized another meeting of polka stars, reassembling some of the participants from that 1948 City Auditorium festival, including Yankovic, Gosz, and Bashell, along with younger bandleaders, Gene Heier and Georgie Cook. The purpose of this gathering, however, was not to have a throng choose a king. This congregation was more nostalgic, seeking to make an-all star record recalling the ethnic musical genre's popular past.[3]

Still, with all this evidence of decline one could not say that the 1960s were marked by total abandonment of ethnic music. Welk, even if he had switched from the Trianon Ballroom to television, did continue to play his polkas to a devoted audience Saturday nights. Frankie Yankovic was able to maintain a touring schedule for years, even through the 1980s. And regional ethnic music bands like Wojnarowski, Witkowski, and many easterners were still able to find bookings at clubs and halls and to appear on radio and records. In fact, as we have seen, Wojnarowski's biggest hit "Matka" (Mother) came in 1961 for Dana and made it to golden status.

This residual ethnic music activity of the 1960s and later was especially evident, of course, in the genre's old epicenters, the upper Midwest area, Cleveland, Chicago, Minnesota, and the East. A source of this continuing regional support was the revival of ethnic consciousness in the late 1960s and thereafter. While some Americans, chiefly those of southern and eastern European background, were experiencing a new sense of identity and demanding increased cultural recognition and expression, a growing number of community and parish festivals responded to that sentiment. This atmosphere of the late 1960s encouraging ethnic pluralism provided the kind of greater opportunity the ethnic bands sought. New Ulm, for example, that longtime center of "Dutchman" music, had actually started its annual Polka Day long before the "ethnic revival," with its several area bands performing in late July 1953. They drew a modest 10,000 over several days. But through the 1960s that attendance exploded, reaching about 33,000 in 1966.[4]

Other evidence, too, indicated that the general public had not totally forgotten its earlier enthusiasm for the genre. Will Glahe could still get a hit polka record in 1957 with his "Lichtensteiner Polka" on the London label.[5] And Welk, too, was able finally to produce his first and only golden disc in that time of declining ethnic music. That was his 1961 hit, "Calcutta," which was appropriately a tune of German origin.

During the years after 1960 the polka community itself did not disappear but experienced a certain renewal of energy and creativity, particularly from Chicago. An important element in this resurgence was the new type of Polish polka music offered by "L'il Wally" (Władziu Jagiello). His songs echoed the original rural *wiejska* (village) music that was reminiscent of the Windy City in the 1920s. Becoming prominent in the 1950s by recording mostly on his own

Jay Jay label, Jagiello offered highly unusual polka pieces for the time, virtually all of them sung in Polish. While he was no American pop star, he nonetheless captured a large and devoted ethnic following with a style that was slower and earthier than that of the more commercialized Polish easterners. In addition, "L'il Wally" was an artistic success.[6]

Undoubtedly, another aid to Chicago's growing dominance was the existence of a lively center for its Polish polka musicians, much as Cleveland had provided in the 1940s. That was Antonina Blazonczyk's Pulaski Village, which opened in 1948 and which she later replaced with her Club Antoinette in 1967. These night spots became hangouts and magnets for local ethnic musicians, men like the button box virtuoso Eddie Zima, Steve Adamczyk, Johnny Bomba, and of course her son who today has one of the leading polka ensembles, Eddie Blazonczyk.[7]

Still another development which shifted more polka music westward to Chicago in the postwar era was organizational. That was the coming together of certain polka supporters, led mainly by Leon Kozicki, to assure the preservation and protection of that music for posterity. He and his colleagues saw in the early 1960s that some kind of institutionalization, in the form of associational backing, was necessary. Thus in 1968, after sponsorship of annual polka conventions since 1963, these Chicago musicmen formed the International Polka Association. Since then the IPA has been holding its annual summer conventions in particular to bestow awards on various deserving polka musicians and entertainers. The Association has memorialized some of the winners by including them in a Polka Hall of Fame in a museum it established.

All these events carry the story down to the present, when it appears that a current revival of interest in the musical genre is taking place. Other supporters have recently formed other promotional societies, such as the United States Polka Association, the Polka Lovers' Klub of America (Po.L.K. of A.), centered in Minnesota, and the Wisconsin Polka Boosters. Two promoters have also established other Polka Halls of Fame, one in Cleveland, mostly under the efforts of the leading promoter there, Tony Petkovsek, and another in Chisholm, Minnesota. A 1985 observer counted at least sixty active polka bands in the Cleveland area alone.[8]

Further, the major genre communication, *The Polka News*, has helped maintain support. It often publicizes the many radio stations offering ethnic music programming, which actually have grown over the past few years, especially on the AM band and over public radio networks. Several surveys have documented the growing health of that kind of media support for the genre, especially in the 1980s. One listed 227 radio stations offering old-time ethnic music in 22 states; another in 1980 showed 189 outlets in 20 states offering 566 hours, which had grown to 201 stations in 27 states and 640 hours in 1990; and a third counted 291 stations playing polka music in 31 states in 1988, which had increased to 354 stations in 32 states in 1989.[9] Still another recent boost to the genre was the formation of a polka disc-jockey association, organized largely by Robert Norgard of Clinton, Ohio.[10] Finally, certain European ensembles have also aided the music's continuance in America, especially the high-quality performances of the Slavko Avsenik group from Yugoslavia, which since 1970 has occasionally toured the United States.[11]

It is no wonder, then, that the National Academy of Recording Arts decided to add the polka category in 1985. The winners who followed Yankovic (through 1988) were Eddie Blazonczyk and Jimmy Sturr. Sturr, of Irish descent from Florida, New York, has won the award most often, in 1986, 1987, and 1988.[12]

If one had to select the most important factor in the dissemination of ethnic music among all Americans, it would have to be the powerful capitalistic value in our culture, the desire to make money. As we have seen, such an urge overrode all other concerns, even including ideology with respect to assimilation of the many immigrants. I am not citing the drive for profit as preeminent among all ethnic bands; certainly many were content to play locally at local and private affairs for not much more than expenses. But it is clear that polkas and other ethnic music forms became nationally popular chiefly as a result of the efforts of individuals who saw large income in making that music popular. One can simply not underestimate the power of money-making in American society, which in this case promoted cultural change in contravention of national social policy, as in the 1920s.

That irresistible drive for profits affected our national musical culture from nearly the beginning. From the mid-1800s, the new profit-oriented commercial concert bands, heavily made up of immigrants, especially Italians, played ethnic tunes such as Italian arias because they thought such music would be popular. And they were successful, as the stardom of Giuseppe Creatore signified.

In the next era, too, from the early 1900s into the 1920s, the new arbiters of American popular music, national phonograph companies, also earnestly sought enlarged profits by recording ethnic pieces for a certain, if modest, market. Unconcerned with whether that action would hasten or retard their customers' assimilation, these firms went ahead and cut even the most ethnic pieces, folk and dance tunes as well as comic skits, especially wedding songs. Overall, these records may well have acted more to preserve than to do away with the many group cultures.

This segment of American business, led by companies like Victor and Columbia, found allies in their marketing to ethnic groups in another business community harboring equally powerful entrepreneurial and commercial objectives, the ethnic music storeowner. Almost every group had at least one, such as the Poles' Sajewski, the Ukrainians' Surmach, the Irish DeWitt, the Jews' Katzenellenbogen, the Italians' Di Martino, and above all, the fabulously successful Czech firm of Vitak and Elsnic. These proprietors were particularly important figures in the interwar era as they sought to preserve their ethnic cultures by selling books and records or, perhaps, sought to make money by promoting their groups' artistic heritage. Whatever their motivation, these ethnic businessmen acted as both middlemen and impresarios for resident ethnic composers, arrangers, musicians, and entertainers. Especially in the 1920s and 1930s they helped get their artists on record and radio.

In the depression a new force appeared, promoting a new type of ethnic music. This was a group of agents both within and without the ethnic groups who sought to broadcast that kind of music widely, to more than a single ethnic community. If the music businessmen could make money promoting their own music, some now thought, along with new musicians and entertainers, that they could make more from a multi-ethnic and general American audience. Fortunately the timing was perfect; by the depression and war eras, the consumers themselves had changed to be more receptive to a more synthetic music—these were younger, American-born children of immigrants, who largely had retained a love for some of the traditional polkas and waltzes but also had developed a love for the more indigenous jazz, had learned the English language, and had even developed familiarity with elements of other ethnic cultures. A newer communications technology and a more popular form of recreation among both the ethnic and general American population also supported the entrepreneurial urge to create a mass audience for ethnic music. In the depression especially, the entire public had taken to dancing as a universal recreational form, and they avidly listened to radio and danced to the jukebox, seeking inexpensive fun in hard times.

When the consumers of popular music sought happy, lively dance music wherever they could find it, the producers and the musicians offered it. Some of the old ethnic performers and many new ones now became "crossover" musicians. Their arrangers were now borrowing tunes from other ethnic groups and even from indigenous American songs. Tin Pan Alley, the American music publishers, just like the earlier American recording companies, were always desperate for a hit—within the musical formula, to be sure—and they began pushing "international" tunes, which could appeal to all. Even more than the performers, certain music industry promoters, such as Kapp, Mills, Shapiro, Demetriades, Shapiro, Gabor, Dana, and Porges, were centrally responsible for bringing about ethnic music's golden age at midcentury. It was that group behind the scenes who realized the great commercial potential of ethnic dance and vocal music in the American mass market.

Ethnic performers, of course, also played a role in this ethnic impact on American popular music, necessitating a shift in their philosophy. The most successful practitioner of popular polka music was Frankie Yankovic, a Cleveland Slovenian who worked with the promoters to gain a national audience. He spoke for many of his colleagues and associates when he identified as the key to success the ethnic performer's ability to change, to fit the pieces played for new audiences under new conditions: "I wanted the polka to reach all ethnic groups, and all teenagers, as well . . . I got rid of the brass and tried to get a smoother . . . more elegant sound by filling in with two accordions. Later I started using [an] electronic keyboard. You've got to stay up to date."[13] Those popular ethnic tunes with foreign titles were actually Americanized pieces reworked by the ethnic music industry to make them broadly appealing.

New communications technology also played a role in this attempt to be more eclectic and universal. Radio for example, could break the parochial world of its listeners during the depression in a way the older entertainment form, the record, could not. Apparently, the reach of radio in the United States in the 1930s was probably greater than in any other country, quite possibly making American ethnic music more open to outside influences than that elsewhere in the world.

World War II only added to that awareness, increasing the influence of and interchange among many ethnic cultures. What had once been discrete musical communities became musically assimilated, and previously segregated American ethnic musicmen could now see wider musical and especially commercial opportunities.

By 1948 Frankie Yankovic's ethnic band proved that it could become a leading popular *American* ensemble by performing modified ethnic tunes. At the same time, it demonstrated that it could become popular by doing the reverse, by taking an indigenous, older American song like "Just Because," rendering it in a particular ethnic style—in that case, Cleveland Slovenian—and still make it a hit.

While Yankovic, the polka king, may not have been aware of it, naming his band the "Yanks" had a particular irony. No ensemble could have been more thoroughly American than these "Yanks," musicians who had emerged from an ethnic community and who played essentially ethnic music. In the present as in the past, our nation produces popular music that remains pluralistic.

Notes

Introduction

1. *Webster's Ninth New Collegiate Dictionary* (Springfield, Mass.: G. & C. Merriam, 1983).

2. I am following the musical genre first laid out in the pioneering volume edited by Judith McCulloh, *Ethnic Recordings in America: A Neglected Heritage* (Washington, D.C.: American Folklife Center, 1982).

3. From the late 1930s RCA Victor designated its purple-label ethnic recordings as its "International Series," and both *Billboard* magazine and the Standard Recording Company used the term "international" at that time. Note also "Eric Olzen" in *Eric Olzen's Scandinavian Dance Album* (Chicago: Chart Music Company, 1937); Janet Ann Kvam, "Norwegian-American Dance Music in Minnesota and Its Roots in Norway: A Comparative Study," (Doctor of Musical Arts diss., University of Missouri–Kansas City, 1986), p. 152, has the general definition.

4. E.g., Bill C. Malone, *Country Music USA: A Fifty-Year History,* rev. ed. (Austin: University of Texas Press, 1985), pp. 39ff. Regrettably, the distinction may remain a bit ambiguous because country music is Anglo-Celtic in origin, and some may insist that like polka music it can be designated "ethnic old time." Ibid., pp. 1, 4. For more on "old time" as country-western, see Charles Wolfe, "Columbia Records and Old Time Music", *John Edwards Memorial Foundation Quarterly* 51:118 (1978); Simon J. Bronner, *Old Time Music Makers of New York State* (Syracuse: Syracuse University Press, 1987), pp. xiii–xv; Robert Cantwell, *Bluegrass Breakdown* (Champaign: University of Illinois Press, 1984), esp. 195; and R. P. Christeson, ed., liner notes to *Old Time Fiddlers Repertory: Historic Recordings of Forty-One Traditional Tunes,* phonograph record (Columbia: University of Missouri Press, 1976). The editorials in *Polka and Old Time News* (Min-

neapolis–St. Paul) 1 (June 1964): 3; and Brian Juntikka, "The Year of the Polka," *Entertainment Bits* 17 (December–January 1990): 5, show the difficulty of identifying "polka" music discretely.

5. Music of these ethnic groups is included in McCulloh, *Ethnic Recordings.*

6. Charles Keil, "People's Music Comparatively: Style and Stereotype, Class and Hegemony," *Dialectical Anthropology* 10: 119.

7. For typical recent discussions of polka music's continued low status in the eyes of the middle class, see Bill Richards, "Put Aside the Tuba: These Folks Insist Polka Has Panache," *Wall Street Journal,* June 28, 1989, pp. 1, A9; and Robert P. Crease, "In Praise of the Polka," *Atlantic,* August 1989, p. 78. Crease refers to polka's "reputation as a moronic form of recreation."

8. Leading polka bandsmen who performed in this manner, probably beginning in the 1930s, were "Whoopee John" Wilfahrt, Johnny Pecon, Freddie "Schnickelfritz" Fisher, and especially Walt Solek, known as the "Clown Prince" of Polish polka music.

9. T. W. Adorno, with the assistance of George Simpson, "On Popular Music," *Studies in Philosophy and Social Science* 9 (1941): 17–25; T. W. Adorno, "A Social Critique of Radio Music," *The Kenyon Review* 7 (Spring 1945): 208–17. For a thorough review of Ortega y Gasset's supporters and of the ensuing debate on massification, see R. Serge Denisoff, "A Sociology of Popular Music: A Review," in Denisoff, ed., *Sing a Song of Social Significance* (Bowling Green, Ohio: Bowling Green State University Press, 1983), pp. 199–201; and R. Serge Denisoff, "Massification and Popular Music," *Journal of Popular Culture* 9 (Spring 1976): 881–88.

10. Dwight Macdonald, "A Theory of Mass Culture," reprinted from *Diogenes* (Summer 1953): 59–60, in Bernard Rosenberg and David Manning White, eds., *Mass Culture: The Popular Arts in America* (New York, Free Press, 1957), pp. 59–67. A recent review of the debate sympathetic to Macdonald and Adorno is Richard H. King, "Modernism and Mass Culture: The Origins of the Debate," in Heinz Ickstadt et al., eds., *The Thirties: Politics and Culture In a Time of Broken Dreams* (Amsterdam: Free University Press, 1987), pp. 120–24, 126, 128, 132–34.

11. David Manning White, "Mass Culture: Another Point of View," in Bernard Rosenberg and David Manning White, eds., *Mass Culture: The Popular Arts in America* (New York: Free Press, 1957), pp. 14–18; and Gilbert Seldes, "The People and the Arts," in Rosenberg and White, ibid., pp. 83–85.

12. Herbert Gans, *Popular Culture and High Culture* (New York: Basic Books, 1974), pp. vii–xi, 10, 13, 19, 27, 44, 75ff; Denisoff, "Massification," p. 890; and Denisoff, "A Sociology of Popular Music," p. 202.

13. Gans, *Popular Culture,* pp. 41–44, 102–03.

14. Herbert Gans et al., eds., *On The Making of Americans: Essays in Honor of David Reisman* (Philadelphia: Univerity of Pennsylvania Press, 1979), pp. 193–208.

15. For a recent influential and representative statement of the folklorists' position, see Stephen Stern, "Ethnic Folklore and the Folklore of Eth-

nicity," *Western Folklore* 36 (1977): 7–14ff. An excellent survey is John Higham, "Ethnic Pluralism in Modern American Thought," in Higham, ed., *Send These to Me: Jews and Other Immigrants in Urban America* (New York: Atheneum, 1975), pp. 196–230, esp. 217–25. A more recent review is Julie Leininger Pycior, "Acculturation and Pluralism in Recent Studies of American Immigration History" in *Economic and Immigrant Groups: The United States, Canada, and England* (New York: Haworth, 1983), pp. 21–27.

16. Maurice R. Davie, "Approaches to the Study of Nationality Groups in the United States," in Caroline F. Ware, ed., *The Cultural Approach to History* (New York: Gordon Press, 1974), pp. 74–75, 78.

17. W. D. Borrie, *The Cultural Integration of Immigrants: A Survey Based Upon Papers and Proceedings of the UNESCO Conference Held in Havana, April, 1956* (Paris: UNESCO, 1959), pp. 93–94.

18. Anthony Smith, *The Ethnic Revival* (Cambridge: Cambridge University Press, 1981), chapter 8, esp. pp. 155–59. Stern, "Ethnic Folklore," pp. 14ff. especially relevant here.

19. Lizabeth Cohen, "Encountering Mass Culture at the Grassroots: The Experience of Chicago Workers in the 1920s," *American Quarterly* 41 (March 1989): 6ff. Cohen criticizes theorists who accepted the idea of mass culture's "embourgeoisement" of the working class. Although she suggests how elements of black culture strongly affected mainstream American life through jazz, she omits discussion of any similar impact on white ethnics, evidence of which I hope to present here. Ibid., pp. 24–25.

20. Lawrence W. Levine, *Black Culture and Black Consciousness: Afro-American Folk Thought from Slavery to Freedom* (New York: Oxford University Press, 1977), p. 228.

21. Charles Hamm, *Yesterdays: Popular Song in America* (New York: Norton, 1979), p. 475. He excludes the indigenous music of American Indians.

22. Carl H. Scheele, "American Entertainment—An Immigrant Domain," in Peter C. Marzio, ed., *A Nation of Nations* (New York: Harper & Row, 1976), p. 410. The best account, for example, of the Jewish ethnic influence on the American cinema is probably Neal Gabler, *An Empire of Their Own: How the Jews Invented Hollywood* (New York: Crown, 1988).

23. Theodor Reik, *The Haunting Melody* (New York: Farrar, Straus & Young, 1953), pp. 8–9, 15, 222, 241. He specifically referred to the mother's lullaby sung to a child; ibid., p. 243.

24. Frances Hannett, "The Haunting Lyric: The Personal and Social Significance of American Popular Songs," *Psychoanalytic Quarterly* 33 (April, 1964): 226–28, 237.

25. N. Cazden in Paul Farnsworth, *The Social Psychology of Music,* 2d ed. (Ames: Iowa State University Press, 1969), pp. 70–71.

Chapter 1

1. Hamm, *Yesterdays,* p. 327 and passim.

2. See in particular Lawrence Levine, *Highbrow/Lowbrow: The Emergence*

of Cultural Hierarchy in America (Cambridge: Harvard University Press, 1988), pp. 85–86, 96–97, 165. Levine observes that no distinction existed in the nineteenth century between popular and classical music as played by bands; opera arias, for example, were mixed in performance with contemporary American tunes. The elite began to develop a distinction between classical and popular music around the turn of the century. I would extend Levine's early period into the first decade of the twentieth century, as popular bands continued to perform their opera repertoire into the early 1900s. Note the role of the Italian touring bands in Chapter 2.

3. I am combining the observations of Margaret Hindle Hazen and Robert M. Hazen, *The Music Men: An Illustrated History of Brass Bands in America, 1800–1920* (Washington, D.C.: Smithsonian Institution Press, 1987), p. 6, and William Carter White, *A History of Military Music in America* (New York: Exposition Press, 1975), p. 13.

4. Bernard J. Pfohl, *The Salem Band* (Winston-Salem, N.C.: Winston Printing Co., 1953), pp. 8–12; Hazen and Hazen, *Music Men,* pp. 6–8, 53; and Richard D. Wetzel, "Frontier Musicians on the Connoquenessing, Wabash, and Ohio: A History of George Rapp's Harmony Society (1805–1906)" (diss., Ohio University, 1976), p. 140; Harry Hobart Hall, "The Moravian Wind Ensemble: A Distinctive Chapter in America's Music" (diss., George Peabody College for Teachers, 1967), pp. 56–57, 79, 81–83; James Wesley Herbert, "The Wind Band of Nineteenth Century Italy: Its Origins and Transformation From the Late 1700s to Mid-Century" (thesis, Columbia University, 1986), pp. 53–54.

5. Hazen and Hazen, *Music Men,* pp. 11–12; Christine Condaris, "The Band Business in the United States Between the Civil War and the Great Depression" (dissertation, Wesleyan University, 1987), p. 4.

6. Stephen Erdely, "Ethnic Music in the United States: An Overview," in Israel J. Katz, ed., *1979 Yearbook of the International Folk Music Council* (offprint), pp. 117, 119–20. Erdely considers these choruses central to the immigrant communities' values and tastes.

7. As early as the mid-eighteenth century one observer had labeled Bohemians as "the most musical people of Germany, or, perhaps all of Europe." Charles Burney, *The Present State of Music in Germany, The Netherlands and United Provinces: A Facsimile of the 1775 London Edition,* 2 vols. (New York: Broude Brothers, 1969), 2:3–4. With respect to German traditions, see especially Theodore John Albrecht, "German Singing Societies in Texas" (diss., North Texas State University, 1975), pp. i–iii, and an excellent discussion in Philip Vilas Bohlman, "Music in the Culture of German Americans in North Central Wisconsin" (thesis, University of Illinois, 1979), pp. 120–22, 142, 447ff. Interestingly, the well-known early historical works on German settlement in America do not mention the brass-band tradition; they emphasize the German contribution to classical music in America. See Albert Bernhardt Faust, *The German Element in the United States With Special Reference to its Political, Moral, Social and Educational Influence,* 2 vols. (1909; reprint ed., New York: Steuben Society, 1969), 2:251–53, 375; and Carl Wittke, *We Who*

Built America: The Saga of the Immigrant, rev. ed. (Cleveland: Western Reserve Univ. Press, 1969), pp. 370–73, 374–79.

8. Wetzel, "Frontier Musicians," pp. x, 20–29.

9. Hazen and Hazen, *Music Men*, p. 167. Note especially the typical prominence of the brass band at Frankentrost, near the heavily German Michigan settlement of Frankenmuth in the late 1800s. Letter to author from Leonard Reinbold, Frankenmuth, Mich., Feb. 2, 1990.

10. Hazen and Hazen, *Music Men*, p. 53. For a challenge to Gottschalk's comment, see Raoul F. Camus, "The Influence of Italian Bandmasters on American Band Music," paper presented at July 1990 meeting of the International Society for the Promotion of Wind Music meeting in Dobbiaco, Italy, pp. 1–2 and passim.

11. See the listings in Hazen and Hazen, *Music Men*, pp. 112ff, and references below.

12. Pauline Norton, "Nineteenth Century American March Music and John Philip Sousa," in John Newcom, ed., *Perspectives on John Philip Sousa* (Washington, D.C.: Library of Congress, 1983), pp. 43, 50. Norton asserts the preeminence of band music among the public in that century.

13. Condaris, "Band Business," p. 6; Leon Mead, "The Military Bands of the United States," *Harper's Weekly Supplement*, Sept. 28, 1889, p. 785; Hazen and Hazen, *Music Men*, p. 8.

14. Hazen and Hazen, *Music Men*, pp. 43–60. Note especially that Chinese bands in San Francisco performed at mid-century for Chinese funerals, but later, American brass bands were included at those events. Ronald Riddle, *Flying Dragons, Flowing Streams: Music in the Life of San Francisco's Chinese* (Westport, Conn.: Greenwood Press, 1983), pp. 120–23.

15. Frederick Crane, "A Short History of Bands in Iowa," *The Iowa Music Educator* 33 (1980): 10–12.

16. Hazen and Hazen, *Music Men*, pp. 76–77.

17. New Prague had a population of fifteen hundred in 1895. *New Prague, Minnesota: Brief Sketches of Its History* (New Prague, Minnesota: New Prague Times, 1895), p. 5. Early musical activities in the town are the subject of "Individual Achievement Punctuates Musical History," *New Prague Times*, Aug. 27, 1931, pp. 36, 48.

18. Evan Jones, "Oompah Town," *Collier's* 134 (August 20, 1954): 26. See also Robert Andresen, "Traditional Music: The Real Story of Ethnic Music and How It Evolved in Minnesota and Wisconsin," *Minnesota Monthly* 107 (October 1978): 12. Note also a more recent illustration of the town's old time character; it is the home of one of the nation's leading concertina makers, Christy Hengel, "New Ulm Concertina Maker Chosen for Honors," *Entertainment Bits* 17 (August–September 1989): 1–2.

19. Information obtained from the Band File of the Brown County Historical Society, New Ulm, and La Vern J. Rippley, "The German Oldtime Orchestra in Southern Minnesota," typescript kindly supplied by the author. See in particular *New Ulm Review*, May 5, 1950; manuscript, WPA Writers' Project, "History of Brown County," 56; Allan Gebhard, "Band History in New Ulm," typescript; "Bands Have Played Big Role in New Ulm,"

Historical Notes (Feb. 11, 1982), 187, all in Brown County Historical Society.

20. See Frank Benes, *Czechs in Manitowoc County, 1847–1932* (Manitowoc, Wis.: Manitowoc County Historical Society, 1979), passim.

21. "Manitowoc—Always a City of Splendid Musical Organizations— Takes Lead in State," *Manitowoc Herald-News,* Oct. 28, 1922, p. 14.

22. "Manitowoc Very Musical," *Chicago Chronicle,* June 5, 1905, p. 5. Compare, for example, the item in *Polka and Old Time News* 1 (June, 1964): 15, on Bohemian settlers of Kewaunee.

23. Information on the Manitowoc area brass bands comes from four unnumbered scrapbooks at the Kewaunee County Historical Society. Note also Camille Dushek et al., "Bohemians Prominent in Manitowoc County History," *Manitowoc County Historical Society Occupational Monographs* 38 (1979): 5, 11, 12.

24. "Manitowoc—Always a City," p. 14. See also Kewaunee scrapbooks, especially an unattributed article, "Ramesh Band is Silent But the Melody Lingers On." Another source on the Moser Marine Band is Mary Hinkamp, "Youngsters, Oldsters Toot Together in Manitowoc's 51-Year-Old Band," *Milwaukee Journal* (1949), in the possession of Larry Pagel, Brillon, Wis.

25. From the Kewaunee scrapbooks.

26. Three Rotts made up the six members of the town band in 1888, and eleven of thirteen band members were Rotts in 1916. "Yuba and Its Bands," *The Richland* (Wis.) *Observer,* Feb. 5, 1987, pp. 1–14; James P. Leary, *The Wisconsin Patchwork: A Companion to the Radio Programs Based on the Field Recordings of Helene Stratman-Thomas* (Madison: University of Wisconsin Board of Regents, 1987), p. 48.

27. James Leary, "Early Life Centered Around Bohemian Hall Brass Band," *Folk Life of the Upper Mid-West,* 4 (Summer 1988): 3–4.

28. For the Dakotas, see Tarnar C. Reed, "Reflections from the Festival Director," in Tarnar C. Reed, ed., *Festival of Ethnic Musical Traditions in North Dakota* (Fargo: University of North Dakota, 1983), p. 59 and passim. Reed mentions Czech marching brass bands in two towns at least seventy years ago. Note also the statement of Ed Kudrna, "Czech Days at Tabor, South Dakota," *Polka and Old Time News* 2 (March 1965): 6, and the implication of E. K. Dalstrom and Harl Dalstrom, "From Skylon Ballroom to Oscar's Palladium: Dancing in Nebraska, 1948–1957," *Nebraska History* 65 (Fall 1984): 367ff. For a brief sketch of Czech bands in Nebraska, see Joseph G. Svoboda, "Czechs: The Love of Liberty," in *Broken Hoops and Plains People: A Catalogue of Ethnic Resources in the Humanities: Nebraska and Thereabouts* (Lincoln: Nebraska Curriculum Development Center, 1976), pp. 164, 189–90.

29. See William Phillip Hewitt, *The Czech Texans* (San Antonio: Institute of Texan Cultures, 1972, 1983), p. 3; Roger Kolar, "Early Czech Dance Halls in Texas," in Clinton Machann, ed., *The Czechs in Texas: A Symposium* (Temple, Texas: Texas A&M College of Liberal Arts, 1979), p. 122; and Clinton Machann and James W. Mendl, *Krásna Amerika* (Austin: Eakin

Press, 1983), p. 39. See also Kathleen Conzen, "Germans," in Oscar Handlin et al., eds., *Harvard Encyclopedia of American Ethnic Groups* (Cambridge: Harvard University Press, 1980); and Terry G. Jordan, *German Seed in Texas Soil: Immigrant Farmers in Nineteenth Century Texas* (Austin: University of Texas Press, 1966), p. 57.

30. James P. Leary, "Czech Polka Styles in the U.S.: From America's Dairyland to the Lone Star State," in *Czech Music in Texas: A Sesquicentennial Symposium*, ed. Clinton Machann (College Station, Texas: Komensky Press, 1987), pp. 79–82, 92. Cf. the description of mixed Czech and Western music in Clinton Machann, "Country-Western Music and the 'Now' Sound in Texas-Czech Polka Music," *John Edwards Memorial Fund Quarterly* (hereafter, *JEMF Quarterly*) 19 (1983): 3. On Texas Czech and German music and songs, see also Gilbert Jordan, *German Texas: A Bilingual Collection of Traditional Materials* (Austin: Eakins Press, 1980), and William A. Owens, *Tell Me a Story, Sing Me a Song* (Austin: University of Texas Press, 1983), pp. 193–219.

31. Glen E. Lich, *The German Texans* (San Antonio: Institute of Texan Cultures, 1981), pp. 123, 145, 171, 174.

32. The first state *saengerfest* was held in New Braunfels in 1853. Cf. Gerald R. Reeves, "The Houston Liederkrantz Choir," *The Polka News* 20 (January 10, 1990): 5–6. Note especially, Theodore John Albrecht, "German Singing Societies in Texas" (thesis, North Texas State University, 1975), pp. i–ii; Curt E. Schmidt, *Oma and Opa: German Texas Pioneers* (New Braunfels, Texas: Folkways Publication Co., 1975), pp. 82–86; Lota M. Spell, *Music in Texas . . .* (Austin, 1936), pp. 34, 58, 76, 95; an article, "Brief History of San Antonio Liederkrantz" in the files of Evelyn Kaase, Schulenberg, Texas; and Machann and Mendl, *Krásna Amerika*, pp. 154ff. According to Machann and Mendl, folk music is of "tremendous" importance, the most important indicator of Czech identity. Ibid., pp. 154.

33. Machann, "Country-Western Music," 5.

34. Cat Spring Agricultural Society, *The Cat Spring Story* (San Antonio: Lone Star, 1956), pp. 67–68.

35. From the files of Evelyn Kaase; Jane Knapik, *Schulenberg: 100 Years on the Road, 1873–1973 . . .* (Schulenberg, Texas: Schulenberg Centennial Committee, 1973), p. 54; *History of St. John the Baptist Church, Ammansville, Texas* (La Grange: *La Grange Journal,* 1965). In the early 1900s a musical group appeared under the family name, Kossa's Farmer's Brass and String Band. See also Mary T. E. Hinton, *Weimar, Texas, First 100 Years, 1873–1973* (Austin: Von Boeckmann-Jones, 1973), p. 198.

36. In *Krásna Amerika*, p. 159, Machann and Mendl have compiled eighty-five family names of Texas Czechs who were connected with this band tradition. Unfortunately the authors provide no chronology. Machann, "Country Western Music," p. 5, offers sixty names.

37. Fayetteville retains its ethnic title today. A few years ago a huge road sign on the highway between San Antonio and Houston directed motorists to the town, proudly described as the Czech-American capital.

38. Rose Marie Bača Rohde and Louis Polansky of Fayetteville graciously

allowed me to use Ms. Rohde's collection, which is hereinafter designated RBR. See also Estelle Hudson and Henry R. Maresh, *Czech Pioneers of the South-West* (Dallas: South-West Press, 1934), opposite p. 317; and Machann, "Country-Western Music," p. 3.

39. The best source is *Bača's Musical History, 1860–1968: An Old Texas Czech Band and Orchestra* (La Grange, Texas: *La Grange Journal*, 1968), pp. 4–7. See also Pat Reed, "Is There Another Texas Band That Began in 1892," *Texas Magazine, The Houston Chronicle*, probably in 1967, and *La Grange Journal* (July 17–19, 1933), both in RBR; and Hudson and Maresh, *Czech Pioneers*, opposite p. 317. The date and number in Hewitt, *Czech Texans*, 13, appear to be incorrect. As the number of sources suggests, the Bača family history is legendary.

40. Hewitt, *Czech Texans*, p. 14; *Bača's Musical History*, pp. 7, 12. See also the article in *The Houston Post*, Nov. 7, 1954?, sec. 6, p. 14, and *Brenham Banner Press*, November 21, 1951?, p. 6, both in RBR, for the variety of occasions at which the Bačas performed.

41. *Česka Osada I Její Spolkový Život v Cleveland . . .* (Cleveland: Volnosti, 1895), p. 104. "No major Czech event in Cleveland could be without music . . . vocal, brass band, symphonic, drums and bugle." Taken from C. Winston Chrislock, "The Czech Community of Cleveland," pp. 16–17, typescript paper supplied by the author. Note also several articles in David Van Tassel and John Grabowski, eds., *The Encyclopedia of Cleveland History* (Bloomington: Indiana University Press, 1987), including Nicholas J. Zentos, "The Czechs," pp. 326–27; "Saengerfests," pp. 851–52; and "Lumir-Hlakol-Tyl Singing Society," p. 644.

42. Although it is unclear whether the Great Western Band was indeed a Bohemian band at its start, by 1877 it seems likely that it was. See, in Van Tassel and Grabowski, eds., *Encyclopedia of Cleveland History*, Frank Hruby, "Bands," p. 73, Valencic, "Polkas," p. 777, and Chrislock, "Czech," p. 16.

43. The "Hruby Family" entry in the *Encyclopedia of Cleveland History*, p. 530, labels them "America's Foremost Musical Family."

44. *Česka Osada*, p. 104.

45. "Hruby Family," p. 530. I am grateful to two correspondents in Cleveland, Frank Bardoun and Richard Kolda, who supplied much source material on the Hrubys. A letter from Frank Bardoun to author, March 16, 1988, enclosed newspaper clippings of Frank Hruby's obituary, a *Brief Historical Sketch of Cuyahoga County Soldiers' and Sailors' Monument* (Cleveland, 1942?), a program from the Hruby Family Concert at Bohemian National Hall, Cleveland, Nov. 16, 1913, a speech delivered by John Hruby at Musicians Club of Cleveland, May 19, 1951, a press notice of a Great Western Band concert at Germania Hall, Oct. 4, 1897, and a brochure, *The Hruby Conservatory of Music* (Cleveland 1950), all from the Kolda file.

46. The Lyceum and Chautauqua movements were adult-education and self-improvement programs that had begun in the 1830s and 1870s, respectively. The Chautauqua network had hundreds of local assemblies around the turn of the century, which offered musical entertainment supplied by traveling ensembles. For a good general account, see Alvin F. Har-

low, "Chautauqua Movement," in *Dictionary of American History*, rev. ed., 7 vols. (New York: Charles Scribner's Sons, 1976), 2:1.

47. I am broadening his conclusion to include the ethnic influence on the turn-of-the-century popular music as well. Frank Hruby, "Cleveland: A Cultural Enigma," *Musical America* 81 (September, 1961): 17. See also Valencic, "Polkas," 777. I believe both Hrubic and Valencic would support this assertion. Note, too, "The Hruby Family" in the Bardoun-Kolda file, which states that six of the eight children played for the Cleveland Orchestra. More than one-sixth of the orchestra's first members were Czech. Zentos, "Czechs," p. 327.

48. Texas did have them but apparently only in the more urbanized areas, places "to which the whole family repaired on Sundays and holidays." Spell, *Music in Texas*, 41.

49. "Haltnorth's Gardens," *Encyclopedia of Cleveland History*, p. 483.

50. Hruby, "Bands," p. 73.

51. From "Milwaukee Beer Gardens," typescript #29 at the Milwaukee County Historical Society. See also Harry H. Anderson, "Recreation, Entertainment, and Open Space: Park Traditions of Milwaukee County," in Ralph Aderman, ed., *Trading Post to Metropolis: Milwaukee County's First 150 Years* (Milwaukee: Milwaukee County Historical Society, 1987), pp. 257–59. For a good overall description, see William George Bruce, *A Short History of Milwaukee* (Milwaukee: Bruce Publishing Co., 1936), pp. 202, 206–7.

52. Bruce, *History*, p. 207.

53. Note a similar park in Chicago, Ogden Grove, begun about 1865. Perry Duis, *The Saloon: Public Drinking in Chicago and Boston, 1880–1920* (Champaign; University of Illinois Press, 1983), p. 154. Even Texas had beer gardens in its cities, places "to which the whole family repaired on Sundays and holidays." Spell, *Music in Texas*, p. 41.

54. Klaus Ensslen, "The German-American Working Class Saloon in Chicago: Their Social Function in an Ethnic and Class-Specific Cultural Context," in Hartmut Keil, ed., *German Workers Culture in the United States, 1850–1920*, (Washington, D.C.: Smithsonian Institution Press, 1988), pp. 174–75; and especially Royal L. Melendy, "The Saloon in Chicago," *American Journal of Sociology* 6 (November 1900): 291–93, 295, 298, 300, 302–05. Melendy does make a distinction between the ethnic German and the ordinary American saloon. Haltnorth's Gardens is clearly the former, and I am highlighting here a sort of drinking and music establishment that is really quite different from the den of iniquity Lewis Erenberg refers to in his *Steppin' Out: New York Nightlife and the Transformation of American Culture, 1890–1930* (Chicago: University of Chicago Press, 1984), pp. 20–21. The immigrant saloon was a complex, culturally diverse institution that has yet to be fully explained. Some of these establishments functioned as social clubs, others as theaters, and probably some but not all as centers of vice. The most recent authoritative discussion is probably Duis, *The Saloon*, especially chapter 5.

55. Note also the prominence of German bands in a small town in

eastern Pennsylvania, Honesdale. That community had a "substantial" German population in the middle 1800s and, of course, German amateur bands. Here, too, the bands served as an integral part of the town's identity until they were superseded by singing societies. Kenneth Kreitner, *Discoursing Sweet Music: Brass Band and Community Life in Turn-of-the-Century Pennsylvania* (Champaign: University of Illinois Press, 1989), pp. 132, 133, 186–88.

56. Antanas Kučas, "Shenandoah" in Simas Suziedelis and Antanas Kučas, eds., *Encyclopedia Lituanica,* 6 vols. (South Boston, Mass.: J. Kapocius, 1970–1978), 5:130.

57. *The Path of Progress: Shenandoah, Pennsylvania, 1866–1966* (Shenandoah, 1966), n.p., at Shenandoah Public Library; letters dated July 24 and August 1, 1989, to writer from W. J. Krencewicz, Shenandoah, a Lithuanian band member in the early 1920s.

58. Victor Greene, *The Slavic Community on Strike; Immigrant Labor in Pennsylvania Anthracite* (Notre Dame, Ind.: University of Notre Dame Press, 1968), pp. 195–96; Kucas, "Shenandoah," p. 131 (the year he refers to, 1920, is obviously a typographical error); "Benai," typescript by Juozas Zilevičius at the Lithuanian Cultural Center, Chicago. An assessment of the high quality of the First Lithuanian Band, a brief historical account, and a late 1919 photograph of this ensemble before it disbanded are offered in *Shenandoah, Pa., Lietuvių Kataliku, Šv. Jurgio Parapijos, 50 Metų Sukakčiai, Paminēti Leidinys, 1891–1941* (Shenandoah, 1941), pp. 38, 50, and letter to author from Krencewicz, July 24, 1989. It seems unlikely that the non-Lithuanian repertoire of the band's last years was also representative of its earlier period.

59. By 1911 other such ensembles had been formed in Chicago, and several were started in Philadelphia, Cleveland, Waterbury, Conn., and Lawrence, Mass. It is very likely that the organization of all the group's bands cannot be documented. My references are from the large list in "Band" in *Lithuanian Encyclopedia,* 36 vols. (Boston, Mass.: Lithuanian Encyclopedia Press, 1953–1969), 2:371–72. See also Zilevičius, "Benai."

60. Zilevičius, "Benai."

61. Alaine Pakkala, "The Instrumental Music of the Finnish-American Community" (thesis, University of Michigan, 1983), p. 14; Pekka Gronow, "Finnish American Records," *JEMF Quarterly* 7 (Winter 1971): 177.

62. Gronow, "Records," p. 178; Alaine Pakkala, "The Instrumental Music of the Finnish-American Community in the Great Lakes Region, 1880–1930," *Siirtolaisuus-Migration* 3 (1983): 3–4.

63. The temperance musical band was known as a *soitokunta.* Pakkala, "Music," p. 3; Reino Nikolai Hannula, *Blueberry God: The Education of a Finnish American* (San Luis Obispo, Calif.: Quality Hill Books, 1979), pp. 184–87.

64. The best brief overview is Alaine Pakkala, "The Finnish American Bandsmen," *Suomen Silta* 4:36–38, offprint supplied by author, Walled Lake, Michigan.

65. "Lest We Forget," *Siirtokansan Kalenteri, 1953* (Duluth, Minn.:

1952), p. 62; Alaine Pakkala, "The Humina Band," typescript supplied by author, p. 2.

66. Wahlstrom's accomplishments are listed in "Lest We Forget," pp. 63–65, and John I. Kolehmainen, *A History of the Finns in Ohio, Western Pennsylvania, and West Virginia* (New York Mills, Minn.: Finnish American Historical Society, 1977), 282–84. See also the article on Ashtabula in *Finn Heritage* 3 (Fall 1987): 3.

67. Pakkala, "Bandsmen,," pp. 37–38.

68. Pakkala, "Instrumental Music," thesis, p. 91.

69. Ibid.

70. *Finn Heritage* 3 (Fall 1987): 4.

71. Ibid. 1 (Spring–Summer 1985): 8.

72. Pakkala in *Siirtolaisuus*, p. 4; Pakkala, "Instrumental Music," thesis, pp. 102, 106, 108–11.

73. Quoted in Kolehmainen, *Finns*, p. 289. Note also the pertinent reference and statement of Hazen and Hazen, *Music Men*, p. 52, concerning other nationality bands in New York and California.

Chapter 2

1. Hazen and Hazen, *Music Men*, p. 17.

2. Mead, "Military Bands," p. 785.

3. The best brief biographical sketch is probably H. Wiley Hitchcock, "John Philip Sousa," in Hitchcock and Sadie, eds., *The New Grove Dictionary of American Music*, 4 vols. (London: Macmillan, 1986), 4:272–74.

4. Ibid., p. 273.

5. H. W. Schwartz, *Bands of America* (New York: Doubleday, 1957), pp. 289–290.

6. William G. Huey, "Making Music: Brass Bands on the Northern Plains, 1860–1930" *North Dakota History* 54 (Winter 1987): 4.

7. For example, in 1876 at least one-half of the members of the Seventh Cavalry Band in the Montana Territory were immigrants, including the band's Italian leader, and ten years later about half the Eighteenth Infantry Band in Kansas consisted of immigrants. Huey, "Plains," p. 5; Kenneth Hammer, *Men with Custer: Biographies of the Seventh Cavalry, 25 June 1876* (Ft. Collins, Colo.: The Old Army Press, 1972), pp. 12–16.

8. Hazen and Hazen, *Music Men*, p. 17. American opera singers occasionally assumed Italian names, a practice reflecting the same stereotype of European musical superiority.

9. Ibid.

10. Life in Arizona had a significant impact on Fiorello, as discussed in Huey, "Plains," p. 5; Lawrence Elliot, *Little Flower: The Life and Times of Fiorello LaGuardia* (New York: William Morrow & Co., 1983), pp. 18–23, 25, 28, 38–39; Fiorello H. LaGuardia, *The Making of An Insurgent: An Autobiography: 1882–1919* (Philadelphia: J. B. Lippincott, 1948), chapter 1.

11. Harry C. Freeman, *A Brief History of Butte, Montana: The World's*

Greatest Mining Camp... (Chicago: Henry O. Shepard Co., 1900), pp. 36–37; letter of Sara McLernan, Butte, Montana, May 8, 1989, to author. James Wesley Herbert, in "The Wind Band of Nineteenth Century Italy: Its Origins and Transformation From the Late 1700s to Mid-Century" (thesis, Columbia University, 1986), p. 6, generalizes about the ubiquity of Italian musicians in America.

12. Sverre O. Braathen of Madison, Wis., quoted in Christine Condaris, "The Band Business in the United States Between the Civil War and the Great Depression" (thesis, Wesleyan University, 1987), p. 32. The famous Liberati band, which is discussed below in this chapter, worked for Ringling Brothers in 1895. Ibid., p. 33.

13. The following comes from James Wesley Herbert, "Wind Band," pp. 53–54, 58, 84ff; and Emma Scogna Rocco, "Italian Wind Bands: A Surviving Tradition in the Milltowns of Lawrence and Beaver Counties of Pennsylvania" (thesis, University of Pittsburgh, 1986), pp. 1–9, 15–20, 29–33.

14. Rocco, "Bands," pp. 6, 8.

15. This emphasis on the lyrical instead of the martial aspects of band music was evident in Italian American music. Ibid., p. 34; Liner notes to "Eviva La Banda! The Music of the Feasts Featuring Caliendo's Banda Napoletana: Chicago's Premier Italian Feast Band" (private label, no discographic information; disc in the possession of Philip Balistreri, Milwaukee).

16. Herbert, "Wind Band," pp. 103ff, 110.

17. David R. B. Kimbell, *Verdi in the Age of Italian Romanticism* (Cambridge: Cambridge University Press, 1981), p. 22.

18. Julian Budden, *The Operas of Verdi*, 3 vols. (London: Cassell, 1973), 1:11.

19. Nicholas Till, *Rossini: His Life and Times* (New York: Media Books, 1983), p. 11. Further evidence of Italian opera's popularity among all classes was the mass attendance at Giuseppe Verdi's funeral. Half of Milan paid their respects. Joseph Wechsberg, *Verdi* (New York: G. P. Putnam's Sons, 1974), p. 247.

20. Nicholas Tawa's discussion of the Italian immigrants' attachment to Italian music in *A Sound of Strangers: Musical Culture, Acculturation, and the Post-Civil War Ethnic American* (Metuchen, N.J.: Scarecrow Press, 1982), pp. 30–31, 35, proceeds from the assumption that because most of the emigrants came from rural rather than urban areas of Italy, they had developed no love of opera until after their arrival in the United States. Tawa does not attribute or explain this assertion, and I believe it is mistaken.

21. The role of bel canto in Italian American identity is an important theme that awaits further study. Fragmentary evidence strongly suggests that ordinary Italian immigrants were devotees, often passionate devotees, of bel canto opera in America. The renowned tenor Enrico Caruso, for example, assumed a heroic stature among immigrants from his homeland, not only for his mastery of their beloved music but also for his sensitivity to and fulfillment of the cultural needs of the Italian American masses. "To New York's Little Italy, [Caruso] was far more than a voice; he [was] a symbol

of hope and laughter in adversity. They identified fiercely [and] patriotically with the chubby little man who had escaped from a Neapolitan slum to win storybook success on alien soil." Stanley Jackson, *Caruso* (New York: W. H. Allen, 1972), pp. 208, 210.

For additional evidence of the intense devotion of ordinary Italian American immigrants to opera, see Jerre Mangione, *Mount Allegro* (New York: Columbia University Press, 1981), pp. 15–16, and the description of avid enthusiasm for bel canto music among illiterate fishermen in San Francisco as recounted in Andrew Rolle, *The Immigrant Upraised: Italian Adventurers and Colonists in An Expanding America* (Norman: University of Oklahoma Press, 1968), pp. 261, 266. Gary R. Mormino and George E. Pozzetta, in *The Immigrant World of Ybor City: Italians and their Latin Neighbors in Tampa, 1885–1985* (Champaign: University of Illinois Press, 1987), pp. 182–183, suggest the great appeal of opera in Tampa's Italian community. Another observer spoke of immigrant banana vendors in Chicago who had acquired a better acquaintance with opera than American-born professionals. W. C. Jenkins, "Chicago's Pageant of Nations—Italians and Their Contributions," *Chicago Evening Post*, Nov. 16, 1929, p. 7.

In Philadelphia, beginning at least as far back as World War I and extending into the 1980s, Italian immigrant John Di Stefano and especially his sons Henry and Armand figured prominently in the promotion of Italian opera. The family's Victor Cafe became a famous opera restaurant, and Henry and Armand Di Stefano conducted a long-running opera radio program. In their heavily Italian neighborhood of South Philadelphia, the family amassed an enormous collection of records, numbering 10,000 by about 1950, and the Di Stefanos promoted bel canto among Italian Americans and the entire community. *Il Popolo Italiano*, May 7, 1954, p. 2; newspaper clippings, "Mine Host for a Musical Banquet," Mar. 30, 1940, p. 15, and obituary of John Di Stefano, May 5, 1954, both from the Urban Archives, Temple University; interview, Antoinette (Mrs. Henry) Di Stefano with author, Sept. 5, 1987, Philadelphia; taped interview, "A Tribute to Armand Di Stefano," especially with Armand Di Stefano and Jack McKinney, June 1987 at Philadelphia public radio station WHYY.

22. John Clagett Proctor, "Marine Band History and Its Leadership," *Washington* [D.C.] *Sunday Star*, May 8, 1922, magazine section, p. 6. Jefferson's admiration of Italian band musicians is stressed in Raoul F. Camus, "The Influence of Italian Bandmasters on American Band Music," p. 3, paper presented at July 1990 meeting of the International Society for the Promotion of Wind Music in Dobbiaco, Italy.

23. Camus, "Italian Bandmasters," p. 7; Hazen and Hazen, *Music Men*, p. 53; Rocco, "Italian Wind Bands," p. 155.

24. Glenn Braggs, *Pioneers in Brass* (Detroit: Sherwood, 1965), p. 89, and Frank J. Cipolla, "Carlo Alberto Cappa," in *The New Grove Dictionary of American Music* 1:354.

25. Giovanni Ermenegildo Schiavo, *Italian American History*, 2 vols. (1947: New York: rpt., Arno Press 1975) 1:340.

26. Note especially "Il Ballo Italiano all'Irving Hall," in *L'Eco d'Italia*,

Feb. 18, 1865, p. 1, where Cappa led nationalistic and folk-type selections. See also T. Rossi, "An Educator of the People," *Musical Courier* 25 (1892): n.p.; "Carlo Alberto Cappa," ibid. 26 (Jan. 3, 1893): 9; Mead, "Military Bands," 785; and "Death of Carlo A. Cappa," *American Art Journal,* 60 (Jan. 14, 1893): 307. For his Italian knighthood, see Cipolla, "Cappa," in Hitchcock and Sadie, *Grove Dictionary,* 1:354.

27. David M. Ingalls, "Francis Scala: Leader of the Marine Band From 1855 to 1871" (thesis, Catholic University of America, 1957), pp. 132, 134–35. See also "Scala's Glorious Past," *Washington [D.C.] Morning Times,* Jan. 19, 1896, p. 20; *Washington [D.C.] Star,* April 20, 1903, p. 7; Schiavo, *History* 1:435; Cipolla, "Francis Maria Scala," in Hitchcock and Sadie, *Grove Dictionary* 4:147.

28. Frank J. Cipolla, "Francesco Fanciulli: Turn of the Century American Bandmaster," *The Instrumentalist* 33 (February 1979): 35; "Francesco Fanciulli," *The National Cyclopedia of American Biography,* 74 vols. (New York: James T. White Co., 1891–1986) 16:96; Edward Ellsworth Hipsher, *American Opera and Its Composers* (Philadelphia: Theodore Presser, 1927), pp. 170–71.

29. "Fanciulli," in *National Cyclopedia* 16:96; Letter of Frederick P. Williams, Philadelphia, to author, March 6, 1989; Frank J. Cipolla, "Francesco Fanciulli," in Hitchcock and Sadie, *Grove Dictionary* 2:98.

30. An even fuller roster is in Harry W. Schwartz, *Bands of America* (New York: Doubleday, 1957), pp. 212, 222. See also Kenneth Berger, ed., *Band Encyclopedia* (Evansville, Ind.: Band Associates, 1960), pp. 185, 188; and the list in Camus, "Italian Bandmasters," and esp. p. 10, which notes Phillipini's long and close association with opera music.

31. Schwartz, *Bands,* pp. 177ff.

32. Ibid., pp. 17, 94, 98, 114, 133, 272–73. The Omaha *Bee* reported that he held an audience of twelve thousand "spellbound" at a 1921 concert in an Omaha park.

33. Raoul Camus, "Alessandro Liberati," *Grove Dictionary* 3:44. Frederick P. Williams of Philadelphia, a leading amateur collector of recorded band music, characterized Liberati's style in a letter to author, March 6, 1989, as clearly reflecting his Italian heritage.

34. Curtis H. Larkin, "Last of the 'Old Guard'—Giuseppe Creatore," *School Musician* 157 (November 1945): 15–16.

35. Creatore's obituary in the *New York Times,* August 16, 1952, p. 15, says he was twenty-five years old when he became director of the Naples Municipal Band. My information on his early years is from Fred P. Williams, "Giuseppe Creatore: Chronology of Events," typescript supplied by the author, p. 1; Schwartz, *Bands,* p. 213; Norman E. Smith, *March Music Notes* (Lake Charles, La.: Program Note Press, 1986), p. 93; *Musical America* 72 (September, 1952): 24; and Larkin, "Last of the 'Old Guard,' " 24.

36. Cf. Camus, "Italian Bandmasters," p. 8, on Banda Rossa.

37. Jan Kapusta, *Dechové Kapely Pochod František Kmoch* (Praha: Supraphon, 1974), p. 104. I am grateful to my colleague Karol Bayer for assisting me with the translation.

38. Fred P. Williams, "Giuseppe Creatore: Chronology," p. 1; Williams, "The Willow Grove Park Concerts, 1896–1925," in *Chestnut Hill Local,* Aug. 19, 1982, p. 4. Sources dispute the details; I believe Williams's research is the most accurate.

39. Williams, "Concerts," p. 4; Smith, *Notes,* p. 94.

40. *New York Times,* Aug. 16, 1952, p. 15. James Francis Cooke, in "Musical Showmanship," *Etude* 73 (May 1955): 16, 64, was much less complimentary.

41. Raoul Camus puts the size of Creatore's new band at forty men in "Giuseppe Creatore" in Hitchcock and Sadie, *Grove Dictionary* 1:532; *Musical America* 72 (September 1952): 24, has the figure at fifty-five; my figure of sixty comes from Williams, "Creatore," p. 1, and Smith, *Notes,* p. 93.

42. Fred Williams, "The Times as Reflected in the Victor Black Label Recordings from 1900 to 1930," *Association for Recorded Sound Collections Journal* 13 (1981): 4.

43. Larkin, "Last of the 'Old Guard,' " p. 16.

44. Williams, "Concerts," p. 6; C. Bagley, "In Memory of a Great Conductor," *Overture* 32 (September 15, 1952): 29.

45. Williams, "Creatore," p. 3; official programs from Williams collection, Philadelphia. Cf. "Wagner Program Displays Great Power," *Indianapolis News,* June 6, 1914, p. 4.

46. Condaris, "Band Business," pp. 80ff.

47. Fred Williams, letter to the author, March 6, 1989.

48. Smith, *Notes,* p. 94; *New York Times,* Aug. 16, 1952, p. 15; " 'Carmen' On a Huge Scale," *Musical Courier* 72 (November 9, 1916): 19; "Giuseppe Creatore," in Nicholas Slonimsky, *Baker's Biographical Dictionary of Musicians,* 7th ed. (New York: Schirmer Books, 1984), p. 515. Creatore's later career, in the late 1920s and 1930s, was even more involved with opera; *New York Times,* Aug. 16, 1952, p. 15; Condaris, "Band Business," pp. 88, 166.

49. Figured from Condaris, "Band Business," pp. 59ff.

50. Lawrence Levine, *Highbrow/Lowbrow: The Emergence of Cultural Hierarchy in America* (Cambridge: Harvard University Press, 1988), pp. 85–86, 96–97.

51. Italian American community bands were probably most significant from the 1890s through the 1920s. The quotation is from Hazen and Hazen, *Music Men,* p. 53; see also "Eviva La Banda!," p. 3, for the Chicago area; and especially Rocco, "Italian Wind Bands," p. 156.

52. William J. Schafer, *Brass Bands and New Orleans Jazz* (Baton Rouge: Louisiana State University Press, 1977), pp. 8–10, 19; Gunther Schuller, *Early Jazz: Its Roots and Musical Development* (New York: Oxford University Press, 1986), p. 4; Henry A. Kmen, *Music in New Orleans: Its Formative Years, 1791–1841* (Baton Rouge: Louisiana State University Press, 1966), pp. 203–05.

53. Jeanie Blake, "University of New Orleans Professor Tackles Study of City's Largest European Ethnic Group," *New Orleans Times Picayune,*

Nov. 29, 1981; Evans Casso, *Staying in Step: A Continuing Italian American Renaissance* (New Orleans: Quadriga Press, 1984), p. 26.

54. My information on this distinctive group is from Casso, *Staying in Step*, pp. 102–05; John Pope, "Just Jazzin' Around," *New Orleans States Item*, Jan. 4, 1977, Section B; Dalt Wonk, "Sons of Contessa Entellina," *New Orleans Times Picayune*, Oct. 16, 1983, *Dixie Magazine*, p. 10; and especially Emile Lafourcade, "Italians Fill New Home With Music," *New Orleans Times Picayune*, Aug. 29, 1982, Section 2, p. 6; Lafourcade, "Contessa 'Grad' Played Beside Jazz Greats," ibid., pp. 6–7.

55. Julia Volpelletto Nakamura, "The Italian American Contribution to Jazz," *Italian Americana* 8 (1986): 23; Harry O. Brunn, *The Story of the Original Dixieland Jazz Band* (Baton Rouge: Louisiana State University Press, 1960), pp. 2–4; liner notes to "New Orleans Rhythm Kings, 1934–35" (Swaggie Records 826); Evans J. Casso, "The Dukes of Dixieland and the Lingering Echoes," *Italian American Digest* (Summer 1984): 7; and Casso, "The Metro Impresario," *Italian American Digest* (Fall 1983): 6; and especially Philip Elwood, "Prima's Prime Memories," *San Francisco Examiner*, Sept. 9, 1968, in which Prima told how he developed his early love of music. As a youth, he said he "chased the parade bands and funeral processions."

56. This observation is taken from a newspaper account quoted in Mormino and Pozzetta, *Immigrant World of Ybor City*, (Champaign: University of Illinois Press, 1987), p. 192.

57. Emelise Aleandri, "Little Italy at the Turn of the Century," *Little Italy: Souvenir Book* (n.p., n.d.), pp. 5–8.

58. Rocco, "Italian Wind Bands," pp. 172, 192–93, 199–202, 210, 238, 245–48, 336–38; Mildred Urick, "The San Rocco Festival at Aliquippa, Pennsylvania: A Transplanted Tradition," *Pennsylvania Folklife* 19 (1969): 14–20; Harlan Berger, "The Italo-American Sound: Italian Bands of Western Pennsylvania," *Research, Penn State* (September 1985): 31–32; Rocco, "Italian Bands: A Surviving Tradition," *Pennsylvania Ethnic Studies Newsletter*, Winter, 1984, pp. 1–5. Additional Italian bands are identified in Tontitown, Arkansas, 1905, and Patchogue, Long Island, 1910, in Helen Barolini, et al., *Images: A Pictorial History of Italian Americans* (Staten Island, N.Y.: Center for Migration Studies, 1981), pp. 68, 134, and in Denver, 1901, in *Our Lady of Mount Carmel Church* (Denver, 1975), p. 13.

59. The name of the Verdi Band did indeed reflect the inclusion of bel canto selections in its repertoire. Nicholas Sorgeni, "History of the Verdi Band," *The Verdi Band, 65th Anniversary . . .* (Norristown, 1985), pp. 1–2; Loretta Marsella, Philadelphia, letter to author, Dec. 11, 1985; and *Norristown Times Herald*, Nov. 5, 1964, pp. 1, 3.

60. From liner notes to "Eviva La Banda! The Music of the Feasts Featuring Caliendo's Banda Napoletana: Chicago's Premier Italian Feast Band."

61. Waterbury had at least two other Italian music teachers around the time of World War I. My sources are Frank P. Augustine, "Italians: The Music Makers," *Watertown Daily Times*, Feb. 12, 1989, pp. C1, 7; and Augustine, "Music Makers: Looking Back at Watertown Bands," *Watertown*

Daily Tribune, Feb. 12, 1989, supplied to the author by James Jerome, Watertown, N.Y.

Chapter 3

1. Note, for example, Robert Janda, "Entertainment Tonight: An Account of Bands in Manitowoc County Since 1900," *Occupational Monograph* no. 28 (1976), Manitowoc County (Wis.) Historical Society, p. 2; and Don Sosnoski, "The Story of Matt Hoyer," *The Polka News* 17 (June 24, 1987): 2.

2. Mark Slobin, in *Tenement Songs: The Popular Music of the Jewish Immigrants* (Champaign: University of Illinois Press, 1982), p. 122, refers to the changing circumstances generally, but his focus is limited to Jewish immigrants' songs rather than their involvement in the music industry *as a business.*

3. Cf., especially concerning the Dopjera family firm, John Bazovsky, "Early Slovaks of Los Angeles, 1883–1945," *Slovak Studies* (1973): 206–10.

4. The name of the legendary peasant girl is Anna Slezakova, according to Bruce B. Boettcher, "A Polka Music Story," *The Polka News* 18 (Nov. 23, 1988): 2.

5. For a description of polka's European origins, see Bob Norgard, "Polka Parade," *The Polka News* 20 (Feb. 14, 1990): 4.

6. Other good accounts of its early growth are in Christopher Ann Paton, "Evolution of the Polka from 1830 to 1930 as a Symbol of Ethnic Unity and Diversity" (thesis, Wayne State University, 1981), pp. 1, 13–15; and Pauline Norton, "Polka" in Hitchcock and Sadie, *New Grove Dictionary* 3:585. An extremely thorough review is Janice Ellen Kleeman, "Origins and Stylistic Development of Polish American Polka Music" (Ph.D. diss., University of California, Berkeley, 1982), chapter 2. For a controversial view that the origin of the polka is Polish, see letter to the author from Walter Ossowski, Philadelphia, Feb. 4, 1990, referring to the *The Standard Dictionary of Folklore* (1950).

7. "František Kmoch," *Česko-Slovensky Hudebni Slovnik: Osob a Instituci,* Svazek Prvy A-L (Prague: Statní Hudebni Vydavaelstvi, 1963), 678. I acknowledge the translation assistance of Karel Bayer of Milwaukee.

8. Note especially James P. Leary, "Czech Polka Styles in the United States: From America's Dairyland to the Lone Star State," in Clinton Machann, ed., *Papers from Czech Music in Texas: A Sesquicentennial Symposium* (College Station: Texas A & M University, 1987), p. 81; James W. Mendl, "Interviews With Texas Band Leaders," in ibid., p. 98; Norman E. Smith, *March Music Notes,* pp. 246–47, in the collection of George Koudelka, Flatonia, Texas.

9. "Muziky, Muziky" alone sold 120,000 copies. Kmoch remains a revered legend to rural Czechs. Jan Kapusta, *Dechové Kapely Pochod František Kmoch* (Prague: Supraphon, 1974), pp. 130–31; *Narodni Album Sbirka Podobizen a Životopisu Českych . . .* (Prague: Vilimak, 1899), p. 352; Smith, *Notes,* pp. 246–47; "Kmoch," *Česko-Slovensky Hudebni Slovnik,* pp. 678–79;

Thomas Hancl, "Brass Bands in Czechoslovakia," *Journal of Band Research* 6 (1969): 42.

10. I obtained biographical information on Jiran from two interviews with his son Charles Jiran in LaGrange, Illinois, Dec. 3 and Dec. 13, 1987.

11. A Chicago Czech business directory for 1900 lists Jiran's address as 510 West 19th Street. His firm was one of three listed under "Musical Instruments." *Adresar, Českych Obchodniků, Živnostniků A Spolka . . .* (Chicago: Narodni Tiskarny, 1900), pp. 121–22.

12. Taken from his sampler of printed pieces, *New Bohemian Orchestra Numbers* (Chicago: Jiran, ca. 1938).

13. Interview with Charles Jiran, Berwyn, Ill., Dec. 6, 1987.

14. A Kmoch piece, "Satacek" (The Kerchief), in the author's possession, has Jiran's stamp.

15. From the list in Jiran's catalogue, *New Bohemian Orchestra Numbers.*

16. Interviews with Charles Jiran, Dec. 6, 1988, and with Joseph Divisek, Berwyn, Ill., Jan. 27, 1988.

17. Calculated from Jiran's *New Bohemian Orchestra Numbers* (ca. 1938) and *Sample Parts of International and Old Time Music Published for Band and Orchestra by Vitak and Elsnic Company . . .* (Chicago: Vitak and Elsnic, 1949?). Charles Jiran spoke of Grill's major role in the works his father published in an interview with author, Dec. 6, 1988.

18. I obtained details of Grill's life story from his grandson Myles in an interview March 12, 1989, in Berwyn, Illinois. Myles Grill had a small collection of Andrew Grill's papers, baptismal and death certificates, a passport, and manuscript sheet music.

19. From interviews with Myles Grill and Charles Jiran and the sheet music collection at the Czechoslovakia Society of America Library in the Fraternal Life Building, Berwyn, Illinois.

20. About half of the 170 pieces dated between 1904 and 1937 that appear on Jiran's 1938 list were copyrighted in the 1920s. From *New Bohemian Orchestra Numbers.* Interview with Charles Jiran, Dec. 6, 1987.

21. My sources on Vitak's life are largely oral and indirect, based on interviews with persons who knew only his partner Joseph Elsnic. Interviews with Dorothy Kommer of Fort Myers, Florida, in Whitefish Bay, Wis., Oct. 7, 1985, and with Laurence Musielak, a longtime employee and later owner of the firm, in Berwyn, Illinois, July 26, 1985.

22. Kommer interview; Doris Pease, "Love for the Concertina Builds Family Business," *Entertainment Bits* 14 (November 1986): 4.

23. From *Sample Parts of International and Old Time Music . . . Vitak and Elsnic Co.,* pp. 37, 38. Thus, the incorporation paper dated 1912 that was supplied to me by Mr. Musielak did not represent the beginning of the firm. Interview with Laurence Musielak.

24. Note in particular the catalog, *Sample Parts . . . ,* p. 50, and *passim.*

25. Volumes nos. 1 and 6 are in the CSA Fraternal Life Library, Berwyn, Illinois.

26. This was Grill's objective in his arrangements. Interview with Charles Jiran, Dec. 6.

27. He was in fact the maestro's assistant. Kommer interview.

28. However, retirement for Vitak did not mean inactivity. He was an arranger of German waltzes put out by V-E in 1929, *Lauterbach German Medley Waltzes.*

29. German, Hungarian, and International compilations would appear by 1940. From collections at the CSA Library, Berwyn, and the personal collections of Victoria and Peter Karnish, Rosedale, New York, and Walter Ossowski, Philadelphia.

30. See *Sample Parts* . . . (Chicago, 1954?), and *Sample Parts* . . . (Chicago, 1942?).

31. From his obituary, *Cleveland Plain Dealer,* Dec. 20, 1960, p. 41.

32. From the files at CSA Fraternal Life Library, Berwyn.

33. A. L. Maresh, arr. *Album of Bohemian Songs* (Cleveland: Maresh, 1905).

34. Maresh Obituary, *Cleveland Plain Dealer,* Dec. 20, 1960.

35. Sajewski's son Alvin was interviewed by Richard Spottswood, "The Sajewski Story: Eighty Years of Polish Music in Chicago," in McCulloh, *Ethnic Recordings,* pp. 133–57; I also interviewed Alvin Sajewski in Chicago, May 24, 1983, Dec. 29, 1984, and March 21, 1985.

36. A brief, fragmentary, and really inadequate review is in Sula Benet, *Song, Dance, and Customs of Peasant Poland* (New York: Roy, 1951), pp. 23, 75, 137ff, 152, 160–61, 223, 245–46. See also Helen Wolska, *Dances of Poland* (New York: Crown Publishers, 1952), and Alfred Sokolnicki, "Polish Folk Dancing," in Betty Casey, ed., *International Folk Dancing, USA* (Garden City, N.Y.: Doubleday, 1981), pp. 231–32ff.

37. Spottswood, "Sajewski," pp. 145–47.

38. In addition to the *gorali,* see below the violinists leading the most popular Polish American polka bands, Ignace Podgorski, Josef Lazarz, and Frantiszek Dukla. Kleeman, "Origins," pp. 112–14, 121–22, is an episodic but sound discussion.

39. A good historical account of the early years remains Wacław Kruszka, *Historya Polska w Ameryce,* 13 vols. (Milwaukee: Kuryer Polski, 1905–1908) 4:49–52.

40. My statistics are from Joseph Parot, *Polish Catholics in Chicago, 1850–1920* (DeKalb, Ill.: Northern Illinois University Press, 1981), pp. 234–37; see also my *For God and Country* (Madison, Wis.: Society Press, 1975), p. 46.

41. From my interviews with Sajewski; Spottswood, "Sajewski," p. 133; Howard A. Tyner, "After 84 Years Polish Store Stops Music," *Chicago Tribune,* May 10, 1981, section 3, p. 1; transcript of interview with Theodore Sajewski in the Oral History collection of Chicago Polonia, SAJ 034, at the Chicago Historical Society, hereinafter Polonia/CHS.

42. Spottswood, "Sajewski," p. 133.

43. He had left Russian Poland to work in the Pennsylvania mines and in Cleveland before settling in Chicago. Ibid.; Theodore Sajewski interview, Polonia/CHS.

44. From a collection in the possession of Virginia and Peter Karnish, Rosedale, N.Y.

45. Krygier's *Album Balowy No. 1 Na Orkiestra* has a 1911 copyright

date. The Karnish collection has music publications of the Schunke and Tojanowski firms. Letter from Elizabeth A. Zaremba, daughter of Daniel Schunke, one of the sons of the firm's founder, Mar. 26, 1990, Tonowanda, N.Y. The work of Ignace Podgorski will be considered below.

46. The figure is from Nicholas Tawa, *A Sound of Strangers: Musical Culture, Acculturation, and the Post Civil War Ethnic American* (Metuchen, N.J.: Scarecrow Press, 1982), p. 111.

47. A very good brief explanation is Henry Sapoznik, "From Eastern Europe to East Broadway: Yiddish Music in Old World and New," *New York Folklore* 14 (Summer–Fall 1988): 117ff. See also Maurice Schwartz, liner notes for "Klezmer Music: Early Yiddish Instrumental Music, The First Recordings, 1910–1927" (Folklyric Records 9034).

48. Note especially "Badkhn," in Richard F. Shephard and Vicki Gold Levi, *Live and Be Well: A Celebration of Yiddish Culture in America from the First Immigrants to the Second World War* (New York: Ballantine Books, 1982), p. 19; and Macy Nulman, ed., *Concise Encyclopedia of Jewish Music* (New York: McGraw-Hill, 1975), pp. 22, 24. Note also the general discussion in Mark Slobin, *Tenement Songs: The Popular Music of the Jewish Immigrants* (Champaign: University of Illinois Press, 1982), pp. 14ff.

49. The number of sources on the subject of the Yiddish theater is vast. A good beginning, and probably the most complete text in English, is Nahma Sandrow, *Vagabond Stars: A World History of the Yiddish Theatre* (New York: Harper and Row, 1977). Other works depicting in particular the American Yiddish theater are the contemporary account in Hutchins Hapgood, *The Spirit of the Ghetto: Studies of the Jewish Quarter of New York,* rev. ed. (New York: Shocken Books, 1976), chapter 5, pp. 113–76, and more recent descriptions, such as David Lifson, *The Yiddish Theatre in America* (New York: Yoseloff, 1965); and chapter 14 in Irving Howe, *World of Our Fathers* (New York: Harcourt, Brace and Jovanovich, 1976).

50. Howe, *Fathers,* p. 460.

51. Irene Heskes, "The Hebrew Publishing Company Collection: An Introductory Report," in Glen Loney, ed., *Musical Theatre in America,* (Westport, Conn.: Greenwood Press, 1984), p. 391; Morris Clark, "America As A Cradle of Jewish Music," *Musical America* 33 (June 28, 1913): 25.

52. David Kessler, "Reminiscences of the Yiddish Theatre," *Yiddish* 5 (1983): 48; Mark Slobin, "A Survey of Early Jewish American Sheet Music, 1898–1921," *Working Papers in Yiddish and East European Jewish Studies* no. 17 (New York: Yivo Institute, 1976): 12.

53. Fred Somkin, "Zion's Harp by the East River: Jewish American Popular Songs in Columbus's Gold Land, 1890–1914," *Perspectives on American History,* New Series 2 (1985), p. 183.

54. Moses Rischin, *The Promised City: New York's Jews, 1870–1914* (Cambridge: Harvard University Press, 1962), pp. 133, 136.

55. Michael Gold, "East Side Memories," *American Mercury* 18 (September 1929): 98. Note also the nostalgic discussion in Zelda F. Popkin, "The Changing East Side," ibid. 10 (January 1927): 168ff. The classic Hapgood, *Spirit of the Ghetto,* ch. 5, refers to the Russian cafes as centers of much intellectual exchange but says little about music.

56. Fred Somkin, "Zion's Harp," pp. 184–85.

57. See Katzenellenbogen's obituary in *New York Times,* July 10, 1920, p. 15; and the death notices of Joseph Werbelowsky, ibid., June 12, 1919, p. 15; and David Werbelowsky, ibid., September 18, 1939, p. 19. Oddly, Somkin does not mention the Hebrew Publishing Company or Katzenellenbogen's part in its founding, as mentioned in the latter's obituary. See Somkin, "Zion's Harp," pp. 183–85.

58. Note the contemporary review of Zunser first as a traditional wedding bard and later as a turn-of-the-century Yiddish poet on the Lower East Side, in Hutchins Hapgood, *The Spirit of the Ghetto,* ed., Moses Rischin (Cambridge: Harvard University Press, 1967), pp. 91–98.

59. Charles Madison, *Jewish Publishing in America: The Impact of Jewish Writing on American Culture* (New York: Sanhedrin Press, 1976), pp. 79–81, 206–07.

60. The years are copyright dates, not necessarily the dates of composition. From Slobin, "Survey," and Slobin, *Tenement Songs* (Champaign: University of Illinois Press, 1982), pp. 119ff.

61. An excellent review of the Yiddish songs of this period is Somkin, "Zion's Harp," pp. 183–220.

62. Nahma Sandrow, "Yiddish Theater and American Theater," in Sarah Blacher Cohen, ed., *From Hester Street to Hollywood* (Bloomington: Indiana University Press, 1986), p. 19; Bret Charles Werb, "Rumshinsky's Greatest Hits: A Chronological Survey of Yiddish American Popular Songs, 1910–1931" (M.A. thesis, University of California–Los Angeles, 1987), pp. 4–6; Sapoznik, "From East Europe," p. 121.

63. The Hebrew Publishing Company terminated its music publishing by 1920.

64. Interview with Myron Surmach, Dec. 4, 1984, New York; Mark Slobin and Richard Spottswood, "David Medoff: A Case Study in Interethnic Popular Culture," *American Music* 3 (Fall 1985): 268.

65. The best brief summary in English of Ukrainian music culture is Anisa H. Sawyckyj, liner notes to "Ukrainian American Fiddle and Dance Music; The First Recordings, 1926–1936" (2 vols., Folklyric Records 9014 and 9015). The similarity with the Jews and Poles is obviously controversial, but on this point see Richard Spottswood, "Recordings of Ukrainian and Polish Popular Music in the United States," liner notes to " 'Spiew Juchasa,' Song of the Shepherd: Songs of the Slavic Americans" (New World Records, NW 283).

66. His autobiography, fortunately, was published, *The History of My "Surma"[Bookstore]; Memoirs of a Bookseller* [in Ukrainian] (New York: Surma, 1982), pp. 1–2.

67. Carl Fleischhauer, "Going Through The Same Thing: Alvin Sajewski Meets Myron Surmach," *Old Time Music* 27 (Winter 1977–78): 10; interview with Surmach. He may have already begun to sell sheet music in Wilkes-Barre. Slobin and Spottswood, "David Medoff," p. 268. See also the interview in *The New York Daily News,* Feb. 19, 1983, p. 49.

68. His son continued the business in the same Ukrainian neighborhood in Manhattan. See also Nanette DeCillis, "A Ukrainian Tradition: Myron

Surmach, Sr. and 'Surma,' " in the newsletter of the Ethnic Folk Arts Center of New York (Winter 1989).

69. Another immigrant group with an important cafe or coffeehouse tradition was the Greeks, where such social and entertainment centers first appeared in America about 1910. Sotiros Chianis, "A Glimpse of Greek Music in America," *Greek Music Tour . . .* (New York: Ethnic Folk Arts Center, 1983), booklet, p. 3.

70. My descriptions of these Italian cafes are heavily indebted to the ground-breaking work of Emelise Aleandri. See especially her dissertation, "A History of Italian American Theatre, 1900–1905 (City University of New York, 1983), for an extended discussion of this important institution. For a convenient summary, see Emelise Aleandri and Maxine Schwartz Seller, "Italo-American Theatre," in Maxine Seller, ed., *Ethnic Theatre in the United States* (Westport, Conn.: Greenwood Press, 1983), pp. 237–76. Note also Giuseppe Cautela, "The Italian Theatre in New York," *The American Mercury* 12 (September, 1927): 106. A very good recent review of the Italian ethnic and immigrant comedic tradition is Pamela [sic, Salvatore] Primeggia and Joseph Varacalli, "Southern Italian Comedy: Old to New Worlds," in Joseph V. Scalsa, Salvatore J. LaGumina, and Lydia Tomasi, eds., *Italian Americans in Transition* (Staten Island, N.Y.: Italian American Historical Association, 1990), pp. 241ff.

71. Aleandri, "Italian American Theatre," pp. 40, 43–44, 342, 347; Deanna M. Paoli, "The Italian Colony of San Francisco, 1850 to 1930," (M.A. thesis, University of San Francisco, 1970), pp. 72.

72. Giuseppe Cautela, "The Italian Theatre," p. 106; Aleandri, "Italian American Theatre," p. 316.

73. Aleandri, "Italian American Theatre," 327.

74. Cf. the experience of an entertainer, William Ricciardi, "An Actor Tells His Story," *Atlantica* 17 (May 1935): 135. Performers usually earned $8 per week or less. E. Aleandri, "Farfariello: King of Comedians on the Italian American Stage. But Who Remembers?" in *Little Italy Souvenir Book* (New York), p. 20.

75. Aleandri, "Italian American Theatre," p. 18.

76. Cf. the commedia del l'arte tradition in the Old World, as described in Primeggia and Varacalli, "Southern Italian Comedy," p. 242.

77. Lawrence Estavan, ed., *The Italian Theatre in San Francisco,* San Francisco Theatre Research Monograph XXI. From Theatre Research, vol. 10 (San Francisco: WPA Project 10677, June 1939), p. 24; Paoli, "Italian Colony of San Francisco," p. 73.

78. Aleandri and Seller, "Italo-American Theatre," p. 257; Primeggia and Varacalli, "Southern Italian Comedy," p. 246.

79. Ricciardi, "An Actor," pp. 134–35; Aleandri, "Little Italy at the Turn of the Century," in *Little Italy,* p. 8.

80. Aleandri, "Little Italy at the Turn of the Century," p. 7.

81. Author's interview with Louis Rossi, Ernesto Rossi's son, April 2, 1987, in New York; Michael Schlesinger, "Italian Music in New York," *New York Folklore* 14 (Summer–Fall 1988): 131.

82. "Santa Lucia–Casa Editrice–Napoli," in *Encyclopedia Della Canzone Napoletana*, 2 vols. (Naples: Casa Editrice Torchio, 1968–69), 1:482.

83. He would have had to have been well beyond the age of twenty, so the data in "Santa Lucia," p. 482, is incorrect. From my interview with his daughter, Lyvia, September 27, 1987, Brooklyn, N.Y.

84. Di Martino apparently held the position of company secretary into the 1920s. Vincenzo De Luca was President. Most of the biographical information was obtained from interviews with his daughter, Lyvia Di Martino, Sept. 27, 1987, and with Frank Tudisco, current head of the Italian Book Corporation, June 6, 1987, both in Brooklyn. I am grateful to them both for allowing me to view and copy both family and company files.

85. Tudisco interview.

86. Lyvia Di Martino interview.

87. Tudisco interview; "Santa Lucia," p. 482; *August (1927) Supplement of Italian Style Music Rolls . . . Italian Book Corporation*, in Mr. Tudisco's possession, Brooklyn, New York.

88. Tudisco interview. Mario wrote several tunes about American immigrants, e.g., "L l'America" (1921). From Italian Book Company files in Tudisco's possession. The company eventually (probably in the late 1930s) obtained ownership of about 25,000 titles and was selling sheet music at the rate of 50,000 copies per month. Lyvia Di Martino interview.

89. Tudisco interview.

90. Primeggia and Varacalli, "Southern Italian Comedy," p. 244–45.

91. Tudisco interview.

92. Cf., the Croatian Dobranic & Vardian Co., which by 1895 had probably become the first American firm to manufacture and sell tamburas and printed musical materials. Walter W. Kolar, *A History of the Tambura* (Pittsburgh: Duquesne University, Tamburitzans, 1973), pp. v, 1–3.

Chapter 4

1. I am clearly indebted to observers such as Pekka Gronow, "Ethnic Recordings: An Introduction," in McCulloh, *Recordings*, pp. 3, 5, 7; Richard Spottswood, "Commercial Ethnic Recordings in the United States," ibid., p. 54; and Spottswood, "Do You Sell Your Italians?" *John Edwards Memorial Foundation Quarterly* 15 (1979): 225–26.

2. From Allen Koenigsberg, *Edison Cylinder Records, 1889–1912 . . .* (New York: Stellar Productions, 1989), in the Frederick Williams collection, Philadelphia.

3. From Frederick P. Williams, compiler, "A Discography of the United States Marine Band Recordings", paper, August 1, 1988. I am again grateful to Mr. Williams, Philadelphia. One Felix Iardella was solo clarinetist, for example, in a Verdi piece and a Neapolitan song, and Fanciulli is named as composer of marches recorded in April 1894.

4. Spottswood, "Commercial Ethnic Recordings in the United States," in McCulloh, *Ethnic Recordings*, p. 53.

5. *Berliner Records in the Library of Congress* (brochure), pp. 6, 7, 16; Pekka Gronow, *Studies in Scandinavian American Discography*, 2 vols. (Helsinki: Suomen Aanitearkisto, 1977) 2:6; Koenigsberg, *Edison*, p. 1; R. Spottswood, liner notes to "Folk Music of Immigrants from Europe and the Near East," *Old Country Music in a New Land: Folk Music of Immigrants from Europe and the Near East* (New World Records, NW 264), in the Recorded Anthology of American Music, 1977. Because they are not true ethnic recordings, I am excluding from consideration here vaudeville-style cylinders and discs of stock ethnic stereotypes, which began to appear at this time.

6. Martin W. La Forse and James A. Drake, *Popular Culture and American Life; Selected Topics in the Study of American Popular Culture* (Chicago: Nelson-Hall, 1981), p. 26.

7. The 1903 date is the copyright date. Richard Spottswood, *Ethnic Music on Records: A Discography of Ethnic Recordings Produced in the United States, 1893–1942*, 7 vols. (Urbana: University of Illinois Press, 1990), pp. 635–36. I am grateful to both Mr. Spottswood and the University of Illinois Press for allowing me to see portions of Spottswood's work prior to publication.

8. Interview with Charles Jiran, Dec. 6, 1987.

9. From Stanley Jackson in Martin W. Laforse and James A. Drake, eds., *Popular Culture and American Life: Selected Topics in the Study of American Popular Culture* (Chicago: Nelson-Hall, 1981), pp. 37–42; Michael G. Corenthal, *The Iconography of Recorded Sound, 1886–1986: A Hundred Years of Commercial Entertainment and Collecting Activity* (Milwaukee, 1986), p. 52. Cf. a popular piece in the repertoire of John McCormack in the late 1800s entitled, "The Irish Emigrant."

10. Note the employment of a Slovenian baritone, Anton Schubel, in the late 1920s and early 1930s. Giles Edward Gobetz, *From Carniola to Carnegie Hall: A Biographical Study of Anton Schubel* (Wickliffe, Ohio: Euram Books, 1968), pp. 26, 32–33.

11. Spottswood, *Ethnic Music*, p. 1; Pekka Gronow, "Ethnic Recordings: An Introduction," in McCulloh, *Ethnic Recordings*, p. 5. "Ethnic Recordings in America," in *Folklife Center News* 5 (July 1982): 1, says Columbia's initial catalogue offering was for music in eleven languages.

12. From *Columbia Record* 7 (September 1909), quoted in Pekka Gronow, *Studies in Scandinavian American Discography*, 2 vols. (Helsinki: Suomen Aanitearkisto, 1977) 2:7.

13. Sotiros Chianos, "Survival of Greek Folk Music," *New York Folklore* 14 (Summer 1988): 41; Gronow, *Studies*, 1:8.

14. Foreign Record Field, *Columbia Record* 12 (May 1914), in Gronow, *Studies*, 2:8. See also *Columbia Record* 9 (1911): 7, and "Foreign Records for the Alien," *ibid.*, 10 (December 1912): 15.

15. *Talking Machine World* 11 (June 15, 1915): 31.

16. From *The Voice of the Victor*, September 1917, p. 173, quoted in Richard K. Spottswood, "Do You Sell Your Italians?," *JEMF Quarterly* 15 (1979): 226–27. As the author relates it, in the May 1918 issue of *The Voice* a Milwaukee dealer wrote to urge fellow agents to treat "Tony" as a regular customer. Ibid., p. 228.

17. Spottswood, *Ethnic Music*, p. 1; Norman Cohen, liner notes to "From the Tatra Mountains: Classic Polish American Recordings from the 1920s" (Morningstar Records 45007).

18. Gronow, *Studies* 2:7, 10; *Talking Machine World* 11 (August 15, 1915): 67.

19. *Talking Machine World* 11 (August 15, 1915): 67.

20. Ibid., 68.

21. Spottswood, "Sajewski," pp. 141–42; interview with Charles Jiran, La Grange, Ill., Dec. 6, 1987.

22. This was record E 2221. Spottswood, "Sajewski," pp. 141–42.

23. Carl Fleischhauer, "Going Through the Same Thing: Alvin Sajewski Meets Myron Surmach," *Old Time Music* 27 (Winter 1977–78): 10.

24. Interview with Charles Jiran, La Grange, Illinois, Dec. 6, 1987; *The Columbia Record* 13 (October 1915): 13; interview with Joseph Divisek, Berwyn, Illinois, Jan. 27, 1988.

25. Spottswood, *Ethnic Music*, pp. 609–10. Another Bohemian band that Heindl recorded was the Louis Solar and Concertina Orchestra, which had also made some cuts in New York for Columbia in 1911. Spottswood, *Ethnic Music*, pp. 660–61.

26. Gronow, "Ethnic Recordings," p. 6.

27. Gregory Mumma, "Sound Recording," in Hitchcock and Sadie, *Grove Dictionary* 4:267; Roland Gelatt, *The Fabulous Phonograph*, 2d ed. (New York: Macmillan, 1977), pp. 190, 208.

28. Pekka Gronow, "The Record Industry: The Growth of a Mass Medium," in Richard Middleton and David Horn, eds., *Yearbook, Popular Music* (Cambridge: Cambridge University Press, 1983) 3:59; Joseph Csida and June Bundy Csida, *American Entertainment: A Unique History of Popular Show Business* (New York: Watson-Guptill, 1978), pp. 220, 230–31. This huge growth of the record industry at the start of the 1920s also meant an expansion of other ethnic-related popular music forms, such as jazz, race records for black Americans, and hillbilly recordings; Russell Sanjek, *American Popular Music and Its Business: The First Hundred Years, 1900 to 1984*, 3 vols. (New York: Oxford University Press, 1988) 3:31; Bill C. Malone, *Country Music, USA*, rev. ed., (Austin: University of Texas Press, 1985), pp. 1, 34–35 ff.

29. David Boorstin, *The Americans: The Democratic Experience* (New York: Vintage Books, 1974), p. 383.

30. Gronow, "Ethnic Recordings," p. 15; Kathleen Monaghan, "The Role of Ethnic Recording Companies in Cultural Maintenance," *JEMF Quarterly* 14 (Autumn 1978): 145. Gronow states that more than half of Columbia's popular-music list of 11,000 records before 1923 were ethnic. He provides ethnic totals for both Victor and Columbia but not yearly totals, except for the Finns, 1923 to 1942 and 1952. Note also individual ethnic catalogues, such as the 95 discs in the 1918 *Victor Records paa Danish* (Aug. 1918), the 195 listed in *Norske Victor Plader* (Aug. 1921), the nearly 500 non-opera items in the 1924 *Česke Victor Rekordy*, and the immense numbers in *1920 Numerical List of Victor Records* (Camden, N.J., 1919).

31. Sotiros Chianos, "A Glimpse of Greek Music in America," *Greek*

Music Tour . . . (New York: Ethnic Folk Arts Center, 1983?), 4; Chianos, "Survival of Greek Folk Music in New York," *New York Folklore* 14 (Fall-Summer 1988): 41.

32. Gronow, *Studies* 1:31, 105; Bjorn England, "A Glimpse of the Past: Wallin's Svenska Records," *Storyville* 46 (April, 1973): 134.

33. Composite review, correspondence with Thomas Weber, a relative, Los Alamos, New Mexico, Mar. 3, 1988.

34. *Česke Victor Rekordy,* and the more general catalogue, *1920 Numerical List, Victor Records.* See also the record collection at the Czechoslovak Society of America Library, Berwyn, Illinois. The best biographical material on Kryl is Glenn Bridges, *Pioneers in Brass* (Detroit: Sherwood, 1965), pp. 54–56, which lists 38 of his records; R. Jaromir Pšenky, ed., *Zlata Kniha* (Chicago: Geringer, 1926), p. 252; Schwartz, *Bands,* pp. 17, 164–65, 187, 229–35, 270, 276–77; Kenneth Berger, ed., *Band Encyclopedia* (Evansville, Indiana: Band Associates, 1960), p. 124.

35. All of these are from Spottswood, *Ethnic Music,* pp. 600–05, 609–14, and 629–30. Oddly, I could not find Kryl in his listing. Interview with Joseph Divisek, Berwyn, Illinois, Jan. 27, 1988, helped me identify these musicmen more clearly.

36. Interview with Charles Jiran, Dec. 6. 1987.

37. Frederick P. Williams, "The Times as Reflected in the Victor Black Label Military Recordings From 1900 to 1930," in *Association for Recorded Sound Collections Journal* 13 (1981): 36, 38; materials supplied to me by Mr. Williams; and letter of Frederick P. Williams to author, March 6, 1989, to author.

38. From the files of Philip Balistreri, Milwaukee, and Frederick P. Williams, Philadelphia. Some of the names of the folk and popular recording artists are Nullo Romani, Raoul Romito, Paolo Dones, Voccia Coppia, Gilda Mignonette and Paolo Cittarella.

39. E.g., a contract with De Rosalia dated October 4, 1920, for "Nofrio Soldato," among many others in the Company files. I am grateful to Mr. Frank Tudisco of the Italian Book Corporation, Brooklyn, N.Y., for allowing me to see those files now deposited with the Immigration History Research Center, University of Minnesota.

40. From Spottswood, *Ethnic Music,* pp. 819–25; Spottswood, "Sajewski," p. 143; interview with Sajewski.

41. Record liner notes from Richard Spottswood, "Folk Music in America: Dance Music, Reels, Polkas, and More," 15 vols. (Washington: Library of Congress, 1976), vol. 4.

42. Spottswood, "Sajewski," p. 145; Cohen, "Tatra Mountains"; Sigrid Arne, "One Time Matinee Idol, Polish Arts Mentor Here," *Cleveland News,* March 11, 1959; and Bob Seltzer, "Polish Star Shines Here," newspaper clippings in Don Sosnoski Collection, Parma, Ohio. See also Kleeman, "Origins," pp. 65–66, 76–77, 121–22; Jozef Migała, *Polskie Programy Radiowe w Stanach Zjednoczonych* (Warsaw: Wydawnictwa Radia i Telewizji, 1984), pp. 35–37; "European American Music, Polish," in Hitchcock and Sadie, *Grove Dictionary* 2:81–82; interview with Witkowski's nephew, Bernie, Nov. 4, 1984, Hillside, N.J.

43. He would make many records for that firm in the 1930s and others from the late 1920s with Okeh, Brunswick, and Columbia. *Album Jubileuszowy 25-lecia Istnienia, Stow. Polsko-Amerykanskich Muzykantów* ... *20, 21, i 22-go Stycznia, 1941* (Philadelphia, 1941), pp. 2, 4, 6; Podgorski obituary, *The Philadelphia Evening Bulletin*, Nov. 7, 1957; *Program Booklet, 1978, International Polka Association* (Chicago, 1978), n.p.; Spottswood, *Ethnic Music*, pp. 771–77.

44. Another Philadelphia Polish bandleader who cut almost as many records as Podgorski, though somewhat earlier, and who may have been a colleague was (Władysław) Walter Podoszek. Interviews with Sophie Podgorski, Philadelphia, Oct. 11, 1985, and Walter Ossowski, Philadelphia, Nov. 18, 1989; Spottswood, *Ethnic Music*, pp. 777–80.

45. Chianis, "Survival of Greek Folk Music," p. 41; and Chianis, "A Glimpse of Greek Music," pp. 3–4.

46. A dozen Slovenian singing societies were active by World War I. "Zarja Singing Society," in Van Tassel and Grabowski, *Encyclopedia*, p. 1079; Rudolph M. Susel, "Slovenes," ibid., p. 897; "Slovenian National Home," ibid., p. 899; Richard March, "Slovenian Roots Inspire American Polka Styles," *Expressions* 1 (Summer–Fall 1985): 1; Louis Kaferle, "Iz Kraljestva in Polk v Clevelandu," *Slovenski Iseljenski Koledar* (Ljubljana, 1967), 265. I am grateful to Leo Muskatevc, University of Wisconsin–Milwaukee, for helping me with the translation.

47. Interview with Mervar's daughter, Justine Reber, May 29, 1985; Cleveland; telephone interview with Joseph Valencic, Sept. 6, 1987, Cleveland; letter to author from Joseph Velikonja, Seattle, Washington, Nov. 16, 1988; advertisement, *KSKJ Anniversary Album, 1924* (Cleveland, 1924), p. 223, at Immigration History Research Center, University of Minnesota; Frank Zupancic, "Anton Mervar: Master Accordion Craftsman," *St. Clair and Suburban News*, Jan. 24, 1985, pp. 1, 6; Zupancic, "Mervar Accordions—Unique Instruments," *Ameriska Domovina*, Aug. 30, 1974, p. 1. March, in "Slovenian Roots," p. 1, says button boxes were expensive, costing $200 in the 1920s. This may have been the maximum price. Justine Reber stated that Mervar arrived in 1912.

48. Zupancic, "Anton Mervar," p. 1; interview with Justine Reber.

49. Kaferle, in "Iz Kraljestva," p. 266, lists the major Cleveland ensembles active between World Wars I and II. Other sources are interviews with Sen. Frank and Mrs. Alice Lausche, Euclid, Ohio, Sept. 7, 1987, and with Joe Valencic, Cleveland, Sept. 7, 1987; Van Tassel and Grabowski, *Encyclopedia*, p. 562; and Spottswood, *Ethnic Music*, pp. 1024–25.

50. Vince Gostelna, "Matt Hoyer, Pioneer Polka Accordionist," *American Home* (Cleveland), Nov. 18, 1988, section 2, p. 7; *International Polka Festival ... 1987* (Chicago: International Polka Association, 1987), p. 10; Don Sosnoski, "The Story of Matt Hoyer," *The Polka News* 17 (June 24, 1987): 2.

51. Sosnoski, "Hoyer," p. 2; *International Polka Festival*, p. 10; Gostelna, "Hoyer," p. 7. Spottswood, in *Ethnic Music*, pp. 1018–21, lists none before 1926 and "Dunaj Ostane Dunaj" as recorded ca. 1927. See also Kaferle, "Iz Kraljestva," p. 266.

52. Lawrence McCullough, "An Historical Sketch of Traditional Irish Music in the U.S.," *Folklore Forum* 8 (July 1974): 177–80.

53. Mick Moloney, "Irish Ethnic Recordings and the Irish-American Imagination," in McCulloh, *Ethnic Recordings,* pp. 85, 87; Robert C. Toll, *Blacking Up: The Minstrel Show in Nineteenth Century America* (New York: Oxford University Press, 1974), pp. 173–77, 180.

54. W. H. A. Williams, "Irish Traditional Music in the United States," in David Noel Doyle and Owen Dudley Edwards, eds., *America and Ireland, 1776–1976: The American Identity and the Irish Connection* (Westport, Conn.: Greenwood, 1980), pp. 288–90; Tony Russell, "Irish Music in America: Early Recording History," *Old Time Music* 27 (Winter 1977–78): 15.

55. Moloney, in "Irish Ethnic Recordings," p. 90, provides an account of the incident. See also William Michael Healy, "Traditional Irish Music in the 78 rpm Era: An Analysis of Change of Instrumentation and Repertoire" (M.A. thesis, University. of California at Los Angeles, 1980), pp. 129, 131, and the reference in Rebecca S. Miller, "Our Own Little Isle: Irish Traditional Music in New York," *New York Folklore* 14 (Summer–Fall 1988): 113–14.

56. On the activities of the national labels, see, e.g., Pekka Gronow, comp., *The Columbia 33000F: A Numerical Listing* (Los Angeles: John Edwards Memorial Foundation, 1979), pp. 1–3; Healy, "Traditional Irish Music," p. 139. On the origins of the Irish American labels, see Harry Bradshaw, liner notes to "James Morrison: The Professor" (cassette, Viva Voce 001).

57. Bill Healy, liner notes to "Irish American Dance Music and Songs" (*Folk Lyric Records* 9010, 1977). Healy identifies them and others in more detail.

58. Pekka Gronow, *The Columbia 33000F Irish Series: A Numerical Listing* (Los Angeles: JEMF Center, UCLA, 1979), p. 3.

59. Frank Ferrel, "The Heyday of Michael Coleman," *Seattle Folklore Society* 5 (March 1975): 3; Rob Fleder, liner notes to "The Legacy of Michael Coleman" (*Shenachie Records,* 33002).

60. Mischa Elman referred to him as Ireland's "Kreisler of the Violin." Ferrel, "Heyday," p. 3; Lawrence E. McCullough, "Michael Coleman, Traditional Fiddler," *Eire-Ireland* 10 (Earrach, 1975): 91–92; Fleder, liner notes to "Michael Coleman."

61. The full biography is Bradshaw, "Morrison."

62. John McKenna Traditional Society of Drumkeering, County Lietrim, has put out a cassette, "John McKenna: His Original Recordings," with biographical notes by Frank Flynn and others.

63. There is a monument to him in Tarmon, County Leitrim. See also Harry Bradshaw and Jackie Small, "John McKenna: Leitrim's Master of the Concert Flute," *Musical Traditions* no. 7 (1987): 4, 6, 8, 10.

64. Interview with Surmach, New York, Dec. 4, 1984; Fleischhauer, "Sajewski," p. 10; Pekka Gronow, "Recording for the 'Foreign' Series," *JEMF Quarterly* 12 (Spring 1976): 18.

65. My account diverges in some details but generally follows Spottswood's description of the relationship between Humeniuk and Surmach in "Commercial Ethnic Recordings," pp. 60–61.

66. Letter of Surmach to author, Oct. 17, 1988, Saddle River, N.J.; obituary of Humeniuk in *Svoboda* (Freedom), Jan. 29, 1965, a New York area Ukrainian newspaper, supplied by Surmach.

67. "Pawlo Humeniuk," in *"Surma," Yuvileyniy Kalendar Almanackh Knegarni "Surma". . . 1945 rik* (New York, 1945), in the possession of Stefan Maksymjuk, Silver Spring, Md., to whom I am grateful. See also Anisa F. Sawickyj, liner notes to "Ukrainian American Fiddle and Dance Music: The First Recordings, 1926–1936" (*Folklyric Records,* 9015).

68. These figures cannot be verified, but in this case the general magnitude is more important than the precise number; like any article of popular culture, many more people heard the record than purchased it. My source is "Pawlo Humeniuk," *Almanackh* which is also cited by Gronow, "Recording for the 'Foreign' Series," p. 18.

69. Fleischhauer, "Sajewski," p. 10, quoting from a talk at a conference on recorded ethnic music.

70. "Pawlo Humeniuk," *Almanackh;* "Ukrainian Wedding," *Request Records,* SRLP 8168; Richard Spottswood, *Musical Images of Ellis Island* (Washington, D.C.: Portfolio Project, 1987), pp. 38–39. Still another important Ukrainian musician whom Surmach helped record was violinist Jozef Pizio. Liner notes by Roman Sawycky to "Dance Music, Ragtime, Jazz and More," Spottswood, "Folk Music in America."

71. Spottswood, "Ukrainian and Polish Popular Music." See also the liner notes for the polka piece "Hop Ciup" in Cohen, "Tatra Mountains."

72. Slobin and Spottswood, "David Medoff," pp. 261–66.

73. Interview with Surmach. Records were sometimes reissued to ethnic markets other than the original audience. Cf. Cohen, liner notes to "Tatra Mountains."

74. From *The Columbia Record* flyer of May 1914, quoted in Gronow, *Studies* 2:8.

Chapter 5

1. From my *For God and Country: The Rise of Polish and Lithuanian Ethnic Consciousness in America* (Madison, Wis.: Society Press, 1975).

2. Linda Degh, "Uses of Folklore as Expressions of Identity by Hungarians in the Old and New Country," *Journal of Folk Research* 21 (1984): 194–95; and T.H., "Hungarian Vintage Ball in South Chicago," *The New Hungarian Quarterly* 29 (Autumn 1988): 120–21.

3. A Norwegian American entertainment group contemporary with the Olsons was the Aakhus (family) Concert Company. Little is known about their material except that the father played an instrument and the mother spoke in various ethnic dialects. Apparently they made no records. See LeRoy Larson, "The Aakhus Concert Company: Norwegian-American Entertainers," in *Sacra Profana: Studies in Sacred and Secular Music for Johannes Riedel,* eds. Audrey Ekdahl Davidson and Clifford Davidson (Minneapolis: Friends of Minnesota Music, 1985), pp. 114–18.

4. Most of my biographical material on these Olsons is from their *Yust*

for Fun, Paul Anderson, ed. (Minneapolis: Eggs Press, 1925, 1979), which Mr. Anderson of Minneapolis kindly shared with me.

5. Telephone conversation with Odd Lovoll of Northfield, Minn., April 1, 1990; *Daglid Tidend,* September 14, 1933, fragment supplied by Mr. Anderson.

6. "Scandinavian Fun," *The Voice of the Victor* (August, 1924), 6, supplied to me by Paul Anderson; telephone interview with Odd Lovoll of Northfield, Minn.

7. Victor Record 72183. Apparently, Ethel Olson did the Brunswick version of 1926, no. 40053. From Gronow, *Studies* 1:104. It is possible that this reference is inaccurate, as Eleonora was known as the Sogne woman on stage.

8. Note the cartoon in Anderson, ed., *Yust,* p. 3.

9. *Ibid.,* p. 16.

10. The sampling of the Olsons' repertoire is in *ibid.*

11. Albin Widen, "Scandinavian Folklore and Immigrant Ballads," *Bulletin of the American Institute of Swedish Arts, Literature, and Science* 2 (January–March 1947): 9.

12. Ulf Beijbom, "Olle i Skratthult," *Svenska Amerikanaren Tribune,* May, 2, 1973, supplied by Carl Werner Pettersen, Stockholm; Beijbom, "Olle i Skratthult—Nicolina och Nojeslivet i svensk-amerika," *Svenska Posten,* Portland, Ore., Jan. 23, 1974, pp. 1, 3, 6, both translated by Roy Swanson, University of Wisconsin, Milwaukee, to whom I am grateful.

13. Beijbom, "Nicolina," p. 6; *Teater, Visafton och Bal,* A National Tour of Theatre, Music and Dance Traditions of Swedish America (1982), supplied by Robert Andresen, Duluth, Minn.

14. It may have been 1905. Maury Bernstein, "The Man Who Gave Us Nikolina," *Minnesota Earth Journal* 2 (1972): 18; Robert Andresen, "Traditional Music: The Real Story of Ethnic Music and How It Evolved in Minnesota and Wisconsin," *Minnesota Monthly* 107 (October, 1978): 11.

15. Beijbom, "Olle"; taped interview of Peterson's wife, Olga Lindgren, March 6, 1973, by Carl-Werner Pettersen, Minneapolis, kindly supplied by Anne-Charlotte Harvey of San Diego State University.

16. Pettersen interview; Beijbom, "Olle,"; Anne-Charlotte Harvey, "Swedish American Theatre," in *Ethnic Theatre in the United States,* ed. Maxine Schwartz Seller (Westport, Conn.: Greenwood, 1983), p. 505.

17. Dan Armitage, "The Curling Waters: A West Bank History," *Common Ground* (Minneapolis) (Spring, 1974), pp. 48ff.

18. Henriette C. K. Naeseth, "Drama in Swedish in Chicago," *Illinois State Historical Society Journal* 41 (June, 1948): 164; Ernest H. Behmer, "Seventy Years of Swedish Theatre in America," in *The Swedish Element in America . . . ,* ed. Axel W. Hulten, 4 vols. (2d ed., Chicago: Swedish American Biographical Society, 1934), pp. 111, 117; Harvey, "Theatre," pp. 495–96.

19. Letter from Bob Andresen, Duluth, May 23, 1988; Beijbom, "Olle"; Gareth Hiebert, "Olle Took Snoose Boulevard to the Rest of America," *St. Paul Pioneer Press,* February 15, 1976, Lively Arts section, p. 3. It concludes,

"And so Nikolina and I now are waiting for [her] old man to die" (translation by Swanson). Peterson made over a score of records in his fifteen-year career on stage. Maury Bernstein, "Scandinavian American Vaudeville," from the collection of Paul Anderson, Minneapolis. See also liner notes to "From Sweden to America," Caprice CAP 2011, 17.

20. Letter from Sally Lindholm, St. Paul, April 11, 1988; Peterson interview of Olga Lindgren; Leroy Larson, liner notes to "Early Scandinavian Bands and Entertainers," Banjar Records, BR 1840.

21. Note the 1919 photo in the advertisement in record liner notes, "From Sweden," p. 17; and the advertisement in *Countryside* 4 (September, 1976): 25. The description is a synthesis of Hiebert, "Olle"; Harvey, "Theatre," p. 508; and Beijbom, "Olle."

22. *Teater,* pp. 1, 7; Larsen, "Early Scandinavian Bands"; Armitage, "Curling Waters," p. 49.

23. Howard Pine, "Pine Country Echoes: State Fair Memories of Olle i Skratthult," *Countryside* 3 (August 1975): 30. I am deeply indebted to Mr. Pine of Roseville, Minnesota for his kindness.

24. Beijbom, "Olle."

25. Bernstein, "Scandinavian-American Vaudeville," p. 63, apparently from a translation by Anne-Charlotte Harvey.

26. The critic here is Anne-Charlotte Harvey. See especially Harvey, "Theatre," p. 503 and *passim;* and *Teater,* p. 8. The Depression killed the troupe in 1933, as it killed much of American vaudeville. Also, many Scandinavian Americans were assimilating by then, and fewer were interested in supporting ethnic theater. Peterson himself continued to perform, but by the end of the decade his interest had shifted away from comedy to religious evangelism. He died in 1960. Beijbom, "Olle"; Larsen, "Early Scandinavian Bands."

27. E.g., A. Richard Sogliuzzo, "Notes for a History of the Italian American Theatre," *Theatre Survey* 14 (November, 1973): 71.

28. Deanna M. Paoli, "The Italian Colony of San Francisco, 1850–1930," (M.A. thesis, University of San Francisco, 1970), p. 73; Lawrence Estavan, ed., *The Italian Theatre in San Francisco,* vol. 10, Monograph 21, San Francisco Theatre Research. (San Francisco: WPA Project 10677, June 1939), p. 24.

29. Sogluizzo, "History of the Italian American Theatre," pp. 68–69; and Emelise Aleandri, "A History of Italian American Theatre, 1900–1905 (Ph.D. diss., City University of New York, 1983), p. 130. My enormous debt to Dr. Aleandri for both her pioneering research into the subject and her generous assistance will be obvious in my notes.

30. I. C. Falbo, "Figure e Scene del Teatro Popolare Italiano a New York," *Il Progresso Italo-Americano,* June 7, 1942, p. 5-S; Olga Peragallo, *Italian American Authors and Their Contribution to American Literature,* ed. Anita Peragallo (New York: S. F. Vanni, 1949), p. 152.

31. "Farfariello," *Enciclopedia della Canzone Napoletana,* 3 vols. (Naples: Il Torchio, 1969), 2:151.

32. Peragallo, *Italian American Authors,* p. 152; Aleandri, "Italian Amer-

ican Theatre," pp. 131–33; Sogliuzzo, "History of Italian American Theatre," p. 68.

33. Aleandri, "Italian-American Theatre," p. 266.

34. Falbo, "Figure," p. 5-S; Aleandri, "Italian American Theatre," p. 150.

35. From an interview, "Farfariello," in L'Americolo, 36–37.

36. From a paper titled, "Il Macchiettista Principe" in Box 1 of the Migliaccio Papers, Immigration History Research Center, University of Minnesota (henceforth, IHRC).

37. Most of the following material I obtained from Aleandri, "Farfariello: King of the Comedians on the Italian American Stage—But Who Remembers," in Little Italy, Souvenir Book (New York?, n.d.), given me by Louis Rossi, New York City; New York Times, March 29, 1946, p. 24; and J.A.T., "Italian American Pens," Italian Heritage (May 1971), n.p., in the Migliaccio Papers, IHRC.

38. In Box 1, Migliaccio Papers, IHRC.

39. For example, they appeared at the Dante Theatre in Chicago, August 4, 1917. Program in Box 1, Migliaccio Papers, IHRC.

40. Probably the closest was Giovanni de Rosalia and his comic character, Nofrio, an immigrant half-wit, who became especially well known on records. See E. Falbo, "Giovanni de Rosalia," Il Progresso Americano, June 28, 1942, p. 5-S; Cautela, "Italian Theatre," p. 110; Sogliuzzo, "Notes," p. 67.

41. Except as otherwise specified, most of the skits described below are from the list provided by Aleandri, "History," pp. 455ff. See also the summaries of Edmund Wilson, "Alice Lloyd and Farfariello," The New Republic 44 (October 21, 1925): 230.

42. Generalized from Sogliuzzo, "History of the Italian American Theatre," p. 69; Falbo, "Figure," p. 5-S; and newspaper article on Farfariello in Box 1, Migliaccio Papers, IHRC.

43. As translated by Aleandri, "Italian American Theatre," pp. 462–63.

44. Note the conclusion of Lizabeth Cohen, "Encountering Mass Culture," p. 9, on the group's devotion to the phonograph in Chicago, further substantiated by Michael Schlesinger, "Italian Music in New York," New York Folklore 14 (Summer–Fall, 1988): 131.

45. Contracts dated April 5, 1916, with C. G. Childs, General Director, Victor Talking Machine Co., and August 15, 1917, both in Box 1, Migliaccio Papers, IHRC; Aleandri, "Farfariello," p. 23.

46. Schlesinger, "Italian Music," p. 133; 1920 Numerical List of Victor Records . . . (Camden, N.J.: Victor Talking Machine Company, 1919), pp. 95–96.

47. Ibid.

48. Aleandri, "Farfariello," p. 23.

49. Irving Howe, World of Our Fathers (New York: Harcourt, Brace, Jovanovich, 1976), pp. 480, 485–86.

50. Miriam Kressyn, "Memories of the Yiddish Theater," Famous Records, no catalog number (Kressyn is an old member of the Yiddish musical stage); David Lifson, The Yiddish Theatre in America (New York: Yoseloff, 1965), p. 149.

51. Joseph Rumshinsky, *Klangen Fun Mein Leben* (Pages From My Life) (New York: Vadran, 1944), p. 591. I am grateful to Paul Melrood, Milwaukee, for his assistance in translation.

52. The most detailed biography is in Zalmen Zylbercwajg, ed., *Lexicon of the Yiddish Theatre* (in Yiddish), 4 vols. (Warsaw, 1934), 2:1133–35. See also Helen Stambler, liner notes to "Aaron Lebedeff on Second Avenue," Collectors Guild Record CG663/4, 1968; and B. and H. Stambler, liner notes to "Aaron Lebedeff Sings Rumania, Rumania and Other Yiddish Theatre Favorites," Collectors Guild Record CGY 631.

53. H. Stambler, "Lebedeff."

54. Zylbercwajg, *Lexicon* 2:1135.

55. Rumshinsky, *Klangen*, p. 592. Inexplicably, the major authority on Yiddish musical comedy, Mark Slobin, in one essay slights Lebedeff in his discussion of the development of that entertainment in the 1920s and 1930s, despite citing the significant and novel role of Molly Picon. Despite the difficulty of comparing the two, I would argue that in the 1920s and even in the 1930s Lebedeff was the more important and popular star nationally. See for example Mark Slobin, "How the Fiddler Got on the Roof," in *Folk Music and Modern Sound,* eds. William Ferris and Mary L. Hart (Jackson, Miss.: University Press of Mississippi, 1982), pp. 26–28. Mordecai Yardeni, *Words and Music: A Selection From His Writings,* trans. and ed. by Max Rosenfeld (New York, Yiddisher Kallen Farband, 1986), p. 153, mentions Picon incidentally but lists Lebedeff as one of the three best-selling Yiddish recording stars.

56. Interview with Lotte Weintrop, New York City, October 16, 1988, who participated in Lebedeff's summer workshops.

57. In *Jewish Daily Forward* (Chicago edition), October 8, 1925, p. 1; *Ibid.,* October 11, 1929, p. 3, from microfilm supplied by Center for Research Libraries, Chicago. See also "Lebedeff," in Zylbercwajg, *Lexicon,* 2:1135.

58. James Albert Miller, *The Detroit Yiddish Theatre, 1920–1937* (Detroit: Wayne State University Press, 1967), pp. 43, 78, 94–96, and *passim.*

59. Yardeni, *Words,* 173.

60. From Spottswood, *Ethnic Music,* pp. 151–58, compared with Zylbercwajg, *Lexicon,* 2:1134–35, who lists what appears to be his full dramatic schedule to the mid-1930s.

61. Norman H. Warenblad, *The New York Times Great Songs of the Yiddish Theatre* (New York: Quadrangle, 1975), p. 45.

62. Jacob Katzman, *Song of the Golden Land: The Jewish Immigrants' Experience as Reflected in Their Music,* lecture 7 (New York: Touro College, 1984), cassette recording.

63. A good overview of this feud is in Richard F. Shephard and Vicki Gold Levi, *Live and Be Well: A Celebration of Yiddish Culture in America from the First Immigrants to the Second World War* (New York: Ballantine, 1982), pp. 104–06.

64. Abraham Ellstein, "Reflections of a Composer," in *Jewish Music Programs,* ed. Irene Heskes (New York: Jewish Music Council of the Jewish Welfare Board, 1978), p. 116.

284   Notes to Pages 105–108

65. From Spottswood, *Ethnic Music*, pp. 151–58; Zylbercwajg, *Lexicon*, 2: 1133–35; Max Karper, "Yiddish Theatre Vignettes," *The New York American*, January 26, 1935; *New York Herald Tribune*, Mar. 24, 1935; *New York Times*, May 16, 1941; *New York Post*, February 27, 1937, all clippings in The Billy Rose Collection at the New York Public Library; Miller, *Detroit*, pp. 95, 96. Perhaps his best known and remembered performance, after his first in "Liovke Maladetz," was in "Bublitchki," with Molly Picon in 1938. It was a musical set, like so many others, in the old country. B. and H. Stambler, "Lebedeff." The leading composers are listed in Sapoznik, "From Eastern Europe," p. 121.

66. The years of tunes listed hereafter are dates Lebedeff recorded them. From Spottswood, *Ethnic Music*, p. 154; and sheet music kindly supplied by Nathan Kaganoff, Librarian at the American Jewish Historical Society, Waltham, Mass., to whom I am deeply grateful. The dates of tunes listed below are those of Lebedeff's recordings. Cf. "Mein Shtetele Belz," another example of the genre, though one that Lebedeff did not record. Its music was by Olshanetzky and words by Jacob Jacobs. See Eleanor Gordon Mlotek and Joseph Mlotek, comps., *Pearls of Yiddish Song: Favorite Folk, Art and Theatre Songs* (New York: Education Department of Workers' Circle, 1988), p. 260; Katzman, *Song*, Lecture 4.

67. From sheet music (1933) with music by Sholem Secunda and words by Anshel Schorr, translated by Paul Melrood.

68. Liner notes to "Aaron Lebedeff," Banner BAS 1007; Molly Picon, with Jean Bergantini Galleo, *Molly! An Autobiography* (New York: Simon and Schuster, 1980), p. 74.

69. From Eleanor Gordon Mlotek, comp., *Favorite Yiddish Songs: Mir Trogn a Gezang* (New York: Adama Books, 1972), pp. 40–41.

70. Spottswood, *Ethnic Music*, pp. 151–58; H. Stambler, "Lebedeff," vol. 2.

71. Warenblad, *Songs*, p. 175; Spottswood, *Ethnic Music*, pp. 151–58; cassette recording of lecture given by Henry Sapoznik, "The Mavin's Guide to Jewish Records," Association of Recorded Sound Collections, 1982.

72. Taken from "Roumania, Roumania," Banner BAS 1007; B. and H. Stambler, liner notes to "Aaron Lebedeff Sings 'Rumania, Rumania' and other Yiddish Favorites," Collector's Guild CGY 631; and conversation with Henry Sapoznik, New York, April 6, 1988.

73. "Aaron Lebedeff is Dead; Starred in Yiddish Theatre," *New York Times*, November 9, 1960, p. 35.

74. This follows from Slobin, *Tenement*, pp. 198–200; and his "Klezmer Music: An American Ethnic Genre," *Yearbook for Traditional Music* 16 (1984): 37. Slobin calls Lebedeff, "one of the most beloved and often recorded of Jewish American performers," and a significant agent in creating a common Jewish American identity. See also Sandrow, "Yiddish Theatre," p. 22; and Howe, *Fathers*, pp. 490–91, for overall assessments of Lebedeff.

75. On this general topic see further the vital nature of music among the Finnish lower classes discussed by Keijo Virtanen, "Musiikin Merkitys

Siirtolaisten Kultturotoiminnassa" in Virtanen, *Arja Pilli Auvo Kostianinen, Suomen Surtolaisuuden, Historia,* Osa III (Turku, 1986), pp. 181ff.

76. My biographical information is from Toivo Tamminen, "Arthur Kylander," in a recent article in *Kansanmusiikki* kindly supplied to me by Arne Santa of Duluth, Minn.; a section of *Reisaavaisen Laulu Ameriikkaan, Siertolaislauluju, Toimittanut Simo Westerholm* (Kaustinen, Kansanmusiikki Instituutin Julkaisiija, 1983), pp. 76–77. I am grateful to Ivy Nevala of Milwaukee for her translations. Toivo Tamminen of Eprantie, Finland has also been especially generous.

77. Tamminen, "Kylander."

78. Pekka Gronow, "Finnish American Records," *JEMF Quarterly* 7 (1971): 184.

79. *Ibid.,* p. 179.

80. Kylander recorded it for Victor in March, 1928. See Pekka Gronow, liner notes for "Siirtolaisen Muistoja" (Immigrant's Memories), cassette recording, *Ohjelma* (Helsinki, 1978); *Reisaavaisen,* p. 77. Finding that he could not support himself by his music in the depression, he returned to Hollywood, where he and his wife worked in a restaurant until 1943. They then purchased a farm which, as a result of his occasional performances, became a Finnish American center. He died there in 1968. Tamminen, "Kylander."

81. According to Richard Spottswood, *Musical Images of Ellis Island* (Washington, D.C., Portfolio Project, 1987), p. 31, who quotes one of his prolabor songs, "Varssyja Sielta Ja Taalta" (Verses from Here and There). However, a Radio Finland interview of Niilo and Olli Pekka Ihamaki provided me by Mr. Tamminen, and Juka Niemela, "Hiskias Motto eli Hiski Salomaa," *Amerikan Uutiset,* September 24, 1987, dispute this point, saying he was a labor singer without any political bias.

82. Niemela, "Hiskias."

83. These songs are on the cassette from the Radio Finland interview of the Pekkas.

84. Gronow, "Records," p. 181, provides the descriptions and the figure.

85. From Stasys Santvaras, "Dzimdzi-Drimdzi," in *Encyclopedia Lituanica,* 6 vols. (Boston: Encyclopedia Lituanica, 1972), 2:125–26.

86. See the close descriptions of their acts in Vytautas Alanta, ed., *Antanas Vanagaitis, Jo Gyvenimas ir Veikla* (Tabor Farm, Mich.: Bachunas, 1954), pp. 54–59.

87. Courtesy of Loreta Venclauskas, Executive Director, Lithuanian Research and Studies Center, Chicago.

88. From *Margutis* 1 (July–August 1928), p. 16. The figure in this periodical was probably a claim by Vanagaitis rather than a verifiable number, but certainly it was a hit, nevertheless.

89. Kazys Bielinis, "Jack Sharkey," in *Encyclopedia Lituanica,* 5:129. That he earned an entry in the *Encyclopedia* is additional proof of Sharkey's ethnic appeal.

90. Gronow, "Ethnic Recordings," p. 33.

Chapter 6

1. A recent discussion of Hansen's conclusions is Peter Kivisto and Dag Blanck, eds., *American Immigrants and Their Generations* (Champaign: University of Illinois Press, 1990).

2. The generalization does not require specific documentation, but see as examples the confession of a writer, John Fante, "The Odyssey of a Wop," *American Mercury* 30 (September 1933): 91–93, quoted in Maurice Davie, *World Immigration* (New York: Macmillan, 1936, 1949), pp. 278–79; and the film *The Immigrant Experience: The Long, Long Journey* (1973).

3. Davie, *Immigration*, pp. 174ff.

4. Csida and Csida, *Entertainment*, p. 230.

5. Gronow, "Record Industry," p. 64.

6. The depression was not the sole reason, but it was an important one. Gareth Hiebert, "Olle Took Snoose Boulevard To The Rest of America," *St. Paul Pioneer Press,* February 15, 1976, clipping supplied by Howard Pine, Roseville, Minn.: Armitage, "Curling Waters," p. 50.

7. The term was not in common use in the 1930s, but it is an apt designation for the appearance of musical entertainers who aimed their performance beyond their own ethnic audience. Their intention is further discussed below.

8. From Gilman M. Ostrander, *American Civilization in the First Machine Age* (New York: Harper & Row, 1970), pp. 4, 9–10, 28–29; Richard Weiss, "Ethnicity and Reform: Minorities and The Ambience of the Depression Years," *Journal of American History* 66 (December, 1979): 566–68 and passim; and especially Warren I. Susman, "The People's Fair: Cultural Contradictions of a Consumer Society," in Susman, *Culture as History; The Transformation of American Society in the Twentieth Century* (New York: Pantheon, 1984), pp. 175–76, 206, 212–13.

9. Each did the waltz but in segregated locations. E.g., Lewis Erenberg, *Steppin' Out: New York Nightlife and the Transformation of American Culture, 1890–1930* (Chicago: University of Chicago Press, 1981), chapter 5, especially pp. 148–58.

10. Edith Terry Bremer, *The International Institutes in Foreign Community Work; Their Program and Philosophy* (New York: Woman's Press, 1923), p. 6; Julia Talbot Bird, "The International Institutes of the Young Women's Christian Association and Immigrant Women," (M.A. thesis, Yale University, 1932), especially pp. 17–25, 35ff; and Raymond Mohl, "Cultural Pluralism in Immigrant Education: The International Institutes of Boston, Philadelphia, and San Francisco," *Journal of American Ethnic History* 1 (Spring, 1982): 35–38.

11. *The Book of America's Making Exposition . . . New York, Oct. 29–Nov. 12, 1921* (New York, 1921), and *The Book of All Nations' Exposition* (Cleveland, 1929).

12. Note especially Alice Sickels, *Around the World in St. Paul* (Minneapolis: University of Minnesota Press, 1945); and my "Old Time Folk Dancing and Music Among the Second Generation, 1920–1950," in Kivisto and Blanck, eds., *Immigrants*, pp. 144–48.

13. One of the best recent works on the subject is Betty Casey, *International Folk Dancing, USA* (New York: Doubleday, 1981). See also Martha Graham Hampton, "Pioneers of Recreational Dance," *Viltis* 47 (January–February 1989): 35.

14. An interesting connection between one of these fairs and old-time ethnic music is the sheet-music copy of the Bohemian song, "City of Promise," heralding the Chicago Century of Progress and published in 1934 by the leading ethnic-music house, Vitak and Elsnic. In the CSA Fraternal Insurance Company library, Berwyn, Ill.

15. Mary Wood Hinman, "Educational Possibilities of the Dance," *Journal of Health and Physical Education* 5 (April 1934): 15. She was of course also justifying the cultivation of other folk-art forms by nongroup members.

16. In Mary F. Watkins, "Current Events in the Dance World," *New York Herald Tribune,* May 8, 1932, section 7, p. 9. See also her column, "With the Dancers," ibid., February 26, 1933, section 7, p. 7.

17. Mary Ann Bodnar, "The Pendulum of Percentage," in *What It Means to be a Second Generation Girl . . .* (New York: Woman's Press, 1935), pp. 15–16, 19–21.

18. Small ethnic ensembles had played earlier for outsiders, as at multi-ethnic Wisconsin house parties in the 1920s, but the ensembles cited here had much more commercial aims and played a much more mixed repertoire than the smaller bands playing in farm homes, barns, and lumber camps that were mentioned in Phil Martin, *Across the Fields; Fiddle Tunes and Button Accordion Melodies; Traditional Norwegian-American Music From Wisconsin* (Dodgeville, Wis.: Folklore Village Farm, 1982), pp. 4–10, especially 7. I refer to these musicians below as predecessors of the larger ethnic dance band.

19. Susan G. Davis, "Utica's Polka Music Tradition," *New York Folklore* 4 (1978): 104, 107–10, 114–15.

20. Quoted in Joseph Ficca, "A Study of Slavic American Instrumental Music in Lyndora, Pennsylvania," Ph.D. thesis, University of Pittsburgh, 1980, p. 57.

21. "Mitch Rudiak and The Ambassadors" had existed as a band at least since 1930. Ibid., pp. 69, 204.

22. The second generation apparently was able to accommodate comfortably a simultaneous ethnic and American dance education. From "Muziky, Muziky . . . Muziky," *Wisconsin Slovak* 4 (Autumn, 1983): 2–4. Note, too, the love of Polish music among the ethnic youth in Philadelphia at this time. *Album . . . Stow. Polsko-Amerykanskich Muzykantów,* p. 12.

23. Nancy Ann Kvam, "Norwegian American Dance Music in Minnesota and Its Roots in Norway: A Comparative Study" (doctoral thesis in Musical Arts, University of Missouri, Kansas City, 1986, pp. 109–12); Phil Martin, *Across the Fields,* pp. 6–7; E. K. Dalstrom and Harl A. Dalstrom, "From Skylon Ballroom to Oscar's Palladium: Dancing in Nebraska, 1948–1957," *Nebraska History* 65 (Fall, 1984), 368–71.

24. Cf. Kvam, "Norwegian American Dance Music," p. 20.

25. For similar features in the German sections of Michigan see, Stephen R. Williams, "House Parties and Shanty Boys: Michigan's Musical Tradi-

tions," in C. Kurt Dewhurst and Yvonne Lockwood, eds., *Michigan Folklife Reader* (East Lansing: Michigan State University Press, 1987), pp. 226–27, 236–37.

26. Mrs. Ben Johnson in Kvam, "Norwegian American Dance Music," p. 102.

27. From James P. Leary, "Old Time Music in Northern Wisconsin," *American Music* 2 (Spring, 1984): 75.

28. Paul M. Gifford, "Fiddling and Instrumental Folk Music in Michigan," in Dewhurst and Lockwood, eds., *Michigan Folklife Reader*, p. 193.

29. Folklorist Jim Leary and his colleagues have also referred to the genre as "old time." Leary, "Old Time Music," p. 75.

30. Lewis Erenberg, "Ain't We Got Fun," *Chicago History* 14 (Winter, 1985–1986): 18.

31. Lon Gault, "Ballroom Echoes," mimeographed (Wheaton, Ill.: author, 1983), pp. 40, 191–93, 196, 261; Nancy Banks, "The World's Most Beautiful Ballrooms," *Chicago History* 2 (Fall–Winter, 1973): 207, 209.

32. Gault's work, "Ballroom Echoes," is an encyclopedic national listing. I am deeply grateful to Mr. Gault for his help.

33. Csida and Csida, *Entertainment*, pp. 227, 250.

34. John Mihal, "Radio Stations Here Lead in Old World Music Programs," *Cleveland News*, March 30, 1935, p. 9B. WEVD (New York), the station of the *Jewish Daily Forward*, began in 1926 and shortly thereafter offered programs in many languages. Other ethnic programming in the nation's largest metropolitan area then or by 1930 was on WBNX and WLIB in New York and especially on WHOM in Jersey City. Nanette De Cillis, "A Ukrainian Tradition: Myron Surmach, Sr., and 'Surma,' " *Newsletter, Ethnic Folk Arts Center* (Winter, 1989): 1ff.; Surmach, "Surma," p. 69; letter from J. J. Stukas of Watchung, N.J., to author, August 1, 1989. One should use Migała, *Polskie Programy Radiowe w Stanach Zjednoczonych,* and his *Polish Radio Broadcasting in the United States* (Boulder, Colo.: East European Monographs, 1987), with extreme care. For Chicago, see Spottswood, "Sajewski," p. 148; "Brunswick Company Broadcasts Polish Hours of Music," *Talking Machine World,* February 1928, p. 99; and the Polish programs of 1930 on WEDC conducted by Bruno Z. Zielinski, in *International Polka Association News* 26 (May 1986): 1 and 26 (June 1986): 1; Migała, *Polish Radio,* p. 227. Note, too, the 1930 birth of ethnic radio in Philadelphia on WRAX, in Jack McKinney, "A Guide to Ethnic Radio; or, Now a Few Words from the Old Country," in *Philadelphia Daily News,* in a February 1980 clipping at the Temple University Urban Archives. Theodore C. Grame, *Ethnic Broadcasting in the United States* (Washington, D.C.: American Folklife Center, 1980) is an adequate contemporary aid but offers little historically.

35. Gault, "Ballroom Echoes," p. 50.

36. Carl H. Scheele, "American Entertainment—An Immigrant Domain," in Peter C. Marzio, ed., *A Nation of Nations* (New York: Harper and Row, 1976), p. 443.

37. The standard history is Toni Charuhas, *The Accordion* (New York: Accordion Music Publishing Company, 1955), pp. 9–22.

38. The role in this popularization of Deiro's brother, Guido, another accordion virtuoso, is disputed. Theresa Costello, "Octave Pagani," *Accordion World* 1 (November 1936): 8; "Who Was First; The Deiro Brothers Controversy," ibid. (August 1935): 4–7, 15, in the Eddie Chavez collection, San Antonio, Texas. I am grateful to Mr. Chavez.

39. Chic Winters, "The Trend to Accordions," *Accordion World* 4 (March 1940): 16; "Building Yesterday Into Today," ibid., p. 7; interview with Charles Nunzio, former vice president of the AAA, November 14, 1988, Milwaukee.

40. See Davis, "Utica's Polka Music Tradition," pp. 110–11; and Leary, "Old Time Music," p. 79.

41. Charuhas, *Accordion*, pp. 50–61, has good brief biographies of the stars.

42. *Accordion News* 2 (April 15, 1935): 2.

43. "The Charles Nunzio Story," *The Polka News* 19 (June 28, 1989): 13.

44. Note in particular the experience of the leading virtuoso, Charles Magnante, whose rise paralleled that of his instrument. George M. Bundy, "Just Who Is Charles Magnante?" clipping in the Eddie Chavez Collection; John H. Reuther, "Magnante: Highlights of a Meteoric Career," *The Accordion World* 1 (April 1936): 16; *American Accordion Association Presents the Charles Magnante Memorial Concert, August 6, 1988, passim*, in the Chavez collection. Note especially the quotation, "In 1939 his accordion recital in Carnegie Hall firmly established the instrument as a versatile [and] completely satisfying medium of musical interpretation," in the memorial-concert publication, supplied by Mr. Chavez. For the attempt to obtain recognition for the accordion as an instrument of serious music, see "All Accordion Concert Set for Carnegie Hall," article in the Chavez collection.

45. Jimmy Stewart, Donald O'Connor, Charlie Chaplin, and Ginger Rogers. "Musical Rage in Hollywood," *Accordion World* 3 (December 1938): 8–9.

46. Note the advertisements in issues of *Accordion News* and *Accordion World* in the mid-1930s, and especially, "Gene Warner: Musician and Business Executive," *Accordion World* 2 (February 1937): n.p.; and ibid. 2 (April, 1937): 17, from a file of these periodicals at the American Accordion Musicological Society in Pitman, N.J. I am grateful to Stanley Darrow, director. See also John Krachtus, "Personal Experiences in Accordion Music Publishing," *Accordion World* 1 (June 1936): 6–7.

47. "Eric Olzen," *Accordion World* 1 (June 1936): 17; Ibid. 5 (December, 1940): 10.

48. Calculated from a list in *Accordion World* 5 (December 1940): 17–18. See also Mary Pembroke, "Dorchester's Gaviani is 'Dean' of American Accordionists," *The Boston Seniority*, August 1979, p. 7; "News: The American Accordionists Association is Formed," *Accordion World* 3 (May 1938): 10, 22; and interview with Joseph Divisek, Berwyn, Ill., January 27, 1988; American Accordionists Association, *Fiftieth Anniversary Jubilee* . . . (New York: AAA, 1988), pp. 10–11; Leary, *The Wisconsin Patchwork*, p. 15.

49. Except of course for the war years. "Accordion Music: The Universal Language," *Accordion World* 2 (April 1937): 5; interview with Charles Nunzio, who estimated 150,000 by 1950.

50. February 3. From Russell Sanjek, *American Popular Music and Its Business: The First Hundred Years, 1900 to 1984,* 3 vols. (New York: Oxford University Press, 1988), 3:128.

51. The standard history is Vincent Lynch and Bill Henkin, *Jukebox: The Golden Age* (Berkeley, Calif.: Lancaster-Miller, 1981), pp. 7ff.

52. Ian Dove, "Juke Box, A Brief History on the Medium's 100th Anniversary," *DISCoveries,* December 1989.

53. Robert C. Toll, *The Entertainment Machine; American Show Business in the Twentieth Century* (New York: Oxford University Press, 1982), p. 59; Gordon Mumma, "Sound Recording," in Hitchcock and Sadie, eds., *New Grove Dictionary,* 4:268. Gault, "Ballroom Echoes," p. 47 has faulty statistics; see "Phonograph Boom," *Time Magazine,* September 4, 1939, p. 36, and "America's Jookbox Craze: Coin Phonographs Reap Harvest of Hot Tunes and Nickels," *Newsweek,* June 3, 1940, p. 49.

54. Gronow, *Studies* 1:12.

55. *New York Times,* March 26, 1949, p. 17; Lester Velie, "Vocal Boy Makes Good," *Collier's,* December 13, 1947, p. 123.

56. Velie, "Vocal," p. 124.

57. Quoted in Sanjek, *American Popular Music,* 3:126. Note also "Feathered Kapp," *Time,* July 1, 1940, p. 48.

58. Sanjek, *American Popular Music,* 3:127; "Phonograph Boom," p. 36. For a detailed description of their relationship, see in particular Lewis's memoirs, E. R. Lewis, *No CIC* (London: Universal Royalties, 1956), chapter 7, esp. pp. 52, 57, and 62, where Lewis recounts Kapp's aggressive business competitiveness and his shrewd selection of popular stars to launch his new company. Kapp did a "fine job with the artists. . . .In his own field he stood head and shoulders above the others." Ibid., p. 62.

59. Even though Victor preceded Kapp with its inexpensive Bluebird label. Three-fifths of Decca releases in the late 1930s went into jukeboxes. Velie, "Vocal," p. 125. For Henry Luce's praise of Kapp's business acumen see the former's editorial, "No Frontiers?" *Life,* March 7, 1949, p. 30.

60. Tony Russell, "Irish Music in America; Early Recording History," *Old Time Music* 27 (Winter, 1977–78): 17.

61. "Phonograph Boom," p. 37.

62. Sanjek, *American Popular Music,* 3:137.

63. "America's Jookbox Craze," p. 50.

64. Sholom Secunda, "From the Melody Remains: The Memoirs of Sholom Secunda (as told to Miriam Kressyn)," *Yiddish* 5 (1983): 118. His most complete biography is by his daughter-in-law, Victoria Secunda, *Bei Mir Bist Du Shon: The Life of Sholom Secunda* (Weston, Conn.: Magic Circle, 1982).

65. Michael Mok, "The Sad Story of Thirty Pieces of Silver," *The New York Post,* January 13, 1938, p. 13; James Street, "By Me You Are Grand," *Radio Guide,* February 19, 1938, p. 2, from the Sholom Secunda file at Yivo Institute, New York.

66. Sholom Secunda, "The Real Story of a $30 Tune Smash," in the Secunda Collection at Yivo. Cf. Secunda, *Bei Mir,* pp. 144–50.

67. "The Real Story . . . " and "You're Grand Plays Merry . . . ," newspaper fragments in the Sholom Secunda file, Yivo, have an account that differs somewhat from the version in Secunda, *Bei Mir,* pp. 144–50. See also Sammy Cahn, *I Should Care: The Sammy Cahn Story* (New York: Arbor House, 1974), p. 44; Max Wilk, *They're Playing Our Song* (New York: Atheneum, 1973), pp. 189, 192; Mok, "Sad Story," p. 13.

68. Levy interview, September 22, 1988, New York.

69. Michael Freedland, *So Let's Hear the Applause: The Story of the Jewish Entertainer* (London: Vallentine and Mitchell, 1984), pp. 161–62, 164–66, says that it was Cahn who got the Andrews Sisters to record "Bei Mir."

70. It yielded $3 million in royalties down to 1961. Secunda, *Bei Mir,* pp. 149, 220; "Andrew Sisters," Roger D. Kinkle, ed., *The Complete Encyclopedia of Popular Music and Jazz, 1900–1950,* 4 vols. (New Rochelle, N.Y.: Arlington House, 1974), 2:504; Brian Rust with Allan G. Debus, comps., *The Complete Entertainment Discography from the mid-1890s to 1942* (New Rochelle, N.Y.: Arlington House, 1973), p. 5.

71. Victor Record 25751 A & B. Besides Goodman on clarinet, the others were Teddy Wilson, piano; Lionel Hampton, vibraphone; and Gene Krupa, drums. Donald Russell Connor, *Benny Goodman, Off the Record: A Bio-Discography of Benny Goodman* (Fairless Hills, Pa.: Gaildonna Publications, 1958), pp. 153–54. Elman became especially famous for his other Yiddish source recording with the Goodman Orchestra of "And the Angels Sing," which he cut with them on February 1, 1939, and later in 1943 with the Tommy Dorsey Band. Ibid., p. 169.

72. Although all sales statistics are really tentative estimates, I cite this figure and others to give some idea of the commercial success of the piece. This study is more interested in the latter than the former. The statistic here is from Joseph Murrells, comp., *The Book of Golden Discs: The Records That Sold a Million* (London: Barrie and Jenkins, 1974, 1978), p. 20. See also "Song Becomes Hit in Month After Six Years' Obscurity," *Buffalo Evening News,* February 4, 1938, p. 19; "The Story of A Song . . . ," *Life,* January 31, 1938, p. 39; Street, "By Me," p. 3.

73. "The Story of A Song," p. 39; "Song Becomes Hit," p. 19.

74. They had already cut earlier records, in March and October but the public generally overlooked these efforts. James Robert Parish and Leonard DeCarl with William T. Leonard and Gregory W. Marsh, *Hollywood Players: The Forties* (New Rochelle, N.Y.: Arlington House, 1976), p. 28; Rust, *Entertainment,* p. 5. See also Max Bushwick, "What Records Are Doing For Me," *Billboard,* June 10, 1939, 78.

75. The statistics on total sales from *Time,* May 19, 1967, p. 112, are undoubtedly faulty but certainly suggestive.

76. Because the Andrews singers were quite young in the late 1930s, two of them still in their teens, the decision on what to record was certainly not theirs alone. Levy and likely the Kapps of Decca may have been more responsible. Levy did admit that their goal was to entertain rather than educate their audience. Levy interview; Kyle Crichton, "Sweet and Hot,"

Collier's, October 28, 1939, p. 44; Rex Reed, "Those Boogie Woogie Babies Bounce Back," *Chicago Tribune,* March 3, 1974, section 6, p. 3. See especially David A. Jasen, *Tin Pan Alley: The Composers, the Songs, the Performers, and Their Times* (New York: Donald I. Fine, 1988), p. 246.

77. From "Bei Mir Bistu Shein," sheet music copy (New York: Secunda, 1933) translated by Paul Melrood, Milwaukee.

78. Cf. the explanation by Secunda, *Bei Mir,* pp. 151–52.

79. Levy interview; Rust, *Entertainment,* p. 6; "Andrews Sisters," in Kinkle, *Encyclopedia,* 2:504.

80. Rust, *Entertainment,* p. 9; Kinkle, *Encyclopedia,* 2:504.

81. J. Sterba, "60th Anniversary of the Beer Barrel Polka," *Hlas Naroda,* November 28, 1987, p. 15. The most authentic history appears to be Pavel Vesely, "Life with a Song," trans. Henry Peck, in *Vestnik,* April 29, 1987, pp. 1–4, reprinted in Bob Norgard, "Polka Parade," *Polka News* 17 (Nov. 25, 1987): 3. I am grateful to Robert Norgard of Port Clinton, Ohio, for his kindness in assisting me with these materials. Jan Buberle, "Jaromir Vejvoda, Composer of "The Beer Barrel Polka," *Ceska Muzika* 1 (December, 1973): 45, gives the date of writing as 1929. Vejvoda later went on to compose about fifty polkas. *Viltis: A Magazine of Folklore and Folk Dance* 47 (March–April 1989): 37.

82. For details, see Buberle, "Vejvoda," p. 45.

83. He had collected, recorded, and sung Greek folk music in the 1920s for Victor and started his own Victor label, Orthophonic, in 1932, stressing Greek and Turkish music. He had thought that the cut backing "Beer Barrel"—"Hot Pretzels"—would be the hit. Interview with Walter Eriksson, Brooklyn, N.Y., January 18, 1988; telephone interview with Sam Chianis, Binghamton, N.Y., June 2, 1988; Sotiros Chianos, "Survival of Greek Folk Music in New York," *New York Folklore* 14 (Fall–Summer, 1988): 41; letter from Pekka Gronow, November 1, 1987, Helsinki; Gronow, *Studies,* 2:20; Sterba, "60th Anniversary," p. 15; *International Polka Association News* 22 (October, 1987): 1. For biographical information on Brown, an incredibly prolific songsmith involved with seven thousand popular works, see Edward Pessen, "The Immigrant Contribution to American Popular Music," paper presented at the New York Historical Society, May 16–17, 1986, p. 16; "Lew Brown," in Kinkle, *Encyclopedia,* 2:629–30.

84. Murrells, *Discs,* p. 21; *IPA News,* October 1987, p. 1. Precise dates of its recording and release remain unclear. I am taking the years offered by Spottswood, "Sajewski," p. 149. It seems highly unlikely, therefore, that Timm gave it its English title in 1939, as some sources suggest. Spottswood also has a good firsthand testimonial on the effect of the jukebox on the record's sales.

85. Shapiro, Bernstein and Co., *Ideas* (New York: Shapiro, Bernstein and Co., 1979), pp. 3, 16, 20–21, 29–30. "The Pennsylvania Polka" (1942) was also theirs. Interview with Richard Vollter of Shapiro, Bernstein in New York City, May 12, 1988. Doris Kommer, daughter of Joseph Elsnic, stated that her father, then head of Vitak and Elsnic, had purchased the work from Prague and then sold it to Shapiro, Bernstein, retaining a copyright. Kommer

interview, Whitefish Bay, Wis., October 7, 1985: sheet music, "Beer Barrel Polka" (New York: Shapiro, Bernstein, 1939), p. 1, with Vincent Lopez on cover.

86. Rust, *Entertainment*, p. 6; Kinkle, *Encyclopedia*, 2:504.

87. From Ed Shreppel, " 'Jolly Jack' Robel to be Feted," in (Shenandoah, Pa.) *Evening Herald*, July 4, 1987, p. 3. This latter claim seems plausible, but Robel recorded the piece in March of 1939, three years after Shreppel claims Robel "introduced" it. His date for the Andrews Sisters recording is also inaccurate.

88. "Barrel Song," *Time Magazine*, September 11, 1939, p. 69.

89. Sanjek, *American Popular Music*, 3:143.

90. From Shapiro, Bernstein, *Ideas*, p. 3; Crichton, "Sweet and Hot," p. 44; and Sterba, "60th Anniversary," p. 15. Brown added it to a Broadway musical he helped write, "Yokel Boy," which that summer needed a hit tune. Its inclusion helped its popularity. Sterba, ibid.

91. Quoted in George T. Simon and Friends, *The Best of the Music Makers* (New York: Doubleday, 1979), p. 14.

92. *The Billboard*, June 3, 1939, p. 74.

93. Ibid., June 24, 1939, p. 127.

94. Ibid., July 1, 1939, p. 77. Note similar letters from the same city a month later in ibid., August 5, 1939, p. 72, and "August Holidays," *New York Times*, August 20, 1939, Section 9, p. 10.

95. *Billboard*, January 22, 1949, Jukebox Supplement, pp. 54, 76.

96. *Ibid.*, July 29, 1939, p. 85.

97. Quoted in *Billboard*, July 15, 1939, p. 70.

98. Howard Wilson, "Polkas for Accordionists," *Accordion World* 4 (December 1939): 8.

99. Dave Burt, "Accordion Music Musing," ibid. 5 (December 1940): 18.

100. Howard Whitman, "Profiles: Pulse on the Public," *The New Yorker*, August 24, 1940, p. 24, says Decca made 18 million more records than either of the other two, of the total 50 million sold.

101. Crichton, "Sweet and Hot," p. 16.

102. *Polkarama* (Cleveland newspaper), souvenir edition, February, 1975, n.p., provided me by Fred Kuhar of Cleveland.

103. Spottswood, *Ethnic Music*, uses the term throughout his work to distinguish these bandleaders from those who recorded more traditional or single-group selections. Another student of the subject, Christopher Ann Paton, refers to this genre as a new American polka and ascribes some non-ethnic "sweet" orchestra leaders as its promoters, such as Guy Lombardo. Paton, "Evolution of the Polka," pp. 29–30.

104. For example, to profit from his "Beer Barrel" success he altered the title of his ensemble to the Bee Gee Tavern Band. From Spottswood, "Sajewski," Appendix 1, p. 162.

105. Letter from Rene, of 168 W. 23d St., New York City, in *Accordion World* 9 (September, 1943): 6; "Rene to Coast as RCA Victor A & R Director," *Billboard*, June 24, 1950, p. 11.

106. "Henri Rene," in Kinkle, *Encyclopedia,* 3:1624.
107. From Spottswood, *Ethnic Music,* pp. 2951–55.
108. "Rene to Coast," pp. 11, 16; "Rene," in Kinkle, *Encyclopedia,* 2:1624.
109. From correspondence with author dated Nov. 11, 1987 and Jan. 21, 1988 from Dr. Vladimir Kaiser, Usti Nad Lebem, Czechoslovakia.
110. From Spottswood, *Ethnic Music,* pp. 2941–43.
111. " 'Jolly Jack' Robel and His Band," newspaper clipping from the files of Virginia Souchak, a daughter, Shenandoah, Pa. I am grateful to Mrs. Souchak.
112. The name of the store was Wilde. Interview with Bernadette Walsh, Shenandoah, Pa., July 12, 1989.
113. *The Path of Progress, Shenandoah, Pa., . . . Centennial, 1866–1966,* pp. 1–2, at the Shenandoah, Pa., Public Library; *International Polka Festival . . . 1987* (Chicago: IPA, 1987), p. 11, in the Souchak collection.
114. From a photograph and interview with Lucian Kryger, Wilkes-Barre, interview, July 10, 1989.
115. " 'Jolly Jack' Robel Plays Friday Dances," newspaper clipping in Souchak collection.
116. Spottswood, *Ethnic Music,* p. 2955; Shreppel, " 'Jolly Jack,' " p. 16.
117. Spottswood, *Ethnic Music,* p. 2956.
118. Scheele, "American Entertainment," p. 443; *International Polka Festival . . . 1987* (Chicago: IPA, 1987), p. 11; interview with Mrs. Irene Souchek, Shenandoah, Pa., July 7, 1989. Robel even followed up this hit with a sequel, "Let's Roll Out the Barrel Once Again." " 'Jolly Jack' Provided Plenty of Fodder for the Newspaper," *Shenandoah Evening Herald,* July 4, 1987, p. 15, in the Souchak collection.
119. " 'Jolly Jack,' " p. 15.
120. Shreppel, " 'Jolly Jack,' " p. 3, and other materials from the Souchak file.
121. Shreppel, " 'Jolly Jack,' " p. 3.

Chapter 7

1. This list by no means exhausts the roster of regions that produced popular ethnic bands. Among the areas not covered in depth in this study are the German-Russian settlements of eastern Colorado and western Nebraska, home of the "Dutch Hop"; western New York around Buffalo; Detroit; northern Indiana; and various areas of Michigan. I am limiting my references to places that had significant crossover-band activity and about which I could obtain sufficient information.
2. For a good review, see Malone, *Country Music, U.S.A.,* pp. 158ff.
3. From Machann, "Country Western Music," p. 3; Spell, *Music,* p. 58.
4. Machann and Mendl, *Krásna Amerika,* p. 137.
5. Kolar, "Dance Halls," pp. 123–24; interview with Evelyn Kaase, Schulenberg, Texas, October 28, 1987; and my observation near Fayetteville.
6. Robert L. Skrabanek, *We're Czechs* (College Station: Texas A & M University, 1988), pp. 126–30.

7. *Ibid.*, combined with Calvin C. Cervenka and James W. Mendl, "The Czechs of Texas," MS (Austin: Southwest Development Laboratory, 1975), p. 117, and Machann and Mendl, *Krásna Amerika,* p. 163.

8. *Polka and Old Time News* 2 (November 1964): 13.

9. Newspaper article, "Brief History of San Antonio Liederkrantz," in the collection of Evelyn (Mrs. Milton) Kaase, Schulenberg, Texas.

10. Skrabenek, *Czechs,* p. 81.

11. A 1952 survey identified more than twenty radio stations broadcasting that type of music, with twenty-six daily and eighteen weekly programs. By 1974 the number had declined to seventeen stations offering seven daily and twenty-six weekly programs. Cervenka and Mendl, *Czechs,* p. 15. Polka music broadcasting continues today in the state.

12. Machann and Mendl, *Krásna Amerika,* pp. 155–57.

13. Note for example, *Century of Agricultural Progress* (Cat Spring, Texas, 1956), p. 295; "John R. Bača, 60, Widely Known Band Leader, Succumbs," *La Grange Journal,* April 23, 1953, pp. 1ff.

14. From *The Brenham Banner Press,* probably November 1950, p. 6; *Houston Post,* Nov. 7. 1954?, section 6, p. 14; *Houston Chronicle,* May 10, 1934?, in the Rosemarie Bača Rohde collection, Fayetteville. These and other sources give some indication of the band's immense following in the period.

15. This complicated, amoeba-like proliferation is traced in *Bača's Musical History,* pp. 29–32; and Pat Read, "Is There Another Texas Band That Began in 1892?" *The Houston Chronicle,* n.d., *Texas Magazine* supplement, p. 12, from the Rosemarie Bača Rohde collection. I am most grateful to Ms. Rohde for her help. Interview at Fayetteville, Texas, October 28, 1987. The Bača band tradition was a long and active one, as family members performed at the Smithsonian Institution National Folk Festival in Washington, D.C., as late as 1967.

16. Machann and Mendl, *Krásna Amerika,* p. 163.

17. Cf. The Joe Merlick Orchestra on KFJZ, Fort Worth. Cervenka and Mendl, *Czechs,* pp. 114–15; typescript, "Czech Music Symposium," held at Bryan, Texas, Fall, 1986. I am grateful to Clinton Machann of Texas A & M University for supplying this manuscript.

18. From a newspaper article, "1930s Popular Musicians . . . Remember Adolph and the Boys," in the file of George Koudelka, Flatonia, Texas.

19. This account is from John Lueke, the manager of "Adolph and the Boys," in an interview in Flatonia, Texas, October 28, 1987. I am grateful to George Koudelka of Flatonia for arranging this meeting.

20. "1930s Popular Musicians."

21. Lueke interview; Henry Wolff, Jr., "The Old Minden Hotel," *The Victoria* (Texas) *Advocate,* August 8, 1982, n.p., in the Lueke papers; Jane Knapik, *Schulenberg: 100 Years on the Road, 1873–1973* (Schulenberg, 1973), p. 112; George Koudelka, "Musical Memories of Adolph and the Boys and the Prause Band," in the author's possession, Flatonia, Texas; interview with Mr. Koudelka, July 31, 1986, Flatonia, Texas; Molly Pesek, "Molly's Corner," *Lavaca County Tribune-Herald* (Hallettsville), June 8, 1979, n.p., in Lueke Papers.

22. Lueke interview.

23. From Spottswood, *Ethnic Music,* pp. 599–600, who erroneously refers to "Adolph" instead of Julius Pavias.

24. Lueke interview. Cervenka and Mendl, *The Czechs,* p. 114, state that the band continued broadcasting until 1940.

25. "The Patek Band," a manuscript obtained from Joe Janek of Victoria, Texas, to whom I am indebted.

26. "Patek Day Celebration to Honor Joe Patek Orchestra," *Shiner Gazette,* October 7, 1982, p. 1. John continued to play in the band; he died at the age of eighty in 1953. Ibid., October 29, 1987, p. 8A.

27. Strachwitz, "Texas Polka Music," *American Folk Music Occasional* No. 2 (1970): 73–75.

28. Cassette recording from a radio program conducted by Alfred Vrazel, Cameron, Texas, on November 1, 1987, "Tribute to Joe Patek." I am grateful to Mr. Vrazel for supplying me with the tape.

29. The authoritative study of the genre is Manuel Peña, *The Texas Mexican Conjunto; A History of a Working Class Music* (Austin: University of Texas Press, 1985), pp. 21, 35.

30. Peña contends that conjunto was developed essentially through Mexican rather than American immigrant contact, but the involvement of Martinez with Texas Czechs and Germans, which Peña omits, had to have some influence on his music and perhaps vice-versa. I develop this point below. Ibid., pp. 35–36, 42.

31. Most of my information comes from Chris Strachwitz, liner notes to *Una Historia de la frontera. Texas Mexican Border Music.* Vol. 10, *Narciso Martinez, "El Huracan del Valle," His First Recordings, 1936–1937,* Folklyric Records 9017.

32. Ibid.; tape cassette, "Sabor Del Pueblo," no. 2, National Public Radio SA 830107, interview of Martinez.

33. Manuel Peña, "The Emergence of Conjunto Music, 1935–1955," in Richard Bauman and Roger Abrahams, eds., *"And Other Neighborly Names": Social Process and Cultural Image in Texas Folklore* (Austin: University of Texas Press, 1981), p. 283; Peña, *Conjunto,* p. 57.

34. Strachwitz, *Historia.*

35. "Sabor Del Pueblo." He continued to play and record into the 1960s.

36. Cf. John Morthland, *The Best of Country Music* (New York: Doubleday-Dolphin, 1984), pp. 118, 129; Bill C. Malone, *Country Music U.S.A.* (rev. ed., Austin: University of Texas Press, 1985), pp. 152ff; Machann, "Country-Western Music," p. 6; James P. Leary, "Czech Polka Styles in the United States: From America's Dairyland to the Lone Star State," in Clinton Machann, ed., *Papers From Czech Music in Texas: A Sesquicentennial Symposium* (College Station: Texas A & M University, 1987), especially pp. 91–93. All refer to the mutual intergroup musical exchange.

37. Ron Young, "Adolph Hofner: Sweet South Texas Swing," *Country Sounds,* March 1987, p. 10, copy given to me by Mr. Hofner; interview with Hofner, October 27, 1987, San Antonio, Texas.

38. See the listings in Spottswood, *Ethnic Music,* pp. 632–33.

39. Tony Russell, liner notes to "Adolph Hofner: South Texas Swing: His Early Recordings, 1935–1955," Arhoolie Records, 5020.

40. Richard Spottswood, *Musical Images of Ellis Island* (Washington, D.C.: Portfolio Project, 1987), pp. 46–47; Interview with Hofner.

41. Cf. Leary, "Czech Polka Styles," p. 91, who states the regionally distinctive way in which Texas Czech musicians mastered the strings, especially the guitar, in playing their tunes.

42. Quoted in Craig Phelen, et al., "Three Living Legends of San Antonio Music," *San Antonio Express,* August 8, 1982, p. 8.

43. Strangely enough, while the city of Chicago was the locus of a huge ethnic population and undoubtedly the home of many of their musical groups, it did not produce any major territorial ethnic bands until relatively late, the late 1940s, with the Polish L'il Wally. The only widely known bandleader was Ed Terlikowski, a Pole about whom little information was available.

44. Kvam, "Norwegian-American Dance Music," pp. 151–52.

45. Quite possibly, Skarning was playing before that decade, though the earliest documented reference is 1922. From a communication of James Leary of Madison, Wis.

46. Bob Murphy, "His Own and Others: Skarning Serves Up Music Country Style," *The Minneapolis Star,* July 9, 1956, p. 2B; from an interview with Orville Lindholm, St. Paul, July 28, 1988, and an item from his scrapbook. I am deeply grateful to Mr. and Mrs. Lindholm.

47. *Accordion News* 5 (February 15, 1937): 20. Telephone interview with Olga Hansen, Columbus, N.D., February 17, 1990. Note the photo in Philip Nusbaum, liner notes to "Norwegian American Music From Minnesota" (St. Paul, Minnesota Historical Society, 1989), p. 15.

48. Murphy, "Skarning," p. 2B.

49. Letter from Robert Andresen, Duluth, March 8, 1988, to whom I am indebted; Howard Pine, "Echoes From the Past: The Vagabond Kid," *The (November) Country Music Gazette,* November 1969, p. 6; Bob Murphy, "The Local Yokel," *Minneapolis Sunday Tribune,* June 19, 1949, p. 1.

50. *Slim Jim and the Vagabond Kid: WDGY, Minneapolis–St. Paul* (Chicago: M. M. Cole, 1937), p. 2. Their Hooper ratings were consistently high. Murphy, "Yokel," p. 8.

51. Murphy, "Yokel," p. 1; *Slim Jim Club News,* March 1, 1949, p. 3, in the possession of Howard Pine.

52. From a program list for January and February 1937, in which about one work per program was Norwegian. List in the possession of Howard Pine. Note also *Two Hundred Old Time Favorite Songs As Sung By Slim Jim, the Wandering Cowboy* (Omaha: Ernest Iverson, 1931).

53. Letter from Frances Iverson; letter from Bob Andresen.

54. Ibid.; Howard Pine, liner notes to "The Swede From North Dakota," *HepRecords,* 00228. Bob Andresen kindly supplied me with a tape of thirty-five of Iverson's recorded songs.

55. Ernest continued on his own through the 1950s until his death in 1958. Letter, Andresen.

56. Paul Anderson, "Slim Jim and the Vagabond Kid," typescript. Anderson is a Minneapolis collector of Edith and Ethel Olson material.

57. His age is calculated from an article in *Kvallsposten* (Stockholm), July 25, 1948, translated by Merle Carlsson, Brookfield, Wis.

58. "Sausage Maker from Stockholm," in Charles F. Sarjeant, ed., *The First Forty: WCCO Radio, 1924–1964* (Minneapolis: WCCO, 1964), p. 15.

59. From *The Bar and Tavern Keepers' Review*, October 1940, in the Lavone Johnson collection. I am grateful to Ms. Johnson of Minneapolis, the musician's wife, for her help.

60. From *The Minneapolis Star*, April 9, 1938, in the Lavone Johnson collection.

61. From an interview with Johnson by Carl-Werner Petterssen, March 5, 1973 in Minneapolis. I am indebted to Anne-Charlotte Harvey of San Diego State University for supplying me the tape of the interview and to Ms. Carlsson for the translation. Also note the interviews with Lindholm and Maury Bernstein in liner notes to "Gammaldans," *Nordvest Records,* TJ 4318; and the photo in Vernon Lee Barron, *Odyssey of the Mid-Nite Flyer* (Omaha: Barron, 1987), p. 228.

62. Barron, *Odyssey,* p. 228; letter from Petterssen, Aseda, Sweden to author, February 4, 1988; Bernstein, "Gammaldans"; Andreson, "Traditional Music," *The Minneapolis Star,* April 8, 1938, p. 11, refers to the "borrowing" of American popular and southern music by Johnson and other Scandinavian American bands.

63. Evan Jones, "Oompah Town," *Collier's,* August 20, 1954, pp. 26–27.

64. An excellent description of this Dutchman style are several essays by Jim Leary, including "Minnesota Polka," in manuscript, and "The Cultural Meaning of Dutchman Music," paper presented at the American Folklore Society, Cincinnati, October 19, 1985; and Jim Leary and Richard March, "Dutchman Bands: Genre, Ethnicity and Pluralism in the Upper Midwest," in manuscript. Note also Andresen, "Traditional Music," p. 12. I am indebted to all these individuals for their many kindnesses.

65. One estimate was a $100,000 income by 1954. Jones, "Oompah Town," p. 27; articles in *New Ulm Review,* April 20, 1950, and *New Ulm Journal,* August 5, 1984, both in Old Time Band File at Brown County Historical Society (henceforth, BCHS), New Ulm, Minn.; *12th Annual Polka Day, Monday, July 27, 1964* (New Ulm: 1964), n.p.; interview with Myra Fritsche, New Ulm, October 25, 1985.

66. LaVern J. Rippley, "Status Versus Ethnicity: The Turners and Bohemians of New Ulm," in Charlotte L. Brancaforte, ed., *The German Forty Eighters in the United States* (New York: Peter Lang, 1989), p. 274; *New Ulm Review,* April 20, 1950, n.p., in Old Time Band file, BCHS. Note Domeier's mother's influence in Domeier file, BCHS.

67. *15th Annual Polka Day, Monday, July 31, 1967* (New Ulm: 1967), pp. 11, 12 17; "New Ulm Bands Make City 'Polka Capital,' " *Historical Notes,* February 18, 1982, pp. 188–91, and Hofmeister file, both in BCHS.

Cf. Leary and March, "Dutchman Bands," pp. 4–5, who refer to both Wilfahrt and Loeffelmacher. Once again I must exclude the even better-known "Whoopee John," who I would contend was, after a brief upbringing in the New Ulm area, really a national entertainer working out of Minneapolis. His Dutchman style was more assimilated and American than was Loeffelmacher's.

68. *Fairfax (Minnesota) Standard,* June 18, 1975, p. 1; Bob Norgard, "Polka Parade," *The Polka News,* February 24, 1988, p. 2, in scrapbook of Roland Boeder of La Crosse, Wis., to whom I am grateful. See also Leary and March, "Dutchman Bands," p. 4.

69. *12th Annual Polka Day.*

70. Leary and March, "Dutchman Bands," pp. 10–11.

71. Ellen Thompson, "New Ulm's 'Mr. Polka' is Dead at 82," *St. Paul Pioneer Press,* January 31, 1988, p. 1B.

72. *12th Annual Polka Day.*

73. Untitled article in Boeder scrapbook.

74. Liner notes, Paul A. Votano, "Six Fat Dutchmen: Merry Polkas," RCA Victor LPM-1418, 1957.

75. Ibid.; Donna Weber, "Loeffelmacher's Death Draws Memories of Polka's Glory Days," *Entertainment Bits* 16 (April–May 1988): 40; Thompson, " 'Mr. Polka,' " p. 2B.

76. Interview with Dostal, Glencoe, Minn., October 21, 1987; Jerry S. Dostal, "What A Difference 50 Years Make," *Entertainment Bits* 13 (October–November 1985): 4.

77. Dostal interview.

78. Dostal, "Difference," p. 4.

79. Dostal interview.

80. This information was obtained from a manuscript written by Berg and from an interview October 24, 1985, in Albert Lea, Minn.

81. Berg Interview.

82. Berg manuscript.

83. From a Tama, Iowa, newspaper article in the "Skipper" Berg scrapbook.

84. Berg manuscript.

85. Jim McCloskey, "Albert Lea's Own: Viking Accordion Band Claims Colorful Career," *Albert Lea Tribune,* February 28, 1958, in Berg papers.

86. Berg interview.

87. All these publications were in the Berg collection in Albert Lea.

88. From the Berg collection. It is interesting that at least the agent of one company, Brunswick, encouraged the Vikings to record their material not in the original but in English, a stipulation that Berg apparently accepted. From a 1935 letter from Murray M. Kirschbaum of Brunswick's Chicago office, in the Berg papers.

89. Berg manuscript.

90. John R. Sherman, "Speaking of Music: Minnesota, the Birthplace of Corn," *Minneapolis Tribune,* December 15, 1943, n.p., supplied by Bob Andresen, Duluth, Minn.

Chapter 8

1. Two leading Milwaukee bandleaders around the mid-1940s were the German-styled Sammy Madden, who often appeared with Helene and her accordion, and the Slovenian Louis Bashell. See the Bashell interview by Charles Keil, "Slovenian Style in Milwaukee," in William Ferris and Mary L. Hart, eds., *Folk Music and Modern Sound* (Jackson: University Press of Mississippi, 1982), especially pp. 50–55.

I would still define Gosz and Duchow as essentially "regional," for despite the fact that both were widely known to many aficionados outside the Upper Midwest from records and possibly radio, neither performed for any sustained period of time beyond their region, and both always maintained a particular, dominant ethnic style.

2. From a scrapbook located in the Kewaunee County Historical Society, Kewaunee, Wis. (KCHS).

3. Robert Janda, "Entertainment Tonight: An Account of Bands in Manitowoc County Since 1910," *Occupational Monographs* no. 28 (Manitowoc, Wis.: MCHS, 1976 series), p. 2.

4. Ibid., p. 3.

5. James Leary, "Early Life Centered Around Bohemian Hall Brass Band," *Folk Life of the Upper Mid-West* 4 (Summer, 1988): 3.

6. Janda, "Entertainment," pp. 3–4.

7. Ibid., p. 6.

8. From photograph album at KCHS; Garth Behrendt, "Polka King: Romy Gosz Started at 11, Spent 45 Years as a Music Maker," a newspaper clipping from *The Press Gazette,* in a scrapbook owned by Roland Boeder of La Crosse, Wis., to whom I am grateful.

9. Some dispute exists on the takeover date. I am using the account in Janda, "Entertainment," p. 6, which has the most detail. The 1930 date for Gosz's assumption of leadership is supported by the newspaper fragment in the Boeder scrapbook; Don Dornbrook, "Wisconsin's Romy Gosz is the King of the Polka," *Milwaukee Journal* (April 9, 1945), quoted in liner notes to Polkaland Stereo Record LP 19; photo caption in scrapbook, MCHS; and Eleanor Steckert, "Pride of the Polka Belt," *Coronet* 20 (November, 1945): 100. It is possible that he formed his own band in 1928 and assumed his father's place two years later. See "Romy is Still the Polka King," *Ozaukee Press,* February 19, 1948, n.p.; obituary notice in *Manitowoc Herald Times,* August 29, 1966, p. 2.

10. *Sheboygan Press,* November 6, 1979, p. 15; photo album, MCHS; interview with Greg Leider, Fredonia, Wis., April 6, 1985. Leider's devotion to Gosz enabled me to obtain information and material that was indispensable. I am grateful to him.

11. Photo album, KCHS; Dornbrook, "Gosz."

12. Steckert, "Pride," p. 100.

13. Spottswood, *Ethnic Music,* p. 627.

14. "It sold like hot cakes." Beulah Schacht, "Romy Gosz and His Boys: They Work All Day and Play Polka All Night," *St. Louis Post-Dispatch,*

November 15, 1945, p. 1B; *Milwaukee Journal,* August 30, 1966, part 2, p. 9.

15. Leary, "Czech Polka Styles," 86–87.

16. Dornbrook, "Gosz."

17. Janda, "Entertainment," p. 6, and *Milwaukee Journal,* August 30, 1966, Part 2, p. 9, say 37 records. Spottswood, *Ethnic Music,* pp. 627–29, lists just under 60 cuts.

18. Audiocassette of radio broadcast by Jim Ebner of WYMS, Milwaukee, "Romy Gosz: The Man With the Golden Trumpet," August 30, 1984; Spottswood, *Ethnic Music,* pp. 627–29; Behrendt, "Gosz," Boeder scrapbook.

19. Leary, *Wisconsin Patchwork,* p. 8; *Sheboygan Press,* November 6, 1979, p. 15.

20. Steckert, "Pride," p. 100.

21. The band would also play regularly at Kermiss, a Belgian community festival held regularly near Green Bay. Ebner, "Gosz."

22. Steckert, "Pride," p. 98–99.

23. Ibid., p. 99. The article in the Boeder scrapbook is likely a copy of the Steckert piece. Note also James Leary and Richard March's interview with Jerome Wojta, in "Down Home Dairyland, program 2, WHAD, February 12, 1990; Schacht, "Gosz," 1B; and an interview with Leah McHenry, the daughter of the founder of Polkaland Records of Sheboygan, Milwaukee, July 21, 1990.

24. Note John Sippel's comment in *Billboard,* November 10, 1945, quoted in liner notes to "Polka Time Presents the One and Only Polka King, Romy Gosz," *Polka Time Records.*

25. "King of the Polka," *Time* magazine, June 25, 1945, p. 45.

26. Behrendt, "Gosz," Boeder scrapbook.

27. Ed Arndorfer, "Son, Tony, Takes Hold: Polka, Waltz Music Kept Alive in Traditional Romy Gosz Style," *Manitowoc Herald Times,* May 27, 1969, on file at Manitowoc (Wis.) Public Library.

28. From "Down Home Dairyland," WHAD, Madison, February 12, 1990; James P. Leary, "Polka Music Record Review: Czech and American 'Polka' Music," originally published in *Journal of American Folklore,* 101 (1988), quoted in *The Polka News* 19 (January 25, 1989): 6.

29. Jan Johnson, "Red Raven Leader Joins Polka Hall of Fame," *Green Bay Press-Gazette,* August 21, 1983, in the collection of Larry Pagel of Brillion, Wis.

30. Most of my biographical information on Duchow's early career comes from Larry Pagel, a Duchow sideman in the late 1930s. I am indebted to him for showing me his files.

31. Jo Ann Borchardt, "Lawrence Duchow Inducted Into the Polka Hall of Fame,"*The (Oshkosh) Northwestern,* August 18, 1983, p. 8.

32. Interview with Larry Pagel, Brillion, April 21, 1989.

33. Bob Norgard, "Polka Parade," *The Polka News,* August 23, 1989, p. 13; Pagel interview.

34. From a statement of his daughter, Barbara Kienast, in Borchardt,

"Duchow," p. 8; *Melodies By Lawrence Duchow* (New York: Hill and Range Songs, Inc., 1950), inside cover.

35. Norgard, "Polka Parade," p. 13; letter from Roland Boeder, La Crosse, Wis., to author, October 31, 1987; Pagel interview.

36. Pagel interview.

37. His entering the military was due in part to an arrangement he made in a court case. "Seven to Miss Jail if They Join the Service," *Milwaukee Sentinel,* May 1, 1942, in Pagel collection.

38. Letter from Duchow to Pagel, date unknown but probably just prior to March 16, 1946, in Pagel file. Apparently, two record companies, Victor and Decca, and NBC Radio had made him offers just after he returned from service.

39. Pagel interview; newspaper clipping, "Red Raven Orchestra Popular in Chicago Area," in Pagel collection.

40. Newspaper clipping, likely *Milwaukee Journal* of September 1946, in Pagel collection; Bob Norgard, "Polka Parade," *The Polka News,* August 23, 1989, p. 13.

41. Norgard, "Polka Parade," p. 13.

42. Pagel interview.

43. Duchow sketch published in International Polka Association publication given me by Alvin Sajewski, Chicago.

44. *Billboard,* January 15, 1949, p. 61 (cover page).

45. Pagel collection.

46. Johnny Sippel's column, "On the Stand," in *Billboard,* May 28, 1949, p. 20.

47. Duchow's band broke up in 1953, and he died in California in 1972 at the age of 58. IPA publication in Sajewski file.

48. John Grabowski, "Immigration," in *Encyclopedia of Cleveland History,* p. 543.

49. Don Sosnoski, "John M. Lewandowski: Veteran Broadcaster of Polish Programs," manuscript in possession of Sosnoski, Parma, Ohio, to whom I am grateful. See also Lewandowski's obituary in *Cleveland Press,* January 29, 1967, p. B12.

50. John Mihal, "Radio Stations Here Lead in Old World Music Programs," *Cleveland News,* March 30, 1935, p. 9B.

51. Ibid. Note also Joseph Migała, *Polish Radio Broadcasting in the United States* (Boulder, Col.: East European Monographs, 1987), p. 119. One is advised to use this latter source with care.

52. Interview with Eugenia Stolarczyk, Cleveland, September 6, 1987. Ms. Stolarczyk and her husband followed Lewandowski taking over his Polish radio programs; Bob Seltzer, "Polish Star Shines Here," newspaper article dated January 6, 1966, likely *Cleveland Plain Dealer,* in Sosnoski collection, Parma; Migała, *Polish Radio,* pp. 209–10.

53. *Annals of the Cleveland Newspaper Series, Cleveland Foreign Language Newspaper Digest, 1937.* Vol. 5, Slovenian (Cleveland: WPA District 4, 1940), in Western Reserve Historical Society, Cleveland.

54. Letter from Tillie Mazanec, his wife, to the author, Cleveland, Sep-

tember 30, 1987; "A Musical Tribute to Jerry Mazanec," *The Examiner*, sometime in September, 1975, p. 2, supplied by Ms. Mazanec.

55. Eleanor Prech, "Just Keep on Dancing, Polka Veteran Advises," *The Cleveland Press Community Weekly*, October 10, 1979, p. 2.

56. Ibid.; Bob Norgard, "Jerry Mazanec, Early Polka King Passes," *The Polka News* 2 (January 26, 1983): 1, says only 57.

57. From Spottswood, *Ethnic Music*, pp. 646–47.

58. "A Musical Tribute," p. 2; Norgard, "Mazanec," 1.

59. Louis even greeted some in New York right off the boat. Sigrid Arne, "Lausche's Parents Stirred Melting Pot," *Cleveland News* October 21, 1957, p. 17, in the file of Alice Lausche. I am indebted to Ms. Lausche and Frank Lausche for their extended assistance to me.

60. William C. Bittner, *Frank J. Lausche; A Political Biography* (New York: Studia Slovenica, 1975), pp. 14–15.

61. Arne, "Parents," p. 17.

62. Interview with his wife, Alice, and his brother, Frank Lausche, in Euclid, Ohio, September 7, 1987. Also from cassettes in the hands of the Western Reserve Historical Society and Bruce Berger of Cleveland.

63. Interview with Fred Kuhar and Jeff Pecon, Cleveland, May 29, 1985; Kaferle, "Iz Kraljestva," p. 266; Tony Petkovsek and Joey Tomsick, "Tony's Polka Village," *The Polka News* 19 (December 20, 1989): 11.

64. Valencic, "Polka," p. 4; Kaferle, "Iz Kraljestva," p. 266.

65. Spottswood, *Ethnic Music*, p. 1031; Rudolph Susel, "Slovenes," *Cleveland Encyclopedia*, p. 898; "Slovenian National Home," *Cleveland Encyclopedia*, p. 899; Tony Petkovsek, "The Lausche Story: A Portrait of Dr. William J. Lausche," typescript in the Alice Lausche collection.

66. Petkovsek, "Lausche Story." Lausche's obituary in *Cleveland Plain Dealer*, July 9, 1967, p. 8AA, says he cut only 30 of his compositions, but Alex Zirin, "City Polka Dad to Aid Milk Fund," probably in the *Cleveland News*, about 1950, in Alice Lausche collection, and Spottswood, *Ethnic Music*, pp. 1041–43, estimate about 60. Tony Petkovsek and Joey Tomsick, "Tony's Polka Village," *The Polka News* 5 (December 20, 1989), says 68 in all in his lifetime.

67. Audiocassette taped by Bruce Berger, Cleveland, for his radio show, "The Polka Man," WZAK, 1977.

68. 'Heinie,' Martin Antoncic, "Old Time Days," *St. Clair and Suburban News*, January 24, 1985, p. 1; Berger, "Polka."

69. Berger, "Polka"; letter of Frank J. Chukayne, Cleveland, in "Sounding Board; Concert Revives Memories of Lost Era," *Cleveland News?*, February 1, 1970, in the Alice Lausche collection; interview with Frank Lausche; Petkovsek and Tomsick, "Tony's," p. 11; Petkovsek, "Lausche"; Valencic, "Polkas," p. 4.

70. Petkovsek and Tomsick, "Tony's," p. 11; interview with Justine Reber, Cleveland, May 29, 1985, who was then running a leading music store in the Slovenian neighborhood.

71. Most of my biographical detail comes from the interview with Fred Kuhar and Jeff Pecon, his son, along with Don Sosnoski, "Johnny Pecon,

1915–1975," *Polkarama, America's Polka Messenger* (Cleveland), March 1975. Sosnoski graciously allowed me to consult his vast files and record collection, likely the largest polka music collection in the United States.

72. Notes on Trebar, dated March 20, 1977, Sosnoski file.

73. Berger, "Polka"; Petkovsek, "Lausche"; Sosnoski, "Pecon."

74. Tony Petkovsek, Jr., "Perry Personality," *Perry News,* May, 1968, pp. 1–2, supplied by Fred Kuhar; Sosnoski, "Pecon," p. 2.

75. For Vadnal's tie with Lausche, see Alex Zirin, "City Polka Dad to Aid Milk Fund," newspaper article, probably *Cleveland News,* about 1950, in Alice Lausche collection.

76. Bob Norgard, "Fifty Years of Polkas Vadnal's Style," *The Polka News* 15 (March 13, 1985): 1; Norgard, "Tony Vadnal Still on Bass After 52 Years in Uniform," *The Polka News* 18 (September 14, 1988): 3; and a publicity release sent to me by Vadnal.

77. Tom Bombich, "Iron Range Polka Ditties," *Entertainment Bits* 16 (February–March 1988): 28; Norgard, "Vadnal," p. 2.

78. His records sold worldwide, especially in Asia. *Vadnal–Over Fifty Years; International Polka Festival . . . 1987* (Chicago: IPA, 1987), 7–8; Norgard, "Fifty Years," p. 1. Vadnal retired in 1968, but the Vadnal band continued under his son, Richie. Tony Petkovsek, Don Sosnoski, and John Pestotnik, eds., *Polka Scene* (Cleveland: Polka Scene Enterprises, 1965?), p. 35.

79. An accordionist, Habat formed his first band in 1942 at age 16, took over Pecon's ensemble when Pecon entered the Navy in World War II, and after his association with Sokach organized his own band in 1950. *The Polka Journal: Frank Yankovic—Polka Joe Fan Club,* photocopy from the Sosnoski collection. The story of the "Blue Skirt Waltz" recording is recounted by Yankovic in *The Polka King: the Life of Frankie Yankovic as Told to Robert Dolgan* (Cleveland: Dillon, Liederbach, 1977), 92.

80. Ed Matasy, "Polka Pals Honor Kenny Bass," *The Polka News* 16 (February 26, 1986): 1; interview with Cecilia and Robert Dolgan, Cleveland, September 7, 1987; Petkovsek and Tomsick, "Tony's," p. 11; article on Bass in *The Cleveland Press,* September 28, 1973, p. 16; Bob Dolgan, "Bass Rolled Out Polka Boom Barrel," *The Cleveland Plain Dealer,* August 25, 1978, p. 13; address by Tony Petkovsek at International Polka Association convention, August 5, 1989, Chicago; radio script dated March 20, 1975, in Sosnoski collection.

81. Petkovsek and Tomsick, "Tony's," p. 11; Dolgan, "Bass," p. 13. His radio program was listed as having the third most popular polka dj in 1953. *Cleveland Press,* September 28, 1973, p. 16.

82. John P. Nielsen, "On Listening to Johnny Pecon," in *Ameriska Domovina,* June 29, 1973, n.p, copy supplied by Justine Reber, Cleveland. Nielsen also states that no non-Slovenian could be affected distinctively by Pecon's playing. The assertion may be true, but the nationwide popularity of his Capitol recordings indicates that outsiders could and did enjoy his music.

83. Although this statement came later than the mid-century period with

which I am dealing, I would contend that it represents an opinion shared earlier by many other individuals. Bukac had formed a band with his brother, Rudy, just after World War II and started his Bohemian radio program in 1966 over WXEN-FM. Note his dominant influence in his community in his obituary, *Cleveland Plain Dealer,* June 28, 1979, supplied to me by his family, Cleveland.

84. Appropriate punctuation added. Quoted in Bob Norgard, "Polka Parade," in *The Polka News* 20 (July 11, 1990): 15.

Chapter 9

1. Undoubtedly, European swing bands in the 1920s and 1930s also had an influence on ethnic bands in America, as Janice Kleeman of Providence, R.I., has suggested to me. Immigrant musicians arriving in those decades were surely well aware of the new instrumentation from their European experience. Cf. Albert McCarthy, *The Dance Band Era: The Dancing Decades From Ragtime to Swing, 1910–1950* (Radnor, Pa.: Chilton, 1982), especially pp. 132–40. This influence, too, however, can be considered a form of Americanization taking place abroad. The sources of ethnic bandleaders' new musical ideas have not yet been studied. My contention remains that most of these ideas came from the American experience, especially since the majority of bandleaders were American born.

2. Gronow, "Ethnic Recordings," p. 8.

3. Csida and Csida, *Entertainment,* p. 250. The subject of ethnic radio cries out for a historical study. Most of the few radio histories neglect the topic, and a few attempts have been unsuccessful. Theodore C. Grame, *Ethnic Broadcasting in the United States* (Washington, D.C.: American Folklife Center, 1980), appears promising but is totally ahistorical.

4. Shepard and Levi, *Live and Be Well,* p. 176.

5. Jack Alicoate, ed., *Radio Daily, The 1938 Radio Annual* (New York), p. 309; Alicoate, *1939 Annual,* p. 107.

6. Alicoate, *1938 Annual,* 306–7. Note, too, the outlet for Italians mentioned in Primeggia and Varacalli, "Southern Italian Comedy," p. 248.

7. Letter from Jack Stukas, Watchung, N.J., August 11, 1989; Alicoate, *1942 Annual,* p. 488; *1938 Annual,* p. 306; interview with Bob Norgard, Port Clinton, Ohio, September 8, 1987.

8. From material supplied by Natalie Kecki, Brooklyn; more detail is in Migała, *Polskie Programy Radiowe,* chap. 12.

9. Jack McKinney, "A Guide to Ethnic Radio; or, Now a Few Words from the Old Country," *Philadelphia Daily News,* February 1980, supplied by the Urban Archives, Temple University.

10. Alicoate, *1939 Annual,* 355–67.

11. Ibid.

12. "Fiorani's 'Musical Varieties' Will Be Presented Daily Over Station WSCR," *The Scranton Tribune,* May 10, 1947, p. 3a, photocopy in Fiorani Papers, Box 1, File 2, Balch Institute, Philadelphia; Angelo Fiorani, "Radio,

An Advertising Medium," speech given at Keystone Junior College, La Plume, Pa., April 30, 1948, in Box 1, File 2, ibid.; National Italian Hour ad card in Box 25, File 1, ibid.; *Souvenir Program for the 5th Annual Celebration of North East Penna. Italian Day . . . Sunday, July 1, 1934,* ibid.

13. *Annual Concert and Ball of Italian Radio . . .* (Boston, 1937), in Fiorani Papers, Box 25, File 2, ibid.; Migała, *Polish Radio,* p. 173.

14. Alicoate, *1939 Annual,* p. 213–15; Migała, *Polish Radio,* p. 169.

15. Gronow, "Ethnic Recordings," p. 9.

16. Spottswood, "Commercial Recordings," p. 64.

17. Ibid., pp. 45–49, 64.

18. I am grateful to Mrs. Donald Gabor of Riverside, N.Y., for supplying me with various materials, especially John Conly, "The Bushy Man in the Fuzzy Hat Puts a Bargain Price on Records," *Pathfinder,* April 5, 1952, a newspaper offprint. See also "Donald H. Gabor, 68, Produced Recordings of Classical Music," *New York Times Biographical Service,* November 1980, p. 1540.

19. The exact year is uncertain, so Gabor may have gotten the idea for his company from his former mentor. Demetriades sold out about 1970. Interview with Walter Ericksson, his music director and one of his major musicians, Brooklyn, January 18, 1988.

20. From a brochure, *Standard Records,* dated about 1950, given me by Alvin Sajewski, Chicago. The Standard Phonograph company was located then at 163 West 23d St., New York City. Gronow, "Ethnic Recordings," p. 48. A good early list of about a score of the company's recording artists is in Standard International Records, Release Nos. 6, 7, 8 (F & T Series), *International Novelties,* September 6, 1946, pp. 1–5.

21. "Walter Dana," reprint from an article that appeared in *Polish American World* about 1971, supplied by Walter Dana, Miami, Fla., November 23, 1984. Dana probably terminated his company in the 1960s, when he moved from New York to Florida and shifted his interest from business to composing classical works.

22. I obtained much of my biographical information from LeRoy Larson, liner notes to "Early Scandinavian Bands and Entertainers," *Banjar Records* BR-1840 (1983), which lists a number of instrumentalists.

23. "Eric Olzen," *Accordion World* 1 (June 1936): 17; Gunnar Ohlander, "Amerika Brevet; Eric Olzen," *Frosini NYH* 2 (1987): 1–2; *Eric Olzen's Scandinavian Swedish-Norwegian-Danish Dance Album* (Chicago: Chart Music Company, 1937), p. 1.

24. *Eric Olzen's Dance Album,* p. 1; "Olzen," p. 17.

25. Eddie Jahrl, "Pianoless Orchestra," *Accordion News* 2? (March 1936), fragment at the Music Division, New York Public Library, Lincoln Center.

26. Gronow, "Ethnic Recordings," pp. 15–16.

27. Ibid., p. 16. Note the photograph of the six pieces in Jahrl, "Pianoless," a guitar, string bass, drums, two saxophones, and piano accordion.

28. James Leary, "Reading the 'Newspaper Dress': An Expose of Art Moilanen's Musical Tradition," in C. Kurt Dewhurts and Yvonne R. Lockwood, eds., *Michigan Folklife Reader* (East Lansing: Michigan State University Press, 1987), p. 212.

29. I am especially grateful to folklorist Jim Leary of Mt. Horeb, Wis., for his pioneering field work in rediscovering Turpeinen and his generous help and advice in obtaining biographical information. I also thank Melvin Holli of the University of Illinois at Chicago for his advice and suggestions on Finnish American entertainers and for directing me to some little-known sources.

30. Much of her early life is described in a tape supplied me by Leo Keskinen, entitled "The Viola Turpeinen Story," a radio program on KAXE-FM, Grand Rapids, Minn., June 19, 1988. The most complete biography is Toivo Tamminen, "Viola Turpeinen and Co.," *Kansanmusiikki* 4 (December 1988): 6–17. Leo and Ivy Nevala of Glendale, Wis., helped me with translations of Finnish material.

31. Keskinen, interviewing Turpeinen's sister in "Story."

32. Ibid.; James P. Leary, "The Legacy of Viola Turpeinen," *Finnish Americana* 8 (1990): 7.

33. Tamminen, "Turpeinen," p. 6, says her favorite piece was the prelude from "The Barber of Seville."

34. *Accordion News* 2 (June 15, 1936): 3.

35. Richard Kaumo, "Pietro Deiro, Father of the Modern Day Accordion," *Accordion World* (May 1936) reprinted in *The Polka News* 19 (January 11, 1989): 4; Vienna Laine, "Viola Turpeinen and William Syrala," photocopy of *Finn Heritage* 4 (Spring 1989): 7; Keskinen, "Story"; copy of Sylvia Polso scrapbook supplied by Jim Leary, Mt. Horeb, Wis. The New York Labor Temple had been built in 1921 at a huge cost of $325,000; Timo R. Riipa and Michael G. Karni, "Finnish American Theatre," in Seller, *Ethnic Theatre,* p. 120.

36. Kaumo, "Deiro," p. 4; Tamminen, "Turpeinen," p. 13.

37. Note, for example, Standard International, *International Novelties,* p. 2.

38. Keskinen, "Story"; Leary, "Legacy," p. 7; Pekka Gronow, *Studies in Scandinavian Discography I,* p. 61.

39. Keskinen, "Story."

40. Tamminen, "Turpeinen," p. 13.

41. From a summary of announcements in Polso scrapbook.

42. Helga Koivisto in *Finn Heritage* 4 (Fall 1988): 4.

43. Vera Rivers, "I Grew Up In Hubbardstown, Massachusetts," *Finn Heritage* 4 (Fall 1988): 4–5.

44. From a translation of the piece by Ivy Nevala in *Reisaavaisen,* p. 60; Leary, "Legacy," p. 10; Keskinen, "Story." See also Gronow, *Studies* 1:55; and Gronow, "Ethnic Recordings," p. 10.

45. Toni and Oren Tikkanen, liner notes to *Viola Turpeinen: The Early Days: Finnish American Dance Music, 1928–1938* (audiocassette), Calumet, Mich: Thimbleberry Records, 1989). Note the poem dedicated to her, "To the Singing Maiden," October 8, 1949, in the *New Yorkin Uutisit.* Turpeinen did sing occasionally in her later performances. She moved to Florida with Syrala in 1952 and died six years later at the age of forty-nine. Tamminen, "Turpeinen," pp. 14–15; a segment of the *Iron Reporter,* January 6, 1959, in *The Polka News,* March 22, 1989, p. 19.

46. Keskinen, "Story"; Leary, "Turpeinen," p. 10.

47. Leary, "Turpeinen," pp. 10–11.

48. Toivo Tamminen, "Hannes Laine," *Kansenmusiikki* 1 (1989): 20–22. A good list of others is in Pakkala, "Instrumental Music," pp. 135–36.

49. Note in particular their coming to Buffalo in William Falkowski, "The Polka," in G. David Brumberg et al., eds., *History for the Public: A Report on the Historian-in-Residence Program* (Ithaca, N.Y.: Cornell University Press, 1983), pp. 96–97. Janice Kleeman of Providence, R.I., has suggested to me that the eastern Polish musicians were generally well-trained musically, playing in their area for an upper-class ethnic audience, while westerners from Chicago and that region were more working-class and supported the village style throughout the period. The idea has some merit, but it does not explain the popularity of easterners in the Midwest, as documented below. Also, eastern descendants of Polish immigrant mineworkers and the many factory and textile workers of New England, New Jersey, and New York would be surprised to hear that their ancestors were not unskilled. The eastern style also appealed to blue-collar Polonia.

50. An excellent, comprehensive analysis of this eastern genre and a comparison with the *wiejska* (village) style is in Kleeman, "Origins," pp. 83–85, 112–14, 191–92, 225–31, and passim. For more succinct descriptions, I have used Mary Spaulding, "The Irene Olszewski Orchestra: A Connecticut Band" (M.A. thesis, Wesleyan University, 1986), pp. 11–20; William Falkowski, "The Polka," from an application submitted to the New York Historical Resources Center; Falkowski, "The Polka," pp. 96–97; and my interview with Alvin Sajewski, December 29, 1984, Chicago.

51. Kleeman, "Origins," chap. 2, offers the origins of the American Polish and Czech polka as exclusively European. I suggest below that at least some of those dances have sources in American instrumental music as well.

52. The dispute is between Charles Keil, Angelika Keil and Richard Blau, "Polka Happiness," manuscript chap. 2, especially p. 27, which gives the date as 1892, and Herbert Geller, "Bridgeport's Polka Band Played Everybody's Music," *Bridgeport Sunday Post,* May 21, 1978, p. C-6, which suggests the later date, obtained from an interview with E. Theodore Krolikowski III, Devon, Conn. July 8, 1989. I am indebted to Keil of the State University of New York at Buffalo for allowing me to see his work. I am also grateful to Krolikowski, the bandleader's grandson, for his help and effort in gathering together his collection for me.

53. Rocky Clark, "Polka Here to Stay Says Polka Maestro," *Bridgeport Sunday Post,* July 28, 1940, p. B-2.

54. A mid-1920s photograph inside his store, in the E. T. Krolikowski III collection, shows generally popular music, such as "Smile All the While," "Sleepy Time Gal," "All Alone," and "Yes Sir, That's My Baby."

55. Clark, "Polka," p. B-2.

56. Geller, "Polka," p. C-6.

57. Keil, Keil, and Blau, "Happiness," p. 32. It is debatable that his was the *first* Polish band on radio, as the manuscript suggests considering John Lewandowski's efforts in Cleveland, mentioned above.

58. Spottswood, *Ethnic Music,* pp. 735–36.

59. "Popularity of Polkas Proves a Boon to Edward Krolikowski," *Bridgeport Sunday Post,* February 1, 1942, n.p., copy supplied by Bridgeport Public Library; Charles Keil, "People's Music Comparatively: Style, Stereotype, Class and Hegemony," in *Dialectical Anthropology* 10 (Amsterdam: Elsevier, 1985): 121. Spottswood, *Ethnic Music,* pp. 736–37 supports my contention.

60. Clark, "Polka," pp. B-2, B-4; Spottswood, *Ethnic Music,* p. 735.

61. Clark, "Polka," p. B-4. Spottswood, "Ethnic Music," pp. 735–36, has the complete list down to 1942.

62. Len Grimaldi, *Only In Bridgeport: An Illustrated History of the Park City* (Bridgeport: Windsor, 1986), pp. 132–33; Gault, "Ballroom Echoes," pp. 87–88.

63. Roldo Bartimole, "The Ritz Passes with Demise of Big Bands: Ballroom Leased to Become Furniture Store," *Bridgeport Sunday Post,* October 22, 1961, Joseph Barre file, Bridgeport Public Library.

64. For some time, Massachusetts refused to permit dancing and therefore dance bands performing on Sunday. Interview with Henry Baron, July 7, 1989.

65. Keil, Keil, and Blau, "Happiness," p. 32; Clark, "Polka," p. B4.

66. Advertisements in the E. T. Krolikowski III collection, Bridgeport.

67. *Bridgeport Post,* November 28, 1939, and ticket for the event in E. T. Krolikowski III collection. See also *Bridgeport Post,* November 30, 1935, February 19, November 21, 1936, November 28, 1939; (Bridgeport) *Times Star,* November 30, 1935, July 31, 1936, November 28, 1939, in Krolikowski collection. See also Geller, "Polka," p. C-6.

68. In 1940 a reporter observed that even though "The Beer Barrel Polka" was not a Polish polka, Krolikowski had to include it in his repertoire, likely a common occurrence among popular ethnic musicians. Clark, "Polka," p. B-2.

69. The youngest joined just after his passing in 1951. From a Wilkes-Barre newspaper article by Michael Sydek, dated June 5, 1974; "Spotlight-Brunon Kryger Remembered," *Dyno Polka Newsletter* 1 (September, 1966): 3; biographical entry for "Brunon Kryger" in International Polka Association booklet for 1977, supplied to me by IPA, Chicago. Most of my biographical material I obtained from a collection of clippings and photographs in the possession of his son Lucian, Wilkes-Barre, to whom I am grateful.

70. Telephone interview with a member of his band, Rose Mary Sobol, Naperville, Ill., August 4, 1989; IPA Booklet, 1977.

71. His theme was his own Polish piece, "Hop Siup-Oj Dana" (Happy Polka), recorded in 1941 for Victor. Spottswood, *Ethnic Music,* pp. 736–38; *Cześć Polskiej i Muzyce! Piesn Polskiej z Repertuaru Prof. Brunon Kryger,* in the Lucian Kryger collection.

72. Interview with Lucian Kryger, Wilkes-Barre, July 10, 1989. *Wilkes-Barre Sunday Independent,* November 2, 1941, p. A15, had already bestowed that title upon him earlier. From the L. Kryger file.

73. From *IPA Program Bulletin for 1978.* For a more detailed musicological assessment of his work see Kleeman, "Origins," p. 125.

74. Obituary in *The Philadelphia Evening Bulletin,* November 7, 1957, supplied by Philadelphia Free Library; interview with Sophie Podgorski, Philadelphia, October 11, 1985.

75. Interview with Ossowski, Philadelphia, November 18, 1989.

76. Harvey Wang, " 'Godfather' of Polka Just Fiddles," *The (Chicopee?) Register,* May 31, 1978, p. 7, in a scrapbook in the possession of Al and Lillian Lazarz, Westfield, Mass.

77. Bill Czupta, liner notes to "Joe Lazarz and His International Orchestra," *Polka Music Hall of Fame Album,* LP-4102 (circa 1977). He appeared at the Ritz in Bridgeport and regularly on Saturdays on WSPR in Springfield. Interview with Al and Lillian Lazarz, July 7, 1989, in Westfield, Mass.

78. Johnny Prytko, "Polka Music History," *The Polka News* 19 (May 24, 1989): 16; "Julia and Henry Wegiel," newspaper clipping of 1940, in Lazarz scrapbook.

79. Interview with one of his sidemen, Henry Baron, Chicopee, Mass., July 7, 1989; Spottswood, *Ethnic Music,* pp. 741–43.

80. Falkowski, "The Polka," p. 97.

81. Letter, Fred Robak of Chicopee to author, June 6, 1989.

82. Interviews with Henry Baron and Frank and Fred Robak, Chicopee, July 6–7, 1989.

83. Spottswood, *Ethnic Music,* p. 792.

84. Johnny Prytko, "U.P.B. Polka Pioneer Award, Jan Robak of Massachusetts," *The Polka News* 20 (June 27, 1990): 22. Many Massachusetts polka bands often played just beyond the state line on Sundays because of restrictive state blue laws. Interview with Henry Baron.

85. Keil, Keil, and Blau, "Happiness," pp. 42–46.

86. Clipping from a Leighton, Pennsylvania, newspaper, Jack Yalch, "Polka King Visits the Panther Valley for the First Time," September 30, 1972, p. 11, supplied by Solek, Meriden, Conn.

87. The discrepancy is in Keil, Keil, and Blau, "Happiness," p. 47, and "About Walter Solek," publicity release provided by Solek. An explanation may be that he recorded it on several different labels.

88. Bob Norgard, "Polka Parade," *The Polka News* 20 (February 14, 1990): 4–5.

89. See also Susan Okula, "Solek is King in Polka Music World," 1978? issue of Meriden newspaper, supplied by Solek.

90. At about this time in 1955, Universal Studios asked him to make a feature film for them on the polka. Yalch, "Polka," p. 11. See the ad in *New York Daily News,* January 30, 1950, from the collection of Staś Jaworski of Toms River, N.J. Jaworski was generous in allowing me access to his materials. Other Connecticut contributors in mid-century to the eastern style were Gene Wisniewski and Ray Henry (Mocarski), who also appeared at Roseland. From the Jaworski collection.

91. My information is from *Pierwszy Album Polskich Tanców Ulorzane i Rekordowane przez Bernarda Witkowskiego a Orkiestra "Srebne Dzwony" na Płytach "Viktora"* (New York: Colonial Music Publishing Co., n.d.) in the

possession of "Connecticut" Staś Przasnyski, Bristol, Conn. Kleeman, "Origins," p. 122, is clearly inaccurate regarding Leon's date of death.

92. Interview with Witkowski, Hillside, N.J., November 4, 1984; Kleeman, "Origins," pp. 65–66.

93. Interview with his wife, Mariane Witkowski, Hillside, May 19, 1989.

94. Letter from Bebko, Olean, N.Y., August 31, 1989.

95. Ibid.

96. Ibid.

97. Interview with Teresa Zapolska, Westbury, L.I., February 23, 1989. I am grateful to Peter and Virginia Karnish for arranging this meeting.

98. Mariane Witkowski interview.

99. It is unclear when he received the degree. It must have been sometime before 1942, when he left Witkowski's band. Bebko letter; also see Kleeman, "Origins," 126; communication from Kleeman, August 30, 1990.

100. Kleeman, "Origins," p. 86. Since he also used the name Bernie Whyte, the Latinized polka instrumentalist would read "Bernardo Blanco." Interview with Witkowski.

101. Spottswood, *Ethnic Music,* pp. 835–38.

102. Telephone interview with Bebko, June 12, 1989; Spottswood, *Ethnic Music,* pp. 836–38.

103. From Standard International Records, *Release . . . Sept. 6, 1946,* p. 1; Spottswood, *Ethnic Music,* pp. 835–37. His label was Stella, and he continued it until the mid-1980s. Interview with "Connecticut" Staś Przasnyski, Bristol, Conn., July 7, 1989.

104. She fulfilled her wish. Interview with Ms. Zapolska. Note Dana's moving eulogy at Witkowski's death. From a tape supplied by Bob Norgard, Port Clinton, Ohio.

105. Kleeman, "Origins," p. 131.

106. From a manuscript in the possession of Virginia and Peter Karnish, Riverside, N.Y., and an interview with Wojnarowski there, May 20, 1989.

107. Interview with Michael Violante, a band member, Bridgeport, July 9, 1989.

108. His band usually consisted of the standard eastern instrumentation. At the height of his popularity in the late 1950s he had a sizable ensemble, including 5 saxophones, 3 trumpets, 3 trombones, an accordion, and drums. From a photo dated August 4, 1957 in the possession of Virginia and Peter Karnish.

109. Volante interview.

110. Virginia Seretny, "Review of Frank Wojnarowski at 1970 IPA Convention," copy supplied by Ms. Seretny of Willimantic, Conn.

111. From John Z. Kame, *Polish American Film Productions Presents Jedzie Boat* (brochure) (Bridgeport, ca. 1959); Wojnarowski interview, Rosedale, N.Y., May 25, 1989; "Polka Band Sees New Crowd Mark," *Bridgeport Sunday Herald,* March 21, 1948, supplied by Bridgeport Public Library. Attendance figures were from the 1950s. "State Polka King Asks For Divorce," *Bridgeport Sunday Herald,* February 23, 1958, p. 10.

112. Dana record 561. One estimate was a sale of 300,000 in a short

time. The exact number is of course debatable, but the work's popularity is not. Kame, *Polish American Film; Dana Polkas Combo Book* (New York: Charles H. Hansen Music Corp. 1954?), p. 5; Violante interview.

113. Charlie Barnett was paying his men $18 per night in 1952, when Wojnarowski was offering $25. Lou Plucino, a trumpeter for Wojnarowski, 1951–1964. Interview with Plucino, Bridgeport, July 9, 1989.

114. "Polka King Scores With 'Matka' (Mother) But Photograph is of Somebody Else's Mom," *Bridgeport Sunday Herald,* March 11, 1962, p. 21.

115. Jaworski interview; interview with Virginia and Peter Karnish, February 23, 1989, Rosedale, N.Y.

116. Staś Jaworski's scrapbook lists him at the Roseland's 31st Anniversary in *New York Daily News,* January 30, 1950, and on February 20 and March 6 and 13, 1950.

117. *IPA Program for 1980.*

118. Ibid.

119. Clipping from the *Polish American Journal,* March 3, 1951, supplied by Natalie Kecki of Brooklyn.

120. From Albert Q. Maisel, *They All Chose America* (New York: T. Nelson, 1957), quoted in Gronow, "Ethnic Recordings," pp. 25, 31.

Chapter 10

1. My analysis follows H. F. Mooney, "Popular Music Since the 1920s: The Significance of Shifting Taste," *American Quarterly* 20 (1968): 73; and especially the standard work on country music, Malone, *Country Music, U.S.A.,* ch. 6, especially pp. 177–88.

2. The full influence of the war upon America's recreational life remains to be studied.

3. Mooney, "Popular Music," pp. 73–74.

4. I am grateful to Wolan's daughter, Carole Wolan Gubala, of Cumberland, R.I., for providing biographical information.

5. Robert Wolan and Carole Wolan Gubala, "Resume of Sylvester Filip (Shep) Wolan," typescript (1989), kindly supplied by Carole Gubala.

6. Letter of Carole Wolan Gubala, to author, July 3, 1989.

7. "Resume."

8. Admittedly, the bulk of these discs must have been in the hands of Italian Americans and other group members around the world. I must express my appreciation here to Joseph Bentivegna of Loreto, Pa., for bringing Paone to my attention and promoting long-overdue recognition of this musical genius.

9. Interview of Nicola and Delia Paone, Scarsdale, N.Y., January 16, 1988.

10. Liner notes, David Drew Zing, "The One and Only Nicola Paone," *ABC Paramount Records,* ABC 263; Danton Walker, "Cabarabian Nites," *New York Sunday News,* January 7, 1951, section 2, p. 12.

11. Liner notes to "The One and Only Nicola Paone," ABC Paramount

Records, ABC 263. I am grateful to Philip Balistreri of Milwaukee for allowing me to consult his vast library of Italian records and giving me excellent advice and information.

12. Newspaper article, "Young Singer Starts Tour," approximately 1940, in the possession of Paone, to whom I am grateful. Interview with Paone, Scarsdale, N.Y., May 19, 1989.

13. Wambly Blad, "He Gave Up Opera to Make People Laugh," New York newspaper clipping in the possession of Nick Antonazzo of Hawthorne, N.Y., to whom I am grateful.

14. E.g., "Gli Spettacoli de L'Italia Broadcasting Co. Un Gran Success," *L'Italia* (Chicago), December 3, 1940, and printed announcement, *Our Lady of Sorrows, Auditorium Theatre, Jackson Blvd. and Albany Ave.,* dated probably Sunday, December 1, 1939, in Paone's collection at his home in Scarsdale, N.Y. He was then going under the stage name of "Niki Russo."

15. Paone interview, New York, September 7, 1990.

16. At first he disguised his WBNX appearances because his jewelry store also sponsored his program. He presented himself as "Il Cantante Misterioso (The Mysterious Singer)." Zing, "Paone"; interview with Paone, May 19, 1989 in Scarsdale, N.Y.

17. Paone interview, September 7, 1990. Again, there is obviously no way to document the precise figure, which of course is less important than the certainty of the song's wide popularity.

18. Shapiro, Bernstein and Co., *Ideas,* p. 26; letters from Shapiro, October 3, 1947, and January 3, 1950, to Paone, in Paone collection.

19. From my May 19, 1989, and September, 7, 1990, interviews with Paone; and Walker, "Cabarabian Nites," p. 12.

20. Walter Winchell's January 1956 column in Paone collection, and an article on Paone in (Ebensburg, Pa.) *Mountaineer Herald,* June 15, 1986, provided by Joseph Bentivegna, Loreto, Pa.

21. Talk on Paone given by Joseph Bentivegna at American Italian Historical Association meeting, New York, Octover 15, 1988, draft copy in Paone collection.

22. This list is a compilation of a variety of sources. Note in particular the letter/contract from Shapiro, Bernstein to Paone of July 28, 1955, in Paone collection; Victor Records, *Bulletin* FA 185, April 21, 1952; Etna Records, "The Peak of Pleasure," (1950), in Antonazzo collection; and the talk on Paone given by Bentivegna at the American Italian Historical Association meeting, Chicago, Nov. 14, 1987.

23. From Paone collection. See also liner notes by David Drew Zing to "Down at Paone's Place," ABC Paramount Records, ABC 282, about 1958. This lp record sold about 700,000, Paone interview, May 19, 1988.

24. RCA Victor record 1501-A. Lyrics from Paone collection.

25. *Philadelphia Inquirer,* May 17, 1948; *Pittsburgh Sun-Telegraph,* January 3, 1949; *Buffalo Courier Express,* April 20, 1949, in Antonazzo collection; interview with Paone, January 16, 1988, New York.

26. From article by Lee Mortimer in the New York *Daily Mirror,* March 8, 1948; "The Talk of New York" (brochure), dated November 10, 1948;

New York World-Telegram, December 12, 1948; clipping of Lee Mortimer, "Nicola Paone Opens at the China Doll Wednesday," in a 1950 *Daily Mirror* article; *New York Journal American,* November 9, 1948, p. 13, all in Antonazzo collection. See also *Daily News,* March 7, and March 13, 1948, Paone collection.

27. Hamm Allen, "Guitarist Sets City Record," *Rochester Times-Union,* April 5, 1950, p. 46. The success there is further documented in "The Hey Buddy Man," *Time* Magazine, April 13, 1953, p. 29. I cannot of course agree with its opinion that Paone was not a nationally known artist. See below.

28. Joe Martin, "Paone at Palace," *Billboard,* September 15, 1951, p. 107, stated he "wound up way ahead" after singing his familiar "Telephone No Ring," but felt his voice was lacking somewhat. Phil Strassberg, "Fine Stage Show Jams Palace," New York *Daily Mirror,* September 7, 1951, p. 32, was totally enthusiastic.

29. Paone interview, May 13, 1988, Scarsdale, N.Y.

30. Articles, "L'entusiasmo non conobbe piu limiti," and "La Chitarra di Nicola Paone Culma Gli Anima in Argentinu," from an Italian publication in Buenos Aires, probably LR3 *Belgrano Informa* (Buenos Aires) (March 1953) in Paone collection. See also "The Hey Buddy Man," p. 29; and Zing, "Paone."

31. As "L'Emigrante" (1953) and "Mamma Mia" (1943).

32. The translation is by Paone.

33. The writer was Tom Glazer. Letter from Paone to Shapiro, Bernstein, New York, January 16, 1954, in Paone collection.

34. Interview with Evans Casso, Metairie, Louisiana, November 1, 1987; Casso, "Louis Prima: New Orleans Heartbeat," *Italian American Digest,* Autumn 1978, pp. 1, 4–5; clipping file on Prima at New York Public Library, probably *Life* Magazine article, August 20, 1945, pp. 113–14.

35. Release dates from Steven C. Barr, *The (Almost) Complete 78 rpm Record Guide* (Toronto: author, 1979).

36. But he did not give up composing or even performing. Interview with Paone, January 16, 1988, New York.

37. By 1954 three of his works had sold five million, according to Joseph Bentivegna, "Revitalization of Ethnic Pride Among Young Italian Americans After World War II," paper given at the American Italian Historical Association meeting, Chicago, November 14, 1987. Worldwide, a good guess would be twenty million in all. Paone interview, September 7, 1990, New York.

38. Kip Lornell, "The Early Career of 'Whoopee John' Wilfahrt," *John Edwards Memorial Foundation Quarterly,* nos. 75–76 (Spring–Summer 1985): 51.

39. Anthony M. Gruchot, "The Closing Chord: John A. Wilfahrt," *The St. Paul Musician* 13 (1961): 15.

40. Lornell, "Wilfahrt," p. 51.

41. Compare the similarity of three photos of the band: one in the flyer advertising the band's appearance August 16, 1931, at the American Fur-

nishing Company store, in my possession, with the one of 1940 or 1941 in David Wood, "Yoo Hoo-hoo! Whoopee John Band, An Institution with a Life of its Own," *Minneapolis Tribune*, August 24, 1980, p. 8G; and that of 1954 in Barron, *Odyssey*, pp. 227, 244. The 1954 photo shows twelve members with the same instrumentation as the others except for an added banjo.

42. Letters from Jack Kapp of Chicago to Wilfahrt, forwarded to Minneapolis, July 15, 1930, and from Kapp in New York to Wilfahrt, November 5, 1930, in the Dennis Wilfahrt collection, St. Paul. I am grateful to Dennis Wilfahrt.

43. Kapp to Wilfahrt, October 23, 1934, in ibid.

44. Newspaper clipping in Wilfahrt file at Brown County (Minn.) Historical Society, henceforth BCHS; and *New Ulm Journal*, February 11, 1985, section A, p. 1.

45. Wilfahrt to Kapp, March 25, 1938, in Dennis Wilfahrt collection.

46. The number of 1,000 is suspect, as suggested by *New Ulm Journal*, January 23, 1975, *The Fun Magazine*, part 1, in BCHS, supported by an offprint of the International Polka Association yearbook for 1976, supplied by Leon Kozicki of La Grange, Ill. Gruchot, "Wilfahrt," p. 15, and Bill Kuehn, "West Side Story, Oompah, Oompah, Oompah," (St. Paul) *West Side Voice* (1975), p. 3, have the 300 sum, copy supplied by Dennis Wilfahrt, which appears to be the best guess, as Spottswood lists only 100 to 1941, as stated in Lornell, "Wilfahrt," pp. 54–58.

47. Interview with Verne Steffel, April 17, 1985, Minneapolis. I believe this estimate true but was unable to further verify it.

48. James P. Leary and Richard March, "Dutchman Bands: Genre, Ethnicity, and Pluralism in the Upper Midwest," paper supplied by the authors, Madison, Wis.

49. Leary and March, "Dutchman Bands," p. 18; James P. Leary, "The Cultural Meaning of Dutchman Music," paper presented to the American Folklore Society meeting, Cincinnati, October 19, 1985.

50. Leary, "Dutchman," pp. 1–2, 6. Thus, his band played more varied American pieces than Loeffelmacher's, in that the latter continued to exploit the "Dutchman" image more openly. See also the selections in *The "Whoopee John" Band Book* (Chicago: Vitak and Elsnic, ca. 1938).

51. Wood, "Whoopee John," p. 1G; interview with McLeod in Oshkosh, Wis., June 14, 1987.

52. "Wilfahrt Traveled in Yellow," quoted in *New Ulm Journal*, July 28, 1966, at BCHS.

53. In a group of ten. "Voted Most Popular Twin City Radio Artists," *The St. Paul Shopper*, March 12, 1940, supplied by Dennis Wilfahrt.

54. Wood, "Wilfahrt," p. 8G; Tom Streissguth, "Polka Music Mingled with Spy Fantasies during World War II," *New Ulm Journal*, November 9, 1980; and reprinted article in *New Ulm Journal* of May, 1942, by Paul Light, "Refutes Wild Talk About Whoopee John Orchestra," both in BCHS.

55. MacLeod interview.

56. They had only one open date in 1951. "Interview of Whoopee John

by Glen Reed, Radio Station WMNE Menomonie (Wisconsin)," (February 1952?) supplied by BCHS; interview of Dennis Wilfahrt; Charles F. Sarjeant, ed., *The First Forty: The Story of WCCO Radio* (Minneapolis: T. S. Denison, 1964), p. 15.

57. Louis Sebok of Decca, New York to Wilfahrt, May 20, 1946, in Dennis Wilfahrt collection.

58. Adeline Wilfahrt interview, St. Paul, April 17, 1975; Vern Steffel interview; Gruchot, "Wilfahrt," p. 15.

59. The demise of this last "Whoopee John" band resulted from organizational matters, not a lack of public interest. The demand for bookings far outpaced the number of times the band could play. Interview with Steffel, the leader; Wood, "Wilfahrt," p. 8G; article in *New Ulm Journal,* August 6, 1983, copy supplied by BCHS.

60. The fullest biographical account is Bob Andresen, liner notes to "The Plehal Brothers: Tom and Eddie, Rare Recordings from the 1930s," *Banjar Records,* cassette BR 1850 (1989).

61. One of their best-selling pieces was, as one might expect, "The Beer Barrel Polka." Howard Pine, "Pine Country Echoes," *Countryside* 3 (May 1975): 28.

62. Recording of interview, July 25, 1983, with Ed Plehal, supplied to me by Bob Andresen.

63. From Welk's autobiography, Lawrence Welk with Bernice McGeehan, *Wunnerful! Wunnerful!* (Englewood Cliffs, N.J.: Prentice-Hall, 1971), p. 6.

64. Clarence Shipp, "From Farm Boy to TV Dance King," *American Weekly* 162 (July 1956): 102.

65. William Kaye Schwienher, "A Descriptive Analysis of the Lawrence Welk Show as a Unique Sociological Phenomenon," Ph.D. diss., Northwestern University, 1971, p. 65.

66. I am extrapolating this conclusion from several sources: Welk, *Wunnerful!* p. 138; Lawrence Welk with Bernice McGeehan, *My America, My America* (Englewood Cliffs, N.J.: Prentice-Hall, 1976), p. 34; Shipp, "From Farm Boy," p. 21; Albert Govoni, "The Lawrence Welk Story," *Philadelphia Daily News,* May 4, 1961, p. 34. Govoni refers to the mid-thirties, but I believe Welk had those aims earlier.

67. From Brian Rust, *The American Dance Band Discography, 1917–1942,* 2 vols. (New Rochelle, N.Y.: Arlington House, 1975) 2: pp. 1,909, 1,911.

68. Letters from John Matuska, Yankton, S.D., to author, August 6, November 4, and December 28, 1987, which seem to contradict Welk himself in Welk, *Wunnerful!* p. 79. See also *The WNAX Station Book . . . 1866–1929* (Yankton, S.D.: Gurnee Seed and Nursery Company, 1929), pp. 48, 106; and Reynold M. Wik, "Radio in the 1920s: A Social Force in South Dakota," *South Dakota History* 11 (Spring 1981): 98, 104, both of which depict the two bands well and tend to verify Matuska's version. See also Wynor Speece with M. Jill Karolevitz, *The Best of the Neighbor Lady* (Mission Hill, S.D.: Dakota Homestead, 1987), *passim,* which provides a good overview of the station.

69. Welk, *Wunnerful!* pp. 86–87, and caption under photograph of Archer following p. 182.

70. *Accordion News* 5 (October 15, 1936): 13, referred to him then as "fastly becoming popular in all of the Middle West."

71. Samuel Honigsberg, "Lawrence Welk," (review of his Edgewater Beach Hotel engagement) in *The Billboard,* August 12, 1939, p. 13; and George T. Simon, *The Big Bands,* 4th ed. (New York: Schirmer Books–Macmillan, 1981), pp. 449–51. Simon added that Welk's music "has all the subtlety and polish of a used-car salesman's pitch," p. 451.

72. Lawrence Welk, "Champagne Music," *The Billboard,* August 26, 1939, p. 24.

73. The photo is in the center group of pictures in Welk, *Wunnerful!* after p. 182. Note also the comment in "Lawrence Welk," *Accordion World* 3 (April 1938): 19.

74. "Chicago, Chicago," *Billboard,* September 15, 1939, p. 20.

75. Rust, *Dance Band,* pp. 1,911–12.

76. The Trianon and the Karsas's other dance palace, the Aragon, were nationally famous after they were built in the 1920s. The Trianon was named, of course, for one of the French royal palaces. Nancy Banks, "The World's Most Beautiful Ballrooms," *Chicago History* 2 (Fall–Winter 1973): 206ff.

77. Welk, *Wunnerful!* p. 211; Andrew Hamilton, "Why Lawrence Welk is the People's Choice," *Town Journal (Pathfinder)* 63 (August 1963): 69.

78. Welk, *Wunnerful!* p. 171.

79. *Lawrence Welk's Polka Folio for Piano and Piano Accordion* (New York: Leeds, 1942), p. ii. About half of the pieces were polkas.

80. Welk, *Wunnerful!* pp. 183–84.

81. Ibid., p. 182. In 1948, he replaced Guy Lombardo at the Roosevelt Hotel in New York. Ibid., p. 222.

82. Welk, *Wunnerful!* pp. 215–19.

83. Ted Hilgenstuhler, *Lawrence Welk* (Los Angeles: Petersen, 1956), p. 50, has the figure.

84. In Schwienher, "Welk," p. 198.

85. Welk, *Wunnerful!* p. 183.

Chapter 11

1. The promoter was Ray Mitchell. The detailed description of the festival-competition is in Don Dornbrook, "Roll Out the Polka, Bugs' Jitters Cease," *Milwaukee Journal,* June 10, 1948, p. 1L.

2. *Accordion World* 12 (April 1948): 8. The city was also the home of manufacturers of the instrument, such as George Karpek. From an undated communication with James Leary, Mt. Horeb, Wis.

3. *Billboard* Magazine, January 22, 1949, "Jukebox Supplement," 54, had ranked Godfrey's "Too Fat" as 26th on the jukebox list and the Andrews Sisters' "Toolie Oolie Doolie," Decca 24380, as 14th, over the previous year.

4. Welk, *Wunnerful!,* p. 222.

5. I use the latter term. Dornbrook, "Roll Out the Polka," p. 1L.

6. A possible exception was Sammy Madden of Milwaukee, whose name was probably least known nationally of the contestants.

7. Once more, I consider the claim more significant than the claimed figure. See Dornbrook, "Roll Out the Polka," p. 1L.

8. A chatty, informative, if overly detailed autobiography is Frankie Yankovic as told to Robert Dolgan, *The Polka King: The Life of Frankie Yankovic* (Cleveland: Dillon/Liederbach, 1977).

9. Linda Tyssen, "Ironworld Inducts Yankovic into the Polka Hall of Fame," *Mesabi* (Minnesota) *Daily News,* June 23, 1988, pp. 1, 8; Joe Edwards, "The Band Plays On: Polka King Yankovic Still Squeezing Tunes," *Milwaukee Journal* (1987), p. 1G, copy supplied by Yankovic. See also Frank Smodic, Jr., *The Legendary Frankie Yankovic "Through the Years": The Life and Times of America's Polka King* (Scottdale, Pa.: author, 1991).

10. Collinwood also had a colony of Italians. Van Tassel, *Encyclopedia of Cleveland History,* p. 289; Yankovic, *Polka King,* pp. 14–17.

11. Yankovic, *Polka King,* p. 17; "Frank Yankovic: America's Polka King," typescript supplied by Fred Kuhar of Cleveland, to whom I am indebted. Kuhar and Jeff Pecon aided me with information especially about Pecon's famous father, Johnny Pecon.

12. Clarissa Start, "Frankie Yankovic Confounded Record Industry Experts" (partial title), article in the collection of Mr. Roland Boeder of La Crosse, Wis., to whom I am indebted.

13. Norbert Blei, *Neighborhood* (Peoria, Ill.: Ellis Press, 1987), p. 155; interview with Justine Mervar, Cleveland, May 29, 1985. Trolli died in 1990.

14. He may have begun with a two-man band. See *Polka and Old Time News* 1 (February 1964): 6.

15. Interview with Yankovic, Milwaukee, November 23, 1987.

16. Brian Juntikka, liner notes to "Frankie Yankovic: The Early Years," vol. 1, 1938, 1939, 1940, cassette SNC 109; also in Bob Norgard, "Polka Parade," *The Polka News* 20 (June 27, 1990): 19.

17. Valencic, "Polka," typescript, p. 5, provided by Mr. Valencic; Gene Hersh, "The Revival of the Polka," *Cleveland Plain Dealer,* November 18, 1968, n.p., supplied by Margo Anderson of University of Wisconsin–Milwaukee.

18. My major source of information on Yankovic's recording career is Brian Juntikka of Fort Myers, Florida. His detailed knowledge of Yankovic's recording career in the late thirties and forties is likely unsurpassed. Letters from Juntikka to author, July 28, 1989, and January 10, 1991 (probably February 10).

19. Juntikka letter, July 28, 1989; Yankovic interview.

20. Yankovic, *Polka King,* pp. 47–48.

21. Although some were not released in that time. Juntikka's letters to me of July 28, 1989, and January 10, 1991, clarify the rather complicated details and especially the seizure of Yankovic's recordings by Donald Gabor, head of Continental Records about that time.

22. Juntikka letter, January 10, 1991.

23. Gene Hersh, "The Revival of the Polka."

24. Yankovic, *Polka King*, p. 4.

25. From Robert Dolgan, "Frankie Yankovic."

26. Yankovic interview. The output was prodigious. One estimate is that since 1949 Yankovic and Trolli had written over 300 songs in all. "Frank Yankovic: America's Polka King."

27. My emphasis. Yankovic, *Polka King*, p. 7.

28. From Paton, "Evolution of the Polka," p. 31.

29. The best account of the origins of "Just Because" is "Johnny Pecon, 1915–1975," a typescript biography in the Don Sosnoski collection, Parma, Ohio. I am grateful to Sosnoski for allowing me to consult his material.

30. Tony Petkovich, Jr., "Perry Personality," *Perry (Ohio) News,* May 1945, p. 1.

31. Interview with Fred Kuhar and Jeff Pecon, Euclid, Ohio, May 29, 1985.

32. The dating is unclear for both the composition and the record. Nat Shapiro and Bruce Pollock, eds., *Popular Music,* 9 vols. (Detroit: Gale Research Company, 1985–86) 2:1017, give 1937 as the copyright date. Malone, *Country Music USA,* pp. 169–70, says the brothers issued the record in 1935.

33. Pecon stayed with Yankovic for three years, until 1949, during the time the Yanks had their greatest hits. Unfortunately, after some disagreement with Yankovic, chiefly about business, Pecon left the Yanks. In the 1950s he was very successful in forming an ethnic Slovenian comedy duo with Lou Trebar and an equally successful polka band, making about 50 records for Capitol and others for other labels. He passed away in 1975, much appreciated in the Cleveland community. Kuhar-Pecon interview; and especially Sosnoski, "Johnny Pecon, 1915–1975," in *Polkarama, America's Polka Messenger* (March 1975), copy supplied to me by Sosnoski; clippings supplied by Fred Kuhar, Cleveland. Yankovic tells about his concluding relations with Pecon in Yankovic, *Polka King*, ch. 8.

34. The details are in Yankovic, *Polka King*, pp. 81–82. The record was Columbia 12359-F, released on January 19, 1948. Juntikka letter, January 10, 1991.

35. Yankovic, *Polka King*, p. 83, says 25,000; Bob Dolgan, liner notes to "Seventy Years with Frankie Yankovic," Smash Records, says 38,000; videotape, Joey Miskulin, "Polka Gold" (1984), gives Yankovic's figure as 35,000. Juntikka letter, January 10, 1991, has complementary information.

36. *Billboard* Magazine, January 22, 1949, "Jukebox Supplement," p. 54. Godfrey's "Too Fat Polka" was 26th and the Andrews Sisters' "Toolie Oolie Doolie," 14th.

37. Yankovic, *Polka King*, p. 84, says it was 1949 when Mills first contacted him. However, the copyright date for the English-language piece was 1948. See Shapiro and Pollock, *Popular Music* 1: 243.

38. Juntikka letter, January 10, 1991, provided me with the date.

39. Cf. John Sippel, "On the Stand—Frankie Yankovic," *Billboard*, November 19, 1949, p. 20.

40. The explanation of the "spy" who leaked the Parish version is in Yankovic, *Polka King,* pp. 85, 92.

41. This is a translation provided by Karel Bayer of University of Wisconsin–Milwaukee from a 1947 recording on Columbia 312-F by Jerry Mazanec, vocals by Milada and Zdenek Ptak.

42. Yankovic, *Polka King,* p. 85.

43. From Columbia record 12394.

44. According to Murrells, *Discs,* p. 21.

45. According to a *Redbook* Magazine article, May 1950, in Bill Kennedy, "Hollywood Goes Polka Slap Happy: Dotted Ties and Dresses Worn in Dance Revival," *Los Angeles Herald Express,* June 19, 1950, section B, p. 1.

46. All the above quotations are from Dornbrook, "Roll Out the Polka," p. 1L.

47. This was just behind Russ Morgan and Primo Scala. *Billboard* Magazine, January 22, 1949, p. 56.

48. George Foster, "Polka King Frankie," *American Weekly* in *Milwaukee Sentinel,* July 31, 1949, p. 20.

49. There is some disagreement over the year this occurred; it might have been 1952 or 1957. See *Entertainment Bits* 18 (August–September 1990): 13; *Polka Journal* 3 (1952): 4.

50. *Time Magazine* 55 (April 17, 1950): 92–93.

51. Sippel, "Yankovic," p. 20. Cf. "Polka Gold."

52. Yankovic interview; Dolgan, liner notes, "Seventy Years."

53. *Time* Magazine, April 17, 1950, p. 93; telephone interview with Brian Juntikka, June 25, 1989; Yankovic, *Polka King,* p. 119. The videocassette "Polka Gold" (1984), produced commercially, has these short films.

54. "Gets Columbia Push," *Billboard* Magazine, June 3, 1950, p. 14; Yankovic, *Polka King,* p. 119.

55. Kennedy, "Hollywood Goes Polka Slap Happy," p. B-1; Cobina Right, "Society As I Find It," *Los Angeles Herald Express,* June 19, 1950, p. B-1.

56. Kennedy, "Hollywood Goes Polka Slap Happy," p. 1.

57. Yankovic, *Polka King,* p. 119. Cf. the reference to Emory Lewis's 1950 article in the *New York Mirror,* not more specifically cited, in *Polka Journal* 3 (1952): 4.

58. Interview with Yankovic; "Yankovic Gets Columbia Push," *Billboard Magazine,* June 3, 1950, p. 14. The three pieces he did with Doris Day were "Comb and Paper Polka," "You Are My Sunshine," and "Pumpernickel Polka," Columbia Record 39143-F and another in the 39000 series. Telephone interview with Brian Juntikka, Fort Myers, Florida, March 30, 1988.

59. See *E Z Play Today: Frankie Yankovic Polkas and Waltzes* (Milwaukee: Hal Leonard Publication Company, 1975, 1978), p. 24.

60. Yankovic interview.

61. Yankovic, *Polka King,* p. 196; Yankovic interview. These may have been two separate bookings.

62. For his 1952 trip around the country, particularly the Southwest and Kansas City, where he drew 2,500, as well as a list of his many television

appearances that year, see his letter in *Polka Journal* 3 (1952): 2. It was no surprise, then, that the National Ballroom Operators poll conducted by *Down Beat* Magazine named him the nation's favorite polka band leader for 1953–1954. Ibid., p. 3.

63. My conclusion really follows the brief assessment by Richard March, "Slovenian Polka Music; Tradition and Transition," *The Polka News* 19 (March 22, 1989): 14. See also March, "Slovenian Polka Music: Tradition and Transition," *John Edwards Memorial Foundation Quarterly* Nos. 75–76 (Spring–Summer, 1985): 47–50. I am obviously indebted to March.

Epilogue

1. See the introductory discussion in Robert P. Crese, "In Praise of the Polka," in *Atlantic*, August 1989, pp. 78ff. I am grateful to John Steiner of Milwaukee for directing me to this essay.

2. A complaint of a blue-collar worker quoted in Michael Novak, *The Rise of the Unmeltable Ethnics: Politics and Culture in the Seventies* (New York: Macmillan, 1972), p. 60. Novak refers to polkas explicitly on p. 58. According to Valencic, "Polka," p. 779, a particular piece, "Who Stole the Keeshka?," appeared to give substance to that image. A recent documentary attempt to better inform the public about that musical genre was a film called *In Heaven There Is No Beer*. Unfortunately, it seems to have backfired and had the effect of offering further evidence for the stereotype.

3. Donald H. Dooley, "Royalty Bands Meet in Milwaukee to Make Album," *The Milwaukee Journal*, February 8, 1963, n.p., copy supplied by Robert Kames of Milwaukee.

4. *Polka Day, 1967* (New Ulm, 1967), p. 4.

5. *Polkarama* (Cleveland), Souvenir Edition, p. 6, copy provided by Don Sosnoski, Parma, Ohio.

6. A good review of his work is in Kleeman, "Origins," pp. 95ff.

7. From *International Polka Festival . . .* (Chicago: International Polka Association, 1987), n.p. For further information on the vibrancy of the recent Polish polka community in Chicago, see Margy McClain, *A Feeling for Life: Cultural Identity, Community and the City* (Chicago: Urban Traditions, 1988).

8. Derek Van Pelt, "Polka: The Dance that Refuses to Die," *Cleveland Magazine* (1985), p. 83, copy supplied by Margo Anderson, Milwaukee.

9. My information is from a list provided by Dorothy Wendinger of Minnesota in 1987; Doris Pease, "This Is the Year of the Polka: America's Only Party Music," *Entertainment Bits* 17 (December–January 1990): 1; and Gerald R. Ross, "United Federation of Polkas," *The Polka News* 20 (June 27, 1990): 20. For additional confirmation of this renewed growth from 1969 to 1980, see the surprising anti-assimilationist statistics on Polish polka stations and hours in Migała, *Polskie Programy*, p. 137. Note also Valencic, "Polka," typescript, pp. 7–8, provided by Mr. Valencic; and the later published version, "Polkas," p. 779, where he says the revival occurred in 1965.

Note also Ed Matasy, "Polkas In and Around Youngstown," *The Polka News* 18 (December 21, 1988): 6.

10. This obviously does not exhaust all the promoters of the "industry." One can obtain the most complete picture of the current business from the pages of *The Polka News*.

11. Bob Norgard, "Slavko Avsenik," *The Polka News* 15 (August 28, 1985): 1–2.

12. From Robert Norgard, "Jimmy Sturr Wins Grammy," *The Polka News* 19 (March 8, 1989): 1. For some sense of Sturr's energizing of the genre, see "Polka America is Now Jimmy Sturr TV Show," *Entertainment Bits* 16 (December 1988–January 1989): 5.

13. Quoted in Howard Reich, "Mr. Squeezebox: At 75, Frankie Yankovic is Still the Polka King," *Chicago Tribune*, July 22, 1990, section 13, p. 9.

Bibliographic Essay

The notes direct the interested reader to all sources used in this study and can be readily consulted with the aid of the chapter headings and index. Below, I list and review those sources that may prove especially valuable for future investigations of ethnic music. After identifying reference aids, the essay follows traditional bibliographic form, distinguishing between primary and secondary sources, with subcategories under those headings.

Reference Aids

Any study of ethnic music in America would have to begin with Richard Spottswood's massive discography, *Ethnic Music On Records: A Discography of Ethnic Recordings Produced in the United States, 1893 to 1942,* 7 vols. (Urbana: University of Illinois Press, 1990). The work was many years in the making and was published too late for me to exploit as a whole, but I was fortunate enough to have access to listings in draft form for some of the ethnic groups. An earlier, more limited work, which I used and which because of its high quality may have been a model for Spottswood, is that of Finnish discographer Pekka Gronow, *Studies in Scandinavian American Discography,* 2 vols. (Helsinki: Suomen Aanitearkisto, 1977).

Another indispensable aid is H. Wiley Hitchcock and Stanley Sadie, eds., *The New Grove Dictionary of American Music,* 4 vols. (London: Macmillan, 1986). Unlike earlier Grove dictionaries, which had stressed elite art music, this edition is sprinkled through-out with entries concerning ethnic and vernacular music.

An unusual reference work that devotes considerable space to lower-class music comes from urban historiography, the first of a planned series of several big-city histories: David D. Van Tassel and John J. Grabowski, eds., *The Encyclopedia of Cleveland History* (Bloomington: Indiana University Press, 1987). Future volumes on other cities would do well to use it as a model.

Another important type of reference source includes photographic albums depicting bands. Two that emphasize the ethnic and other old-time bands of the Midwest in particular are *Old Timers Picture Album No. 1: Bands* in the Wisconsin Music Collection, Mills Music Library, University of Wisconsin, Madison; and Vernon Lee Barron, comp., *Odyssey of the Mid-Nite Flyer* (Omaha: Barron, 1987).

The most informative encyclopedia on non-ethnic popular music entertainers is Roger D. Kinkle, *The Complete Encyclopedia of Popular Music and Jazz, 1900–1950*, 4 vols. (New Rochelle, N.Y.: Arlington House, 1974).

Primary Materials

ARCHIVES AND OTHER COLLECTIONS

Because scholars have neglected much of the music of American immigrant groups, few of the well-known general repositories have been collecting source materials on the subject. Most such documents remain in small ethnic-group libraries and cultural centers or in the private collections of the families of music businesspeople, bandleaders, entertainers, and their friends or fans. The citations in this volume clearly show the dispersion. A few "outsider" archives, however, most of them devoted to American immigration and ethnic life, do possess limited and specialized materials on old-time musical entertainment. The best and most extensive file of documentary materials on any single ethnic entertainer is probably the Eduardo Migliaccio Papers at the Immigration History Research Center at the University of Minnesota. The IHRC, the major repository for materials on eastern- and southern-European Americans, also contains at least some of the files of the largest Italian American music company, the Italian Book Company of New York, founded by Antonio Di Martino.

Another good source of materials is the Balch Institute for Ethnic

Studies in Philadelphia, where I found two useful collections: the papers of Elba Farabegoli Gurzau, a still-active promoter of ethnic folk dance, and the Angelo and Rose Florey Fiorani Papers. The Fioranis were active in Italian American radio in northeastern Pennsylvania from the early 1930s. The Balch Institute also offers a helpful reference guide, "Ethnic Sheet Music Collection at the Balch Institute for Ethnic Studies," (August 25, 1984), by Deborah Wong.

A few regional historical societies, especially in polka-music regions, have acquired small amounts of materials on the subject. Among them are the Brown County Historical Society in New Ulm, Minnesota, the hometown or regional center of numerous ethnic bandleaders, notably "Whoopee John" Wilfahrt, and the Western Reserve Historical Society in Cleveland, which houses a file donated by Alice Lausche of musical materials pertaining to her husband, Dr. "Bill" Lausche, who of course was the major early Slovenian American composer and arranger.

In Kewaunee, Wisconsin, I discovered a rich array of carefully arranged photo scrapbooks on local Czech or "Bohemian" musicians at the Kewaunee County Historical Society. Also, James Leary is assembling a collection at the Mills Music Library on the University of Wisconsin campus in Madison that includes material on the state's polka and ethnic bands.

Unfortunately, despite the potential richness of the New York City area for this subject, I was unable to locate any public archive there with many materials. The music, theater, and record divisions of the New York Public Library at Lincoln Center were disappointing; except for a few photographs of Aaron Lebedeff in the musical comedies of the city's Yiddish theater, I found little material on old-time entertainment in the region.

The decline of polka music beginning in the 1950s has paradoxically had a beneficial effect, by stimulating the preservation efforts of genre aficionados and promoters, especially for artifacts memorializing the stars in "halls of fame." The largest of the organizations that have sprung up for that purpose is the International Polka Association, founded in Chicago in 1968 under the leadership of Leon Kozicki. Its Polka Hall of Fame includes a small museum with artifacts. More recently, the Slovenian American promoter Tony Petkovsek started a similar institution, the Cleveland Polka Hall of Fame, in that city. A third Polka Hall of Fame is arising at Cloquet, Minnesota.

Ethnic-group libraries contain a variety of source materials, including periodicals, photos, sheet music, and phonograph records, as well as secondary works. The largest of these is the Yivo Institute in New York, the major American Yiddish depository, where I used, among other files, the collections of Sholom Secunda and Abraham Ellstein. Yivo also has a good collection of Jewish-Yiddish musical materials, especially records. A particularly helpful memoir was a paper by Sholom Rubenstein, "Recollections of Jewish Radio and Television," which was delivered October 21, 1985, at the New School for Social Research.

Two repositories in Chicago had modest but excellent material on Lithuanian ethnic vaudeville: the World Lithuanian Cultural Center and the Balzekas Museum of Lithuanian Culture, both of which hold printed sources, artifacts, and many photos. The collection of a third library and archive in the Chicago area, the Czechoslovak Society of America at the Fraternal Life Company offices in Berwyn, is also rich.

AUTOBIOGRAPHIES AND CONTEMPORARY CRITICS

Considering the plethora of ethnic entertainers and the popularity of their music and dance, it is regrettable that so few decided to write their stories. The most valuable, of course, for this work is Frankie Yankovic, as told to Robert Dolgan, *The Polka King: The Life of Frankie Yankovic as Told to Robert Dolgan* (Cleveland: Dillon, Liederbach, 1977). This memoir is valuable more for Yankovic's expressed rationale for the conduct of his career than for specific details of his life. The several publications of another major polka-style bandleader, Lawrence Welk, are useful along similar lines; the best is Lawrence Welk with Bernice McGeehan, *Wunnerful, Wunnerful!* (Englewood Cliffs, N.J.: Prentice-Hall, 1971). The other life stories by members of the Welk organization, such as Myron Floren and Randee Floren, *Accordion Man* (Brattleboro, Vt.: Stephen Greene, 1981), are less helpful for this work because they deal with a later time period.

The memoirs of Jewish-Yiddish entertainers are greater in number. Two of the outstanding ones are *Words and Music: A Selection from His Writings,* translated and edited by Max Rosenfeld (New York: Yiddisher Kultur Farband, 1986), by Mordecai Yardeni, a music authority who knew many Jewish musicmen; and *Klangen Fun Mein Leben* (Pages from my life) (New York: Verlag Vadran, 1944), by Joseph Rumshinsky, the well-known Yiddish music composer who provides brief biographical and critical reviews of his acquaintances, Aaron Lebedeff and Sholom Secunda.

Three contemporary writers offered particularly trenchant views on old-time ethnic musicians: the anonymous reviewer of a Bohemian band's concert in Cleveland in *Česka Osada I Její Spolkový Život v Cleveland*. . . . (The Czech settlement and its social life in Cleveland) (Cleveland: Volnosti, 1895); John Sippel, music critic for *Billboard* magazine in the late 1940s and early 1950s—see, for example, his "On the Stand–Frankie Yankovic," *Billboard*, Nov. 19, 1949, p. 20; and Eleanor Steckert, whose special interest was in Romy Gosz in "Pride of the Polka Belt," *Coronet* magazine, November 1945, pp. 98–100, and who also contributed a brief review of popular music in Polonia (Polish America) in Albert Q. Maisel, *They All Chose America* (New York: T. Nelson, 1957).

Secondary Works

DISSERTATIONS AND OTHER UNPUBLISHED STUDIES

Occasionally, students of ethnomusicology and theater have turned to old-time ethnic music to provide data on particular ethnic groups. One of the most helpful such studies for this project is Janice Ellen Kleeman, "Origins and Stylistic Development of Polish American Polka Music" (Ph.D. diss., University of California, Berkeley, 1982). A complementary work is Joseph Ficca, "A Study of Slavic American Instrumental Music in Lyndora, Pa." (Ph.D. diss., University of Pittsburgh, 1980). Other valuable works include Janet Ann Kvam, "Norwegian American Dance Music in Minnesota and Its Roots in Norway: A Comparative Study" (Doctor of Musical Arts diss., University of Missouri–Kansas City, 1986); Alaine Pakkala, "The Instrumental Music of the Finnish American Community" (M.M.Ed. thesis, University of Michigan, 1983); Philip V. Bohlman, "Music in the Culture of German Americans in North Central Wisconsin" (M.A. thesis, University of Illinois, 1979); and two studies on the Italians, Emma Rocco, "The Italian Wind Band: A Surviving Tradition in the Milltowns of Lawrence and Beaver Counties of Pennsylvania" (Ph.D. diss., University of Pittsburgh, 1986), and Emelise Frances Aleandri, "A History of the Italian American Theatre, 1900–1905" (Ph.D. diss., City University of New York, 1983).

Another unique work that I used in manuscript is now in print as Lon A. Gault, *Ballroom Echoes* (Wheaton, Ill.: Andrew Corbett

Press, 1987), a huge compendium of historical profiles of the major dance palaces around the country. Also available to me in draft was the first major social study of the polka, Charles Keil, Angelika Keil, and Richard Blau, *Polka Happiness,* which is forthcoming from Rutgers University Press. The study has a provocative theme, rooting the polka in a working-class alternative culture. In its early draft, however, it neglected the more rural polka culture of the Midwest and Texas.

PUBLISHED WORKS

As the subtitle of one of the best anthologies of essays on old-time music aptly suggests—*Ethnic Recordings in America: A Neglected Heritage,* edited by Judith McCulloh (Washington, D.C.: American Folklife Center, 1982)—few substantial publications have addressed this enormously popular music. *Ethnic Recordings* contains excellent articles by Spottswood, Gronow, and others, along with partial discographies finally defining the field of study for scholars. A similar and more recent group of essays is in a special issue of *New York Folklore* 14 (Summer–Fall 1988), entitled "Folk and Traditional Music in New York State," which includes brief studies of the vernacular music of more than ten of the state's ethnic groups. A multicontributor volume on a related topic, ethnic theater, is Maxine Schwartz Seller, ed., *Ethnic Theatre in America* (Westport, Conn.: Greenwood Press, 1983). While the overall tone of the work is generally nostalgic and elegiac, the contributions by Emelise Aleandri on Italian American entertainers and Anne-Charlotte Harvey on Swedish American entertainers are exceptional in their attention to the influences of these entertainers on later developments.

Two rare and particularly authoritative reviews of the musical life of working-class ethnic groups are Manuel Peña, *The Texas-Mexican Conjunto: History of a Working-Class Music* (Austin: University of Texas Press, 1985), and, from a social survey conducted by folklore graduate students in 1977 and 1978, Susan G. Davis, "Utica's Polka Music Tradition," in *New York Folklore* 4 (1978): 103–24. Davis's work includes many interviews describing interest in polka music by individual Polish Americans.

Among the numerous published works on the music industry, few refer to the associations with "international" or ethnic musicians and bandleaders. Probably the most detailed insider account of Tin Pan Alley publishers is Russell Sanjek, *American Popular Music and*

Its Business: The First Four Hundred Years (New York: Oxford University Press, 1988), a huge three-volume work. I used volume 3, covering the period from 1900 to 1984. The work has two problems for scholarly readers: an absence of footnotes and a complex narrative that is difficult to follow. Three good supplementary works are Robert C. Toll, *The Entertainment Machine: American Show Business in the Twentieth Century* (New York: Oxford University Press, 1982); David A. Jasen, *Tin Pan Alley: The Composers, the Songs, the Performers and Their Times* (New York: Donald I. Fine, 1988); and a study emphasizing the activities of one group, Charles Madison, *Jewish Publishing in America: The Impact of Jewish Writing on American Culture* (New York: Sanhedrin Press, 1976).

American brass-band music, as one might expect in light of the enduring popularity of John Philip Sousa, has also been a familiar subject of both amateur and professional writers, particularly in the early years. Fortunately, a recent publication summarizes the history of the subject and provides a rather comprehensive list of the best works: Margaret Hindle Hazen and Robert M. Hazen, *The Music Men: An Illustrated History of Brass Bands in America, 1800–1920* (Washington, D.C.: Smithsonian Institution Press, 1987).

Standard historical surveys of the phonograph industry, such as Oliver Read and Walter L. Welch, *From Tin Foil to Stereo: Evolution of the Phonograph,* 2d edition (New York: Sams and Bobbs-Merrill, 1976), and of American popular music say very little about ethnic influences, except for the valuable retrospective by Charles Hamm, *Yesterdays: Popular Song in America* (New York: Norton, 1979). Hamm, however, does not cover specific immigrant and ethnic entertainers but refers more broadly to the group.

Other helpful monographs include three biographies: Victoria Secunda's story of her father-in-law, *Bei Mir Bist Du Shon: The Life of Sholom Secunda* (Weston, Conn.: Magic Circle Press, 1982); William K. Schwienher, *Lawrence Welk: An American Institution* (Chicago: Nelson-Hall, 1980); and Frank Smodic, Jr., *The Legendary Frankie Yankovic "Through the Years": The Life and Times of America's Polka King* (Scottdale, Pa.: author, 1991).

SOUND RECORDINGS

By far the most fertile source of information of all materials I used are liner notes to individual phonograph records. Lamentably, some of the audiocassettes that have replaced the phonograph records have liner notes that either omit all background detail on the artists and musical works or provide only brief coverage. I list below the recordings with the richest information in liner notes or in the work itself; all items are long-playing records except where the abbreviation (c) designates an audiocassette tape.

Czech-Bohemian

Greg Leider, producer. *The Polka King Romy Gosz: Dance at "Turner Hall."* Polkaland LP 44x.

Tony Russell. Notes to *Adolph Hofner: South Texas Swing, His Early Recordings, 1935–1955.* Arhoolie 5020, 1980.

Chris Strachwitz. Notes to *Texas Czech-Bohemian Bands: Early Recordings.* Folklyric 9031, 1983.

Finnish

Pekka Gronow. Notes to *Siirtolaisen Muistoja: The Immigrants Memories.* Ohelma PK 40115, 1978. (c)

Toni Tikkanen and Oren Tikkanen. Notes to *Viola Turpeinen: The Early Days: Finnish American Dance Music, 1928–1938.* Thimbleberry Records, THC 1006, 1989. (c)

German

Philip Martin and James Leary. Notes to *Ach Ya! Traditional German American Music From Wisconsin,* Wisconsin Folklife Center, 1985.

Irish

Harry Bradshaw et al. Notes to *James Morrison: The Professor.* Viva Voce 001, 1989. (c)

Mary Flynn et al. Notes to *John McKenna: His Original Recordings.* John McKenna Traditional Society, 1982. (c)

Bill Healy. Notes to *Irish American Dance Music and Songs,* Folklyric 9010, 1977.

Italian

Notes to *Eviva La Banda! The Music of the Feasts Featuring Caliendo's Banda Napoletana: Chicago's Premier Italian Feast Band.* [No production company or catalog number.]

Pasquale Conte, editor. Notes to *Rimpianto: Italian Music in America, 1915–1929.* Global Village C-601, 1986. (c)

Jewish-Yiddish

Miriam Kressyn and Seymour Rexsite Sing the Yiddish Hit Parade. Greater Recording Co. GRC 212, 1973. (c)

Henry Sapoznik and Michael Schlesinger. *Jakie Jazz 'Em Up: Old Time Klezmer Music, 1912–1926.* Global Village 101, 1984.

Martin Schwartz. Notes to *Klezmer Music: Early Yiddish Instrumental Music.* Folklyric 9034.

B. Stambler and H. Stambler. Notes to *Aaron Lebedeff Sings Rumania, Rumania and other Yiddish Theatre Favorites.* Collectors Guild CGY 631.

Helen Stambler. Notes to *Aaron Lebedeff on 2d Avenue,* 2 vols. Collectors Guild 663/4, 1968.

Andrew Statman and Walter Zev Feldman. *Dave Tarras, Master of the Jewish Clarinet: Music for the Traditional Jewish Wedding.* Balkan Arts Center 1002, 1979.

Mexican

Chris Strachwitz. Notes to *Narciso Martinez, "El Huracan del Valle": His First Recordings, 1936–1937.* Folklyric 9017, 1977.

Norwegian

Philip Martin. Notes to *Across the Fields: Fiddle Tunes and Button Accordion Melodies; Traditional Norwegian American Music from Wisconsin.* Folklore Village Farm FVF 201, 1982.

Philip Martin. Notes to *Tunes from the Amerika Trunk: Traditional Norwegian American Music From Wisconsin,* vol. 2. Folklore Village Farm FVF 202, 1984.

Philip Nusbaum. Notes to *Norwegian-American Music From Minnesota.* Minnesota Historical Society, C-002A, 1989.

Polish

Norm Cohen. Notes to *From the Tatra Mountains: Classic Polish-American Recordings From the 1920s.* Morning Star 45007.

Bill Czupta. Notes to *Joe Lazarz and His International Orchestra.* Polka Music Hall of Fame, Chicago Polkas Collectors Series LP 4102.

Johannes Secundus. Notes to *Polish American Dance Music: The Early Recordings, 1927–1933.* Folklyric 9026, 1979.

Scandinavian

LeRoy Larson. Notes to *Early Scandinavian Bands and Entertainers.* Banjar BR-1840, 1983.

Slavic

Richard Spottswood. Notes to *"Spiew Juchasa"/Song of the Shepherd: Songs of the Slavic Americans.* New World NW 283, 1977.

Slovenian

Don Sosnoski. Notes to *Joe Sodja: Coast to Coast.* Normandy NL 7164 LPS.

Swedish

Ulf Beijbom et al. Notes to *From Sweden to America: Emigrant and Immigrant Songs.* Caprice CAP-2011, 1981.

Ukrainian

Anisa H. Sawyckyj. Notes to *Ukrainian American Fiddle and Dance Music: The First Recordings, 1926–1936,* 2 vols. Folklyric 9014 and 9015, 1977.

Multi-cultural

Robert Andresen. Notes to *The Plehal Brothers: Tom and Eddie, Rare Recordings from the 1930s.* Banjar BR 1850, 1989. (c)

James P. Leary. Notes to *Minnesota Polka: Polka Music, American Music.* Minnesota Historical Society, 1990.

Richard Spottswood. Notes to Folk Music in America series, vols. 4 (*Dance Music: Reels, Polkas and More,* 1976), 5 (*Dance Music: Ragtime, Jazz, and More,* 1976), and 6 (*Songs of Migration and Immigration,* 1977). Library of Congress LBC.

Richard Spottswood. Notes to *Old Country Music in a New Land: Folk Music of Immigrants from Europe and the Near East.* New World NW 264, 1977.

PERIODICALS

The following periodicals are useful for an understanding of the old time ethnic music industry:

The Polka News. St. Charles, Mich. 48655.

Entertainment Bits. Minneapolis 55433.

IPA (International Polka Association) *News.* Chicago 60632.

Texas Polka News. Houston 77280.

Interviews

Below are listed the ethnic musicians and their family members and employees who shared their memories, records, and other materials with me:

Rosemary Bača-Rohde. Oct. 28, 1987, Fayetteville, Tex.

Henry Baron. July 7, 1988, Chicopee, Mass.

"Skipper" Berg. Oct. 24, 1985, Albert Lea, Minn.

Lyvia Di Martino. Sept. 27, 1987, Brooklyn, N.Y.

Joseph Divisek. Jan. 27, 1988, Berwyn, Ill.

Jerry Dostal. Oct. 21, 1987, Glencoe, Minn.

Myra Fritsche. Oct. 25, 1985, New Ulm, Minn.

Adolph Hofner. Oct. 27, 1987, San Antonio, Tex.

Staś Jaworski. July 13, 1989, Toms River, N.J.

Charles Jiran. Dec. 3, 6, and 13, 1987, Berwyn, Ill.

Dorothy Kommer. Oct. 7, 1985, Whitefish Bay, Wis.

George Koudelka. Oct. 29, 1987, Flatonia, Tex.

E. Theodore Krolikowski III. July 8, 1989, Devon, Conn.

Lucian Kryger. July 9, 1989, Wilkes-Barre, Pa.

Alice and Frank Lausche. Sept. 7, 1989, Cleveland.

Al and Lillian Lazarz. July 7, 1989, Westfield, Mass.

Louis Levy. May 11, 1988, New York.

Orville Lindholm. July 28, 1988, St. Paul, Minn.

John Lueke. Oct. 28, 1987, Flatonia, Tex.

Leah McHenry. July 21, 1990, Milwaukee.

Laurence Musielak. July 26, 1985, Berwyn, Ill.

Charles Nunzio. Nov. 14, 1988, Milwaukee.

Walter Osowski. Feb. 4, 1990, Philadelphia.

Larry Pagel. April 21, 1989, Brillon, Wis.

Nicola Paone. Jan. 16, 1988, New York City, and May 19, 1989,
    Scarsdale, N.Y.

Jeff Pecon and Fred Kuhar. May 29, 1985, Euclid, Ohio.

Lou Plucino. July 9, 1989, Bridgeport, Conn.

Sophie Podgorski. Oct. 11, 1985, Philadelphia.

Stas Przasnyski. July 7, 1989, Bristol, Conn.

Seymour Rexsite. April 7, 1988, New York.

Fred and Frank Robak. July 6–7, 1989, Chicopee, Mass.

Louis Rossi. April 2, 1987, New York.

Alvin Sajewski. May 24, 1983, Dec. 29, 1984, Mar. 21, 1985,
    Chicago.

Verne Steffel. April 17, 1985, Minneapolis.

Eugenia Stolarzyk. Sept. 6, 1987, Cleveland.

Myron Surmach. Dec. 4, 1984, New York.

Frank Tudisco. June 6, 1987, Brooklyn, N.Y.

Michael Violante. July 9, 1989, Bridgeport, Conn.

Richard Vollter. May 12, 1988, New York.

Bernadette Walsh and Virginia Souchak. July 12, 1989, Shenan-
    doah, Pa.

Bernard Witkowski. Nov. 4, 1984, Hillside, N.J.

Mariane Witkowski. May 19, 1989, Hillside, N.J.
Frank Wojnarowski. May 20, 1989, Riverside, N.Y.
Frankie Yankovic. Nov. 23, 1987, Milwaukee.

Index

335

Compositor: Impressions, A Division of Edwards Brothers, Inc.
Text: 10/13 Galliard
Display: Galliard
Printer: Edwards Brothers, Inc.
Binder: Edwards Brothers, Inc.